Elections at Home and Abroad

Elections at Home and Abroad

Essays in Honor of Warren E. Miller

edited by
M. Kent Jennings and Thomas E. Mann

Ann Arbor

THE UNIVERSITY OF MICHIGAN PRESS

Copyright © by the University of Michigan 1994
All rights reserved
Published in the United States of America by
The University of Michigan Press
Manufactured in the United States of America
⊗ Printed on acid-free paper

1997   1996   1995   1994   4   3   2   1

A CIP catalogue record for this book is available from the British Library.

Library of Congress Cataloging-in-Publication Data

Elections at home and abroad : essays in honor of Warren E. Miller /
   edited by M. Kent Jennings and Thomas E. Mann.
        p.   cm.
   Includes bibliographical references.
   ISBN 0-472-10492-6 (acid-free paper)
   1. Elections. 2. Voting. 3. Miller, Warren E. (Warren Edward),
1924–   .   I. Miller, Warren E. (Warren Edward), 1924–   .
II. Jennings, M. Kent.   III. Mann, Thomas E.
JF1001.E362   1994
324.6—dc20   94-11407
                                                                  CIP

Contents

Acknowledgments

The preparation of this festschrift in honor of Warren Miller has been a labor of love for the editors. Each of us has experienced the essence of what Warren has meant to the profession and to individual scholars within it: his keen research skills, his astute management of the research enterprise, his unstinting efforts to facilitate the research of others, and his strong sense of personal loyalty and friendship.

For his part, Kent Jennings would like to acknowledge Warren as an invaluable mentor and gateway to multiple research opportunities; Warren as a lively and dedicated co-investigator and co-author in the party convention delegate studies; Warren as the leader of us all at Michigan in the development of the Center for Political Studies and the Inter-University Consortium for Political and Social Research; and finally, Warren as a long-time personal friend of warmth and good cheer.

Tom Mann reckons that Warren has had a decisive influence at virtually every critical juncture in his professional life: initially, as a disembodied voice from Ann Arbor persuading an uncertain college senior that the University of Michigan was the only graduate program for him; then as professor, mentor, and dissertation advisor encouraging him to think anew about congressional elections; later as president of the American Political Science Association when he selected Mann as executive director; and finally, as founder and principal investigator of the National Election Studies generously involving him in the work of the Board of Overseers.

The first chapter of this volume summarizes our views about Warren's extraordinary contributions to the study of elections. Here we would like to acknowledge a personal debt and deep gratitude to our friend and colleague.

The contributors to this volume have been a joy to work with, no doubt because they too have had enjoyable and fruitful relationships with Warren over the years. Drafts of their essays were presented at a conference preceding the 1992 Annual Meeting of the American Political Science Association in Chicago. Paul Beck, Stanley Kelley, Jr., John Kessel, Donald Kinder, Steven Rosenstone, Bo Sarlvik, Walter Stone, and Rudolf Wildenmann provided critical commentary at the conference that was very helpful in revising the papers.

Philip Converse and Donald Stokes charmed the conferees with reflections on Warren's career and their years together. Ruth Jones offered valuable counsel throughout the conception and implementation of this project.

The Center for Political Studies, situated within the Institute for Social Research at the University of Michigan, provided critical support for this enterprise, including sponsorship of the day-long conference mentioned above. We are grateful to the center and its director, Harold Jacobson, for their enthusiastic commitment to the project.

We would also like to acknowledge the support of The Brookings Institution and the assistance in manuscript preparation provided by Judy Chaney, Inge Lockwood, Cindy Terrels, and Todd Quinn.

Finally, we are indebted to three people in particular at the University of Michigan Press. Colin Day gave us very helpful advice and encouragement at the early stages of planning, and Malcolm Litchfield saw us through the later stages of execution. Susan Whitlock and Christina Milton proved to be most able production editors.

Introduction

CHAPTER 1

Warren Miller and the Study of Elections

M. Kent Jennings and Thomas E. Mann

Warren Miller and the study of elections are synonymous. It is impossible to account for the institutional and intellectual developments that have shaped post–World War II scholarship on voting without acknowledging his crucial role. This book is a celebration of Miller's extraordinary influence on several generations of students of electoral behavior in the United States and in democracies around the world. It includes original research reports and synthetic essays, covering the broad range of topics in Miller's own scholarship, written by political scientists whose work has been stimulated or nurtured by his scholarly and organizational efforts of the last three decades.

By exploring some of the major theoretical, methodological, and substantive issues that motivate the field, this volume touches most directly on Miller's scholarly contributions to the study of voting behavior. But it would be a mistake to overlook the ways in which his entrepreneurial talent—his penchant for inventing and building institutions that foster research on elections—has left a distinctive mark on the scholarly enterprise.

Miller played an instrumental role in organizing the biennial national surveys of the American electorate carried out at the University of Michigan, initially by attracting ad hoc financial support to continue the series begun in 1952 and eventually by transforming what had been a Michigan property into a national resource. Created in 1977 with long-term support from the National Science Foundation, the National Election Studies shifted direction and control of the surveys from a handful of scholars at the University of Michigan to a national community of users. Through a board of overseers, study committees, and research conferences, scores of scholars have participated in decisions regarding the maintenance of time-series measures and the development of new survey instrumentation. NES has become the social science equivalent of the national laboratory in the physical sciences and the major research resource for hundreds of public opinion and voting specialists.

Generating systematic survey data was a necessary element in the development of the voting behavior subfield, but it was not sufficient. Miller and his colleagues recognized from the outset that individual scholars needed help if they were to exploit fully the research potential of the national studies.

Gaining timely access to the data was essential; so too was training in the modern techniques of data management and data analysis. In the early 1960s, with seed money from the Stern Family Fund, Miller launched the Inter-University Consortium for Political (and now Social) Research (ICPSR) to provide the archival and training assistance then in very short supply. The rest is history. The ICPSR has become an indispensable resource to thousands of social scientists at hundreds of colleges and universities (Eulau 1989).

A final example of Miller's success in building and strengthening institutions that facilitate research on elections is the creation of the Center for Political Studies within the Institute for Social Research at the University of Michigan. While less obviously tied to the larger community of scholars, the formation of the Center coincided with the initiation of a series of studies of elections, participation, and representation in democracies around the world and, equally important, of collaborative relationships between scholars in the United States and abroad. What followed was an enrichment of the comparative analysis of elections and the further development of national election studies in many countries, along with archiving and training activities, particularly through the European Consortium for Political Research (Crewe 1989).

Each of these organizational innovations served a public purpose in the political science and social science communities: individual scholars acquired skills and data with which to engage in large-scale empirical research; institutions on the periphery of scholarship were able to move to the center; study design and instrumentation decisions once made by the few became the province of many. But rather than diluting the intellectual influence of the Michigan school, Miller's institution building actually had the opposite effect. Ann Arbor became Mecca to a generation of scholars from the United States and abroad, and the approaches to the study of elections advocated by Miller and his colleagues gained enhanced visibility and influence.

Indeed, one need only peruse a list of Miller's publications over the last forty years to appreciate how fertile and consequential for the study of elections the interaction between his scholarship and entrepreneurship has been. An early interest in the relationship between social structure and political choice, reflected in his first published article (Janowitz and Miller 1952), presaged a lively debate on the group basis of electoral behavior. The idea of social-psychological predispositions toward politics, originally introduced by Miller in *The Voter Decides* (Campbell, Gurin, and Miller 1954) as orientations toward issues, candidates, and parties, was elaborated and extended into a more explicit causal structure of decision making in *The American Voter* (Campbell, Converse, Miller, and Stokes 1960). The remarkable (and wonderfully serendipitous) collaboration of Angus Campbell, Philip Converse, Warren Miller, and Donald Stokes, together and in various combinations, produced an outpouring of original thinking and methodological innovation in the study of elections and representation. During this early period Miller also made singular contributions to the study of contextual effects (Miller 1956) and presidential coattails (Miller 1955–56).

The tumultuous politics of the 1960s and 1970s led electoral analysts to rethink the basis of individual vote choice and the sources of aggregate shifts in election outcomes. The accumulating time series in the national election studies, as well as the successive surveys of national party convention delegates, provided an empirical basis for sorting elements of continuity and change and for uncovering the underlying dynamics. Miller played a crucial role during this period in measuring and interpreting electoral change (Miller and Levitin 1977; Miller, Miller, and Schneider 1980; Miller and Jennings 1986; Miller 1988; Miller and Traugott 1989).

Recent years have afforded Miller the opportunity to join several ongoing controversies in the field of electoral behavior. These include an assessment of the long-run significance of party identification (Miller 1991), the sources of declining turnout (Miller 1992), and the relative importance of partisanship, policy, and performance in the Reagan and Bush elections (Shanks and Miller 1990, 1991).

The contributions in this volume reflect several themes and foci found in Warren Miller's scholarship. In some instances the indebtedness and lineage are quite direct, as in the chapters dealing with contextual effects, political representation, and issues about the study of voting preferences. Other chapters address topics on which Miller has made major contributions, as in those dealing with partisanship, the national nominating conventions, and the development and utility of longitudinal databases. Still others provide examples of issues and controversies in the study of elections that could have arisen only in the context of the ongoing national election studies in the United States and other countries that were so assiduously encouraged and nourished by Miller and his Michigan colleagues. We have grouped these contributions under four headings, though a good deal of overlap is present.

Theories of Voting

Voting behavior is not only one of the most (if not *the* most) common objects of empirical political research in the United States but also one of the liveliest in terms of theory and interpretation. So central is voting to the democratic process that theories and interpretations involving the vote go well beyond the relatively simple matters of voter turnout and voter preferences. Nevertheless, even these two topics have served as vehicles for theories and approaches ranging all the way from the strongly empirical ones anchored in social psychology—often called the Michigan model—to the more abstract, formal models characteristic of the rational choice approach—sometimes known as the Rochester model (Weisberg 1986). This continuing diversity provides a backdrop for the three chapters in this section.

Perhaps no issue of greater controversy marks this field than that of explaining the vote. This topic commands the attention of observers all the way from scholars and pundits, for whom it is a consuming passion, to millions of ordinary citizens who ponder, if only in passing, why their candidate lost or won. As J. Merrill Shanks demonstrates in chapter 2, explaining the vote is not simply a question of allocating the determinants of the vote across a set of variables for any given election. Influenced in part by the work in which he has been engaged with Miller, Shanks posits six unresolved issues in the study of choice, some of which hinge on the level at which choice itself is defined. He may find more disarray than some observers, but his discussion highlights, in a particularly acute way, the inextricable linkage of theory, method, and substance and the vital importance of the assumptions that researchers bring to the task of explaining choice.

The accumulation, archiving, and dissemination of the ongoing American election surveys—activities in which Miller's entrepreneurial and leadership roles were without parallel—opened up vast new possibilities for looking at elections from a temporal perspective. Fascination with the election at hand will always be evident, but the capability of ranging over a multiplicity of election surveys, of comparing and contrasting, of looking for trends and deviations has not only proved attractive but has also yielded valuable contributions to the field of electoral behavior. Heinz Eulau reflects on these capabilities and their applications in an essay enriched by the insights derived from his long association with the Michigan studies and the behavioral movement more generally. In addition to calling for more historical and contextual sensitivity in the analysis of longitudinal data, Eulau also draws attention to the problem of how to address time-oriented questions in election surveys, the development and inclusion of questions that will be useful for some (unknowable) future, and the fractious issue of question retention over time.

Among the several camps in the study of elections, none is as clearly marked as that of rational choice. Nor has any other camp received quite the critical examination and skepticism heaped upon the rational choice advocates. Although there now appears to be a more common meeting ground for these advocates and those representing the more empirically driven approaches, the contrasts in initial assumptions continue to be substantial and, for some of the empirically inclined, at least, quite vexing. Among the latter is Raymond Wolfinger, who, in chapter 4, takes up the cudgels against a rational choice approach to turnout, in sharp contrast to such advocates as Aldrich (1993). Choice outranks turnout as a subject of research in the field of electoral behavior, but there has been a steady stream of literature on the latter, especially in the wake of declining turnout figures in the United States. For Wolfinger, the rational choice approach offers little guidance for understanding why people do or do not vote because of its miscalculations about, or nonrecognition of, the costs and benefits of voting, including those associated with the concrete rewards and penalties of voting, the multiplicity of contests on the ballot, the levels and use of electoral information on the part of the voter, and the up-front costs of registration.

Party Identification and Partisanship

If any single concept came to represent the so-called Michigan model of voting behavior, it was that of subjective party identification and partisan orientations more generally. As a raft of recent review essays (e.g., Beck 1986; Dalton and Wattenberg 1993; Niemi and Weisberg 1993), obligatory references, and subsequent applications continue to demonstrate, the origins, dynamics, and consequences of partisanship at the individual and system levels became and still remain key elements in most efforts to understand voting behavior in the United States. Among the several controversies and questions which sprang up in this area were those dealing with the application of the concepts and methods of the Michigan approach in other venues, most obviously across nation-states but also across electoral domains within the United States.

Despite the reservations held by many students of elections outside the American setting, it is rather remarkable how many national election studies throughout Western Europe, in particular, initiated, and have continued to include, a measure of subjective party identification in their surveys. At the very least these replications make it possible to chart the fate of announced loyalties within a given country and to compare countries diachronically and synchronically. In this respect, the fact that the traditional Michigan party identification measure captures intensity as well as direction has proved fortuitous. The intensity component stands as one indicator of political party strength. Although Sören Holmberg uses both components of the party identification measure in chapter 5—and differs from many European scholars in his defense of the directional component—he concentrates on the intensity element. His attempts to explain the mainly declining rates of attachment in western democracies by employing political (as distinct from social) factors meets with only modest success. However, in one of the most egregious cases of decline—that of Sweden—the political explanations appear to be robust and are exemplified by the long-term movements of the four categories contained in the typology that he developed.

Especially ripe opportunities for investigating the workings of party identification and party images occur with new electorates, represented either by the newly enfranchised in established democracies or by entire electorates in new or reestablished democracies (e.g., Converse 1969; Niemi, Stanley, and Evans 1984). In an amazingly short passage of time the appearance of competitive elections in Eastern Europe and the former Soviet Union has provided electoral analysts with an unsurpassed opportunity in these regards. Within this set, the unification of the two Germanies, with its attendant reintroduction of free elections into the former GDR, presents a unique opportunity to observe the dynamics of partisan orientations at an early stage of democratic transition. In chapter 6, Max Kaase and Hans-Dieter Klingemann take advantage of the dramatic historical events, a firm base of prior surveys in West Germany, and timely new studies in East Germany to study the emergence of partisanship in the former GDR. The rapidity with which East Germans adapted to the party system "imported" from West Germany provides the basis for a provocative discussion of the alternative processes by which this happened. Among the many questions raised by this chapter is that of how the East German experience compares with that of newly enfranchised nations and territories in Eastern Europe and the Soviet Union that were less proximate to a democratic neighbor with a common ancestry.

While the cross-national aspects of partisan orientation continue to command attention, especially in the wake of the diffusion of free elections, withinnation variations also continue to come under scrutiny. The presence of different levels and arenas of office holding, especially prominent under federalism and in nonparliamentary systems, offers up lively possibilities of multiple levels of party identification, regional parties, and split-ticket voting. The substantial increase in the latter in the American electorate over the past few decades has not only raised questions about the vitality of the political parties as instruments of aggregation and articulation, but has also resulted in long reigns of divided government in Washington, D.C., as well as an upsurge of divided governments at the state level (Beck et al. 1992). In a more fundamental sense, perhaps, the rise in split-ticket voting challenges some of the basic tenets of party identification as a guiding principle for electoral choice in the American public. Among the several possible explanations for this upsurge in split ballots is that of generational replacement. In chapter 7 Richard Brody, David Brady, and Valerie Heitshusen argue that the lesser partisan attachments of newer generations have at least indirectly contributed to the rise in split-ticket voting at the national level. An intriguing question raised by their conclusions is whether the widespread decline in partisan attachments, as observed in several other countries, has resulted in similar increases in ticket splitting, or whether the institutional context of elections in the United States makes it sui generis in this respect.

The Context of Voting

In one sense electoral context is inevitably present once we begin to engage in comparative or longitudinal research. But contextual factors are often treated in an informal and qualitative fashion, especially when contrasted with the great specificity attached to properties of the individual voter. Despite occasional substantive and methodological outcroppings, it is only in recent years that systematic attention has been devoted to contextual effects and to the related phenomena of networks (Huckfeldt and Sprague 1993). One of the fascinating, yet bedeviling, aspects of contextual analysis is the variable nature of the geopolitical space that defines context. Investigators often make necessary compromises between a theoretically preferred space and data availability. In this section we have two examples of the importance of context, examples that illustrate the range of contextual boundaries, the specificity of contextual measurement, and the kind of analytic tools that can be brought to bear.

One of the issues involved in the larger sense of contextual effects is the way innovations are molded and shaped by particular environments. Modern campaign practices are a case in point. In the United States they seem to have facilitated an increase in candidate-centered campaigns. In what might be termed a "soft" application of the context perspective, Ivor Crewe and Anthony King examine a growing belief that British elections are somehow becoming more presidential-like in nature, that is, that the contenders for the prime ministership are beginning to serve a campaign function for their parties and the voters similar to that purportedly played by presidential contenders in the United States. Crewe and King first conceptualize just what "presidentialization" would mean, and then carry out a variety of tests, including two provocative "thought experiments," to determine whether the perception is, in fact, true. Their largely null findings point toward contextual features of longstanding significance that situate campaigning and voting behavior in the British electorate and, not so accidentally, raise the question as to just how presidential American elections really are.

In a radically different illustration of how context makes a difference, John Sprague combines an early Miller (1956) contribution on the impact of local partisanship distributions with seminal work by Herbert Tingsten ([1937] 1963) to serve as a launching pad for his mathematically oriented exposition. Part of the charm of chapter 9 lies in its use of old data to elaborate a new approach to contextual analysis. In particular, Sprague is concerned with problems of cross-level inference and demonstrates how aggregate data and survey data can be combined to address identification problems in the modeling of contextual effects, with particular attention being devoted to linear and nonlinear effects and the difference between social contexts and political contexts. This chapter also alerts us to the underused potential of the national election studies as sources for developing and testing models of contextual effects and cross-level inferences.

Elites and Representation

One of the more theoretically charged domains of political life that fell prey to the behaviorally oriented inquiries of the post–World War II era was that of political representation. Among the three most seminal works in the United States were the McClosky, Hoffman, and O'Hara (1960) comparisons of party elites and rank and file; the Wahlke, Eulau, Buchanan, and Ferguson (1962) inquiry into representational roles among state legislators; and the Miller and Stokes (1963) investigation of congruence between congressional representatives and their constituents. To a large extent these, and a small handful of other studies, shaped the research agenda on representation for at least two decades. Their residues continue to be reflected in contemporary scholarship, which sometimes challenges and at other times elaborates upon the earlier work.

The Miller and Stokes "diamond model" of representation, with its interconnecting lines between the four components of constituents' attitudes, representatives' attitudes, representatives' perceptions of constituent attitudes, and the representatives' behavior (votes), posed a number of theoretical, substantive, and methodological questions for observers of the electoral process. This was another Michigan model which would undergo rigorous examination, both in the United States and abroad. As with party identification, strong reservations were raised about the exportability of the diamond model, especially in view of the widespread presence of parliamentary governments, proportional representation, and disciplined parties. These and other considerations prompt Jacques Thomassen to question, in chapter 10, whether any of the models of representation are adequate to the task and to explore the problematic connection between empirical models of representation and normative conceptions of representative democracy. In so doing, he suggests a research agenda for the future.

Although the linkage between elected representatives and their constituents has provided most of the grist for the mill of representation studies, the political nominating conventions have also proved irresistible, as chronicled in Leon Epstein's tracing of a variety of approaches to the study of conventions and their delegates. This attraction stems in part from the centrality of parties in the electoral process and in part from the accessibility of party delegates and the rank and file. As with studies of the electorate, the study of party elites via the nominating conventions has aptly demonstrated the importance of replicated designs, for the patterns which characterized the 1950 studies differed considerably from those of the early 1970s, which, in turn, were substantially revised by those pertaining to the 1980s (McClosky, Hoffman, and O'Hara 1960; Kirkpatrick 1976; Miller and Jennings 1986; Miller 1988). These studies of party elites were conducted during a period of time in which fundamental changes in the functions and composition of the party conventions were occurring. These changes have led to suggestions about new research questions and research strategies, topics taken up in the latter part of Epstein's essay.

Rules and formulas under which representatives are elected have obvious implications for the electoral process and mass-elite linkages (e.g., Powell

1982). Manifestations of these implications include the strategies pursued by party elites and the responses of the electorate to those strategies. A standard way of assessing the consequences of electoral rules and formulas—net of other influences—is to make comparisons across countries for some given period of time. Occasionally, however, the real political world presents electoral researchers with a more or less natural experiment in which an intervention takes place and is then subsequently withdrawn with, under the best of circumstances, other conditions remaining stable. These requirements were approximated in Norway when, for the 1985 election, it was possible to form a list alliance, a proviso whereby parties could agree to present separate lists on the ballot and to pool their votes afterwards. Drawing upon electoral returns, survey data, and information about party elites, Henry Valen describes, in chapter 12, the strategies pursued by the parties, the responses of the electorate, and the likely impact of the experiment on the electoral outcome. The relatively modest effects of the proviso should caution against easy extrapolations based on assessments of voting arrangements in laboratory experiments, hypotheticals in survey research, and computer simulations.

Conclusion

The essays in this volume provide a sample of the extraordinarily rich scholarly offerings that now characterize the study of elections at home and abroad. The work is increasingly comparative and historical, theory-driven and empirical. The attitudes of citizens are more explicitly linked to the behavior of elites and the operation of political institutions. Survey data are analyzed in context, along with aggregate measures of political and social structures and content analysis of campaigns and media coverage.

As we write this introductory essay, Warren Miller continues to work actively and productively on the frontiers of electoral research. As such, he is more inclined to look forward than back. Nonetheless, we hope this volume, and the broad community of scholars it represents, evokes within him recognition of and satisfaction with what his unique intellectual and entrepreneurial talents have wrought.

REFERENCES

Aldrich, John. 1993. "Rational Choice and Turnout." *American Journal of Political Science* 37:246–78.
Beck, Paul Allen. 1986. "Choice, Context, and Consequence: Beaten and Unbeaten Paths toward a Science of Electoral Behavior." In *Political Science: The Science of Politics,* ed. Herbert F. Weisberg. New York: Agathon.

Beck, Paul Allen, Lawrence Baum, Aage R. Clausen, and Charles E. Smith, Jr. 1992. "Patterns and Sources of Ticket Splitting in Subpresidential Voting." *American Political Science Review* 86:916–28.

Campbell, Angus, Gerald Gavin, and Warren E. Miller. 1954. *The Voter Decides.* Evanston, Ill.: Row, Peterson.

Campbell, Angus, Philip E. Converse, Warren E. Miller, and Donald E. Stokes. 1960. *The American Voter.* New York: Wiley.

Converse, Philip E. 1969. "Of Time and Partisan Stability." *Comparative Political Studies* 2:139–71.

Crewe, Ivor. 1989. "Innovation, Ideas, and Institutions." In *Crossroads of Social Science,* ed. Heinz Eulau. New York: Agathon.

Dalton, Russell J., and Martin P. Wattenberg. 1993. "The Not So Simple Act of Voting." In *Political Science: The State of the Discipline,* II, ed. Ada W. Finifter. Washington, D.C.: American Political Science Association.

Eulau, Heinz, ed. 1989. *Crossroads of Social Science: The ICPSR 25th Anniversary Volume.* New York: Agathon.

Huckfeldt, Robert, and John Sprague. 1993. "Citizens, Contexts, and Politics." In *Political Science: The State of the Discipline,* II, ed. Ada W. Finifter. Washington, D.C.: American Political Science Association.

Janowitz, Morris, and Warren E. Miller. 1952. "The Index of Political Predisposition in the 1948 Election." *Journal of Politics* 14:710–27.

Kirkpatrick, Jeane. 1976. *The New Presidential Elite: Men and Women in National Politics.* New York: Russell Sage and Twentieth Century Foundation.

McClosky, Herbert, Paul J. Hoffman, and Rosemary O'Hara. 1960. "Issue Conflict and Consensus among Party Leaders and Followers." *American Political Science Review* 54:406–27.

Miller, Warren E. 1955–56. "Presidential Coattails: A Study in Political Myth and Methodology." *Public Opinion Quarterly* 19:353–68.

———. 1956. "One Party Politics and the Voter." *American Political Science Review* 50:707–25.

———. 1988. *Without Consent: Mass-Elite Linkages in Presidential Politics.* Lexington, Ky.: University Press of Kentucky.

———. 1991. "Back to Basics: Party Identification, Realignment, and Party Voting." *American Political Science Review* 85:557–68.

———. 1992. "The Puzzle Transformed: Explaining Declining Turnout." *Political Behavior* 14:333–52.

Miller, Warren E., Arthur H. Miller, and Edward J. Schneider. 1980. *The American National Election Studies Data Sourcebook 1952–1976.* Cambridge, Mass.: Harvard University Press.

Miller, Warren E., and Donald E. Stokes. 1963. "Constituency Influence in Congress." *American Political Science Review* 57:45–56.

Miller, Warren E., and M. Kent Jennings. 1986. *Parties in Transition: A Longitudinal Study of Party Elites and Party Supporters.* New York: Russell Sage.

Miller, Warren E., and Santa Traugott. 1989. *The American National Election Studies Data Sourcebook, 1952–1986.* Cambridge, Mass.: Harvard University Press.

Miller, Warren E., and Teresa E. Levitin. 1977. *Leadership and Change: Presidential Elections from 1952–1976.* Cambridge, Mass.: Winthrop.

Niemi, Richard G., Harold Stanley, and Charles L. Evans. 1984. "Age and Turnout among the Newly Enfranchised." *European Journal of Political Research* 12:371–86.

Niemi, Richard G., and Herbert F. Weisberg. 1993. "Is Party Identification Stable?" In *Controversies in Voting Behavior,* 3d ed., ed. Richard G. Niemi and Herbert F. Weisberg. Washington, D.C.: Congressional Quarterly Press.

Powell, G. Bingham. 1982. *Contemporary Democracies: Participation, Stability, and Violence.* Cambridge, Mass: Harvard University Press.

Shanks, J. Merrill, and Warren E. Miller. 1990. "Policy Direction and Performance Evaluation: Complementary Explanations of the Reagan Election. " *British Journal of Political Science* 20:143–235.

———. 1991. "Partisanship, Policy and Performance: The Reagan Legacy in the 1988 Election." *British Journal of Political Science* 21:129–97.

Tingsten, Herbert. [1937] 1963. *Political Behavior: Studies in Election Statistics.* Trans. Vilgot Hammarling. Totowa, N.J.: Bedminster.

Wahlke, John C., Heinz Eulau, William Buchanan, and Leroy C. Ferguson. 1962. *The Legislative System.* New York: Wiley.

Weisberg, Herbert F. 1986. "Model Choice in Political Science: The Case of Voting Behavior Research, 1946–1975." In *Political Science: The Science of Politics,* ed. Herbert F. Weisberg. New York: Agathon.

Theories of Voting

CHAPTER 2

Unresolved Issues in Electoral Decisions: Alternative Perspectives on the Explanation of Individual Choice

J. Merrill Shanks, with the Assistance of Douglas A. Strand

The occasion for which these chapters were prepared took place on the fortieth anniversary of the biennial surveys now called the National Election Studies (NES), all of which have been carried out under the direction of Warren Miller. Since 1952, substantial changes have been introduced in the content and format of the questions asked of NES respondents, as well as in the explanations of electoral decisions that are based on the resulting data. Throughout this period, NES surveys have been the primary resource for political scientists who study voting behavior in American national elections, and NES materials have played a prominent role in the improvement of our measurement and analytic procedures. Despite this progress, however, several issues have persisted that make it possible for different researchers to reach strikingly divergent conclusions about a given election based on analyses of the same NES data.

The most visible recent disagreements of this sort have concerned the role played by policy-related preferences in the elections that Ronald Reagan and George Bush won in 1980, 1984, and 1988.[1] No report can identify (much less resolve) all of the conflicts among electoral analysts who have based their conclusions on the same NES surveys.[2] Rather than reviewing specific conflicts, this chapter discusses the underlying issues that may be responsible for divergent interpretations of the same election, including the degree to which such conflicts may be resolved by examining additional kinds of evidence.

Unresolved Issues: An Overview

Differences between analysts in their substantive conclusions may be inevitable in the electoral field, for every survey-based analysis rests on a variety of conceptual and methodological assumptions that may not be explicitly stated. To be sure, conflicts concerning electoral interpretation can occasionally be resolved by clarification of technical details concerning measurement or analytic procedures. In most instances, however, differences between researchers' substantive conclusions can be attributed to their contrasting (but often implicit) assumptions concerning one or more of the following aspects of electoral explanation.

Alternative Conceptualizations of Choice. Political scientists and journalists appear to rely on somewhat different assumptions about the meaning of their central dependent variable—that is, about the nature of individual electoral decisions, as well as the processes (or mechanisms) by which such decisions are produced. These differences concern the extent to which voters make choices that are consciously based on comparative evaluations of the candidates with respect to a set of specific criteria and the way in which those evaluations are combined or weighted to produce voters' final decisions.

Diversity in the Content of Potential Explanatory Variables. Several academic disciplines and the media have produced a large repertoire of potential types of explanatory variables. This diversity in explanatory themes includes variables that are defined in terms of basic values, ideological predispositions, group identifications, policy preferences, economic interests or benefits, perceptions of current economic (and other) conditions, and explicit evaluations of presidential or party performance and personal qualities of the candidates, as well as long-term partisan identification. All of these potential sources of political influence compete for attention or credit in interpretations of electoral decisions in a given year, and analysts exhibit widely divergent views concerning the relevance of particular explanatory themes.

Explanation of Individual vs. Collective Decisions. In addition to their often implicit assumptions concerning the meaning of choice or the types of explanatory factors to be considered, analysts can also reach contrasting interpretations of electoral decisions in a given context because they are trying to explain different aspects of that election. In particular, such differences can easily arise when one analyst is trying to account for differences between voters in their individual decisions and another is trying to interpret the aggregate result of the election.

Explanations Based on Reasons vs. Variables. Conceptual differences concerning the meaning of choice also reflect persistent differences between analysts concerning the degree to which they believe that voters (or respondents) can describe the causes of their own choice. Since Lazarsfeld,[3] social scientists have disagreed about the comparative validity of explanations based on reasons (or respondents' own explanations of their preferences) versus explanations based on the analysis of variables. This fundamental difference in explanatory strategy plays an important role in many conflicts concerning electoral interpretation among analysts who rely on both academic and media surveys.

Alternative Assumptions about Causal Sequence or Structure. Electoral analysts also disagree about the most appropriate type of causal and statistical model for survey-based electoral explanation. The core of these differences concerns the number of causal stages that can be distinguished in the overall process culminating in the vote—a process that was described as a "funnel of causality" in *The American Voter.* This kind of disagreement is fundamentally tied to analysts' divergent beliefs concerning the extent to which some effects may be confounded by reciprocal causation or other relationships between measured and omitted causes of the vote.

Causal Heterogeneity among Voters. Finally, many analysts believe that voters are not the same (as one another) in the causal processes that are responsible for their opinions and behavior, and that such differences are difficult, if not impossible, to incorporate into our explanatory models. Such differences between voters may involve the magnitude of "true" effects for specific factors or considerations, as well as the causal sequence that governs relationships between explanatory variables. Furthermore, as suggested above, analysts do not agree on the extent to which survey respondents can be trusted to describe the factors that influenced their own vote. As a consequence, analysts are unlikely to agree on any solution to the problem of variation (between voters) in causal structure that relies on voters' own reports concerning the weights assigned to specific considerations.

Based on this summary, an attentive and not necessarily unfriendly observer might conclude that researchers who use survey data to explain electoral decisions are certain to have difficulty in agreeing upon the most appropriate account of a given election. Such disagreements may be inevitable because (1) we don't agree on the sense in which voters actually choose; (2) we have assembled an unwieldy collection of potential causal factors based on competing theories and academic disciplines; (3) we don't agree on whether respondents can be trusted to provide valid descriptions of the causes of their own decisions; (4) we have very different views concerning the most appropriate causal model for analyzing electoral decision making, including the number and sequence of distinguishable stages in such a model; (5) we are unsure about the magnitude and consequences of undetected variation between voters in the causal effects we are trying to estimate; and (6) we tend to confuse conclusions that account for differences between individuals in the choices they make in a given election with conclusions about the aggregate results of that election. No wonder we find it easy to disagree. Each of these potential sources of divergent electoral interpretations is discussed below, in the order in which they were introduced.

Alternative Conceptualizations of the Vote: Deliberate Choice versus Evolution of Preference

Conflicts in electoral interpretation may be partially caused by implicit differences that are definitional in character, for the analysts involved may be using different conceptualizations of the individual-level choices they are trying to explain and the kinds of processes which shape those choices. In an effort to provoke debate about these issues, I have occasionally argued against any electoral explanation that requires a deliberate or conscious choice by the voter that is based on comparative evaluations of the candidates concerning specific criteria—whether or not such choices are described as rational. In such discussions, my deliberately extreme position has resembled that of the lawyer for the defense who doesn't want to neglect any arguments that might be helpful to the client. In this story, the lawyer is prepared to state that the defendant couldn't have done it because he wasn't present at the scene of the crime; that if he was present, he didn't do it because he had no motive; and that if he did do it, it was an accident.

In a similar fashion, any attempt to explain the vote as a deliberate choice that is based on a conscious weighing of all the relevant considerations may encounter the following sequence of arguments from analysts who make very different assumptions about the causal processes involved:

> According to this contrary view, most voters do not consciously choose between candidates at a specific point in time by considering all of the apparent differences between those candidates that may be relevant. Instead, their preferences evolve over time in response to the accumulation of positive and negative impressions about the candidates, many of which were created by specific experiences or events that are no longer remembered by the voter. To be sure, voters are eventually required to make a decision by election day, but all they do at that point is reveal the result of evaluative processes that have been going on for some time. In this formulation, all that is left from many (if not most) of a voter's experiences concerning a specific candidate is a residual positive or negative impression, whether or not the voter was ever aware of which aspect of a given experience was responsible for its residual impression. At the time of decision (or the survey interview), voters simply identify the candidate about whom their cumulative impression is the most positive or least negative.
>
> If some voters did make a decision by consciously reviewing and weighing their evaluations of the candidates with respect to a list of specific criteria, this type of analyst would not expect such voters to remember all the factors or considerations that produced positive or negative impressions. In this formulation, such voters would be influenced by that conscious review, but their final choice would also be influenced by other factors that were not remembered at the time of their decision.
>
> If some voters made a conscious decision and remembered all the factors or considerations that produced their impressions of the candidates, this type of analyst would assume that such voters differed signifi-

cantly from each other in the causal weights that were attached to specific factors or considerations, and that they would not be able to recall accurately which ones had a major influence on their choice and which ones were of less or trivial importance.

Finally, in this formulation, even if some voters remembered all of the factors involved and their associated weights, they would be unlikely to report accurately those factors and weights when asked by an interviewer, because of either the tendency for respondents to report such causes in ways that make them appear in a favorable light or other deficiencies in our measurement procedures.

In general, analysts of election surveys who believe in deliberate or conscious choice are likely to rely on respondents' explanations of their own preferences[4] or on structured questions which provide comparative evaluations of the candidates concerning specific criteria. In contrast, analysts who are persuaded by the above arguments may pay less attention to direct measures of the proximate impressions which presumably control the vote in favor of other (less proximate) variables, whose indirect effects may be easier to describe.[5]

Alternative Causal Mechanisms. Journalists, politicians, and scholars share an intense interest in why individual voters chose one candidate over another, with an emphasis on the intentional or deliberate character of that choice. As suggested in the above arguments, however, it may also be necessary to understand how voters' impressions of the candidates came to be as positive or negative as they were at the time they made their decision (or were interviewed). In particular, the following possibilities should be considered in describing the processes by which a given voter or respondent arrived at a preference for candidate A over candidate B that is reported in a survey interview.

(R)espondent never knew—or was no longer aware of—the causes of his or her impressions of the candidates, but has the clear impression that "A was better";

R was not aware of very many specific reasons for that preference (at the time of the decision or interview), but did retain a conscious preference for A over B with respect to a few specific considerations or criteria;

R had some residual positive and negative impressions that were not visibly "connected" to any specific criteria, but was aware of conscious or deliberate preferences for A over B with respect to many specific concerns; or

R's preference was entirely caused by a conscious (weighted) combination of comparative evaluation of the two candidates with respect to specific substantive criteria, all of which are reported in the interview.

The above possibilities focus on the degree to which impressions of the candidates are caused by voters' conscious evaluations of the candidates with respect to specific criteria. Insofar as a voter's evaluation of a candidate was not based on specific criteria of this sort, such a voter may still have acquired positive or negative impressions of that candidate through some combination of the following alternative processes.

> Such impressions may have been the result of simple or immediate reactions to some aspects of the campaign or candidate that seemed either attractive or not right, in a way that was influenced by the voter's general outlook, values, or preferences, without the voter being aware of or remembering the specific issues or criteria involved; or

> Such impressions may have been transferred from some influential source that shares the same general outlook as the respondent, such as family members, friends, local leaders, or national organizations.

The above distinctions between causal processes are primarily based on the kind of information that voters acquire before they come to a stable preference or choice. Most of these distinctions concern the degree to which positive or negative impressions can be traced to conscious evaluations based on specific criteria. In addition, however, electoral analysts should consider the possibility that some impressions about candidates, regardless of content, may be acquired from other influential sources, instead of the voter's own exposure to the campaign or media.

Diversity in the Content of Potential Explanatory Variables

In general, apparent conflicts in the interpretation of specific elections may also be attributed to the remarkable variety of explanatory ideas or themes that have been suggested by several academic disciplines, as well as politicians and journalists. It is easy for analysts to disagree when they are trying to explain only a single decision or preference for each voter and can select their preferred explanations from so many potential factors, issues, or considerations, all of which compete for explanatory credit in accounting for electoral decisions in a given campaign. As described in the following paragraphs, electoral analysts have described some types of potential causes as more important than others based on several different ways of classifying those causes, including distinctions between political versus nonpolitical variables, parties versus issues versus candidates, short-term versus long-term forces, and issues that are defined in terms of policy-related conflict versus performance or results.

Nonpolitical versus Political Variables. One of the earliest and most persistent distinctions between alternative types of explanatory variables rests on the assumption that voter characteristics that are not defined in political terms can nevertheless play an important (although indirect) role in influencing their candidate preference. At one point, the electoral field was described in terms of a competition between sociological explanations based on effects that are defined in terms of social or economic characteristics, and psychological explanations based on attitudes toward various aspects of the campaign. In contemporary research, however, social or economic characteristics are often included as explanatory variables because they are exogenous to political or electoral preferences and are assumed to have an indirect impact through their influence on a variety of political attitudes that, in turn, determine the vote. The most frequently used characteristics of this sort are the voters' race or ethnicity, gender, age (or generation), religion, level of education, family income, union membership, and the region of the country in which they live. Each of these variables also represents a characteristic that is highly stable, in the sense that voters' current positions on that variable were established long before the election—although the electoral effect of that characteristic may not have appeared until the current campaign.

Parties versus Issues versus Candidates. The most frequently used distinction between different explanatory variables concerns the object of the attitude involved—for example, whether a specific opinion is about the parties, about an issue that has arisen during the campaign, or about a given characteristic of the candidates. No matter what other distinctions are used, these traditional categories are reflected in most, if not all, comprehensive explanations of the vote.[6] As with the other distinctions in this section, the primary purpose of this classification has been to assess the relative importance of these three types of election-related attitudes in shaping electoral decisions in a given campaign.

Long-term Predispositions versus Short-term Forces. The distinction between opinions that are about parties and those that are about issues or candidates is hard to separate from the suggestion that some political opinions have a long-term influence on the vote—in the sense that they were acquired before the current election and have a continuing impact on partisan evaluations— while other opinions have an impact that was created (or generated) fairly recently in response to short-term forces in the current campaign. To qualify as a long-term force, a given characteristic must both be stable (or resistant to change from campaign-specific forces) and have a continuing impact on other partisan attitudes on the vote. In contrast, the short-term forces in a given campaign can be activated by both stable predispositions and highly contemporary or volatile issues in the current campaign.

In principle, any voter characteristic that might be used to explain the vote can be assigned to a position on a continuum from extremely stable to highly volatile. Based on over three decades of NES-related publications, many analysts have concluded that the NES root question concerning partisan identification represents the most stable political attitude, that measures based on perceptions or evaluations of specific candidates represent the most volatile potential causes of the vote, and that issue-related opinions occupy an uncertain intermediate position in this respect. As emphasized below, however, electoral analysts do not agree about the degree to which these three types of attitudes are influenced by other short-term forces in the current campaign.

Two Major Types of Issues. In reports defining many of the issues that still dominate the electoral field, researchers at both Columbia and Michigan suggested that the impact of campaign issues should be described in terms of two types of political evaluation.[7] This dichotomization of issue content has been described in various terms, including distinctions between candidate evaluations that are defined in terms of conflict versus consensus concerning specific governmental objectives, candidates' positions on a given issue versus their style or valence, and voters' preferences concerning policy versus their evaluations of candidate (or incumbent) performance. This basic distinction between alternative types or sources of candidate evaluations may be clarified by suggesting that some evaluations appear to be based on the voter's belief that a controversial policy or objective is right or wrong, while other evaluations appear to be based on the voter's perception of a candidate's or party's success or failure concerning some noncontroversial or consensual objective. Contemporary analysts do not agree on the necessity or viability of this kind of conceptual distinction, but it persists as a common approach to allocating explanatory credit for electoral decisions.

Other Competing Distinctions. The above paragraphs identify only a few of the distinctions that have been used to classify and summarize the political attitudes or forces that influence electoral decisions in a specific campaign. To emphasize the role played by particular types of factors, analysts have also suggested distinctions based on voters' economic interests, defined in terms of individual or group benefits; their evaluations of personal versus national conditions; the degree of specificity versus generality in their preferences (or perceptions); the degree to which preferences are based on ends versus means; and the degree to which evaluations represent retrospective evaluations of the past performance or positions of the candidates versus prospective expectations concerning their future characteristics, if they are elected.

In our essays on the 1980, 1984, and 1988 elections, Warren Miller and I have presented a series of multistage models that incorporate most of the above types of distinctions between competing explanatory variables or themes. All three essays concentrate on the distinction between political variables that are based on policy-related preferences and those based on performance evaluations, but we have also emphasized the relationships between such opinions and other types of factors that may have influenced the vote. Any explanation of electoral decisions must consider the potentially confounding effects of causes of the vote that have been omitted from that account but are related to variables that *have* been included. For that reason, our analyses have included an increasingly diverse set of explanatory themes as well as a growing attention to issues concerning the underlying causal structure.

Explanation of Individual versus Aggregate Decisions

Most of this essay concentrates on conflicting descriptions of the role played by specific types of variables or explanatory themes in determining individual voter decisions. It should be noted, however, that academic, journalistic, and political use of such descriptions is often linked to a different, but related, question about the aggregate result of the election. In particular, many observers want to understand why the victorious party won and why their margin of victory was as big or small as it was. Because of that impulse, analysts often try to decompose the winner's plurality into a set of positive and negative components that, in combination, produced the collective electoral decision. Unfortunately, this distinction between explanations of individual decisions and aggregate results is often lost in discussions about the relative importance of specific explanatory variables. Electoral analysts and their readers should be certain that they are trying to answer the same questions before debating the validity of specific statistical results.

This distinction between the explanation of differences in individual preferences and the interpretation or decomposition of aggregate results has a long history in the electoral field. The rationale and procedures for assessing the importance of specific factors with respect to these two aspects of a given campaign are discussed extensively elsewhere.[8] The present essay concentrates on the explanation of individual preferences or decisions, but the following points should be emphasized.

Variables or factors that played a major role in determining individual choice may not make a significant contribution to the winning candidates' victory if the distribution of voters' opinions with respect to that factor were evenly balanced so that neither candidate had an advantage in that area. Preferences concerning policy direction may often have this quality, where opposing parties advocate policy alternatives about which voters are approximately evenly divided.

Factors that play only a modest role in explaining individual differences in voting behavior may still make a major contribution to the aggregate result if the distribution of opinions in that area are heavily skewed to favor one of the candidates. A clear example of this possibility can be seen in the 1980 electorate's nearly unanimous view that the national economy had worsened since the year before. Such a factor, however, must exhibit some cross-sectional variation (between voters) if we are to estimate its contribution to the winner's plurality.

All techniques for interpreting the aggregate results of a single election are necessarily based on some kind of explanation at the individual level, and will be suspect insofar as that individual-level account is incorrect.

In particular, interpretations of the aggregate result of elections are subject to the same controversy, previously discussed in this essay, concerning the validity of respondents' self-reports about the reasons or causes for their own choice. Analysts who are confident about the validity of voters' reports concerning the determinants of their own candidate preferences are likely to adopt a method for interpreting the aggregate result of a given election that is based on those self-reported reasons. Analysts who are not persuaded of the validity of self-reported causes must rely on some other, less direct, approach to explain both individual decisions and aggregate results.

Explanations Based on Reasons versus Variables

As suggested above, conflicts in electoral interpretation can often be traced to disagreements between analysts that might be called substantive, because of their conceptualization of choice, the types of explanatory variables they have examined, or their concentration on individual decisions versus the aggregate results of an election. Some differences in conclusions or interpretation, however, can be traced to methodological or technical differences between analysts in the assumptions they have made about causation, measurement, and the effects of omitted variables. Furthermore, substantive issues are often confounded by simultaneous differences in the types of measures and statistical procedures involved. The most important of these differences concern the alternative strategies that can be used to explain any choice or behavior with survey data.

The introduction to this essay emphasized a simple dichotomy between the use of reasons and variables as alternative survey-based strategies for explaining individual vote choice. Although easy to state and remember, it may be helpful to replace that dichotomy with a continuum that suggests the variety of strategies which analysts have adopted concerning information provided by respondents about their own decision-making processes.[9] Such a continuum ranges from complete reliance on respondents' reports concerning the causes of their own choice, on one end, to a complete disregard of any information from the respondent concerning the causes of their evaluations of the candidates. In particular, a continuum of this sort would include the following specific strategies.

A pure reasons-based strategy would rely entirely on respondents' answers to questions concerning the reasons for their preferences, without any multivariate analysis to estimate differential weights for specific areas. This method is often used in exit polls because of its simplicity and efficiency.[10]

In *The American Voter,* explanatory variables were constructed from responses to open-ended questions concerning those aspects of the candidates and parties which were liked and disliked, but multivariate analyses were used to assess the overall importance of measures which summarized such responses in specific domains or issue areas.

Alternatively, structured questions might be used to construct comparative evaluations of the candidates with respect to prespecified criteria or areas, as well as ratings of the importance, or weight, of each such area, as exemplified in the standard NES measures of issue proximity and the importance ratings which were introduced in the 1980 NES surveys. With such variables, vote prediction equations can be estimated that multiply comparative evaluations (or proximity scores) by salience weights based on respondents' own reports concerning the importance of each issue area. In this approach, as in the first two above, the analyst is still trying to describe the individual-level forces that produced the vote, but the explanatory variables are constructed from responses to structured questions about prespecified criteria for choice, instead of open-ended questions about reasons.

Analysts could decide to use respondents' perceptions or evaluations of candidates with respect to specific criteria but *not* to trust salience weights based on respondents' own reports concerning the importance of those areas. In such analyses, each coefficient for a specific area presumably represents an average effect across respondents, for whom the true effect is somewhat variable.

Finally, analysts could decide not to trust any placements, ratings, or comparative evaluations of the two candidates, in order to estimate the overall (average) impact of respondents' own positions in each area.

Warren Miller and I began our essays on the Reagan/Bush elections with an implicit assumption that we would produce a more accurate explanation of electoral decisions if we estimated the apparent effects of specific voter characteristics based on answers to structured questions in each such area, rather than relying on the open-ended questions that analysts use to make inferences about the reasoning of respondents. As our work has evolved, we have changed our definition of several explanatory themes and shifted our analytic emphasis away from the direct measurement of individual-level evaluations of the candidates. Because of a growing concern about the distortions or biases associated with those reports, we now concentrate on the voters' own policy-related preferences, instead of using any respondent-supplied information about candidates' positions or the causal weight of specific factors.

As we begin our analysis of the 1992 election, however, we are reconsidering the potential relevance of respondent-based reasons for any comprehensive explanation of the vote. In particular, we have begun to compare the descriptions of vote choice in the 1980, 1984, and 1988 elections that emerge from our analysis of explanatory variables at various stages in the "funnel of causality" with alternative portraits based on responses to the open-ended "likes and dislikes" questions about the candidates and parties that were featured in *The American Voter*. To what extent do analysts get the same impression concerning the impact of a specific topic or issue on the vote, when they switch from an analysis of variables based on structured questions about that topic to a summary of responses to open-ended questions involving that topic?

Our experience to date suggests that the results produced for this kind of comparison will be difficult to interpret, because of built-in differences between the two methods in their assumptions about causal order or sequence, as well as their obvious differences in measurement and the conceptualization of choice. Despite these obstacles, however, we are extending our comparisons in this area because many observers are curious about the degree of similarity between these two approaches to survey-based explanation. For the foreseeable future, both approaches will continue to be used, based on media polls, as well as NES surveys. As a consequence, we need to know much more about the circumstances under which the apparent causes of the vote are fairly similar or quite different when the analyst's approach to explanation shifts from voters' own reasons to the multivariate analysis of variables.

Alternative Assumptions about Causal Sequence or Structure

Several of the issues discussed above have also contributed to long-standing conflicts between analysts in their assumptions about the direction of causality, relationships between included explanatory variables and other omitted causes of the vote, and the magnitude of errors in survey measurement. Such assumptions are often regarded as technical instead of substantive, but they have had a powerful influence on the statistical procedures which electoral analysts have chosen and, because of those choices, on their conclusions about the causes of individual decisions. In particular, survey-based electoral explanations rest on markedly different assumptions concerning the number and meaning of the causal stages that can be distinguished in the many individual-level processes which culminate in the vote.

In *The American Voter,* each voter's decision was seen as determined by a field of psychological forces that were created by that person's reactions to the current campaign. Such forces were measured by categorizing responses to open-ended questions concerning those aspects of the candidates and parties that the voter liked and disliked. In this approach, the relative importance of alternative types of forces (e.g., domestic policy or group benefits) was assessed by describing the statistical connection between the vote and attitudinal components that summarized the psychological forces in each such area. Each component variable was constructed by counting the number of responses that could be classified in that substantive area (e.g., domestic policy).

It was acknowledged that many other characteristics of the voters besides their campaign-specific evaluations or forces might have an indirect impact on the vote by influencing some of these evaluations, but it was assumed that all of the statistical information needed to explain the vote could be captured in proximate variables constructed from voters' own reports concerning the nature of these psychological forces. *The American Voter* introduced the concept of a funnel of causality to suggest ways in which causally prior variables might have indirect impact on the vote by influencing proximate, psychological forces, but party identification was the only such variable whose indirect and direct effects on the vote were examined in any detail.

For many years, critics of *The American Voter* concentrated on the possibility that its conclusions were misleading because of its conceptualization and measurement of the individual-level forces involved. In particular, advocates of rational or policy-based choice suggested that responses to open-ended questions did not accurately capture the impact of voters' preferences on policy issues, so that new, structured questions were introduced that described respondents' own preferences concerning specific policy alternatives and their perceptions of the candidates' positions concerning the same policies. Vote choice could then be explained in terms of a linear combination of variables that were defined in terms of issue proximity, each of which assessed the degree to which respondents saw their own preferences in that area as closer to the perceived position of one candidate than the other. Since 1968, analyses based on issue proximities have been a standard, if not dominant, approach to explaining vote choice in terms of policy-related preferences.

From the beginning, however, other analysts have been concerned that effect coefficients for issue proximities, or any other comparative evaluations of the candidates, would be biased if they were estimated in a single-equation model. Such concerns are frequently discussed in terms of simultaneity, whether they involve reciprocal causal relationships between explanatory variables and the vote or relationships between such variables and omitted causes of the vote, but the same kinds of problems or biases may also arise because of nontrivial measurement error in the explanatory variables. Based on such assumptions of reciprocal causation, correlated disturbances, or measurement error, several analysts have suggested that effect estimates for endogenous explanatory variables that are themselves caused by contemporary or short-term forces will be seriously biased if they are based on a single equation model.[11]

Such analysts have typically noted that believable estimates of causal effects may still be possible in models which involve reciprocal causation, measurement error, or unavoidable relationships between measured and omitted causes of the vote—provided that the analyst is willing to endorse a different set of assumptions. To produce such estimates, analysts must adopt a simultaneous-equation model that includes assumptions, usually called exclusion restrictions, that assign some potential effects to a nonexistent status (i.e., zero). The history of simultaneous-equation models of the vote has been as controversial as the two single-equation traditions based on open-ended questions and issue proximities they were designed to replace. Disagreement about such models has been primarily based on the validity of the essential exclusion restrictions involved, each of which stipulates that the impact of one explanatory variable on the vote (or on party identification) is entirely mediated by other, endogenous, variables in the model.[12]

As mentioned above, Warren Miller and I have gradually moved away from explanatory models that rely entirely on explicit evaluations of the candidates by concentrating on the total effects of variables that are presumably located further back in the funnel of causality. In particular, we have shifted our policy-related analysis from issue proximities to measures of voters' general predispositions and current preferences concerning policy direction—all of which are defined without any reference to the candidates or parties. In our current work, we have characterized the overall causal structure that culminates in the vote as consisting of four distinct stages. In sequence, these four prevote stages are defined in terms of (1) stable social and economic characteristics, (2) partisan identification and policy-related predispositions, (3) preferences concerning current policy issues and perceptions of current conditions, and (4) all explicit evaluations of the candidates concerning policy, performance, or personal characteristics.

In our current work, we continue to use a block recursive model to estimate the total effects of specific variables in each of our four stages because of concerns about the consequences of false exclusion restrictions in any alternative model based on simultaneous equations. Our use of the above multiple-stage and block recursive model is based on a growing conviction that respondents' own policy preferences and perceptions of current conditions are only moderately affected by persuasion effects from the campaign of the candidate, who they have selected because of other factors, and that all candidate evaluations are subject to substantial projection effects, in which evaluations in one area are affected by candidate preferences that were really based on other considerations. As suggested in the conclusion of this essay, these assumptions should be challenged through a variety of procedures based on panel and experimental designs. In the meantime, our results should be interpreted in ways that underscore their dependence on the validity of our assumptions about causal structure.

Causal Heterogeneity among Voters

In interpreting the results of any equation-based explanation of the vote, readers are often tempted to interpret specific coefficients as apparent effects that represent a kind of summary or average, each concealing an unknown amount of underlying variation in the true impact or relevance of that variable. This informal practice is itself a point of contention among election analysts, although its consequences are not as dramatic as those discussed above.

Consider the simplest type of explanatory variable X, such as gender, which is a simple dichotomy scored as a "dummy," or "indicator," variable [scored 1 for a designated category (e.g., female) and 0 for the other, or base, category (e.g., male)]. Analysts and readers are tempted to interpret the value of any effect coefficient that is estimated for a variable in a linear explanatory model as the apparent average effect on the vote of being in the designated category of that variable (e.g., female), instead of being in the other category (e.g., male), regardless of whether any other explanatory variables are included or held constant in the same equation. By describing such a coefficient as an apparent average effect, the analyst is clearly suggesting that the average of the individual true level effects may be different from the observed coefficient. In addition, the apparent average expression may also be intended as an abbreviation for two other assumptions concerning the sample-specific meaning of the designated coefficient—that the true impact of differences between voters on a variable is not presumed to be invariant for all pairs of persons within the current sample (who differ in the given explanatory variable) and that the average of those true effects within the given sample need not be the same within some larger population from which that sample was drawn.

In the simplest possible case, where we believe that two categories of X are at least approximately equal with respect to the combined influence of all other causes of the vote, we do not need to include or control for any other explanatory variable. In such cases, we can interpret the simple difference between these two categories' means or average scores on the vote as a satisfactory estimate of the apparent effect of X. That simple difference in means is also the average of the differences in the vote between two cases that differ in X over all such pairs of cases that can be drawn from the current sample. This convergence in interpretation is complicated by the extension of this logic to continuous variables and the presence of other variables in the same explanatory equation, where the coefficient produced by ordinary least squares, or some related multivariate procedure, is no longer identical to a strict average of all the individual-level effects involved. Warnings about this kind of discrepancy between estimated coefficients and the average of varying individual-level true effects have recently become visible within the electoral field,[13] but we know fairly little about the magnitude of biases associated with the interpretation of regression-type coefficients as some kind of average.

If the analyst believes that the true effect of being in one category of X is invariant within the population from which the current sample of respondents has been randomly selected, then the potential complications in presentation and inference associated with average effects can be avoided. In survey-based electoral research, however, many analysts and readers are interested in coefficients that are difficult to interpret in any way except as approximations of the apparent average effect of a one category (or one unit) difference in the given explanatory variable. The assumption that effect estimates must represent some kind of average is based on a pervasive belief that the true effects involved are subject to unmeasured and unmeasurable variation between individuals, rather than fixed or invariant parameters, because of the variety of campaign-related processes that may be involved in activating such an effect for a given individual.

In our previous essays, Miller and I did not emphasize this issue concerning the interpretation of effect estimates in any explanation of the vote, in order to concentrate on the overall importance of general explanatory themes. In our current work, however, we have characterized our motivation in generating such coefficients in terms that require they be interpreted as an approximation of the apparent average impact of differences in that explanatory variable in the population from which the current sample has been drawn. In this formulation, each unknown individual-level effect of a given explanatory variable is the result of the activation of that characteristic (for that individual) in the current campaign. Different individuals with the same partisanship, policy preferences, and perceptions of current conditions will be influenced by somewhat different aspects of the campaign because of differences in exposure or attention, as well as unmeasured differences in the importance or centrality of specific issue-related topics. This shift in the rationale and imagery for interpreting explanatory effects is fairly recent, with as yet untested consequences for the clarity and persuasiveness of our substantive conclusions. Such assumptions are often seen as technical rather than substantive, but differences between analysts in this area are difficult to ignore, for they are responsible for continuing disagreements concerning the types of results that should be taken seriously within the electoral field.

Summary: How Should We Deal with Conflicting Explanations of Electoral Decisions?

Given all of the issues discussed above, what should an informed reader make of apparent conflicts between two explanations or interpretations of a given election that rely on survey data from the same context? What kinds of conflicts are we likely to resolve, and which ones are likely to persist in competing accounts of the same political phenomena?

In general, political scientists have devoted more of their efforts to generating alternative interpretations of specific elections than to discussing, much less resolving, apparent conflicts between them. Indeed, one of the purposes of this essay is to encourage that kind of discussion. To succeed, however, such discussions must be based on a better and common understanding of the ways in which analysts' often implicit assumptions influence the kinds of questions they try to answer, as well as their survey measures and statistical procedures. At a minimum, such an understanding would include the following general points.

Readers should never forget the difference between a given variable's importance in explaining individual-level variation in vote choice and the potentially quite different role the same variable played in generating the aggregate results of that election. In this sense, two analysts who appear to have reached opposite conclusions about the importance of a particular explanatory variable or theme can both be right (or wrong), because they are trying to answer different questions about the same election context.

Analysts who see the vote as the behavioral expression of preferences that have evolved over a period of time are likely to consider explanatory variables that are located further back in the funnel of causality, on the grounds that a variety of predispositions acquired before the current campaign may have had an impact on those preferences at different stages of the campaign. On the other hand, analysts who see the vote as a conscious, if not necessarily rational, decision that is made by weighing all of the relevant considerations will attempt to describe the role played by variables that are highly proximate to that decision, each of which is defined in terms of evaluations of the candidates with respect to specific criteria. Analysts who believe in voters' ability to describe the "field of forces" that determines their own vote are likely to rely on responses to open-ended questions that ask each respondent to identify the reasons why they like or dislike particular candidates. Analysts who do not believe that voters can accurately describe the causes of their own behavior or preference will rely on structured questions about the respondent's opinions in specific areas rather than open-ended questions about the reasons for choice, and will be reluctant to ask respondents for the causal weights that describe the importance of each specific area.

Analysts who believe that voters' decisions have feedback effects on many of the attitudinal variables that are used to explain the vote, that those attitudes share common causes with the vote that cannot be included in the analysis, or that some explanatory variables are subject to significant measurement error will prefer simultaneous-equation models, rather than effect estimates based on a recursive system of equations. (In order to use a simultaneous-equations model, the analyst must make assumptions that include some exogenous variables to be excluded from each of the equations involved.) Analysts who reject such exclusion restrictions will be prevented from using procedures based on simultaneous-equation models. Instead, such analysts may concentrate their explanatory effects on exogenous and semiexogenous variables that are located further back in the underlying causal structure, especially if they are persuaded that the effects of feedback or correlated disturbances are relatively minimal for those variables.

Differences between analysts in these kinds of assumptions are impossible to resolve within the confines of a single cross-section survey. Such issues must be addressed on the basis of outside information obtained from longitudinal or experimental designs. For example, any assumption that policy-related preferences are relatively immune to campaign-related persuasion can be tested in panel designs that include frequent reinterviewing, or experimental studies that randomly assign persons with the same initial preferences to different persuasive circumstances.

In evaluating any interpretation of a given election, readers should compare the analyst's apparent assumptions concerning the above basic issues with their own beliefs concerning the same topics. In some cases, a given interpretation may be easy to accept or reject because of the reader's own convictions concerning causal structure and measurement. In many cases, however, the often implicit and overlapping nature of these basic assumptions may make it difficult to arrive at decisive conclusions.

Miller and I are presently restating and elaborating an approach to the explanation of individual decisions and aggregate results that rests on explicit assumptions concerning each of the issues discussed above. In particular, our approach to electoral explanation is based on the assumption that individual votes should be seen as the behavioral expression of preferences that have evolved over a period of time, and that such preferences are shaped by the campaign through the activation of a variety of predispositions and perceptions concerning conflicts or conditions in the society, most of which were already in place before the current campaign began. Within that framework, we have also assumed that four general stages can be distinguished in the causal processes that produce voter preferences or vote choice, beginning with (1) social or economic characteristics, followed by (2) party identification and other general, policy-related dispositions, through (3) preferences concerning current policy issues and perceptions of current conditions, to (4) proximate explanatory variables that are defined in terms of explicit political or partisan evaluations.

We have constructed our analysis upon this sequence of stages because we are convinced that total effect estimates for variables located further back in the funnel of causality provide a better description of the sources, or origins, of current preferences than either reasons for choice that were provided by the voters or a reconstruction of those individual-based reasons from a battery of proximate evaluations. We are interested in the way current conflicts and conditions appear to influence preferences through proximate evaluations of the candidates in specific areas, but we have based our estimates of the impact of these conflicts or conditions on the statistical connection between the vote and voters' own preferences (concerning policy) or perceptions (concerning conditions), and we have relied on single-equation estimates of these total effects, rather than simultaneous-equation models, because we believe they are less vulnerable to serious bias because of misspecification.[14] Analysts who prefer other sets of assumptions are likely to reach different conclusions, based on a different selection of explanatory variables and statistical procedures.

In some cases, differences between rival interpretations of a given election can be seen as the inevitable result of the fact that the analysts involved were trying to answer different questions, rather than coming to divergent answers to a single question, at least one of which is presumably wrong. This approach to apparent conflicts in electoral interpretation, which may permit both interpretations to be equally right or wrong, is particularly relevant when one analyst has concentrated on explaining individual differences in vote choice while another has attempted to interpret the aggregate results of the election by assigning contributions to specific explanatory variables or themes, or when one analyst is only interested in proximate effects, while another is trying to describe the direct and indirect effects of variables that are located further back in the causal structure.

In other instances, however, we may not be able to decide whether two apparently conflicting conclusions are really compatible, because they represent answers to different questions or represent rival claims to the true answer to a single explanatory question. For example, differences between analysts concerning the quantitative importance of ideological or policy-related preferences in the explanation of individual differences in the vote may be hard to separate from implicit differences between the same analysts concerning the extent to which the vote should be seen as a deliberate choice based on a conscious weighing of all relevant considerations at the same point in time. At this point, we can only note that some observers would explain (and tolerate) divergent conclusions concerning the importance of policy- or conflict-related preferences on the grounds that the two analysts chose to assess the importance of such considerations at two different stages in the funnel of causality, while other observers would insist on resolving the apparent conflict in conclusions by first settling the definitional and causal issues associated with the concept of deliberate choice.

In any event, all analysts' conclusions are powerfully shaped by the assumptions they have made concerning the unresolved issues discussed throughout this essay. To be sure, the validity of their conclusions should be partially judged in terms of the appropriateness of their measures and statistical procedures, given their assumptions in each of the above areas. Equal attention, however, should be given to the meaning and validity of these assumptions. Much more discussion, and fundamental research, is needed on the ways in which individuals arrive at their final choice or preference before the electoral field attempts to resolve conflicts between results that are based on very different assumptions about that process.

NOTES

1. See Asher 1992, 177–95, for a summary of conflicting views concerning the role of policy- or ideology-related preferences in those elections.

2. Despite this cautionary note, the author and Warren Miller are currently engaged in a comprehensive review of alternative conclusions about the 1980, 1984, and 1988 elections and an extension of our existing analyses of those elections to include the 1992 campaign. My colleague will recognize some of what follows, and parts of it may have an impact on our continuing collaboration. As with the other contributions to this festschrift, however, he is not responsible for any of the arguments that follow.

3. The distinction between causal inferences based on reasons versus variables is discussed by Lazarsfeld and his colleagues in several places. For a general discussion in the context of consumer behavior, see Kornhauser and Lazarsfeld 1955.

4. Voters' own reasons for preferring one candidate over another were featured in *The American Voter* (Campbell et al. 1960) and numerous subsequent publications, including Asher 1990, Kelley 1983, and Wattenberg 1991. For an impressions-based approach that addresses the validity of self-reported causes, see Lodge et al. 1989.

5. This formulation reflects the approach taken in the author's current work with Warren Miller. Over time, we have increasingly emphasized the role played by variables that are presumably located further back in the causal process, whose impact should be mediated by proximate evaluations of the candidates.

6. Almost every analysis of presidential elections includes a discussion of partisanship (if not party identification) and various types of issues. See Kinder 1980 for a review of measurement objectives and strategies concerning perceptions or evaluations of presidential candidates.

7. See Stokes 1966 and Shanks and Miller 1990 for a review of these alternative formulations.

8. These issues are discussed at length in all three of the essays on U.S. elections in the 1980s written by the author and Warren Miller. See Miller and Shanks 1982 and Shanks and Miller 1990 and 1991.

9. For an influential critique of explanations based on respondents' own accounts, see Nesbitt and Wilson 1977.

10. For an illustration of this procedure in the explanation of individual and aggregate choice in the 1992 election, see Pomper et al. 1993.

11. For an influential discussion of these potential problems, see Page and Brody 1972. In their formulation, simultaneity effects concerning issue proximities can occur through two clear substantive processes as well as through unspecified correlations between the disturbances for each dependent variable in the model. In the first of these confounding processes, usually called projection, respondents who do not know the position of a given candidate simply attribute their own preference to that candidate, thereby maximizing their apparent proximity to that candidate. In the other confounding process, usually called persuasion, respondents shift or create their own policy preferences to match the position of the candidate they have already chosen because of other factors.

12. For analyses which consider the endogeneity of party identification based on reciprocal causation or correlated disturbances, see Fiorina 1981, Jackson and Franklin 1983, and Green and Palmquist 1990. The most frequently cited simultaneous-equation models of the vote can be found in Franklin and Jackson 1983, Page and Jones 1979, and Fiorina 1981. Simultaneous-equation models may also be used to correct for bias in effect estimates caused by measurement error in the explanatory variables. See Green and Palmquist 1990 and Rosenstone et al. 1988 for examples of this kind of rationale and analysis.

13. See Rivers 1988.

14. See Bartels 1991 for a discussion of tradeoffs or risks associated with the use of instrumental variables as simultaneous-equation models.

R E F E R E N C E S

Asher, Herbert. 1992. *Presidential Elections and American Politics*. 5th ed. Pacific Grove, Calif.: Brooks/Cole.
Bartels, Larry M. 1991. "Instrumental and 'Quasi-Instrumental' Variables." *American Journal of Political Science* 35:777–800.

Campbell, Angus, Phillip E. Converse, Warren E. Miller, and Donald E. Stokes. 1960. *The American Voter.* New York: Wiley.

———. 1966. *Elections and the Political Order.* New York: John Wiley and Sons.

Fiorina, Morris P. 1991. *Retrospective Voting in American National Elections.* New Haven: Yale University Press.

Franklin, Charles E., and John E. Jackson. 1983. "Dynamics of Party Identification." *American Political Science Review* 77:957–73.

Green, Donald P., and Bradley Palmquist. 1990. "Of Artifacts and Partisan Instability." *American Journal of Political Science* 34:872–902.

Kelley, Stanley, Jr. 1983. *Interpreting Elections.* Princeton, N. J.: Princeton University Press.

Kinder, Donald R., Mark D. Peters, Robert P. Abelson, and Susan T. Fiske. 1980. "Presidential Prototypes." *Political Behavior* 2:315–38.

Kornhauser, Arthur. 1955. "The Analysis of Consumer Actions." In *The Language of Social Research: A Reader in the Methodology of Social Research,* ed. Paul F. Lazarsfeld and Morris Rosenberg. New York: Free Press.

Lazarsfeld, Paul F., and Morris Rosenfeld, eds. 1955. *The Language of Social Research: A Reader in the Methodology of Social Research.* New York: Free Press.

Lodge, Milton, Kathleen M. McGraw, and Patrick Stroh. 1989. "An Impression-driven Model of Candidate Evaluation." *American Political Science Review* 83:399–420.

Miller, Warren E., and J. Merrill Shanks. 1982. "Policy Directions and Presidential Leadership: Alternative Interpretations of the 1980 Presidential Elections." *British Journal of Political Science* 12:299–356.

Page, Benjamin I., and Calvin C. Jones. 1979. "Reciprocal Effects of Policy Preferences, Party Loyalties, and the Vote." *American Political Science Review* 73:1071–90.

Page, Benjamin I., and Richard A. Brody. 1972. "Policy Voting and the Electoral Process." *American Political Science Review* 66:979–95.

Pomper, Gerald M., et al., eds. 1993. *The Election of 1992.* Chatham, N. J.: Chatham House.

Rivers, Douglas. 1988. "Heterogeneity in Models of Electoral Choice." *American Journal of Political Science* 32:737–57.

Rosenstone, Steven J., John Mark Hansen, and Donald R. Kinder. 1988. "Measuring Change in Personal Economic Well-being." *Public Opinion Quarterly* 50:176-92.

Shanks, J. Merrill, and Warren E. Miller. 1990. "Policy Direction and Performance Evaluation: Complementary Explanations of the Reagan Elections." *British Journal of Political Science* 20:143–235.

———. 1991. "Partisanship, Policy, and Performance: The Reagan Legacy in the 1988 Election." *British Journal of Political Science* 21:129–97.

Stokes, Donald E. 1966. "Spatial Models of Party Competition. "In *Elections and the Political Order,* by Angus Campbell, Philip E. Converse, Warren E. Miller, and Donald E. Stokes. New York: John Wiley and Sons.

Wattenberg, Martin P. 1991. *The Rise of Candidate-centered Politics: Presidential Elections of the 1980s.* Cambridge, Mass.: Harvard University Press.

CHAPTER 3

Electoral Survey Data and the Temporal Dimension

Heinz Eulau

Who would have thought, forty years ago, that surveys on voting behavior conducted in 1948 and 1952 would still be sources of political analysis in 1992?[1] Well, there were two people who have left a record of having thought so—one who mostly wrote about it, another who did something about it. One was an Austrian-born sociologist; the other was a midwestern political scientist. The first was Paul F. Lazarsfeld; the second was Warren E. Miller.

There was no end to the argument, then and later, that surveys were unreliable (disaster had struck in 1948);[2] undemocratic and destructive in their influence (a voice of authority, Columbia University political scientist Lindsay Rogers [1949], had said so);[3] and, above all, superficial, transient (or temporally flat), and devoid of intellectual depth, whatever that may have meant (Berns 1962).[4] Polling the voters was a one-shot affair, perhaps entertaining for the public interested in the current horse race for the presidency, but of no further theoretical or historical significance or use. After all, the real election returns would tell all that had to be told or explained. Surveys of public attitudes or opinions had nothing to do with the inherited wisdom of Aristotle, James Madison, or that later English James, Lord Bryce.[5]

With this as the point of departure, I want first to say something about the evolution of the SRC, CPS, and NES studies as sources of data of use to the historian or time-conscious social scientist.[6] I shall do so against the background of Paul Lazarsfeld's early articulation of some of the problems involved in making survey data "historically useful."[7] This frame of reference is ironic because it has been argued, quite wrongly I think, that "because of its tautological overtones, the motivation model [the SRC model] did not have the intellectual relevance and durability of the Lazarsfeld approach" (Janowitz 1978, 98).[8] The statement is especially wrong because (and this adds paradox to irony) Lazarsfeld's two famous Columbia-based and community-centered election studies (Lazarsfeld, Berelson, and Gaudet 1948; Berelson, Lazarsfeld, and McPhee 1954) were substantively atemporal and have not given rise to a research tradition, while the SRC studies of the 1950s, as will be noted, had a temporal vision and became institutionalized, with a large research community making use of the data.[9]

After these for-the-historical-record preliminaries, my concern will primarily be the relationship between electoral surveys—especially those spawned by what are often simply called the "Michigan" studies—and political futures.[10] In particular, I will deal with some problems involving issues of survey research's temporal dimensions. One problem concerns the *omission,* in surveys, of historically desirable questions or of previously-used questionnaire items that might be useful in subsequent time-series analysis.[11] A second problem deals with the *inclusion,* in the interview, of *new* time-relevant items from the perspective of the future analyst who looks backward on some past events. A third problem exemplifies ignorance or neglect of time-relevant components in the actual wording of a questionnaire item, especially as this influences the construction of causal models.

The problems involved, as I propose to develop them, go beyond the familiar interest of the historically-minded social scientist in the analysis of time-series survey data. The creation and protected continuity of time series are important considerations, but these are not the only problems that face historically-oriented survey research. Equally important, it seems to me, are the temporal aspects of the questions asked of the survey respondent. Some questions refer to past, some to present, and some to future events.[12] I have the very strong impression that, while sophisticated analysis of survey data by way of fancy statistics has reached almost orbital successes (but possibly also failures), the simple art of question wording has become something of a stepchild in the training of survey analysts. In part, it has become so as a result of the very triumph of the poll or survey in both politics and political science. Data from both commercial and scientific polls or surveys are so abundant and readily available for statistical analysis that it may, and, in fact, does, lead to overlooking such fundamentals as question wording, question location, question bias, question stability, question salience, question response, and so on and so forth.[13] Yet, as any electoral and legislative field worker (rather than data analyst) knows from experience, the formulation of proper questions is as critical in the design of a study as is the definition of the sample. And all of the concerns with the questions in the survey instrument impinge on the proper manipulation and interpretation of the data. I shall therefore retrogress (to avoid "regress" in either its statistical or pathological sense) to some rather rudimentary, but, I think, neglected, issues in the formulation of survey questions, with particular emphasis on the temporal or historical aspects of survey research.

Of Accident, Opportunity, and Project

It has sometimes been remarked that the early Michigan SRC studies were designed to at least partially refute the studies that had been conducted at Columbia, especially by confronting Lazarsfeld's social stratification model of the voter's choice with alternative social and psychological variables (Janowitz 1978, 98; J. Converse 1987, 364). This may have been so, but I am inclined to think that to make the difference between the two types of study a difference between sociology and psychology is a mistake (see Converse, Eulau, and Miller 1982). The approaches of both schools were "social-psychological," with somewhat different emphases that were occasioned, probably, by the different social and educational backgrounds of their principal investigators and, as a result, by their different "reading of the times" (Lazarsfeld having been an Austrian socialist, Campbell being an American liberal). If the former was more likely to see conflict among groups and classes as motivating factors in the voters' political choice, the latter was more likely to see the voting decision in individualistic-consensual terms. To pose the differences between the Michigan and Columbia schools in these terms is to pose a false dualism. As Miller and Shanks show in their analyses of the 1980, 1984, and 1988 presidential elections, a complex multivariable, multistage model can easily accommodate both schools by way of theorizing in conflict-and-consensus terms (Miller and Shanks 1982; Shanks and Miller 1990, 1991).

In any case, I don't think that the SRC studies were initiated on the scientific grounds of either refuting or sustaining the approaches or findings of the Columbia studies. They were, initially, an accident. I suspect that this is not widely known, for the SRC/CPS/NES studies of voting behavior and elections have come a long way since 1948, when Angus Campbell and Robert Kahn, social psychologists, undertook the first in the series of remarkable national election studies that nowadays serve hundreds of scholars, to pursue their interests in a complex field of investigation. For the overwhelming majority of today's research community in the field, the scientific survey-based study of the electorate began with the publication of *The American Voter* in 1960. A few may have heard of, if not read, *The Voter Decides,* published in 1954. But there was also a little monograph entitled *The People Elect a President,* by Campbell and Kahn, published in 1952.[14] The president about whom Campbell and Kahn were writing was Harry Truman, whose election victory was probably as stunning to them, at least before they could look at their own data, as it was to the commercial pollsters who, in September, had given the election to Thomas Dewey of New York and then stopped interviewing. But if Truman's election was no fluke, the Campbell-Kahn investigation was something of a serendipitous event. An SRC study of public attitudes toward foreign policy, in the field in October 1948, included a couple of questions about respondents' political interest and general political orientations.[15] Although the October sample was small (N = 610), luck or, better, the SRC's probability sampling method, got the election outcome right. This, in turn, led to a grant from the Social Science Research Council to conduct a postelection panel study in November, designed in part to shed light on why the commercial pollsters had so dismally failed in forecasting the vote.[16] The interesting thing about all this is that if the pollsters had not erred (for whatever reason) in 1948, there would probably have been no concern with their work at the SSRC, probably no grant from the SSRC to the SRC for a postelection study, probably no funding for a study in 1952, and probably no Warren E. Miller at the University of Michigan.

Looking at the Campbell and Kahn monograph today, it serves to remind one of the humble beginnings of survey-based electoral research. It is "surprising," the two authors wrote in the 1952 edition of their study, that elections have been "the subject of relatively little scientific study." They continue:

> One would expect that a social phenomenon as important as the presidential election would have attracted a corps of social scientists, armed with their crude instruments, intent on laying bare the forces which underlie this vast outpouring of political activity. There have been many speculations about the democratic ethos, but empirical analyses of the vote have been notably infrequent. One finds a handful of studies, based on aggregative election records, and, in most cases, limited to local or state elections. (1952, 1)

Counter to those who see the Michigan studies as a response to the Columbia research, Campbell and Kahn paid homage to Lazarsfeld's 1940 Erie County study, which "demonstrated for the first time something of the range of possibilities which this research method promises in the analysis of political behavior," and they remarked that a similar study of the national electorate "as yet . . . has not been done" (1952, 2)—a statement that was not altogether accurate.[17]

It is impossible to say, in retrospect, whether Campbell (and perhaps Kahn) ever suspected that what began accidentally in 1948 would become the large collective enterprise it is today. Their comments were somewhat ambiguous. On the one hand, they seem to have envisaged only one follow-up study. A single sentence is not much of a crutch to lean on, but they described their research as "a pilot study to the definitive investigation which needs to be done" (1952, 2). The reference, in the singular mode, to the definitive investigation, would seem to suggest that these investigators were not looking, then, beyond the upcoming 1952 election. However, from one perspective I'm pursuing here—the importance of building constructs of the future into the chain of national election studies—it is of special interest that Campbell and Kahn also saw their modest research on the 1948 election "as a small-scale forerunner to more substantial studies of the presidential vote in subsequent elections" (1952, 61). Other internal evidence thus allows the conclusion that Campbell and Kahn saw the study of elections not just as a "scientific" but also as a historical enterprise, which meant that there had to be time series and that the good contemporary survey would have the future in view. Outlining a number of objectives that some future presidential election study might have in view, they suggested comparison of voters' socioeconomic, attitudinal, and perceptual attributes to "the corresponding groups in the 1948 election" (1952, 62). In today's perspective this sounds rather simplistic, but elaboration by way of a question shows otherwise:

> Would the hypothesis that the attitudes taken publicly by party leadership are followed by party rank-and-file be supported by data on foreign policy issues from two campaigns, in 1948 when foreign policy was not a prominent issue and in the later election when it might be? (1952, 63)

This sentence signals the possibility of a loss of knowledge through omission. What Campbell and Kahn are hinting at here is a generic point: just because some theoretically plausible effect is not present in a current and given election, it might be in the future and, therefore, should not be overlooked in a study design and the construction of a questionnaire.

The community-based research on voting behavior conducted by the group of sociologists around Lazarsfeld at Columbia University had a short-term longitudinal dimension, in being in the panel mode, but it was essentially ahistorical—something of a curiosity because Lazarsfeld was an articulate spokesman for the view that the polls should be constructed to benefit the future historian. By way of contrast, the Michigan studies from 1952 on had the potential of serving the future historian, even if this potential was not as noticeable as it is today.[18] V. O. Key, Jr., referred to this potential in his foreword to *The Voter Decides,* noting that the study's analytic scheme "will differ markedly from simpler voting behavior theories which so often seem to hold good for only one election" (1954, xi). The potential was also sensed by sociologist Peter Rossi (1959) in a critical overview of modern electoral research. Unlike *Voting* (Berelson, Lazarsfeld, and McPhee 1954), "whose results," Rossi wrote, "strictly speaking, can only be used to interpret the victory of Dewey in Elmira, *The Voter Decides* performs a greater service to the historian of the future by providing national projections of its sample findings" (Rossi 1959, 38). And again contrasting the two studies (both published, by chance, in the same year, 1954), Rossi noted that *The Voter Decides* "can deal with the Eisenhower victory with confidence in its statistical basis. In addition, the comparative frame of reference afforded by the Center's [SRC] previous survey of the 1948 election lends an historical depth to the data" (Rossi 1959, 39). Rossi was critical, however, of what he called the "static character" of the Michigan group's research design. Rossi had in mind that, unlike the Columbia group's multilevel approach to the individual person's voting behavior, the Michigan study remained on the single level of the person:[19]

Because, as has been indicated, the major explanatory variables and voting are roughly on the same level, it is difficult to understand how changes over time come about. However, from the analysis and interpretations one cannot be sure that this is a peculiar characteristic of this election or common to elections of this historical period. (Rossi 1959, 42)

This comment was not well considered. Obviously, no matter which or how many levels are brought to bear on research design or analysis, if there is only one case treated, as is true of the 1952 election in *The Voter Decides,* one can never be sure whether a finding is peculiar or common in a given historical period.

What followed is, as the saying has it, history. By the time of the 1952 study that led to *The Voter Decides,* Warren Miller had come aboard the Survey Research Center and, after serving the proper apprenticeship,[20] became the engine that drove the SRC election studies in three major, overlapping, and ascending, directions: first, seeing to it that the studies would continue through time, even if it required endless and often frustrating fund-raising efforts; second, providing that the data from the studies would be available to the research community at large (accomplished through the creation of the Inter-University Consortium for Political and [later] Social Research); and, finally, with the NSF's funding of what became known as the National Election Studies, stimulating and maintaining the active participation of the research community in the design and analysis of the studies.

Of History, Politics, and Values

I don't know how it came about that Paul Lazarsfeld (I almost said "of all people") concerned himself with the problem of the uses that historians could make of survey data. The Erie County study of the 1940 and the Elmira study of the 1948 elections, though dealing in time-dependent microchanges in the voters' choice by way of panel surveys, were not inspired by a passion for history or writing about history on a grand scale. However, it is well to keep in mind that, as Philip Converse once noted, "the founding fathers of survey research and opinion polling in the 1930s were persons of profound democratic convictions." He continues:

For them, the combination of population sampling with survey interviewing was not just a methodological development. It was a major political breakthrough. It could remove the chief barrier to true democracy and thereby assure that the voice of the people would be heard in the land. (Converse 1982, 150)

There is no indication that Lazarsfeld, at the time of the Erie County study or even later, when the second edition was published, thought of a time series as being of historical use. Rather, he spoke of scientific validation of findings through replication that, in permitting comparison, serves three functions: corroboration, specification, and clarification (Lazarsfeld et al. 1948, xiv–xv). The changes observed in the panels were really measured in microtime, but microtime was not what Lazarsfeld later had in mind when talking about the potential uses of survey research to the historian. By way of contrast, the two major pre-NES Michigan panel studies covered several years (1956–58–60 and 1972–74–76) and, as Warren Miller informed me, "the manifest interest in both cases was in the temporal dimension and the study of change through time. This was not in the name of history per se, but certainly in the conviction that microhistory was relevant to social science, even in the short run" (pers. com., 1992).[21]

Lazarsfeld's initial thrust was a theme familiar to critics of conventional history: that, with some exceptions, few historians make "elaborate efforts to document their statements about public attitudes. It is much more likely that we shall find statements which read like a Gallup release, except, of course, that the tables are missing" (Lazarsfeld 1957, 244). There are three areas in which the historian can use opinion data: First, when "prevailing values" are themselves the objects of study (1957, 246). Second, in studying new institutions or major legislative developments, the historian "would be greatly helped by data on the interaction between the diffusion of attitudes and the sequence of social actions" (1957, 247). Third, the historian would benefit from polling in connection with writings "in which specific events [like presidential elections] are to be explained," though Lazarsfeld warns (with the 1948 fiasco of the polls in mind) that "even with poll data it is not easy to arrive at safe conclusions" (1957, 248).

Let me sharpen this point by referring to two explanatory tasks historians have traditionally set for themselves. One task is to explain "how things have really been," the classical Rankean formulation. The other task is to explain "how things have come to be what they are"—a formulation that, I would think, is more congenial to the social scientist.[22] From the Rankean formulation it follows that the survey researcher as contemporary historian should include in his study questions that produce answers which his successor, tomorrow's historian, will need in order to write yesterday's history (i.e., the history of the pollster's time) in the retrospective mode of Ranke. An excellent example of the contemporary history approach is Miller's analytic use of his construct of the "new politics" in examining the electorate's responses to the events of the late 1960s as they impacted patterns of public attitudes and voting patterns in the early 1970s. Miller was most sensitive to the problem that he might be seen as a "historicist."[23] He described what he was doing as "somewhat unusual," because his classification of the respondents in terms of the new politics theme deviated from conventional membership group definitions and was not explicitly guided by social theory, but rather by a "speculative idea." By the turn of the decade, he wrote,

> the idea of the New Politics as a phenomenon of theoretical interest had been widely discussed but not systematically studied. The pragmatic political importance of various aspects of the New Politics had been debated by politicians and political observers, but their disagreements were evidence that the importance of the New Politics for practical politics had not been clearly established. And yet, the events of the late 1960s were so vivid and compelling, the response to those events was so pervasive and so impassioned, that it seemed likely the New Politics had had a significant impact on a significant portion of the electorate. (Miller and Levitin 1976, 66–67)

On the other hand, when the survey researcher omits certain questions about his own time, perhaps because a topic may not seem immediately salient, or for any other reason, the future historian is prevented from explaining how things have come to be in *his* own time in the prospective mode of Teggart. The dilemma involved faced Miller and his collaborator, Merrill Shanks, in trying to locate their wide-ranging analysis of the 1988 NES election data in historical time. Referring to their statistical summary of the effects of explanatory themes on the outcome of the 1988 election, they suggest that the summary "is more revealing (and informative) when it can be compared to similarly structured results from past elections." They are forced to acknowledge, however, that "because of the substantial differences in the NES questions, we have not as yet settled on a version of this explanatory model which can be used to compare the important analysis for 1988 with those from other elections" (Shanks and Miller 1991, 193).

Historical data—and, in some respects, all data about human or social behavior are historical—are usually employed in two analytic modes. The first is a comparative-analytic mode, in which the emphasis is not on the study of change over time but on generalization from cases collected at different time points, the order of the time points being unimportant. The other mode is self-consciously historical, in that the appearance or disappearance of a phenomenon over time is in itself of interest.

Both modes are beset by one of the most serious dilemmas of electoral survey research—the fact that theoretical and methodological innovations make both comparison and trend analysis difficult. The resulting methodological and theoretical indeterminacies have as yet unexplained effects on cross-sectional data collected over time, as the controversies over the effects of issue orientations and voter rationality that broke out in the 1960s and 1970s have shown.[24] Unless both measures and methods used in comparisons of cross sections remain identical, one cannot say whether changes in findings are artifacts of research instrumentation or real-world outcomes.

It requires great analytic sensitivity to avoid the pitfalls implicit in these theoretical and methodological dilemmas. I have a sense that analysts who *are* sensitive have relied all too often on statistical tricks to get around them. Miller and his associates have recognized for some time that the most effective way to have confidence that analyses are not artifacts of the measures involved requires the creation of new and alternative questions in the survey instrument itself—for instance, in the matter of such controversial matters as policy preferences, evaluations of national conditions, or presidential performance (Shanks and Miller 1991, 130). But atemporal comparative analysis, on the one hand, and historical, or trend, analysis, on the other hand, make different empirical demands on the investigator because they are predicated on different assumptions. Comparative analysis, seeking to find general or lawlike phenomena in electoral behavior, is interested in regularities of one sort or another. It is willing, therefore, to ignore departures from hypothesized propositions or expectations that do not fit. Historical analysis, however, is interested not only in regularities and continuities but also in those unique events that do not fit in a scientific mode of analysis but are of great interest as real-world political conditions or outcomes. While, in some recent writings, Miller speaks of the "political interpretation" of a given election, the cumulation over time of such interpretations necessarily leads to historical analysis. In his collaborative work with Merrill Shanks, the question is raised how the importance of explanatory variables is to be assessed:

> When our own analysis [of the 1980 election] reached the point where we began presenting results to interested audiences, we quickly rediscovered the urgent need to distinguish between two generically different functions or types of interpretation for our results. The first function, and that which was foremost in the considerations of those designing the study, is that of extending our *understanding* of human behaviour. The second function is that of utilizing our basic knowledge of human behaviour in order to choose among plausible interpretations of an election outcome which are offered to guide subsequent political or practical decisions. (Miller and Shanks 1982, 301)

In the course of the last forty years, but especially in the last fifteen years or so, electoral research, especially as conducted in the NES, has sought to come to grips with these contrary demands by providing for both possibilities in the survey instrument and subsequent analysis and interpretation. As Shanks and

Miller have put it, "Over the years it has become evident that some aspects of social science theory can be applied to some elections, but not to every election" (1991, 136). A good example appears in the initial analysis of the 1988 election by Shanks and Miller. The investigators were confronted by what they called an *anomaly* (a concept that makes sense only if one presumes the existence of a lawlike phenomenon, or *nomos*). There was a substantial drop in the Republican presidential margin of victory in spite of the fact that, by 1988, the Democratic advantage in party identification had vanished and conservative ideological inclinations had measurably increased over previous years. To cope with this anomaly, they took the route of the traditional historian in examining four "*unique* features" in the data.[25]

The admission that every election outcome may be partly determined by events unique to a given election is certainly a softening of the early behavioralists' hopeful expectation that, because elections themselves are regularized events (which makes them institutions), electoral research would also yield behavioral regularities and, hence, lawlike propositions. Indeed, Shanks and Miller seem to welcome this intellectual-scientific development as progress: "One measure of progress is provided by our growing understanding of the conditions under which different explanatory themes become more (or less) relevant . . . " (Shanks and Miller 1991, 136). Miller and Shanks return to the historical theme in even more sophisticated fashion. It is not only that events (like a stock market crash, the taking of American hostages abroad, or the collapse of the Soviet hegemony in Eastern Europe) have immediate implications for national policy and action; in the historical perspective they also give rise to competing interpretations that "may overtake the events themselves, so that it becomes pointless to wonder whether the interpreted events constitute part of the context for an election campaign or a part of the campaign itself" (Shanks and Miller 1991, 151).

The interest in the varying conditions under which electoral research is conducted and findings are interpreted leads to considerably more emphasis on contextual or exogenous variables than had been the case in the first two decades of behavioral research, and makes time itself a conditional factor: "The explanatory logic is the same, regardless of whether we are talking about contextual variation *between* elections, *over time* in a given election, or between different subpopulations within a single cross-section survey" (Shanks and Miller 1991, 137; emphases added).

Part of what one might almost call a *contextual revolution* in electoral research has been the effort to synchronize traditionally individual-level, or micro, and aggregate, or macro, analyses. Perhaps *revolution* is too strong a term.[26] In fact, it was thirty-five years ago that Warren Miller (1956) pioneered this kind of analysis with national survey data.[27] By attributing to survey respondents the aggregate partisan tendencies of their counties of residence,

Miller demonstrated that the rate of partisanship at the micro level of individual behavior was systematically conditioned by the partisan environment produced at the aggregate level. This early study is of particular interest in the perspective of the theme I'm pursuing here, for it also reveals Miller as a future student of historical change. Referring to the persistence of one-party politics, Miller wrote: "Since this analysis does not, at this point, deal directly with the *development* and *evolution* of the political structure, we are limited to speculation concerning *tides* and *trends* in politics" (Miller 1956, 716; emphases added).[28]

The major theme I am pursuing in this essay (as well as the obvious space limitation) does not permit me to expand on the micro-macro problem that has clearly come to play an increasing role in Miller's thinking about, and analysis of, elections. While the Miller-Shanks methodological restatements of the problem are at times tedious and redundant, they clearly point to the importance of the problem when it comes to over-time, or historical, analysis and interpretation of elections as macropolitical events.[29] As they instruct,

> there is a sharp conceptual boundary separating the *context* for voters' decision making from the *process* of their coming to election-day decisions. Thirty years ago, *The American Voter* was appropriately ambiguous about the process of providing a politically meaningful translation of events external to the voter, because it was, and still is, an incompletely understood process. (Shanks and Miller 1991, 152)

I don't know how historians nowadays feel about the utility of survey research on elections in their own work, but I'm inclined to take a dim view, reminding myself of an exchange of a few years ago between a once–Young Turk historian, Lee Benson, and Warren Miller. Benson, once an enthusiastic practitioner of quantitative history who had sat at Lazarsfeld's feet, had soured on the social sciences for one reason or another, I don't know which, though he offered, of course, his own rationalization: American social science, across the board, had made basic errors stemming from its "intellectual miscegenation represented by the mating of French positivist scientism and German idealist historicism on native American ground—miscegenation because they not only were individually erroneous but radically incompatible, given their different assumptions" (Benson 1978, 436).

There is no need here to review all of Miller's responses to this ideological polemic. However, there was one observation in Benson's article—to the effect that "human behavior cannot be studied scientifically when researchers who study *past* human behavior become effectively isolated from researchers who study *present* human behavior" (1978, 436)—that struck a sympathetic chord in Miller. He refers to "the values of one of the primary methodological options for social research; that is, the option of studying variation in human behavior across time" (Miller 1978, 446). After mentioning another option—cross-national and cross-cultural comparisons—Miller is more explicit:

> History, properly conceived, presents the other major alternative for increasing variation in the testing of scientific propositions. Indeed, change across time is rapidly coming to be recognized, as in the increased use of the techniques of cohort analysis, as presenting one of the great opportunities for truly significant theory testing. (447)

Taking scientific advantage of the change-through-time phenomenon, he claims, depends on two conditions: first, more interaction between historians and social scientists; and second, "the retrieval and reconstruction of the data" that will serve their joint purposes (Miller 1978, 447). Miller then scolds social scientists for being "too often ahistorical because they suffer from temporal myopia and a time-bound parochialism." His stricture of historians is equally severe: "Without some appreciation of the social scientific perspective, the historian is not likely to recognize the relevance of historical materials for hypothesis testing" (447).

It remains an open question, it seems to me, how, or in fact whether, what Miller referred to as "reconstruction of the data" can shed light on the macropolitical attempts to explain secular changes in the American electoral system. An enormous literature, deriving from V. O. Key's seminal studies of the 1950s and based on aggregate-areal election statistics, concerns the issues of realignment and dealignment in the American party system. It is clear enough that a given hegemonic system constitutes the most significant interpretative context in the analysis of the microphenomena with which survey research deals. Obviously, micromodeling and the analysis of individual-level data should be "contextual," a prescription that, in the last ten years or so, has become something of a social-scientific bromide because it has implications for the measurement of the exogenous conditions needed to make causal modeling persuasive. The problem is, of course, that the aggregate election data of yesteryear do not give unambiguous answers as to just when a realignment or dealignment process began or when it was consummated (see Clubb, Flanigan, and Zingale 1980). Ultimately, in some distant or not-so-distant future—fifty years from now, or one hundred years—survey research with its individual-level data will undoubtedly be able to pinpoint with considerable exactitude the process of transformation of one hegemonic party or electoral system into another—a transformation that may be rapid or prolonged.

Because any unknown number of biennial elections may be involved in the transformation, proper prognostication of the rates of micropolitical change requires the kind of developmental construct of the future that, as will be noted,

Harold D. Lasswell had in mind, and that must be built into the voting model and cannot be treated as an exogenous or contextual variable. This, it seems to me, is the only way that any voting study conducted in any particular year can escape the charge that it was dominated by the wrong party or electoral system variable, as may have been the case with the SRC studies when, in the 1950s, the New Deal system no longer provided the appropriate contextual variable. In hindsight it is perhaps true that the questions and variables one finds in the early SRC studies reflected the investigators' acceptance of the "Roosevelt coalition" as providing the sociopolitical base of the electoral party system. While this condition undoubtedly has made some of the earlier questions of the SRC studies obsolete, it symbolizes a condition that, I fear, will never be overcome but that, I hope, can be at least partially remedied by the survey researcher being something less of a contemporary historian and perhaps something more of a futurist.

Of Past, Present, and (Missing) Future

A single election survey can never tell the story of an election as a whole or even of the electorate's behavior as a total entity. As V. O. Key, Jr., in his wisdom, put it when writing the foreword to *The Voter Decides,* "The survey apparatus, unlike a camera, does not record an image of the entire scene toward which it is aimed, but only of those parts that have been singled out in advance" (Key 1954, xi). What, then, can be singled out in advance? And how does one go about doing it? Among the possibilities, Lazarsfeld suggested "efforts to guess what the future will want to know about today" (Lazarsfeld 1957, 255).

Lazarsfeld is not asking us to predict the future, but to guess what a future historian may want to know about today—that is, the time when a survey is conducted or, put differently, our own present that is his past. This immediately creates a dilemma, for what the future historian wants to know about today is likely to be influenced, in part, by his own time's cultural, social, economic, or political conditions and circumstances. This brings us right back, of course, to predicting the future. Lazarsfeld recommended that "we should form expectations of what major changes might come about within the next decades." He was not unaware of this being a "most difficult task. It not only requires . . . that we translate more or less vague ideas into specific instruments of inquiry; there is so little thinking along this line that we shall even have to assume some responsibility for guessing what will be of importance a few decades hence" (Lazarsfeld 1957, 255–56).[30] Guessing is not really the right word for what is involved. Although Lazarsfeld does not elaborate on this, he gives a brief quote from Harold D. Lasswell—unfortunately not the best that could be cited as an example of Lasswell's idea of developmental constructs—which suggests that something more disciplined is involved than mere guessing.

In the practice of social science, . . . we are bound to be affected in some degree by our conceptions of future development . . . What is the function of this picture for scientists? It is to stimulate the individual specialist to clarify for himself his expectations about the future, as a guide to the timing of scientific work. (H. D. Lasswell, quoted in Lazarsfeld 1957, 255)

A survey as an instrument of social-scientific inquiry is eminently oriented toward past, present, and future, though until recently only a few practitioners were sufficiently sensitive to all three dimensions of time. Survey questions are not made of thin air. The well-trained social scientist making use of the survey instrument knows that much of what he or she knows is experiential, and that his or her questions and subsequent analyses are necessarily rooted in events of the past. The problem is, of course, to be selective, for not all the questions that the past may suggest can be transformed into survey items. So selection has to be made, and the preferred criterion has been some theory, theoretical framework, or propositional inventory whose hypotheses have at least some chance of being falsified by the contemporary data that the survey enables us to collect. Here the major problem is, of course, that the writers of survey questions—in order to make it possible to confront hypotheses with empirical data—will allow their sense of what questionnaire items are viable *now*, in the present, to determine what theoretical propositions to investigate. It would surely be a waste of valuable space and time in a survey instrument to ask questions that, however theoretically attractive or useful to the future historian, are unlikely to be meaningful to respondents and, therefore, cannot be meaningfully answered in the present.

Yet, the present is at best a transitional way station between past and future. It is, in fact, rather infirm ground on which to stand in testing theoretical notions. Today's proof with today's data may be invalidated by tomorrow's proof with tomorrow's data. My hunch is that until very recently, and only after the power of time-series data had been recognized, social scientists generally allowed their analyses to be overdetermined by the present or, to a more limited extent, by a phenomenon's past. A classical example of overdetermination, noted by Miller, comes from the early Michigan studies of the 1950s, when there were no prior trend data available and, hence, the current data were the sole bases for inference and interpretation. Miller notes that "in documenting the relatively major importance of party in the 1950s, many political analysts also concluded that the relatively minor role of issues indicated the usual state of political affairs." He continues: "In the absence of comparable survey data about citizen interest in questions of public policy in previous elections, it was perhaps too easily assumed that the readings of that period were typical of most other elections" (Miller and Levitin 1976, 50). Miller's caveat pertains not only to studies conducted at one point in time, but also to trend studies based on time series. Even if trend data are available, overdetermination is always a fallacy to be guarded against, for it is all too human to believe that present trends will continue indefinitely into the future. In human affairs, today's proofs can never be treated as eternal verities.[31] Straight-line, cyclical, or any other dimensional extrapolations of trends are as subject to modification by the vicissitudes of time as are one-shot investigations limited to one point in time. Miller has illustrated this point in a reference to the 1964 presidential election campaign, "generally credited with providing a turning point in the growth of public concern with policy questions." He considers this conclusion "debatable," even though "by 1964 issue concerns had taken on a new political meaning." However, he continues,

> it is virtually impossible to determine precisely when between 1960 and 1964 such change began. It seems most unlikely that the brief two or three months of election campaigning in 1964 alone could have been the source of the changes in the structure of public opinion that took place between 1960 and 1964. (Miller and Levitin 1976, 54)

To escape these vicissitudes of inference and interpretation, surveys may incorporate, if only inadvertently or invisibly to the naked eye, some questions that are guided by the prognoses of the future that, linked with the data on the present, might be of possible use to the future social science–oriented historian. This is not to underestimate the difficulties involved in prognostication, as Converse amply demonstrated some years ago. The opening paragraph of his disquisition on prognosis is suggestive:

> Any prediction of the likely state of public opinion in 1980 is bound to be hazardous and, in a sense, quite foolish without foreknowledge of the surrounding political conditions that might pertain. If we were sure that a new storm of troubles would be gripping the electorate five or ten years hence, we would have quite different expectations than if we could be certain that a period of more routine politics would develop. (Converse 1975, 107–8)

Converse's crutch for appraising past, present, and future developments is the well-known instrumental construct of the "normal vote" (Converse 1966).[32] With this construct in hand, then, he would probably ask of the contrast between the present and the future the same kind of questions he could ask of the contrast between the past and the present: "Were the 1950s not only quiescent but ridiculously so? Or is it the 1960s that were abnormal in terms of these properties of public opinion?" (Converse 1975, 108).

In general, while there has been some sermonizing in this matter, building time-series investigations on Lasswell-type "developmental constructs" of the future has not been widely or intentionally practiced. I think the original Michigan studies of voting behavior and the later National Election Studies have been rare exceptions in political science in anticipating the dynamics of continuity and discontinuity in social and political changes through time. Indeed, Miller (in collaboration with Shanks) has made "stability" the critical criterion for ordering the variable themes of the causal models in the various analyses of the 1980, 1984, and 1988 elections: the more stable the variable, the more prior its location in the causal model. The best example is the discussion of the 1980 NES study, which differed from its predecessors in collecting data at six points in time, allowing the analyst to "follow a year-long time-series of sequential indicators of citizens' perceptions, aspirations, and assessments" (Miller and Shanks 1982, 300). Making a hypothetical temporal ordering of the variables, the critical mode of ordering in the final causal model, and observing the stability of partisan and ideological predispositions throughout the year, they suggest that "these same patterns of stability and change in perceptions are important because they strongly support the particular sequential ordering of causal factors that we have proposed" (1982, 332–33). Moreover, aware of competing models, they emphasize that "it is clear that quite different prescriptions for the *future* would follow from establishing the relative merits of the two broad competing 'explanations' of the 1980 results" (1982, 301).

There is also a negative side to including a future orientation in the construction of a survey. A developmental construct is supposed to be a reasonably believable image of what tomorrow may bring, but sometimes the picture may be wrong, and we are investigating things that might just as well not have been looked at (from the perspective of the future historian). Although the NES study of the 1988 election included many new questions, Shanks and Miller, after analyzing the data in great detail, complained about lacunae that would make historical reconstruction difficult:

> In addition, we believe that perceptual assessments of current conditions should ideally cover other substantive areas, *as well as other time periods.* Such questions should also assess the absolute level of *current* conditions, *as well as change* from the previous year. We are concerned that the existing measures miss politically relevant perceptions. . . . Because of these potential omissions, we may have underestimated the role played by perceptions of current conditions. (Shanks and Miller 1991, 175; emphases added)

There is the additional problem of dropping questions from the survey instrument that, though useful in the past, do not seem useful in the present, but may be relevant again in the future. Let me give an example of this problem from the SRC studies of 1952 and 1956. These studies included a rich portfolio of questions about social class, class perceptions, interclass perceptions, class interests, and expectations.[33] These questions were omitted in all later SRC, CPS, and NES studies, with the result that if class as a psychological phenomenon should ever be of interest to the future historian (as, in fact, it seems to be of interest again today, in 1992), he or she will find only the familiar (and, I think, unsatisfactory) "class identification" question to work with.

Of Time, Invention, and Aggregation

As I read the hundreds of methodologically sophisticated books and research articles on voting behavior and elections based on survey data, I'm more often than not disappointed by their cavalier treatment of time in human behavior and social relations. As to cavalier treatment, there are two opposite modalities. Many analyses give the impression of saying the last word about voting, and elections in general, for all times. There simply seems to be a lack of a sense of time. Many other analyses are exclusively devoted to historical specificity and uniqueness, as if time stood still and the event were not just an incident in the infinite chain of moments that is time. These, too, really have no sense of time. To appreciate time, and change through time, one must have a feeling for chronicity and historicity.

I can best illustrate what I have in mind by some historical observations made by Miller in connection with the apparent shifts in party identification that occurred between Ronald Reagan's election in 1980 and his reelection in 1984. Miller here comments on the magnitude of change in the partisan balance within the older generation, when contrasted with the younger generation. The evidence, he writes,

> constitutes an anomaly which may force us to reexamine our assumptions about some of the regularities we have assumed governed changes in party loyalty. We are indeed confronted with a series of anomalies that are particularly noteworthy in the face of growing evidence that the crises invoked by the Great Depression of the early 1930s were primarily responsible for an asymmetrical *mobilization* on behalf of the Democratic party *rather* than for any enduring *conversion* of pre-Depression Republicans into post-Depression Democrats. Against that backdrop it is puzzling, at least, to observe 50 years later a partisan balance in mobilization accompanying unidirectional conversion among older citizens. (Miller 1986, 106)

It is, of course, a very disputatious sort of thing to know in the present what one can learn from the past, especially in science, which is immanently future-oriented in seeking to predict or explain in the present an effect (a future) by discovering a cause (the past). For survey-dependent social scientists working with data created in the present (for that is the characteristic feature of the survey), both the past, where causes occur, and the future, where effects occur, can only be hypotheticals.

It is important to remember that the social survey was one of the great scientific inventions that advanced the social disciplines by an order of magnitude yet to be appreciated by our friends, the philosophers (see Deutsch, Markovits, and Platt 1986; and the interesting little book by Dogan and Pahre 1990). Let us listen to Harold Lasswell, who was there when there was no "there":

> When I first became acquainted with the field of public opinion and communication research there was no Roper, no Gallup, no Cantril, no Stouffer, no Hovland. Lazarsfeld was neither a person, nor a measuring unit; or even a category. There was no survey research, content analysis, or quantified depth analysis; no computerized system of storage, retrieval, and utilization; no interuniversity networks of cooperation; no training institutes, research bureaus, professional bibliographies, magazines, or associations. (Lasswell 1972, 301)

Now, it is well for users or consumers of survey data to recognize and keep in mind that a survey's questions are also inventions, at that point in time when new and innovative questions are entered into a survey instrument. Like any invention, the new question needs to be handled with tender care. It seems to me that it behooves the user of survey data to know something about and understand the origins, purposes, and implications for analysis *and* interpretation of the questions from which the data are derived. Miller, in his collaborative work with Merrill Shanks, has been highly sensitive to such considerations. In general, Miller and Shanks, in their various studies of the 1980s, made temporal priority (rather than some theory-dependent logical argument) the plausible criterion for ordering the variables. In their report on the 1988 election, they were confronted with a great many new and various questions in the interview schedule that were likely to have some impact on the ordering of variables in the complex, but recursive, causal model intended to explain the November vote. It is interesting to note how they coped with this problem:

> The 1988 NES interview schedules contain several new questions which ask for the respondent's perceptions of personal or national conditions. These expanded measures may be used to clarify the difficult problem of *temporal perspective,* for some questions ask for retrospection about changes since the previous year, while other (equally retrospective) ques-

tions ask about changes that have taken place since Reagan took office, and still others call for prospective assessments of conditions likely to prevail in the coming year. (Shanks and Miller 1991, 174; emphasis added)

Miller and Shanks found that the eight-year retrospective perceptions of conditions were "indistinguishable from explicit performance evaluations," and, for this reason, did not make use of the data.

Every question asked in a survey had a past, has a present, and is likely to have a future. The future is often also implicit in what is called *reconceptualization,* which may be conscious or not but, in either case, can distort the question's meaning as it had been originally intended. As an example, I shall give the Michigan question on the respondent's "party identification." Perhaps no question in the Michigan surveys has had a more illustrious, but also victimized, history than this question. The research and literature on and around party ID is a cottage industry within a cottage industry. What created this cottage industry is the fact that the question was an invention that came to serve many purposes and, in the course of time and for any number of reasons, may have been misread, misunderstood, misapplied, or misinterpreted. One reason for this has been, and possibly still is, that both advocates and critics of the party ID measure were overlooking the fact that the question has a temporal component that is critical for its proper usage, whether in analysis or interpretation. Ignoring the orthodox interpretation of the party ID measure (Miller 1991a) has had the effect of making for all kinds of havoc in the measurement of "party-related personal attributes."[34]

In operationalizing their concept of party ID as a long-term attribute of a person, the inventors had to format the time component into their question. For party identification was thought of as a product of a person's life space and career. They did this by using two words that are easily overlooked but are important in interpreting the meaning of the measure. The question asks: "*Generally* speaking, do you *usually* think of yourself as a Republican, a Democrat, an Independent, or what?" Now, admittedly, the time referent here is vague or inchoate—for some people, thinking of themselves as *usually* a Democrat or Republican may mean a lifetime of consistent self-identification, in terms of the particular label; for others it may mean simply a convenient and rather temporary self-identification rather than one standing for some long-term commitment.[35] Nevertheless, the long-term component is clearly built into the question and cannot be ignored without creating conceptual confusion.

Of particular interest here is the question of how the time dimension plays out when it comes to comparing the micromeasurement of party-related personal attributes with some macromeasurement of partisanship. As this is not intended to be a literature review, I'll just deal with this matter by way of one illustration. A few years ago, a team of investigators (MacKuen, Erikson, and Stimson 1989) used a Gallup question to measure something that Gallup himself had called *party affiliation,* but that they conflated with the term *party identification.*[36] They wanted to demonstrate that, at least at the aggregate level, whatever it is that is measured as a party-related attribute is less constant than traditionally or conventionally assumed, and that it is more responsive to certain short-term fluctuations, also reported at the aggregate level, like citizens' economic evaluations and incumbent presidential approval ratings. Whatever the virtues of the analysis, the major trouble is that what was being measured as a party-related attribute of citizens had nothing to do with party identification as traditionally conceptualized and measured. For, rather than asking the respondent how he or she *usually* thinks of him- or herself, *generally speaking,* the Gallup question asked just the opposite: "In politics, *as of today,* do you consider yourself a Republican, Democrat, or Independent" (emphasis added). In other words, the Gallup question sought specificity and immediacy in the respondent's self-definition, whereas the Michigan question sought generality and continuity. Converse, some time ago and in another connection, noted the difference in question wordings:

> The items [Gallup's and SRC's] appear almost identical to casual glance. However, the "generally" and "usually" qualifiers in the SRC question were originally intended to broaden the time reference and properly classify the long-term identifier who is momentarily piqued at his own party, or tempted to defect temporarily. . . . A verb like "consider" in the Gallup question has somewhat parallel, if perhaps weaker, overtones; but the "as of today" invites in the baldest way a very transient frame of reference. (Converse 1976, 35)

This is not a latter-day rationalization in defense of the standard measure. It strikes me as rather ironical, therefore, that statistical virtuosi as sophisticated as MacKuen, Erikson, and Stimson can be so mistaken in their cavalier attitude toward the meaning of the party identification question, designed to measure what in *The American Voter* (Campbell et al. 1960, 121) was called "party attachments that persist through time," or "lasting attachments."[37]

There has been, in recent years, a tendency among analysts to interpret the notion of party identification at the aggregate level of national samples. Deriving meanings of party identification from or imputing them to aggregated survey data at the national level just doesn't make sense to me. While, even in presidential elections, the aggregate vote outcome may be driven by aggregate long-term or short-term forces—a horrible concept, anyway—the voter (that's I or me, depending on how I look at myself as a self) isn't driven by these aggregations. Aggregation of survey data may serve the virtuous purpose of unravelling causal relations at the aggregate level, but the aggregation in this case is just as exposed to the sundry fallacies that occur in the use of aggregate data obtained for other units of analysis—"states, counties, wards, precincts, or other political units one may care to examine." This quote is taken from *The American Voter* (Campbell et al. 1960, 121) to make a point: the party identification question was not invented or intended to serve as a substitute for the insight the authors of *The American Voter* started with—that in the various units of aggregation mentioned here "the correlation of the party division of the vote in *successive* elections is likely to be high" (Campbell et al. 1960, 121).

Rather, it was this condition that suggested to Campbell and company that "great numbers of voters have party attachments that persist through time" (Campbell et al. 1960, 121). The party identification question was designed to shed light on what is going on *within* the aggregates, not to serve the purpose of aggregation. I have the uncomfortable feeling, however, that after having been told about the behavior of aggregates, however conceptualized, and measured at whatever level, I have not learned anything about the historically emerging relationship between voters or nonvoters as living organisms with hearts (party identifications) and souls (issue orientations), interacting with one another and politicians (or rather candidate images) in something called *the electoral process.*

Both Converse and Miller have recently argued against treating national electorates as holistic units that can be expected to provide much understanding of politics at that level. Converse, in the context of writing about the high variance of the distribution of information in electorates, notes:

> The steep stratification of the electorate jointly in terms of both information possession and information receptivity is well worth keeping in mind in analyzing electoral data. I think of it often when I see coefficients bearing on information processes that are calculated for the electorate as a whole. (Converse 1990, 374)

Converse also notes that the electorate is not only highly stratified in information levels, but also "at least partially differentiated into 'issue publics' that have somewhat specialized interests. . . ." (Converse 1990, 375). Both considerations suggest disaggregation, rather than aggregate analysis. Warren Miller, the other major custodian of the evolving Michigan dispensation, has in recent years devoted much analytic effort to a fuller understanding of the continuing genesis and emergence of party identification at both the micro and macro levels. He distinguishes between two kinds of shift in identification, one called "distributional," the other "relational." Space limitations do not allow me to elaborate this suggestive distinction here, but it served Miller to explain (counter to what higher-level aggregation would conceal) why, in 1984, the "politicized young actually shifted their party identification to give slightly *greater* support to the *Democratic*—not the Republican—party . . ." (Miller 1986, 117).[38] Even more recently, Miller (1991a) has called for "Back to Basics" in the use of the party identification measure by disaggregating the electorate along politically significant social group lines. Such disaggregation shows that there is no evidence of partisan realignment between 1952 and 1980, counter to findings for the electorate as a whole that suggested volatility in response to short-term influences.

Conclusion

The behavioral analysis of politics "has been largely a-historic (though not anti-historic). The defense, or better, the rationalization, has been that, in any case, the task of behavioral research is to establish functional rather than causal relations between variables. This is a rather disingenuous avoidance of the causal challenge" (Eulau 1963, 128).[39] In the thirty or so years since this was written, electoral research has confronted the causal challenge with a vengeance, much of it making sense but some of it being nonsense, especially those studies that claimed the superiority of nonrecursive simultaneous equations over recursive models in explaining the electoral decision process.

Time is the essence of cause, as Aristotle might say if he were living today. Most of us would probably agree, even if we disagreed with the sage on other matters. Today's voting research at the level of individual persons is almost unthinkable except in terms of some kind of sophisticated multivariate analysis, mainly making use of some statistical regression model. The model is assumed to capture causation in the real world. This is all to the good, were it not for the fact that the conditions for causality to operate do not seem to be altogether met when the analysis is based on cross-sectional data, even if collected at different points in time. Meritorious and enormously useful as time series based on many cross sections are to the historically-minded scholar, they do not meet the conditions for causal inference, and only longitudinal data coming out of panel studies permit legitimate causal inference.

Causation is intrinsically a phenomenon of time. Cross-sectional data measured at only one point in time are, therefore, suspect candidates for causal analysis: the sequencing of the independent variable and the dependent variable is theoretical, and while the analyst may be able to give a plausible reason for the ordering, the reason can never be convincing, *even if there is a satisfactory fit between the model and the data.* This is of course precisely the reason why cross-sectional data can be so easily thrown into the cauldron of nonrecursivity—another way would be to say that "anything goes." Moreover, in using cross-sectional data, causal analysis is necessarily based on the assumption that the values for the dependent variable were identical *before* the effect of the independent or causal variable on the dependent variable was measured. Only if this condition is met can one give some credence to the plausibility criterion.

As one reads the regression-spiced research reports on voting behavior, one seems to lose a sense of historical reality. As far as I can make out, few of the studies worry about a simple—perhaps it is thought of as simplistic—thing like whether the causal model is sufficiently isomorphic with the temporal-behavioral processes in the real world to warrant confidence (of a nonstatistical sort) in the inferences being made about electoral politics.

The dilemma in using either correlation or regression in causal inference from data based on cross sections is that causal findings based on cross-sectional data may be modified or even reversed in a longitudinal analysis based on panel data. Nevertheless, there remains the question of whether cross-sectional data, properly conceptualized, cannot be treated as if some of them preceded others in time because, in spite of the availability of panel data for some election cycles, the great bulk of the research on voting at the micro level is likely to continue to be cross-sectional rather than longitudinal. In this regard, electoral analyses making use of aggregate electoral statistics clearly have an advantage over those using survey data: the units of analysis of the aggregate studies remain the same over relatively long periods and, though boundaries are redrawn occasionally, relatively constant—census tracks, cities, counties, states, legislative districts, school districts, and so on. As a result, causal analysis is on firmer ground in aggregate-longitudinal than in cross-sectional studies based on individual behavioral data: it is always clear that a presumed causal or explanatory variable measured at t1 precedes an observed or dependent variable at t2. There cannot be such a thing as nonrecursive (reciprocal) causation over time.

It has been Warren Miller's great contribution to social-scientific sanity in electoral research, and with it to historical scholarship, that he has always kept one foot in the real world of politics while the other foot ascended to the next step on the ladder of methodological sophistication, rather than—to change the metaphor—jumping with both feet into the deep waters of the latest methodology that is likely to be of limited use to the future historian.

N O T E S

1. This is not a rhetorical question. Listen to a reminiscence from the beginnings by Samuel J. Eldersveld (1951), whose inventory of electoral research in that year was probably the first of its kind. "In early September, 1949, a conference sponsored by the Social Science Research Council was held at the University of Michigan for the purpose of discussing techniques for the study of political behavior. . . . Although there was

much disagreement as to whether political behavior could best be studied at election time, it was one of the concrete proposals advanced and generally accepted by the conferees." *O Tempora! O Mores!*

2. The disaster was so great that the usually quiescent and politically passive Social Science Research Council felt impelled to set up a committee of inquiry into the failure of the polls in 1948. See Mosteller, Hyman, McCarthy, Marks, and Truman 1948.

3. Recent generations of political scientists find it sometimes hard to understand that well into the late 1940s and early 1950s political science, with a few exceptions, was an essentially ministerial discipline. You were not trained to be a research scholar but ordained, upon proof of "knowing the literature" (and that's what most Ph.D. examinations were about).

4. Berns's (1962) "Straussian" critique was primarily addressed to the Elmira Study (Berelson, Lazarsfeld, and McPhee 1954), and its (admittedly myopic) interpretation of citizen competence, but it is quite clear that Berns would have said the same things about political survey research generally.

5. On a personal note, I'm recalling that James Bryce's *The American Commonwealth,* first published in 1888 and reissued for many decades later, had an almost biblical impact on the senior member of the teams that conducted the 1952–1960 election studies of the Survey Research Center at the University of Michigan. When I first met Angus Campbell in the early 1950s, he would often refer to something or other he had read in Bryce. When, in November, 1977, the Inter-University Consortium for Political and Social Research honored him at the meeting of its Official Representatives from member colleges and universities in the United States and abroad, he was presented a two-volume, leather-bound copy of the first edition of *The American Commonwealth.* I can now add a postscript: Lazarsfeld (1957, 252) once referred to Bryce as "the patron saint of modern public opinion research," a latter-day beatification of the Englishman that Angus Campbell evidently shared.

6. In the course of this chapter, I shall refer to the Michigan studies between 1948 and 1970 as SRC (Survey Research Center) studies; to those conducted between 1970 and 1976 as CPS (Center for Political Studies) studies; and to those since 1978 as NES (National Election Studies) studies.

7. As far as I know, Lazarsfeld was the only social scientist among the first generation of pollsters and survey researchers who wrote about the question of making survey research useful to the historian. However, in a personal communication of February 24, 1992, Warren Miller informed me that "Angus [Campbell] and Al DeGrazia had a grand plan to capture the interviews of a national survey on video film. I think they actually asked for a large grant to do this. Their idea was to record the dialects, accents, and ordinary language of respondents answering interviewers' questions, while at the same time filming the interiors of homes to capture all of the ethnic and cultural variety that characterized the mid-twentieth century. The idea reflected many of Angus's interests as an anthropologist, but both of them [were] committed to preserving a unique historical record."

8. My unhappiness with this most unfortunate, invidious, and incorrect judgment by my good friend, the late sociologist Morris Janowitz, was aggravated by a footnote

reference ("for a critical assessment") to my review of *The American Voter* (Eulau 1960). I certainly did not make the comparison between the Michigan and Columbia approaches that the footnote gives the impression of my having made. Moreover, the Janowitz text refers exclusively to the 1952 SRC study as reported in *The Voter Decides* (Campbell, Gurin, and Miller 1954), and nowhere to *The American Voter* (which, moreover, is not mentioned at all by Janowitz).

9. It may be that, as is so often the case in the social sciences after a discontinuous interval, a revival of the "Columbia tradition" is in the offing. See Popkin 1991.

10. I want to emphasize that I shall not be dealing here with the enormous contribution that Warren Miller has made to social science history by way of his organizational and administrative talents. In the early 1960s, he encouraged quantitatively-inclined historians to associate their own efforts with those of the new Inter-University Consortium for Political and (later) Social Research by sponsoring seminars on historical data in Ann Arbor and, in 1964, starting a historical archive. Later, Miller was active in organizing the Social Science History Association (serving as its president in 1979–80) and creating the journal *Social Science History.*

11. This problem should not be confused with the familiar empirical "missing data" problem.

12. Needless to say, perhaps, yet in need of being said in this connection, I mean by "events" everything that occurs—situations, actions, predispositions, or all the other things on the agenda of electoral survey research.

13. At least it is my impression that third-, fourth-, or fifth-generation electoral analysts are rarely as careful as is Warren Miller, notably in the series of three articles on the 1980, 1984, and 1988 elections published in the *British Journal of Political Science* in collaboration with Merrill Shanks. To give just one example where I could give many, Shanks and Miller (1991, 169), discussing a 1988 NES preelection question on whether respondents were willing or not willing to "pay more in federal taxes . . . in order to reduce the size of the federal budget deficit," write: "To be sure, such a question is at least potentially erroneous as a measure of 'true' tax preferences because respondents may not understand or accept the hypothetical premise of the question—i.e., that a tax increase is or might be necessary 'in order to' reduce the budget deficit." But this is really only part of the problem. Shanks and Miller assumed that voters willing to have their taxes increased would be more likely to vote for Dukakis than Bush. They expressed surprise that, after controls were introduced, the hypothesized relationship was reduced to "substantive insignificance." The problem, of course, was that the interview question was double-barreled. It was not only a question about willingness to pay taxes (in general) but also about one's attitude in the matter of budget deficits. A believer in deficit spending, for instance, would give a negative answer on willingness to pay more taxes for the purpose indicated by the question, yet favor more taxation for other purposes.

14. The major findings of the 1948 study were actually first reported in April 1949, in a mimeographed report entitled "A Study of the Presidential Vote: November 1948."

15. The questions were: (1) "In the presidential elections next month, are you almost certain to vote, uncertain, or won't you vote?" (2) (if certain or uncertain) "Do

you plan to vote Republican, Democratic, or something else?" I do not have the vaguest idea of how and why these two questions were inserted in the survey.

16. The fiasco of the commercial polls was a potential threat to the reputation of all the social sciences, leading the Social Science Research Council to set up a committee to investigate. The Campbell-Kahn study was part of this investigation. See Mosteller et al. 1948.

17. In fact, a national study of the 1944 presidential election had been conducted by NORC (National Opinion Research Center). The data from this survey were used in an unpublished Ph.D. dissertation by Korchin (1946).

18. When I served on the Board of Overseers for the National Election Studies (1976–84), now conceived as a national resource rather than a Michigan operation, it was one of our primary missions to protect certain questions—called "core"—from shortsighted elimination due to pressure for new questions occasioned by the events of the day that, quite naturally and legitimately, fascinate students of voting behavior.

19. Rossi was not quite correct. The research design of the 1952 study allowed for multilevel analysis, but this opportunity was not utilized in the main text of *The Voter Decides*. However, there are two appendices that attest to this, one entitled "Primary Group Influences and Political Behavior," the other "The Perceived Political Relevance of Demographic Groups." The 1952 data were also used in a more sociologically-inspired manner by Morris Janowitz and Dwaine Marvick, *Competitive Pressure and Democratic Consent* (1956), and in Heinz Eulau, *Class and Party in the Eisenhower Years* (1962).

20. I've always found it fun to speculate on what is implied by the ordering of names in multiauthored books when the alphabetical order of authors's names, as in *The Voter Decides,* coincides with their academic ranks, and what it means when this subtle equilibrium is upset—say Gurin, Campbell, and Miller, or even Miller, Gurin, and Campbell. Who knows? By 1960, the alphabetical/academic conflation was worse: Campbell, Converse, Miller, and Stokes.

21. Using the word *micro* here is something of a literary license. It is a relative term, its meaning always depending on its antonym *macro*. Lazarsfeld was interested in behavior change over a relatively short period of time. In the Erie County study there were seven monthly interviews with panel respondents, from May to November 1940. By way of contrast, the Michigan panel studies covered four years each and, as the text shows, can also be called *micro,* but in comparison to the Columbia studies they are (relatively) *macro.*

22. I first heard about this formulation while in college during the 1930s from a maverick social scientist, Frederick Teggart, who could not find a home in the departments of History, Sociology, or Economics, and who, for this reason, was given his own department, called "Social Institutions," that also included just one associate professor and, later, one instructor. See Teggart 1960. Teggart's formulation seemed, at the time, quite radical.

23. This is my attribution, not a Millerian self-designation.

24. The relevant literature is enormous, but see Niemi and Weisberg 1976, which includes some of the best articles on these controversies, as well as many insightful commentaries by the editors themselves.

25. The four features were: (1) counter to conventional wisdom, Dukakis was not a less attractive candidate than Bush when it came to personal traits or leadership-related characteristics; (2) while evaluations of Reagan's performance helped the Republican cause in 1988, they were smaller than in 1984 and thus made a smaller contribution to the Bush victory; (3) a decline in positive evaluations of the state of the nation between 1984 and 1988 was "consistent with, if not necessarily a third cause of, the Republicans' reduced majority at the polls"; and (4) partisan divisions in the vote of white citizens seemed "to have been shaped by differences in their sentiments toward blacks to only a minor extent—and in a highly indirect fashion," so that Bush did not benefit from this division (Shanks and Miller 1991, 131–33).

26. Within the community of scholars that now constitutes the clientele of the National Election Studies, none has been more important in sponsoring contextual analysis than John Sprague, a member of the NES' original Board of Overseers. I have in my files a memorandum prepared by Sprague entitled "Contextual Effects and the National Election Studies" and dated October 1976 (a time when the "board" was only a "planning committee" and had not as yet been formally established). See chapter 9 in this volume.

27. Context was, of course, an important consideration in the Columbia studies of personal influence of the 1940s and 1950s, but these studies, like an important study by Putnam (1966) were all community studies of one kind or another. See Eulau 1980.

28. Miller speculated that "if—through whatever course of events—one-party dominance becomes established in a county, its very existence works against a redressing of the political balance and a revival of two-party competition. . . . It may be that, *barring the intervention of events of major social or economic importance*, the second party in local politics fights not for eventual primacy and dominance, but merely to avoid extinction as a real political force" (Miller 1956, 716; emphasis added).

29. In the last of their three articles on the "Reagan-era elections," Miller and Shanks elaborate the problem as follows: "In one analytic mode we are trying to understand (or explain) individual-level differences between voters in their vote choice; in the other, we are primarily interested in the aggregate election outcome and in accounting for the overall margin of victory. Both types of analysis rest on the same estimates of the effect for each of our explanatory variables, but they emphasize different kinds of statistical information about those variables—i.e., their means and their standard deviations. Traditionally, academic electoral analysis has centered on individual-level differences and the objective of giving a summary explanation of differences between voters. To this analysis of the importance of variability across voters, we have added our interest in the objective of determining why one group of voters (who voted for the winner) was larger than the other. In pursuing this latter interest we combine the mean value—or *central tendency*—of each explanatory variable with our assessment of its effects on the vote decision" (Shanks and Miller 1991, 139).

30. As one example of this kind of "guessing," Lazarsfeld offered "the problem of class tensions" (1957, 238). The other example Lazarsfeld gives is the reaction to rapidly increasing industrialization through strong religious movements (Lazarsfeld 1957, 256–57).

31. It is extremely hazardous nowadays to make any generalization about the scientific quality of research in the electoral field—one of the few fields of political science that can boast to be populated by a genuine research community—because the number of investigators is very large and the number of publications even larger. I have the feeling, however, that the electoral research community is somewhat solipsistic, with some analysts even operating on the assumption that the latest is always the best. While there are occasional publications that try to serve as critical inventories of research development in the field, they are rather narrow gauged and do not match the kind of diagnostic appraisal that Philip Converse (1975) wrote some years ago, and that certainly disabuses the reader from overestimating any certainties he or she might be inclined to attribute to electoral research.

32. There is, Miller informed me recently, "an interesting tidbit" about the notion of the "normal vote" apart from its usefulness in his own work. "The Concept of a Normal Vote," authored by Converse, was chapter 2 in Campbell et al. 1966. Miller writes: ". . . *Elections and the Political Order* came into being in large part because no one seemed to share our sense of its [the normal-vote concept's] possible analytic contribution. The manuscript was turned down by APSR [*American Political Science Review*], JOP [*Journal of Politics*], and AJPS [*American (Midwest) Journal of Political Science*], and so I cajoled the others [Campbell, Converse, and Stokes] into doing a book in which it could be a lead piece. However, I am not sure any of us thought of this as a contribution to history" (pers. com., 1992).

33. I used these questions in a monograph (Eulau 1962) that, until recently (Haas 1992), has been largely (and perhaps properly) ignored by the research community, social class not being a variable high in the esteem of American political scientists. My objective in this research was to say something about class consciousness and electoral behavior, knowing full well that it is most difficult to get operational measures for this variable in the American environment. A composite index of *objective* components (income, education, occupation) coupled with the well-known *subjective* class identi-fication measure served as a necessary but not sufficient starting point to "get at" class consciousness. There were other measures as well. One question asked the respondent (who had identified him- or herself as belonging to the middle class or working class) how he or she thought his or her *own* class would vote and how he or she thought the *other* class would vote. The respondent was also asked *why* he or she thought the middle class or working class would vote for one or the other of the two major political parties. The answers to this question were coded into two categories: *interested-oriented* and *not interest-oriented.* The data then permitted analysis of what I called "class salience" (in order to avoid having to quarrel with the ambiguous concept of "class consciousness").

34. I'm using the expression *party-related personal attributes* as a generic term to cover all of the terms described in the text as often being conflated or confused. Over the years, one finds in the literature a veritable beehive of words sometimes treated as synonyms, sometimes not; sometimes deliberately, sometimes not: in addition to party identification, one encounters terms like *partisanship, party attachment, partisan loy-alty, partisan support* (Dennis), *partisan preference, party affiliation,* etc. Sometimes these terms are associated with unique measures; sometimes they are attributed to the same measure. This is not the place to sort out this sort of thing.

35. My use here of the word *inchoate* needs some explication. The word presumably means that something is imperfectly formed or formulated, or that it only partly exists. There may be a better word for what I have in mind, but I want to note that every question has a questioner, and that a question's understanding depends not only on how it is heard but also on how it is asked. In print, underlining the key words *generally* and *usually* makes it pretty clear what the question means. But in the interview situation, different interviewers may well put different *stresses* on these words, so that the respondent may hear the question only *partially* and, hence, respond partially.

36. The words *conflate* and *conflation* should not be confused with the words *confuse* or *confusion.* Conflation refers to combining or linking two or more terms into a composite conception. Conflation thus refers to the process of bringing together things into a composite whole. Confusion refers to the process of making things indistinct and failing to distinguish between them. I'm using the word *conflation* in the text because I assume that the investigators referred to were well aware of what they were doing in conflating the concepts of party identification and party affiliation.

37. When, two years later, Abramson and Ostrom (1991), in a partial replication and extension, compared the statistical results obtained for the Gallup question by MacKuen and colleagues with their own results for the party identification measure used in the SRC/CPS/NES surveys as well as in NORC's General Social Survey, they found exactly what they should have expected to start with, given the different temporal frames of reference provided to respondents by the Gallup and Michigan questions— that the Gallup affiliation measure has "built-in short-term volatility," compared with the party identification measure.

Unfortunately, in the end, Abramson and Ostrom contribute their own obfuscation. The Gallup measure, they write, "may well prove to be useful." The causal analyses by MacKuen and associates "suggest that we may need to combine such measures as presidential approval, the ICS [Index of Consumer Sentiment], and partisanship" (Abramson and Ostrom 1991, 191). Just how this minestrone will taste is left to the imagination.

38. By *politicized* is meant here *more ideologically sophisticated;* by *young* is not meant absolute age, but an age cohort's entry into the electoral process. Miller mentions (in various places) that "national totals may at times conceal more than they reveal about the dynamics of political change" (Miller 1986, 107–8). What he calls "disaggregation" into subpopulations may, however, be a deceptive expression: the data really remain aggregated at the national level, if for units other than the population as a whole (in this case, the politicized grouping or the young cohort). Such disaggregation creates a new problem: because of smaller numbers in the subunits, the sample estimates become more unreliable. Rather than "disaggregation," the analytic process involved is one of "reduction": the unit (the national sample) is reduced to lower-level subunits (the politicized or young subsamples).

39. My own thinking about causation had been influenced by an unfortunately little-noted book of the Columbia University sociologist and political scientist Robert M. McIver, *Social Causation* (1942). I still recommend the book, even though it may displease causal enthusiasts when McIver concludes that "the goal of causal knowledge is never attained, though our endeavors can bring us always nearer" (1942, 392).

The person who brought us nearer was Herbert Simon, who, like any good scholar trained by Charles Merriam and Harold Lasswell at Chicago in the 1930s, would note that unless political science can solve the problem of power, "political science, defined as the study of power, cannot be said to exist." As power involves an asymmetrical relationship, the problem of power "was identical with the general problem of defining a *causal relation* between two variables" (Simon 1957, 4–5). Then along came Hubert M. "Tad" Blalock (1964), solving all our causal problems by way of statistical regression models—or so it appeared.

R E F E R E N C E S

Abramson, Paul R., and Charles W. Ostrom, Jr. 1991. "Macropartisanship: An Empiri-cal Reassessment." *American Political Science Review* 85:181–92.
Beck, Paul Allen. 1986. "Choice, Context, and Consequence: Beaten and Unbeaten Paths toward a Science of Electoral Behavior." In *Political Science: The Science of Politics,* ed. Herbert F. Weisberg. New York: Agathon.
Benson, Lee. 1978. "Changing Social Science to Change the World." *Social Science History* 2:427–41.
Berelson, Bernard R., Paul F. Lazarsfeld, and William N. McPhee. 1954. *Voting: A Study of Opinion Formation in a Presidential Campaign.* Chicago: University of Chicago Press.
Berns, Walter. 1962. "Voting Studies." In *Essays on the Scientific Study of Politics,* ed. Herbert J. Storing. New York: Holt, Rinehart and Winston.
Blalock, Hubert M., Jr. 1964. *Causal Inferences in Nonexperimental Research.* Chapel Hill: University of North Carolina Press.
Campbell, Angus, Gerald Gurin, and Warren E. Miller. 1954. *The Voter Decides.* Evans-ton, Ill.: Row, Peterson.
Campbell, Angus, Philip E. Converse, Warren E. Miller, and Donald E. Stokes. 1960. *The American Voter.* New York: Wiley.
Campbell, Angus, and Robert L. Kahn. 1952. *The People Elect a President.* Ann Arbor: Survey Research Center, Institute for Social Research.
Clubb, Jerome M., William H. Flanigan, and Nancy H. Zingale. 1980. *Partisan Realign-ment.* Beverly Hills: Sage.
Converse, Jean M. 1987. *Survey Research in the United States: Roots & Emergence 1890–1960.* Berkeley: University of California Press.
Converse, Philip E. 1975. "Public Opinion and Voting Behavior." In *Handbook of Political Science,* ed. Fred I. Greenstein and Nelson W. Polsby, vol. 4. Reading, Mass.: Addison-Wesley.
———. 1976. *The Dynamics of Party Support: Cohort-Analyzing Party Identification.* Beverly Hills: Sage.
———. 1982. "The Impact of the Polls on National Leadership." In *The Social Sci-ences: Their Nature and Uses,* ed. William H. Kruskal. Chicago: University of Chicago Press.
———. 1990. "Popular Representation and the Distribution of Information." In *Infor-*

mation and Democratic Processes, ed. John A. Ferejohn and James H. Kuklinski, Urbana: University of Illinois Press.

Converse, Philip E., Heinz Eulau, and Warren E. Miller. 1982. "The Study of Voting." In *Behavioral and Social Science Research: A National Resource,* ed. Robert McC. Adams, Neil J. Smelser, and Donald J. Treiman, part 2. Washington, D.C.: National Academy Press.

Deutsch, Karl W., Andrei S. Markovits, and John Platt. 1986. *Advances in the Social Sciences, 1900–1980: What, Who, Where, How?* Cambridge, Mass.: University Press of America.

Dogan, Mattei, and Robert Pahre. 1990. *Creative Marginality: Innovation at the Intersections of Social Sciences.* Boulder, Colo.: Westview.

Eldersveld, Samuel J. 1951. "Theory and Method in Voting Behavior Research." *Journal of Politics* 13: 70–87.

Eulau, Heinz. 1960. Review of *The American Voter,* by Angus Campbell, Philip E. Converse, Warren E. Miller, and Donald E. Stokes. *American Political Science Review* 54:993–94.

———. 1962. *Class and Party in the Eisenhower Years.* New York: Free Press.

———. 1963. *The Behavioral Persuasion in Politics.* New York: Random House.

———. 1980. "The Columbia Studies of Personal Influence." *Social Science History* 4:207–28.

———. 1986. "Developmental Analysis and Constructs." In *Politics, Self, and Society.* Cambridge, Mass.: Harvard University Press.

Haas, Michael. 1992. *Polity and Society: Philosophical Underpinnings of Social Science Paradigms.* New York: Praeger.

Janowitz, Morris. 1978. *The Last Half-Century: Societal Change and Politics in America.* Chicago: University of Chicago Press.

Janowitz, Morris, and Dwaine Marvick. 1956. *Competitive Pressure and Democratic Consent.* Ann Arbor: Institute of Public Administration, University of Michigan.

Korchin, Sheldon J. 1946. "Psychological Variables in the Behavior of Voters." Ph.D. diss., Harvard University.

Lasswell, Harold D. 1972. "Communications Research and Public Policy." *Public Opinion Quarterly* 36:301–10. Reprinted in Dwaine Marvick, ed., *Harold D. Lasswell on Political Sociology* (Chicago: University of Chicago Press, 1977).

Lazarsfeld, Paul F. 1957. "History and Public Opinion Research." In *Common Frontiers of the Social Sciences,* ed. Mirra Komarovsky. Glencoe, Ill.: Free Press.

Lazarsfeld, Paul F., Bernard Berelson, and Hazel Gaudet. 1948. *The People's Choice.* 2d ed. New York: Columbia University Press.

MacIver, Robert M. [1942] 1964. *Social Causation.* Reprint. New York: Harper Torchbooks.

MacKuen, Michael B., Robert S. Erikson, and James A. Stimson. 1989. "Macropartisanship." *American Political Science Review* 83:1125–42.

Miller, Warren E. 1956. "One-Party Politics and the Voter." *American Political Science Review* 50:707–25.

———. 1978. "Some Reflections on 'Changing Social Science to Change the World.'" *Social Science History* 2:442–48.

————. 1986. "Party Identification and Political Belief Systems: Changes in Partisanship in the United States, 1980–84." *Electoral Studies* 5:101–21.

————. 1989. "Research Life as a Collection of Intersecting Probability Distributions." In *Crossroads of Social Science,* ed. Heinz Eulau. New York: Agathon.

————. 1991a. "Oral History." In *Political Science in America: Oral Histories of a Discipline,* ed. Michael A. Baer, Malcolm E. Jewell, and Lee Sigelman. Lexington: University Press of Kentucky.

————. 1991b. "Party Identification, Realignment, and Party Voting: Back to the Basics." *American Political Science Review* 85:557–68.

Miller, Warren E., and J. Merrill Shanks. 1982. "Policy Directions and Presidential Leadership: Alternative Interpretations of the 1980 Presidential Election." *British Journal of Political Science* 12:299–356.

Miller, Warren E., and Teresa E. Levitin. 1976. *Leadership and Change: The New Politics and the American Electorate.* Cambridge, Mass.: Winthrop.

Mosteller, Frederick, Herbert Hyman, Philip J. McCarthy, Eli S. Marks, and David B. Truman. 1948. *The Pre-election Polls of 1948.* New York: Social Science Research Council.

Niemi, Richard G., and Herbert F. Weisberg, eds. 1976. *Controversies in American Voting Behavior.* San Francisco: W. H. Freeman.

Popkin, Samuel L. 1991. *The Reasoning Voter: Communication and Persuasion in Presidential Campaigns.* Chicago: University of Chicago Press.

Putnam, Robert D. 1966. "Political Attitudes and the Local Community." *American Political Science Review* 60:640–54.

Rogers, Lindsay. 1949. *The Pollsters: Public Opinion, Politics, and Democratic Leadership.* New York: Alfred A. Knopf.

Rossi, Peter H. 1959. "Four Landmarks in Voting Research." In *American Voting Behavaor,* ed. Eugene Burdick and Arthur J. Brodbeck, Glencoe, Ill.: Free Press.

Shanks, J. Merrill, and Warren E. Miller. 1990. "Policy Direction and Performance Evaluation: Complementary Explanations of the Reagan Elections." *British Journal of Political Science* 20:143–235.

————. 1991. "Partisanship, Policy, and Performance: The Reagan Legacy in the 1988 Election." *British Journal of Political Science* 21:129–97.

Simon, Herbert A. 1957. *Models of Man.* New York: Wiley and Sons.

Teggart, Frederick J. 1960. *Theory and Processes of History.* Berkeley: University of California Press.

CHAPTER 4

The Rational Citizen Faces Election Day or What Rational Choice Theorists Don't Tell You about American Elections

Raymond E. Wolfinger

Anthony Downs wrote in *An Economic Theory of Democracy* that "every rational man decides whether to vote just as he makes all other decisions: if the returns outweigh the costs, he votes; if not, he abstains" (Downs 1957, 260). In the ensuing thirty-five years, innumerable scholars have attempted to confirm, refute, or modify this formulation. Their efforts occupy such a conspicuous place in political science that one recent president of the American Political Science Association called public choice a "hegemonic subdiscipline" and "probably the hottest thing going in political science today" (Lowi 1992, 4). The growing popularity of Downs's book is attested by Wattenberg's finding (1991, 18–19) that "In the late 1960s it was cited . . . half as often as *The American Voter;* now it is cited . . . more than twice as often. . . ."

Attempts to give empirical validity to rational choice theories of turnout have failed to acknowledge or take proper account of several important aspects of American elections. Oddly, these include some circumstances where the costs and benefits of voting are tangible and evident. The more consequential overlooked phenomena include multiple contests on the ballot; extensive, but far from universal, ignorance about the electoral system and any contemporary campaign; and, most telling of all, the importance of registering to vote. My first purpose, then, is to criticize the existing body of rational choice scholarship by pointing out some of the gaps between its view of turnout and the real world of American elections.

This criticism of existing work leads in some cases to suggestions about how rational choice researchers could do a better job. But better is not good enough; all the problems cannot be fixed. Real-life elections pose insuperable problems for rational choice explanations of turnout. The inescapable conclusion is that rational choice theory is inherently unsuited to illuminating voter turnout.

Defining the Rational Voter

Downs's rational voter "compares the utility incomes he believes he would receive were each party in office" (Downs 1957, 39). He votes for the party that he expects to provide more utility; if the parties seem tied, he abstains.[1] But the rational person also recognizes that the benefits he anticipates from the victory of his preferred party or candidate do not depend on his behavior; they will come whether he votes or stays home on election day. Only if his vote can make a difference will his behavior affect his chances of getting the desired benefits. "But in fact his vote is not decisive; it is lost in a sea of other votes" (Downs 1957, 246).

So far, the benefits of voting depend on a preferred electoral outcome. There are, however, other rewards from voting:

> The advantage of voting *per se* is that it makes democracy possible. If no one votes, then the system collapses because no government is chosen. We assume that the citizens of a democracy subscribe to its principles and therefore derive benefits from its continuance; hence they do not want it to collapse. For this reason they attach value to the act of voting *per se* and receive a return from it. (Downs 1957, 261–62)

However, this "long-run participation value" (Downs 1957, 270) also is subject to the free-rider problem; the citizen receives the reward irrespective of his own behavior (Feeley 1974, 237).

In summarizing his argument, Downs seemed to shrink from accepting its stark implication that voting is irrational for any citizen because the rewards from his vote will never match the costs of casting it:

> The total return each citizen receives from voting depends on (1) the benefits he gets from democracy, (2) how much he wants a particular party to win, (3) how close he thinks the election will be, and (4) how many other citizens he thinks will vote. These variables insure a relatively wide range of possible returns similar to the range of voting costs. (Downs 1957, 274)

William H. Riker and Peter Ordeshook, the authors of the other landmark in the field, recognized that Downs's argument leads

> . . . to the conclusion that voting, the fundamental political act, is typically irrational. The function of theory is to explain behavior and it is certainly no explanation to assign a sizeable part of politics to the mysterious and inexplicable world of the irrational. . . . We describe a calculus

of voting from which one infers that it is reasonable for those who vote to do so and . . . we present empirical evidence that citizens actually behave as if they employed this calculus. (Riker and Ordeshook 1968, 25)

Riker and Ordeshook's empirical analysis used the 1952, 1956, and 1960 National Election Studies samples. The questions they chose to measure the rational citizen's calculations are, to say the least, inapposite. For example, each respondent's anticipated reward from the success of his favored candidate was measured with a question asking if he personally cared which party won the presidential election. Estimates of the probability that one's vote would be decisive were measured with a question about how close the respondent expected the election would be. This is quite a reach from one vote changing the outcome. In 1960, the closest presidential election in this century, there were still 119,000 votes between winner and loser. It strains credulity to assume that many citizens expecting a similarly close outcome in an imminent election would believe that their own votes would make a difference. (The electoral college will be discussed in due course.) In any event, henceforth rational choice theorists usually estimated the citizen's expectation of being decisive by the closeness of the election, either anticipated by survey respondents or measured in the outcome.

Perhaps Riker and Ordeshook's most noteworthy innovation was an attempt to measure the benefits of performing the voting act, irrespective of any outcome. Unlike Downs's notion of the benefits of "voting *per se,*" which concern the survival of democracy and therefore depend on the behavior of other citizens, Riker and Ordeshook's formulation truly did address some intrinsic benefits of voting, irrespective of the outcome or the actions of others. These were emotional satisfactions, including those derived from "compliance with the ethic of voting . . . affirming allegiance to the political system . . . affirming a partisan preference" (Riker and Ordeshook 1968, 28). This collection of subjective states, called "the D term," was measured by four NES questions on "citizen duty," none of which they quoted, that solicited agreement or disagreement with normative statements about one's duty to vote in various contexts. The citizen duty scale is remarkably ill-suited to its place in Riker and Ordeshook's model. For one thing, none of the four items concerns expressive gratification. Moreover, one statement dismisses many local elections as not "important enough to bother with," which seems beside the point when studying voting in a presidential election.

Riker and Ordeshook handled the question of costs by saying that "the citizen who believes it is terribly important to vote is likely to minimize costs of voting while the citizen who thinks voting is unimportant is likely to maximize costs of voting" (1968, 37). Hence they omitted any direct measure of cost.

Their data analysis, a series of cross-tabulations with the independent variables all dichotomized, indicated generally positive relationships between turnout and both anticipated rewards and expectations that one's vote would be important to the outcome. As a number of later scholars noted, however, "most of the action is in the D term" (Ferejohn and Fiorina 1974, 525; see also Mueller 1989, 355).

Electoral Records Are Public

In the rational choice school, intrinsic rewards, those that come from performing the act of voting and do not depend on any electoral outcome, are either indivisible and remote, as in the case of the Downsian goal of saving democracy, or intangible and expressive, as in the case of various explanations emphasizing remorse, catharsis, group solidarity, or other subjective states.[2] It must be a bittersweet experience to salvage formal choice theories of turnout with such squishy variables.

All the more amazing, then, that no toiler in this vineyard seems to have considered any of the more concrete rewards and penalties that may be an intrinsic result of electoral participation or nonparticipation. These depend, one way or another, on the simple truth that while how one votes is secret, the fact of having voted is, with rare exceptions, a matter of public record. By the same token, registration records are available for inspection.[3] One implication should be obvious to any accountant of costs and benefits: people who hope to get or keep something of value by virtue of their political fidelity cannot afford to abstain in an election that is important to those who have the power to dispose of these valued goods and services. In plain English, this means, for example, that in places where patronage and favoritism influence governmental decisions, only the most foolhardy public jobholders would stay home on election day.

This proposition was handsomely affirmed in the only empirical study of this topic that I am familiar with. Using various methods of identifying such jobholders and holding constant other demographic and legal variables, Steven Rosenstone and I found that their turnout was up to thirteen percentage points higher than that of public employees where patronage was unimportant, and as much as eighteen points higher than that of private workers (Wolfinger and Rosenstone 1980, 97–101). Of course, patronage employees are expected to contribute more to the cause than merely their own votes, but these are not scorned.

At the lowest level of machine politics, one finds the exchange of votes for favors: fixed tickets, fixed building inspectors, better apartments in housing projects, and so on. One leader in New Haven described his modus operandi this way: "I do a lot of things for people. I keep working at it. . . . I just keep piling up good will. . . . People never forget" (quoted in Wolfinger 1974, 84).

What people should never forget to do is vote, a point made clear in this description of a local boss in Boston:

> When people wanted help from the organization, they would come right up here to the office. . . . If a man came in to ask Matt [the boss] for a job, Matt would listen to him and then tell him he'd see what he could do; he should come back in a couple of days. That would give Matt time to get in touch with the precinct captain and find out all about the man. If he didn't vote in the last election, he was out. Matt wouldn't do anything for him— that is, unless he could show that he was so sick he couldn't get to the polls. (quoted in Whyte 1955, 194)

Now it is easy to believe that expectations of votes for favors are widespread in those places where machine politics flourishes. Indeed, if this expectation were not pervasive, the machine's retail representatives would be remiss. What we have here, then, is another example of very tangible rewards for intrinsic voting. How many people are we talking about? In absolute numbers, I do not know. Relatively, I am persuaded that patronage employees and denizens of machine politics communities far outnumber citizens who think that their own vote might decide a presidential election.

Registration records are not only public, they are made available to organizations and individuals for a variety of political, commercial, and judicial purposes. Almost everywhere they are a principal source of jury lists; in some places, the only source. Many people know this, and many are averse to serving on juries. There is a wealth of anecdotes about citizens declining to register or asking that their names be deleted from the rolls in order to avoid literally costly absences from work. My impression that a great many election officials believe that fear of jury duty depresses turnout is supported by a survey making the same point conducted in the 1970s by the General Accounting Office (U.S. Senate 1975). One would think that such a clear example of a cost of voting would have engaged the attention of rational choice theorists; but one would be wrong.

The first systematic empirical study of this hypothesized relationship was Stephen Knack's analysis of 1988 National Election Studies data supplemented by state- and county-level data on the sources of jury lists (Knack 1993). On the basis of this analysis, Knack reported a depressive effect on turnout of seven to nine percentage points. Knack's work helped induce the NES to include questions about the sources of jury lists and willingness to serve on juries in its 1991 Pilot Study.[4] Initial analyses of the 1991 Pilot Study data provided one estimate that fear of jury duty had a very modest deterrent effect on registration (Oliver and Wolfinger 1992) and another estimate that the effect was somewhat more pronounced (Knack 1992). In either case, one might consider these findings a modicum of support for rational choice theories of turnout.

Many Contests Are on Each Ballot

In the formal theorist's world, a citizen looking toward election day contemplates his alternatives in a single contest: vote for A, vote for B, or stay home. But of course American voters typically make several choices in each election.[5] This abundance probably reaches a peak in California, which averaged thirteen statewide propositions on the ballot from 1974 through 1988 (Bowler, Donovan, and Happ 1992, 559). Local propositions, designated by a letter to differentiate them from the numbered statewide measures, give Californians further opportunities for public choice. These range from highly tangible refinements of rent control ordinances to expressions of discontent with U.S. foreign policy. In Alameda County, beyond all the candidates and the twenty-nine statewide propositions, there were more local measures on the ballot in November 1988 than letters in the alphabet to designate each proposition. Fear of polling place gridlock led to suggestions of an express lane for citizens who had filled in their sample ballots at home. One county's proposed ten-minute limit in the voting booth was enjoined by a federal judge's ruling that it would violate the Fourteenth Amendment, which evidently guarantees equal protection of the laws to slow voters.

We can assume that the presidential race is supreme to most potential voters, if only because turnout for presidential elections is almost always higher than that for elections held at other times. Nevertheless, every four years two to three million Americans go to the polls with so little regard for the top contest that they fail to vote for any presidential candidate (Wolfinger and Rosenstone 1980, 116). A fair number of Californians seem to care more about county supervisor than president: "in a typical supervisorial district with a November supervisorial contest in 1980 and 1984, the number of people voting for board candidates actually exceeded the number casting ballots for U.S. presidential candidates" (Lascher 1991, 666–67). The importance of nonpresidential elections is also attested by the consequences of television networks' early projections of the presidential election winner and, in 1980, President Jimmy Carter's concession of defeat three hours before the polls closed on the West Coast. For present purposes, the interesting finding is not the apparent effect of these events, but its modest dimensions, generally found to be a turnout reduction of less than five percent (Wolfinger and Linquiti 1981; Tannenbaum and Kostrich 1983).

Even if a ballot presented just one choice between two alternatives, people might differ in the rewards they expect should their preferred alternative win: enactment of a desired policy, recognition of their ethnic group, pleasure at a friend's success, influence at city hall, adjustment of a formula for assessing residential real property, purely symbolic expressions of approbation or disapprobation, and so on. Readers who wonder what common currency could be used to measure such disparate choices will not find clear answers in the rational choice literature. A typical discussion: " . . . the differential benefit, in utiles, that an individual voter receives from the success of his more preferred candidate over his less preferred one" (Riker and Ordeshook 1968, 25).

The multiplicity of choices on real-world ballots poses a challenge of model specification that would frustrate even the most ingenious formal theorist. Nevertheless, I suggest that rational choice theory leads ineluctably to one proposition: the more choices on the ballot, the higher the turnout.

There are half a million elected officials in the United States, many chosen concurrently with national officials. Just the parents, spouses, significant others, siblings, and adult children of the candidates add up to a sizable number of voters. Even for nonrelatives, the benefit—psychic or otherwise—of being an infinitesimal part of the winning coalition of a presidential candidate may pale beside the rewards from making a larger contribution to the success of a minor but not wholly trivial candidate or cause.[6] The more contests, the greater the chances of finding a candidate the voter knows or an issue he cares about.

There is no reason, at least in principle, why a detailed questionnaire could not winkle out all the benefits that a respondent expected from a favorable outcome to each and every one of the contests on his ballot. If aggregating these anticipated benefits into a comparable index proved daunting—as I expect it would—differences in kind among benefits could be overlooked in favor of adding them up as positive values. Or one could just assume, ceteris paribus, that more choices would increase the probability of benefits.

By the same token, as the number of contests increases, so do the chances that one contest will be close. And as the relevant political unit becomes smaller, the likelihood of being decisive increases.[7] The multiplication of a tiny probability times, say, forty still might not elevate that probability to the point where it could realistically be considered any sort of reasonable bet. Nevertheless, the odds would be much more favorable than those that rational choice theorists now take as providing a reasonable incentive to vote.

Calculations on the cost side also suggest that turnout will vary with the length of the ballot. To be sure, information costs will reflect the number of choices, but the more direct way to avoid paying the cost is not to vote on that contest, a common response in California (Bowler, Donovan, and Happ 1992). On the other hand, major cost factors include registration, locating the polling place, and taking the time to go there. These are the same regardless of the length of the ballot.[8]

Because the costs of voting do not increase in proportion to the number of choices, while the probabilities both of rewards and of casting a decisive vote are proportionate to the number of choices, rational choice theory must predict that longer ballots produce higher turnout. I have no explanation for the absence of this simple and verifiable proposition from the work of rational choice theorists.

Misinformation Is Widespread and Indeterminate

Rational choice theory does not assert that citizens are well informed, but only that their behavior is appropriate to their understanding of the situation. This consideration is perhaps most apposite to beliefs about casting the decisive vote, which have been measured by the closeness of the outcome in empirical applications of rational choice. Someone who believed that presidents are popularly elected and that the 1984 election was too close to call nevertheless could base his decision to vote in that election on a rational calculation of his chances of being decisive. In order to learn whether respondents' turnout is rational, it is necessary to learn what they know about the electoral college.

Unfortunately, empirical applications of rational choice theory have failed even to acknowledge the possibility of widespread ignorance of the electoral college. Some attempts to test rational choice theory with survey data ignore the electoral college (e.g., Riker and Ordeshook 1968) or specify the model incorrectly: "In this context, the rational voter hypothesis implicitly assumes that, because of the electoral college system and its winner-take-all or unit rule, it is appropriate to measure the expected closeness of the state, rather than national, election outcome" (Foster 1984, 682n). Actually, the objective importance of a presidential vote depends not only on the closeness of the race in the state, but also on the contribution of that state to a candidate's electoral vote total and the national balance of electoral votes. A well-informed rational citizen would take all three variables into account when deciding whether to vote.

It seems safe to assume that a great many Americans are not very clear about the electoral college and that even some who do understand it would be taxed to make the three-variable analysis described in the previous paragraph. At the same time, some citizens doubtless do grasp what must be ascertained to make a fully informed decision. How might a public choice theorist incorporate such widespread but not universal ignorance into a model? The proposition to be tested is not that turnout will be higher in close elections, but that people who think an election will be close will be more likely to vote. Data from recent National Election Studies will illustrate some of the complexities behind this apparently straightforward assertion.

The important outcomes in presidential elections are the state-by-state totals. One might think that it would be easier for most people to pick the winner in their own state than in the country as a whole. This seems not to be the case, however. In 1984, for example, 7 percent of NES respondents declined to express an opinion about who would be elected president, compared to 12 percent who refused to predict the winner in their state. Of those who did venture a prediction, only 13 percent thought that Walter Mondale would be elected, but fully 32 percent said that he would carry their state. Just 54 of the 2257 NES respondents were residents of Minnesota, the only state Mondale carried.

This raises the question of how individuals form their impressions of likely electoral winners and, hence, how observers of this process—rational choice theorists or not—might attribute predictions to the citizens whose behavior they try to explain. Preelection polls are an obvious source of information (Riker and Ordeshook 1968, 33n). Perhaps the lower accuracy of citizens' state-level predictions reflects the relative obscurity of statewide polls in the mass media. What is more, public statewide surveys are not available in some states. Thus the public's greater capacity to project the national popular-vote winner may reflect the innumerable nationwide polls that have come to occupy such a prominent place in presidential campaign reportage.

The limits of this line of argument demonstrate the difficulty of ascertaining the effect of preelection polls on public expectations of the outcome. In 1980, 85 percent of the NES sample were willing to pick a winner; 55 percent of them said it would be Jimmy Carter. About two-thirds of the sample reported that they had paid some attention to the polls. Of these, 56 percent said that Ronald Reagan was ahead in the polls. In fact, most polls reported a dead heat. The more interesting point is that 39 percent of those who said that Reagan was leading in the polls thought that Carter would win the election.[9]

The key point, of course, is not who picks the winner, but expectations about the likely margin of victory that help the citizen estimate whether his vote will be necessary to help bring about the desired outcome. The empirical studies of this point (a number are summarized by Mueller 1989, 354–61) reach disparate conclusions; sometimes a belief in a close margin is associated with higher turnout and sometimes it is not.[10]

Although researchers who study this topic differ in their conclusions, they seem united in the assumption that respondents' beliefs about closeness can be put into an equation without regard to their relationship to reality. This is not to say that public opinion about the likely margin is wholly unrelated to news about who is ahead. My point is that people who think that an election will be close when all signs point to a landslide are likely to differ from those who expect a narrow margin when all signs indicate a horse race. This can be demonstrated easily enough by comparing respondents who thought the 1980 presidential election would be close with those who had the same impression in 1984. Although Reagan actually led Carter by nearly 10 percentage points in the 1980 popular vote, virtually all preelection polls showed the two men in a dead heat until the last few days before the election. Small wonder, then, that 84 percent of the NES preelection sample with an opinion on the point expected a close election.[11] Four years later, on the other hand, informed opinion, buttressed by public and private polls, expected that Reagan would easily defeat Walter Mondale. The only suspense was whether Reagan would carry every state (he missed one) and set a modern record for the winning share of the popular vote (he missed by 2.3 percentage points). The people were more out of step with the cognoscenti in 1984; just over half the NES sample with an opinion thought the election would be close.

People who think an impending landslide will be close differ from those who have this opinion of an election that is neck and neck until the last minute. Moreover, they differ in ways that are related to turnout. The 1980 election was expected to be close by 76 percent of respondents who had not graduated from high school, 87 percent of those who had, and 86 percent of people with at least some exposure to college. The corresponding figures for 1984 were 59 percent, 53 percent, and 44 percent. In other words, education was positively related to expectations of closeness in 1980 and negatively related in 1984. This would lead one to think that plausible estimates of the likely margin might have a different relationship to turnout than would implausible estimates, if only because of the different educational attainments of the two groups. And indeed they do. In 1980, 62 percent of those expecting a close race voted, compared to 54 percent who disagreed. The relationship in 1984 went the other way: 61 percent of people expecting a close race voted, compared to 65 percent of those with a more realistic view of the campaign.

Variations in education are not the complete explanation, as can be seen from table 1, which compares the turnout in 1980 and 1984 of respondents who did and did not expect a close election, at three different levels of education. In 1980, with education thus controlled, people who anticipated a close election were still more likely to vote, except for those who had not graduated from high school. In 1984, on the other hand, among respondents with at least some

TABLE 1. Education, Beliefs about Closeness, and Turnout, by Percentage Voting, 1980 and 1984

Education	1980 Believe Election Will Be		1984 Believe Election Will Be	
	Not Close	Close	Not Close	Close
Under 12 years	47%	48%	48%	51%
12 years	49	60	58	59
Over 12 years	67	73	76	69

Source: National Election Studies.
Note: Figures given are validated turnout percentages.

college education, those who expected a close outcome were less likely to vote; there were no significant differences among those with less education.

My guess is that beliefs about the likely margin reflect more general information and political sophistication. An equation properly estimating these attributes probably would wash out any relationship to turnout, irrespective of the plausibility of the respondent's expectations.

I have argued in this section that empirical applications of rational choice theory have failed even to acknowledge widespread ignorance about the electoral college and about electoral margins. Solutions to these deficiencies are easy to prescribe, but a bit more difficult to execute. The National Election Studies may continue to ask questions about the likely state and national victory margins in the presidential election, but there is no practical way to obtain views about many other concurrent contests.[12] Questions to ascertain respondents' understanding of the electoral college and the relationship to it of an individual vote could be added to survey questionnaires. The result might be discontent from the field staff because interviewers do not like to ask a series of questions that are likely to embarrass most respondents.

Registration Is a Prerequisite to Voting

Public choice theorists analyze the rewards from voting and the probabilities of affecting the attainment of these rewards because they posit that voting—like any act—has costs, which may offset the rewards. Yet none of them have much to say about costs. Almost all assume, and some say explicitly, that costs concern the act of voting.[13] Most seem oblivious to registration, and all of them contemplate rewards and probabilities that may become evident only in the latter stages of the campaign, if not on election day itself.[14]

This lack of attention to costs is in striking contrast to non–rational choice empirical research, which has been more successful in identifying variations on the cost rather than the benefit side.[15] Analysis of the demographic correlates of American voter turnout "emphasizes the costs of performing the minor bureaucratic tasks required to cast a ballot and asserts that ability to surmount these hurdles is aided by skills learned in school" (Wolfinger and Rosenstone 1980, 62). Variations in the relationship to turnout of other demographic variables are most plausibly explained by differences in individuals' ability to bear the costs of voting. Analysis of the relationship of state registration laws to turnout shows that raising the cost of voting lowers the likelihood of doing it (Wolfinger and Rosenstone 1980, chap. 4). The same point emerges from comparisons with Europeans, who seem less motivated to vote, but on the other hand are more likely to do so (Glass, Squire, and Wolfinger 1984; Powell 1986; Wolfinger, Glass, and Squire 1990). The difference between the United States and Europe in this respect comes down to a higher threshold that Americans must cross compared to Europeans, who for the most part are automatically registered to vote.

Registration is arguably more difficult than voting. It often requires more obscure information and a longer journey at a less convenient time.[16] Registration deadlines pass quietly and the experience of registering usually is a solitary one. On the other hand, it is difficult to ignore election day, and the expressive gratifications of participating are doubtless more evident than those of signing up to vote. Notwithstanding all the rational choice talk about the information costs of voting, these seem less consequential than the costs of registering. Indeed, much of the mental furniture that guides many electoral choices can scarcely be called either information or costly: ethnic resentment, dissatisfaction with economic conditions, religious commitment, historic memory. Registration, on the other hand, often requires a level of accuracy about where and when to go that cannot be satisfied by gossip, communal loyalties, and casual exposure to the media. As for ballot decisions, the continued strong link between party identification and vote choice (Miller 1991; Keith et al. 1992, chap. 10) suggests one economizing device that can save a good deal of time on information gathering.

Once Americans are registered, they are very likely indeed to vote in presidential elections. About 85 percent of NES respondents whose registration was verified actually voted in each of the three presidential elections of the 1980s.[17] Moreover, some variables that are strongly related to turnout, such as age, are wholly unrelated to the turnout of the registered; other variables, such as political interest and education, have only a weak relationship (Squire, Glass, and Wolfinger 1987). Researchers and interest groups interested in increasing turnout are largely in agreement that this can most easily be accomplished by lowering the costs of registration (Piven and Cloward 1987; Gans 1991; Wolfinger 1991).

For all intents and purposes, registration is permanent for those who do not move.[18] Even readers who reject my assertion that registration is more difficult than voting will agree that in any national election the majority of voters will be registered in advance of the campaign, indeed, in advance of the presidential nominating conventions. Therefore costs and rewards occur in quite different time periods. The rewards, whether from the act of voting itself or consequent to the outcome, are received no earlier than election day. A major part of the cost, on the other hand, was paid years, or decades, earlier, when the citizen registered. The incentives to that earlier registration may have nothing to do with the contemporary election. Perhaps they were Harold Washington's 1983 Chicago mayoralty campaign, or an antinuclear referendum in 1978, or some other long-forgotten issue or hero that moved the citizen to pay the cost of registration. Thus a consequential part of the cost of participating in the current election, having already been paid, need not be set against any benefits likely to ensue from that election.

If only for this reason, the rational choice apparatus is better suited to analyzing the turnout of the registered. The only wielders of rational choice theory I came across who seemed to recognize this point were Ferejohn and Fiorina (1975), whose dependent variable was the nonvalidated turnout of the registered in several NES samples. This measure had the great advantage of being relevant to judgments about closeness of the outcome and the great disadvantage of being a variable with little variation.[19]

Many of the calculations attributed to the rational citizen concern matters that change over the course of the campaign, including the likely closeness of the outcome and the comparative advantage to the citizen of the alternatives. For example, the reportedly fateful debate between Carter and Reagan occurred just a week before the election in 1980 (Lanoue 1992). Thus the information the rational citizen needs to make a decision about voting or abstaining may not be apparent until the last few weeks or days of the campaign. By this time, *it is too late to register.* Unlike citizens of most other democracies, where registration is automatic, voting is not a matter of acting on impulse for most Americans, who must register well in advance of election day if they wish to vote. In 1984, for example, 62 percent of voting-age citizens lived in states with a registration deadline at least four weeks before the election.

Because of registration deadlines and the very high turnout of the registered, all the intricate and imaginative formulations about casting a decisive vote, comparing the benefits of A's victory to a triumph for B, and so on, can help predict the turnout of only that small minority of registrants whose participation is in doubt. Most nonvoters are beyond the reach of such calculations. They cannot vote because they are not registered.

What Is to Be Done?

In view of the foregoing, I find it easy to accept, at least when it comes to turnout, Green and Shapiro's verdict that "rational choice has yet to deliver on its promise to advance the scientific understanding of politics" (1993, 2). To date, rational choice research has not helped explain variations in turnout from group to group, place to place, contest to contest, or election to election. There is no more striking way to illustrate its failure than to contrast the rational choice literature to the wealth of insight and explanatory hypotheses in Warren Miller's meticulous tracing of the turnout of different age cohorts from the Eisenhower elections to the post-Reagan era (Miller 1992).

At least some rational choice researchers acknowledge the disappointing returns from the genre. John Aldrich, a sympathetic and experienced surveyor of the field, recently wrote that "In rational choice theory, turnout holds a special place, as the most commonly used example of a major theoretical puzzle. So important is this puzzle that some see turnout as the major example of the failure of rational choice theory" (Aldrich 1993, 246). But after many sensible comments about the flaws in rational choice models, Aldrich nevertheless recommended more attempts to apply such models to the study of turnout.

There is no question that rational choice models could be made a good deal more realistic, but data gathering difficulties would remain. The price of reducing the disparities between the model and reality is likely to be impracticably cumbersome data collection. To mention just one example, how could any interviewer elicit, even from a sympathetic and self-aware respondent, all the assorted rewards anticipated from the several dozen contests on a California ballot?

If these empirical problems could somehow be solved, however, an intractable theoretical difficulty remains: for most people, costs and benefits are temporally separated by years, if not decades. I see no way to solve this problem, and therefore no hope for rational choice approaches to the study of turnout.

NOTES

My greatest debt is to Bernard Grofman, who invited me to a conference on applications of rational choice theory and encouraged me to write down the comments I made there. I am grateful for assistance and advice on earlier drafts of this paper from Martin I. Gilens, James M. Glaser, Michael G. Hagen, Benjamin Highton, and Theodore L. Lascher, Jr. John H. Aldrich, James E. Alt, John A. Ferejohn, Stanley Kelley, Jr., Jan Leighley, J. Eric Oliver, and Randolph M. Siverson have helped make my argument clearer. Earlier drafts of this article were delivered at the 67th Annual Conference of the Western Economic Association International and the Conference on Warren E. Miller's festschrift.

1. Some public choice theorists (e.g., Mueller 1989) use the female pronoun for the hypothetical citizen. In recognition of Downs's seminal role, I will follow his practice in this respect.

2. Gary Jacobson wittily summarized the latter school: "It's the California model; people vote because it makes them feel good."

3. The near-universal availability of information on registration and electoral participation is the basis of the National Election Studies' Vote Validation studies: interviewers verify each respondent's claims about registration and voting by inspecting the relevant records at the county courthouse.

4. Items about jury duty were deleted in the last stage of preparing the 1984 NES questionnaire. This might not have happened if their advocate had thought to play the rational choice card, thus providing unimpeachable theoretical relevance.

5. Aldrich (1993) acknowledged this fact. So did Riker and Ordeshook (1968, 36), who ignored it in their data analysis.

6. Triviality is in the eyes of the beholder. In November, 1988, a hot issue in my hometown was whether Berkeley would add a Palestinian refugee camp to its list of impeccably politically correct sister cities. Expenditures on this issue were believed to exceed the budget for any other proposition or candidate, including the presidential contenders. A get-out-the-vote drive was organized by the successful opponents of the measure. Four years earlier, Berkeleyans mobilized to support or oppose a measure that would require the mayor to convey to President Reagan the city's endorsement of a formula for restricting American aid to Israel (Polsby 1986). Luckily for American foreign policy, this proposal also was defeated.

7. The generally lower turnout in nonconcurrent local elections, where the chances of casting a deciding vote are so much greater, requires modification of propositions linking closeness and turnout. Aldrich (1993, 252) is one of the few rational choice researchers to mention this point.

8. Aldrich (1993, 261) says that there should be "economies of scale for voting in several contests at the same time."

9. Willingness to disregard the polls is not limited to the mass public. In 1980, the last preelection poll by the National Broadcasting Company/Associated Press partnership showed Ronald Reagan pulling five points ahead of Jimmy Carter. Just after these results were in, on the Saturday night before the election, a group from the NBC Election Unit, the Associated Press's election reporters, and four political science consultants made their predictions of the outcome. All but one of us thought that Carter would win. The exception was the Radcliffe intern at NBC.

10. In his recent review essay, Aldrich (1993, 252) reports that the anticipated margin has been found not to be related to turnout, while the actual margin "is a significant predictor." A plausible explanation for this pattern is supplied by Cox and Munger (1989), who show that campaign spending goes up in close elections, thus stimulating turnout. The relationship between campaign intensity and turnout is a major theme in Rosenstone and Hansen 1993, especially 179–83.

11. Nine percent of the 1980 sample and 7 percent of those in 1984 did not know or failed to answer this question.

12. This leaves unresolved the weakness of measuring a respondent's belief that he might cast the decisive vote by asking him if he thinks the election will be close.

13. Although Downs alludes in passing to registration as a cost (1975, 265, 266), his references to ways to reduce costs (1957, 266) are mostly concerned with the act of voting itself. His major emphasis is on the costs of acquiring useful information about the alternatives facing the citizen. Riker and Ordeshook (1968, 26) are more categorical: "[cost] is the collection of time spent on the voting decision, the act of voting itself, etc." Most other scholars in the genre followed these early precedents. Ferejohn and Fiorina (1975) are one exception. Another is Aldrich, who analyzed registration at some length, but treated "registration and voting as subsumable under one model of decision making" (1975, 719). The problem with this assumption is discussed below. In his recent survey of the literature, Aldrich (1993), when talking about the costs of voting, referred ex-

clusively to the costs of registering. He did not, however, draw any of the conclusions advanced in this article.

Another problematic aspect of rational choice theorists' attempts to allocate costs to predict variations in turnout is the apparently eclectic character of the enterprise. For example, does more education lead to higher or lower turnout? We know from observation that the answer is higher, but most applications of cost-benefit analysis point the other way. Because better-educated people usually enjoy higher pay, their time is more valuable and, hence, the opportunity cost of voting is greater. Such people also have less free time and, probably, more attractive uses of that time other than voting. They are more able to make these calculations and also to realize the improbability of actually affecting the outcome of an election. Being better informed, they are more likely to recognize the complexity of most public policy issues, and thus be unable to make a decision. Compared to all these reasons for expecting educated people not to vote, the countervailing speculations that they can more easily arrange to take time out to vote and that their greater information makes them more confident about their vote choices and more aware of the personal impact of public policy are unimpressive.

14. One last-minute rational choice scenario (Glazer 1988, 17) has Jones driving by his polling place at 7:10 A.M. and seeing a line made longer by the presence of his neighbor Smith, which causes him to decide not to invest the extra time to vote. With a little more imagination, one might attribute other concerns to Jones—can he find a place to park? will he be late to work? can he stand to be in Smith's company so early in the morning?

15. Unlike rational choice theorists, researchers in this genre do not say that costs generally are consciously calculated, that costs are compared to the rewards that would result from the success of favored candidates, or that many "people are brought to the polls by the belief that their vote will make the difference between any candidate's victory and defeat" (Wolfinger and Rosenstone 1980, 7).

16. Registration may also reflect nothing more than being home when a canvasser calls; sharing shelter from the rain with a registration table; or applying for a driver's license in Oregon, Washington, or Montana, where this action is also an application to register to vote. Also excepted from these remarks about the difficulties of registration are citizens of North Dakota, where registration is not required, and of Maine, Wisconsin, and Minnesota, where one may register on election day.

By the same token, the growing liberalization of procedures for obtaining and using absentee ballots is also lowering the cost of voting, at least for the bureaucratically adept. Absentee ballots accounted for fully 17 percent of all votes cast in the 1992 presidential election in California.

17. I say "about 85 percent," because the exact number depends on decisions about classifying those few respondents whose records are ambiguous.

18. To be sure, most states purge registrants who have not voted for various lengths of time. The grace periods involved, together with Americans' high level of residential mobility (Squire, Wolfinger, and Glass 1987) doubtless are responsible for the finding that variations in purge laws have no discernible effect on turnout (Wolfinger and Rosenstone 1980, 76).

19. At least one public choice critic of Ferejohn and Fiorina seems not to have taken proper notice that their dependent variable was the turnout of the registered: "In their sample, about 90 percent of the respondents claimed to have voted. This is a much higher percentage than is typical of the United States and suggests a nonrandom sample or misrepresentation of voter behavior" (Mueller 1989, 354).

REFERENCES

Aldrich, John H. 1976. "Some Problems in Testing Two Rational Models of Participation." *American Journal of Political Science* 20:713–33.

———. 1993. "Turnout and Rational Choice." *American Journal of Political Science* 37:246–78.

Bowler, Shaun, Todd Donovan, and Trudi Happ. 1992. "Ballot Propositions and Information Costs: Direct Democracy and the Fatigued Voter." *Western Political Quarterly* 45:559–68.

Cox, Gary W., and Michael C. Munger. 1989. "Closeness, Expenditures, and Turnout in the 1982 U.S. House Elections." *American Political Science Review* 83:217–31.

Downs, Anthony. 1957. *An Economic Theory of Democracy.* New York: HarperCollins.

Feeley, Malcolm M. 1974. "A Solution to the 'Voting Dilemma' in Modern Democratic Theory." *Ethics* 84:235–42.

Ferejohn, John A., and Morris P. Fiorina. 1974. "The Paradox of Not Voting: A Decision Theoretic Analysis." *American Political Science Review* 68:525–36.

———. 1975. "Closeness Counts Only in Horseshoes and Dancing." *American Political Science Review* 69:920–28.

Foster, Carroll B. 1984. "The Performance of Rational Voter Models in Recent Presidential Elections." *American Political Science Review* 78:678–90.

Gans, Curtis B. 1991. "Anatomy of a Bill or The Education of a Student of Politics." In *Registering Voters: Comparative Perspectives,* ed. John C. Courtney. Cambridge, Mass.: Harvard Center for International Affairs.

Glass, David P., Peverill Squire, and Raymond E. Wolfinger. 1984. "Voter Turnout: An International Comparison." *Public Opinion* 6:49–55.

Glazer, Amihai. 1988. "Why Do People Vote?" University of California, Irvine.

Green, Donald P., and Ian Shapiro. 1993. "Pathologies of Rational Choice Theory: A Critique of Applications in Political Science." Paper presented to the meeting of the Public Choice Society, New Orleans.

Hinich, Melvin J. 1981. "Voting As an Act of Contribution." *Public Choice* 36:135–40.

Keith, Bruce E., David B. Magleby, Candice J. Nelson, Elizabeth Orr, Mark C. Westlye, and Raymond E. Wolfinger. 1992. *The Myth of the Independent Voter.* Berkeley and Los Angeles: University of California Press.

Knack, Stephen. 1992. "Deterring Voter Registration through Juror Source Practices: Evidence from the 1991 NES Pilot Study." Memorandum to the Board of Overseers of the National Election Studies.

———. 1993. "The Voter Participation Effects of Selecting Jurors from Registration Lists." *Journal of Law and Economics* 36.

Lanoue, David J. 1992. "One That Made a Difference: Cognitive Consistency, Political Knowledge, and the 1980 Presidential Debate." *Public Opinion Quarterly* 56:168–84.

Lascher, Edward L., Jr. 1991. "The Case of the Missing Democrats: Reexamining the 'Republican Advantage' in Nonpartisan Elections." *Western Political Quarterly* 44:656–75.

Lowi, Theodore J. 1992. "The State in Political Science: How We Become What We Study." *American Political Science Review* 86:1–7.

Miller, Warren E. 1991. "Party Identification, Realignment, and Party Voting: Back to the Basics." *American Political Science Review* 85:557–68.

―――. 1992. "The Puzzle Transformed: Explaining Declining Turnout." *Political Behavior* 14:1–44.

Morton, Rebecca B. 1992. "Groups in Rational Turnout Models." *American Journal of Political Science* 35:758–76.

Mueller, Dennis C. 1989. *Public Choice II.* Cambridge and New York: Cambridge University Press.

Oliver, J. Eric, and Raymond E. Wolfinger. 1992. "Jury Duty as a Deterrent to Voter Registration." Memorandum to the Board of Overseers of the National Election Studies.

Piven, Frances Fox, and Richard A. Cloward. 1987. *Why Americans Don't Vote.* New York: Pantheon.

Polsby, Nelson W. 1986. "Late Bulletin from the Independent Nation of Berkeley." *California Magazine* 11:72, 81.

Powell, G. Bingham. 1986. "American Voter Turnout in Comparative Perspective." *American Political Science Review* 80:17–43.

Riker, William H., and Peter C. Ordeshook. 1968. "A Theory of the Calculus of Voting."*American Political Science Review* 63:26–42.

Rosenstone, Steven J., and John Mark Hansen. 1993. *Mobilization, Participation, and Democracy in America.* New York: Macmillan.

Sanders, Elizabeth. 1980. "On the Costs, Utilities, and Simple Joys of Voting." *Journal of Politics* 42:854–63.

Squire, Peverill, Raymond E. Wolfinger, and David P. Glass. 1987. "Residential Mobility and Voter Turnout." *American Political Science Review* 81:45–65.

Tannenbaum, Percy H., and Leslie J. Kostrich. 1983. *Turned-On TV-Turned-Off Voters.* Beverly Hills: Sage.

U.S. Congress. 1975. *Congressional Record,* 94th Cong., 1st sess., April 15, 10238–40.

Wattenberg, Martin P. 1991. *The Rise of Candidate Centered Politics.* Cambridge and London: Harvard University Press.

Whyte, William F. 1955. *Street Corner Society.* Enl. ed. Chicago: University of Chicago Press.

Wolfinger, Raymond E. 1974. *The Politics of Progress.* Englewood Cliffs, N.J.: Prentice-Hall.

―――. 1991. "The Politics of Voter Registration Reform." In *Registering Voters: Comparative Perspectives,* ed. John C. Courtney. Cambridge, Mass.: Harvard Center for International Affairs.

Wolfinger, Raymond E., David P. Glass, and Peverill Squire. 1990. "Predictors of Electoral Turnout: An International Comparison." *Policy Studies Review* 9:551–74.

Wolfinger, Raymond E., and Peter Linquiti. 1981. "Tuning in and Turning Out." *Public Opinion* 4:56–60.

Wolfinger, Raymond E., and Steven J. Rosenstone. 1980. *Who Votes?* New Haven, Conn.: Yale University Press.

Party Identification
and Partisanship

CHAPTER 5

Party Identification Compared across the Atlantic

Sören Holmberg

The authors of *The American Voter* introduced the concept of party identification with great claims. The words they used and the conclusions they drew were practically cut in stone: "Evidently no single datum can tell us more about the attitude and behavior of the individual as presidential elector than his location on a dimension of psychological identification extending between the two great parties" (Campbell, Converse, Miller, and Stokes 1960, 142–43).

The introduction was very successful. Later, political scientists in America talked of party identification as "the glory variable of the 1950s and early 1960s" that "brought fame to the Michigan group, provided the basic structure for most studies of voting over a decade or two, and provided a key element in the revision of democratic theory . . . " (Shively 1980, 219). Not everybody agreed, however, that the Michigan Four somehow had discovered the Holy Grail of voting studies. Critical voices began to be heard, especially after partisanship started to decline in the late 1960s. Between 1964 and 1972, the proportion of Americans identifying with the Republican or Democratic party decreased from 77 to 64 percent (Wattenberg 1990, 23).

The main critique against the concept of party identification was leveled on the theoretical front. In *The American Voter,* party identification had been defined as a psychological phenomenon located near the middle of the funnel of causality at a distance from the ultimate dependent variable, the voting choice. The Michigan group used the concept "to characterize the individual's affective orientation to an important group-object in his environment." (Campbell et al. 1960, 121).

Affective orientation are the key words in the definition, and since they refer to something that could be construed as irrational, they have been the prime target of the theoretical critique against the concept of party identification. Under the influence of rational choice models, party identification has been reinterpreted as an information-economizing device (Goldberg 1969; Robertson 1976) or as a weighted average of past evaluations of the parties. Fiorina, the father of the retrospective evaluations approach, maintains that party identification is "the difference between an individual's past political experiences with the two parties . . . " and past political experiences are "simply the voters subjectively weighted retrospective evaluations formed while observing the postures and performances of the contending parties during previous election periods" (Fiorina 1981, 89–90).

The location of party identification farther back in the funnel of causality, with the status of almost an exogenous variable, with a high degree of stability, and produced, to a large extent, by socialization within the family, is another feature of the Michigan construct that has been hotly debated.

It will take too long to try to cover that discussion here; suffice it to say that the critics downplay the role of family socialization and point to the flexibility of party identification, long-term as well as short-term. In general, they tend to view party identification as more of an endogenous phenomenon, closer to the voting decision and affected by short-term forces (Brody 1977; Shively 1980; Franklin and Jackson 1981; Markus 1979; Jennings and Niemi 1981; Wattenberg 1990).

In the European context, the critique against the concept of party identification has been both more technical, dealing with problems of how to render the directional component of party identification unidimensional in multiparty systems, and more fundamental, questioning the usefulness of the concept altogether.[1]

As Budge, Crewe, and Farlie put it in *Party Identification and Beyond:* "Its [party identification] weakness . . . lies in its lack of theoretical or even temporal antecedence to the voting decision itself." And they continue by asking the sarcastic question: "Even if it is accepted that party identification is not exactly the same as past regularity or present intention, one must still ask how theoretically interesting is the statement that electors vote for the party to which they feel closest?" (Budge, Crewe, and Farlie 1976, 11). Thomassen, another European critic, sums up his reasons why "the use of party identification in relation to voting behaviour in the Netherlands [is] very doubtful: (a) party identification is less stable than the vote; (b) what little evidence exists to the effect that party identification and vote preference can be distinguished can also be explained as unreliability of measurement; (c) there is strong evidence that party identification is not causally prior to vote preference." (Thomassen 1976, 77).

In his 1976 article, Thomassen also points out that only a few attempts have been made to validate the concept of party identification outside the United States. In this chapter I will try to alleviate that problem by introducing results on party identification from a non-Dutch and non-American setting. That setting is Sweden.

Sweden has two important assets when it comes to studying party identification in a comparative perspective. First, Sweden has a multiparty system, which, at least up until recently, has proved to be extremely stable. Second, there is an old established program of National Election Studies in Sweden, dating back to the mid-1950s, meaning that access is available to academic voter surveys dating almost as far back as that in the United States (Särlvik 1970). An added advantage with the Swedish Election Studies is that they contain a large number of panel studies. Thus, the question that has loomed high in the European debate, whether party identification or vote is more stable over time, can be studied based on a rich data source.

The emphasis of this chapter, however, will not be on the directional component of party identification. Instead, the other Michigan invention, the intensity dimension of party identification, will be the focus of analysis. This is done in full awareness of Thomassen's critique that studies of the strength of party identification tend to be an escape from studying the real thing, that is, the directional component (Thomassen 1976, 64). But the two concepts are closely related, and if Thomassen is right in his critique against the directional component of party identification, then the intensity component is the more meaningful analytical tool in the European multiparty context.

Too Close for Comfort?

The European answer to the question in the above heading has tended to be yes; the directional component of party identification is too close to the voting choice. The correlation between measures of party identification and vote are too high. Usually, of course, we want high correlations between our independent and dependent variables, since the typical problem in most of the social sciences is that relevant coefficients are too low. But in this case, the paradox is that we want high correlations, but not too high.

The results in figure 1 illustrate the problem. The Swedish correlations between the direction of party identification and the vote are contrasted to the corresponding American correlations. (See also appendix to this chapter.) The analysis spans over twelve parliamentary elections between 1956 and 1991 in Sweden and ten presidential elections between 1952 and 1988 in the United States. The U.S. correlations have changed somewhat over the years, from about .68 in the 1950s, to two low points of .57 and .52 in 1964 and 1972, and back to an all-time high of .75 in 1988.

Judging from these particular results, the decline of American political parties is not an apparent conclusion on the mass level.[2] On the contrary, with 1964 and 1972 as the two exceptions, the relationship between party identification and presidential vote has been remarkably stable among American voters, with a mean correlation of about .70 through the years.

The size of that correlation explains the success of the concept of party identification in the United States. It is not too high; the concept cannot be accused of merely measuring current voting intentions, and a correlation of .70

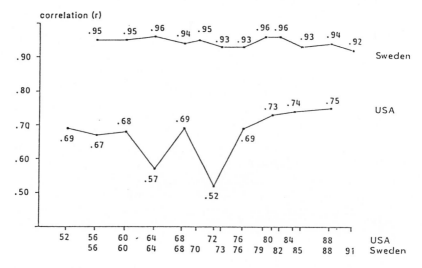

Fig. 1. Correlations of party identification with presidential voting choice in the United States and with party choice in parliamentary elections in Sweden. In order to facilitate the correlational analysis, the Swedish parties have been scored unidimensionally on a left-right scale based on people's perceptions of how the parties are located on the left-right continuum. (American results are taken from Miller 1991 and are based on the American National Election Studies; The Swedish results are from the Swedish Election Studies.)

allows for additional explanatory factors, like candidates, issues, and other short-term forces, to have an impact. And it is not too low; a correlation of .70 is always a substantial relationship whenever cross-sectional survey data is being used. It is clearly high enough to keep researchers' and politicians' interest.

The Swedish results are quite different, and underscore rather drastically why European political scientists have problems using the directional component of party identification. All the correlations between party identification and the final vote choice are extremely high, with coefficients hovering between .92 and .96.[3] With correlations like these it is, of course, difficult to keep the two phenomena apart. However, if one wants to be positive, maybe there is some light at the end of the tunnel for the directional component, even in Sweden. After all, the lowest correlation (.92) appeared in 1991, after having been on the way down all through the 1980s. Party identification and vote have slowly become more disentangled in Sweden. The background to this process is the breaking up of the old, stable, Swedish party system.

What used to be one of Europe's most stable party systems has come apart in the last two elections. The successful entry into Parliament of the Greens in the election of 1988 was the first indication that something new was happening. For the first time in seventy years, a new party managed to gain representation in the Swedish *Riksdag*. The real upheaval came in the 1991 election, however. Two additional parties—the Christian Democrats and New Democrats (a populist party on the right)—won enough votes to enter Parliament, while the Greens narrowly failed to get more than 4 percent of the vote, as required by the Constitution, and had to leave the Parliament after only one term. Thus, in just three years, the old, stable, five-party system has become a volatile, eight-party system, with seven parties represented in Parliament and an eighth outside, trying to get back in.

Looking at percentage breakdowns instead of correlations, it is evident that the appearance of the new parties has loosened somewhat the tight fit between party identification and vote in Sweden. The proportion of Swedish voters who have *not* voted their party identification has developed in the following manner since the late 1970s: 1979, 5 percent; 1982, 6 percent; 1985, 9 percent; 1988, 8 percent; and 1991, 11 percent.[4] Various forms of tactical voting, to get small parties over the 4 percent threshold required for parliamentary representation, is one explanation for the increase. The availability of new parties makes it possible for voters to occasionally deviate from their previous voting habits and support fresh blood and new ideas in the Parliament, thereby sending a message to their old parties.

This pattern of behavior was evident in 1988, when a fair proportion of voters identifying with other parties, especially the Social Democrats and the Center Party, voted for the Greens. No less then 25 percent of the Green voters in 1988 identified with some other party (Gilljam 1990, 291). Similar patterns are also discernable in the election of 1991, especially for the New Democrats. An impressive 38 percent of the voters for New Democracy were identified with other parties, most noticeably with the Conservative Party.

The conclusion is obvious. Compared to the old, stable, days, the appearance of new (flash?) parties has made the directional component of party identification a more interesting and viable analytical tool in the Swedish context. A look at the over-time stability of party identification in Sweden, and the turnover of party identification and the vote in election panels, tends to give further credence to that conclusion. If party identification is a lasting, affective orientation towards a party, it should be highly stable across time and relatively insensitive to short-term factors. Thomassen and others have specified that it should at least be more stable than the voting choice (Thomassen 1976, 68).

The results in table 1 indicate for the Swedish case, as for Canada, Britain, and the United States, but not for the Netherlands, a higher stability across elections for party identification than for vote. The outcome is especially clear

TABLE 1. Stability of Party Identification and Vote in Election Panels

Country	Party Identification		Party Vote	
	Stable	Variable	Stable	Variable
Sweden				
1973–76	85%	15%	82%	18%
1976–79	83	17	83	17
1979–82	84	16	83	17
1982–85	83	17	81	19
1985–88	84	16	82	18
1988–91	79	21	75	25
Britain				
1970–74	85	15	80	20
Canada				
1974–79	80	20	75	25
The Netherlands				
1971–72	75	25	78	22
1981–86	76	24	77	23
United States				
1972–76	93	7	75	25

Source: The British, Canadian, and American results (vote for the House of Representatives) are from Le Duc 1981, 261. The Dutch data for 1971–72 is also from Le Duc, while the Dutch results for the 1981–86 panel is from Visser 1992, 7. The Swedish Election Studies have provided the Swedish data.

Note: Across all countries, all respondents indicating a partisan attachment have been classified as party identifiers. The analysis is restricted to people with party identificatons and who voted in the relevant pairs of elections.

in Sweden for the most recent election panel of 1988–91, but it is also evident in earlier panels.

Expressed in terms of continuity coefficients, the panel correlations for the directional component of party identification have been .87–.88 in the Swedish election panels of 1979–82, 1982–85, and 1985–88. In the latest panel, 1988–91, it was slightly lower, .84. The corresponding coefficients for the stability of the vote have been somewhat lower, usually .01 correlational units lower. Although, in the 1988–91 panel, the continuity correlation for the vote was .06 units lower.[5]

Compared to American results, panel stability of party identification is a little higher in Sweden. The average two-year continuity correlation for party identification in the United States was .84 in the 1956–60 period and .81 in the 1972–76 period (Converse and Markus 1979, 32–49). The average three-year correlation for the four Swedish panels in the period 1979–91 is .87.

The results for the turnover of party identification and vote, once more, show the same outcome for Sweden, Canada, Britain, and the United States, and a deviant outcome for the Netherlands (table 2). In the four countries, vola-

TABLE 2. Turnover of Party Identification and Vote in Election Panels

Country	Party Identifications/Party Vote				Sum Percent
	Stable/Stable	Stable/Variable	Variable/Stable	Variable/Variable	
Sweden					
1973–76	78%	7%	4%	11%	100
1976–79	78	5	5	12	100
1979–82	79	5	4	12	100
1982–85	76	7	5	12	100
1985–88	77	7	5	11	100
1988–91	69	10	6	15	100
Britain					
1970–74	75	10	5	10	100
Canada					
1974–79	70	10	5	15	100
The Netherlands					
1971–72	71	4	7	18	100
1981–86	69	7	8	16	100
United States					
1972–76	71	22	4	3	100

tile voters behaved more according to the postulates of the theory of party identification than against the postulates—that is, more people changed their vote without changing their party identification than the other way around. In the Netherlands the result was the reverse. More Dutch voters changed their party identification while retaining their voting choice than changed their voting choice while keeping the old party identification intact.[6]

However, the United States, not the Netherlands or any of the other countries, is clearly the deviant case if we look at the proportions of voters with a stable party identification; over 90 percent in America compared to about 75 to 85 percent in the other countries. The same is true if we look at the percentage of voters who exhibit what could be called double volatility, that is, who change both party identification and vote. Double volatility is extremely rare in the United States; only 3 percent of the 1972–76 American panel behaved in this manner. In the other countries, double volatility was the most common pattern of change among voters who were exhibiting any form of movement. About 10–18 percent of the respondents in the Canadian, Dutch, British, and Swedish panels reported some kind of double volatility.

Double volatility, per se, is not a phenomenon that disproves the Michigan version of the theory of party identification. But of course there cannot be too much double volatility, and not too often. According to a strict interpretation of the Michigan model, party identification tends to be a life-long attachment that is expected to change only under extraordinary circumstances, such as those of a critical election or a realignment period (Key 1955; Shafer 1991). Naturally, the prevalence of double volatility in Europe and Canada do not reconcile with such a model.

If, however, we are willing to accept a revisionist version of the original model—a version that conceptualizes party identification less as a fixture and more as an endogenous variable, amenable to some forms of short-term change—then the non-American results do not automatically fall outside the ballpark. This is especially true if we recognize the fact that the systemic disparity between the candidate-centered American electoral system and the more party-dominated European systems do make a difference. In the United States, people vote for individual candidates, while in Europe, and certainly in Sweden, people vote for parties. One profound consequence of this difference is that Europeans regularly, at every election, have to consider their party attachment, while Americans do not. For Europeans, party identification and the parties are constantly on the line and are not sheltered from various kinds of short- and long-term forces, as, to an extent, is the case in America, where the individual candidates are the principle actors and take most of the heat (Granberg and Holmberg 1988).

Given these system disparities, the differences between the outcomes of our analyses of the directional component of party identification in America and in Sweden become more accessible. The higher correlation between party identification and the vote in Sweden, as compared to America, and the more frequent occurrence of double volatility, is only to be expected, given the fact that Swedish voters evaluate parties when they vote, while American voters evaluate candidates. Party identification and the vote are closely related in Sweden because both elections and survey questions on party preference are good measuring devices of the same phenomenon, the party attachment of Swedish voters. Thus, the fact that party identification and the voting choice is strongly related in many non-American settings cannot be used as a self-evident justification for the conclusion that European voters have not developed lasting psychological attachments to the political parties (Thomassen 1976, 77–78; Shively 1980, 226).[7]

A more plausible conclusion is the opposite—that is, that European voters do indeed have lasting, affective identifications with the parties and that party identification measurements, as well as elections, register this quite well. The circumstance that a fair minority of voters change their vote and party identification at election times does not disprove the theory of lasting party identifications. Instead, it proves that lasting party identifications do not mean impregnable party identifications in political systems where people vote for parties, not for candidates.

The Strength Component

Fundamental questions of the life and death variety raised against the directional component of party identification have not been leveled against the intensity component. There has been a general agreement that a variable measuring degree of party attachment is quite useful, no matter how we interpret party identification. Consequently, the debates surrounding the strength component (for example, concerning the development of the strength of party identification over time, or the extent to which intensity of partisanship has a cognitive dimension related to policy evaluations) have been less heated. This does not mean, however, that the strength component is somehow less important than the directional component. Theoretically, the two components are closely linked, and what is true for the strength component reflects on the directional component.

The usefulness of studying the strength component of party identification, especially in a comparative perspective, will hopefully be proved in this part of the chapter. Using indicators of the strength of party identification as the analytical tool, the development in some fifteen party systems will be analyzed. The focus will be on changes across time and on country-wise comparisons. Special attention will be devoted to the Swedish case.

Political parties' depiction as dinosaurs is not yet part of everyday parlance on parties in Europe or America. Parties are experiencing problems in many countries, but so far, the prospect of becoming extinct is not one of them. The problems are serious though, especially on the mass level. Voting turnout is on the downturn in many countries, and trust in parties and governments tends to be lower than ever before. The development of the aggregated levels of the strength of party identification bears witness to the same process. The strength of party identification is decreasing in the majority of countries for which we have measurements.

Data availability restricts our analysis to countries with old established Election Studies (United States, Great Britain, Germany, The Netherlands, Norway, Denmark, and Sweden), and to countries who participate in the Eurobarometer Studies (all EC countries). The biyearly Eurobarometers include a question on party attachment, dating back to the late 1970s for many EC countries.

Measurement problems—especially in the National Election Studies—are severe, since the strength component most often has been monitored differently across countries as well as sometimes also within single nations. In this respect, the Eurobarometer surveys are less problematic. Identical questions are used across participating countries in the Eurobarometers. Language differences and translation difficulties cannot be overlooked, however. Achieving the identical meaning of words like *very strong party attachment* is very difficult across European languages. Consequently, level estimates and comparisons across countries have to be used with care.

Figure 2 contains results based on Election Studies in seven countries, while figure 3 presents the results from the Eurobarometers and the twelve EC countries. The Election Studies data have been dichotomized in two different ways, creating two subgroups of citizens—strong party identifiers and party identifiers. The subgroup of strong identifiers consists of those people in each country who, when answering the survey question, chose the highest possible level of intensity of partisanship, while the subgroup of party identifiers comprises persons who chose one of the two top levels. The Eurobarometer results are presented for 1980 and 1990 only.[8] Strong party identifiers are people who answered the question "Do you consider yourself to be close to any particular party?" with "yes, very close." The other response alternatives in the Eurobarometer questionnaire were: fairly close, merely a sympathizer, and close to no particular party. Persons who chose the alternatives "very close" or "fairly close" have been classified as party identifiers. The data presented in figure 3 show the change in the proportion of party identifiers in the EC countries.

A simple visual inspection of figures 2 and 3 reveals that the strength of party identification is decreasing in most countries in Western Europe and in America. Quick glances could give exaggerated impressions, however. In order to help the eyes and give the conclusions a firmer footing, two types of analyses have been performed. One is a readily accessible computation comparing the respective proportions of strong party identifiers and ordinary party identifiers between the oldest and the most recent measurements in the time series. The other is a regression analysis treating strength of party identification as the dependent variable and year as the independent variable. A simple linear trend line is fitted to the curves. The regressions and the computations of the differences in proportions of identifiers across first and last years in the time series have been performed separately for the data based on the Eurobarometers and the Election Studies, and for two different time periods—first, for the longest possible time series in each country, and second, for the period of the 1980s.

The details of the analyses are presented elsewhere (Holmberg and Schmitt 1992). The results are fairly uniform, however, and point to a decline in partisan ties in most of the analyzed countries. The results based on the Eurobarometer data show a downward trend in a clear majority of the EC countries.

The decrease is even more pronounced if we look at the results for the Election Studies, where the longest time series is available. The trend for strong party identifiers points down in six of the seven countries (the Netherlands is the exception), while the percentage of party identifiers points down in all seven countries.

An indication that many of the trend lines—both long-term and for the period of the 1980s—are fairly shaky and irregular is the fact that only a minority of the linear b coefficients associated with the trends were statistically significant (p = .05). Out of a total of seventy-six coefficients, only twenty-one were significant.

The countries with the clearest long-term downward trends in the aggregate level of the strength of party identification are Ireland, Britain, and Sweden. Other countries with clearly decreasing trends, but with some uncertainties, are Denmark (rather pronounced trend down in EB data, especially for strong party identifiers, less clear pattern for ES data), the United States (clear long-term decrease, but an increase in the percentage of strong party identifiers in the last fifteen years), Norway (sharp drop in the last years of the 1980s, but a weak long-term trend), West Germany (clear downward trend in ES data, with the exception of a sharp upturn in 1990 [reunification euphoria?], less evident patterns in the EB data, but the proportion of party identifiers is clearly going down in the 1980s), and Italy (clear drop in the last years of the 1980s, stability earlier).

The remaining countries do not reveal any clear trends, either up or down. They belong to two specific regions of Europe: the southern part (Spain, Portugal, France, and Greece) and the Benelux area. Among these countries, Greece comes closest to showing an increase in the percentage of party identifiers (a clear increase in the last part of the 1980s). In Luxembourg, there are also some signs of an upward trend. The Spanish and Portuguese results are only based on a limited number of studies in the last couple of years, but so far the proportions of party identifiers have been fairly stable on a very low level. The same can be mentioned for the French and Belgian results. No clear trends up or down are evident.

The Dutch case, finally, is more complicated. There is only a weak sign of a long-term decline (EB as well as ES data). In the Dutch Election Studies of the 1980s, however, there is a clear indication of a sharp downturn in the percentages of both strong and ordinary party identifiers. A comparable downward trend is also noticeable in the Dutch Eurobarometer measurements, but much less so. Consequently, the Netherlands should probably be moved to the column of countries where the strength of party identification is on its way down.

In summary, it is evident that we are witnessing a falling-off in partisanship in many Western democracies. The downward trend should not be exaggerated, however. The average decline of the proportion of party identifiers has

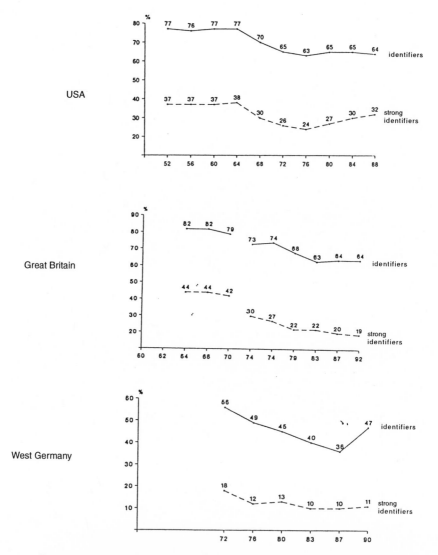

Fig. 2. The development of party identification in seven Western countries. Strength of party identification is measured somewhat differently across the seven countries; in some cases it is also measured differently across time within countries. In the figures, "strong identifiers" comprise the proportion of eligible voters in each country who indicate the highest possible level of strength of party identification, while "identifiers" comprise the combined proportion of people indicating the two highest levels. (Data from National Election Studies and Holmberg and Schmitt 1992.)

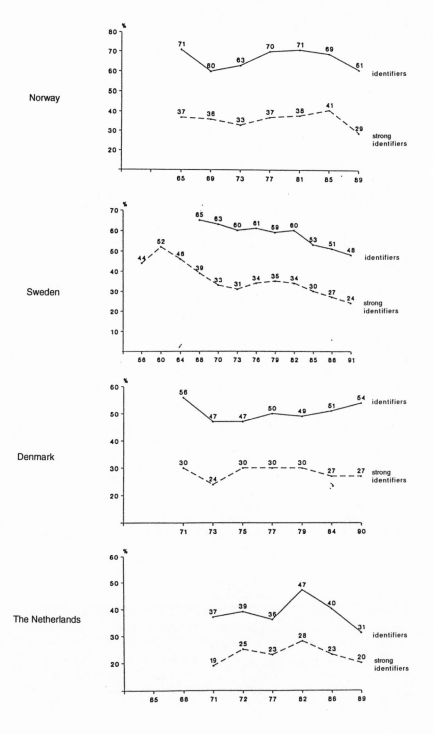

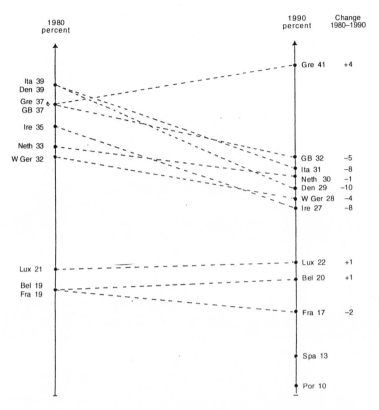

Fig. 3. The strength of party attachment in the twelve European Community countries. The party attachment question has been dichotomized; the results show the proportion of Eurobarometer respondents (aged 18 and over) who indicated a very strong or fairly strong attachment. Results from bi-yearly Eurobarometer Studies have been collapsed and a mean result has been computed. Where available, sociodemographic weighting has been applied. For two countries, Luxembourg and Greece, the results are from 1981 Eurobarometer, not from 1980.

only been three percentage points in the EC countries in the 1980s. If we look at the results for those countries with the longest time series and established Election Studies, the decrease becomes a bit more impressive. Compared with the late 1960s or early 1970s, the proportion of party identifiers has declined by six percentage points in the United States (by thirteen if we compare all the way back to 1952), by nine percentage points in Britain and West Germany, by six percentage points in the Netherlands, and by seventeen percentage points in Sweden.

Political and Other Reasons for the Decline in
Partisan Ties

Explaining the decline in partisanship is no easy business, especially since we are not dealing with smooth and uniform downward trends all over Western Europe and America. On the contrary, the downturn in partisan ties is mainly a Northern European and Anglo-Saxon phenomenon. Strength of party attachments are not on the decline to the same extent in Southern Europe. Paradoxically, Northern Europe leads the way in weakening partisan ties of voters by adjusting to levels already existing in Southern Europe. On the mass level, strong Northern European parties are becoming weaker, while weaker Southern European parties remain weak, but are not becoming weaker.

Looking at the relevant literature, there is, unfortunately, not much help to be found. The most popular explanations in the field are a veritable snake's nest of interrelated processes of social and political change. The downturn in the strength of party identification is said to have been caused by, among other things, such diverse factors as the growing reach of mass media, the expansion of mass education, the change in values toward postmaterialism, the proliferation of political skills and new forms of societal participation, and the overreach of the political system. The basic argument is that the emerging class of young, educated, politically skilled, and self-confident new citizens have less need of organized political groups and, therefore, less often establish durable ties with political parties.

Sweeping macrosociological explanations of this sort, which emphasize the importance of elevated educational levels, increased penetration of mass media, or the coming of the new postindustrial age, cannot do justice to our diverse results. In saying this, I am not arguing that sociological macroexplanations of the indicated variety are irrelevant. In all likelihood, they do play a role as driving forces behind the long-term trend.

In the context of this chapter the sociological macroexplanations are set aside, however. Instead, often overlooked political explanations will be discussed. Clearly, political factors such as the extent of party competition, the emergence of new parties, changes in political leadership, and the scope of politics are relevant if we want to understand shifts in mass partisan ties—both in the long- and the short-term perspective.

An unsystematic glance at the relationship between political factors and the development of partisan ties across the countries investigated highlights the importance of political reasons for the downturn in partisan ties.

> The increase in the percentage of strong party identifiers in the United
> States happened in the 1980s, when Reagan polarized American poli-
> tics and party differences became more clear.

The sharp downturn in partisan ties in the late 1980s in countries like Sweden, Norway, and the Netherlands is coupled with setbacks at the polls for (at least in Scandinavia) hegemonical Social Democratic parties.

The short-term downward dips in the Danish and Norwegian curves in the beginning of the 1970s had to do with the evolution of new parties and referenda on EC membership.

The upturn in the West German curve in 1990 is not restricted to Christian Democratic voters. The same phenomenon is also noticeable among Social Democratic voters. A transient political fallout of the German unification process is a possible explanation.

The decline in the strength of party identification in Sweden in the 1980s and early 1990s coincided with the rise of three new parties, the Greens, the Christian Democrats, and the New Democrats.

The examples indicate that the decline of mass support of parties, to an important degree, is a political phenomenon. But, as always, the proof of the pudding is in the eating, and systematic analyses, across time and countries, of political correlates of the strength of party identification are extremely difficult to perform due to the lack of adequate measurements of relevant independent variables.

In a modest attempt performed by Holmberg and Schmitt (1992), four hypotheses were tested comparatively and across time. The first stated that the degree of political polarization in a system is related to the mass support of parties. A decrease in polarization leads to a loosening of partisan ties among people. The second and third hypotheses dealt more directly with the heart of the matter, that is, the level of political conflict in a system. Decreasing levels of ideological (hypothesis number two) or issue conflicts (hypothesis number three) undercut the relevancy of both parties and partisan ties, meaning that decreasing levels of conflict should affect the strength of party identification negatively. The fourth hypotheses dealt with the structure of the party system and the number of parties. An increasing number of parties was expected to lead to declining intensities in partisan ties, since adherents of new parties, compared to supporters of old parties, have had less time to develop strong party attachments. Another, equally plausible process that yields the same result, involves turning the argument around. Decreasing mass support for established parties makes for easier ascent of new parties.

The outcome of the testing of these hypotheses on data from thirteen European countries was not impressive. All relationships were very weak. But, on the other hand, a majority of the countries behaved according to what was hypothesized. Between 58 and 69 percent of the cases ended up as predicted in the tests, and all four hypotheses were supported. Given the shaky measurements of the independent variables and the rather crude dichotomization of all variables, this is perhaps the best we could expect, and, consequently, a fairly positive result. Especially since there was not much to explain to begin with. The dependent variable—the percentage of party identifiers—did not change very much in most countries during the period of investigation. In the EC countries, the proportion of party identifiers, according to the Eurobarometers, went down by an average of only three percentage points in the 1980s.

If we want more encouraging results, and a better variance in the dependent variable, we have to leave the European Community and look at the Swedish case. Among the countries in our study, Sweden has the steepest downturn in the strength of party identification; a decrease of no less than seventeen percentage points in the proportion of party identifiers in the last two decades.

Political correlates of the intensity of partisanship tend to be much clearer in Swedish data than for the other European countries. For example, a correlational analysis (to test our second hypothesis above) between the movement of a variable measuring degrees of ideological conflict and the change in the proportion of party identifiers, yields positive coefficients in most of the old EC countries with fairly long time series. The size of the coefficients are not overwhelming though, about +.20 as a maximum.

In Sweden, a comparable time-series analysis results in a much higher correlation. Based on data from the Swedish Election Studies, the correlation between an ideological conflict variable and the aggregate level of the strength of party identification is +.75 for the period 1979–91 (five elections).[9] If, instead of using left-right self-placement data to construct the ideological distance variable, we use more appropriate data on how people perceive the location of the parties on the left-right continuum, the correlation increases even further, to +.82.

In Sweden, it is evident that there is a strong relationship between the dramatic downturn in partisan ties of voters (faster than in any other Western democracy) and a lessening of ideological conflicts between the political parties. Based on data on how people perceive the left-right distances between the parties, there is little doubt that ideological conflicts have become less pronounced in Sweden. The average distance between how people locate the Conservatives and the Social Democrats from 0 to 10 on the left-right scale, for example, has gone down from 6.1 in 1982 to 5.7 in 1988, and to 5.1 in 1991. The Social Democrats are located more to the right today, compared to ten years ago, while, at the same time, the Conservatives are located somewhat more to the left.

A sometimes overlooked, but essential, individual-level prerequisite for all kinds of political explanations of the decline of partisan ties is that the strength component of party identification has to have a political content. Strength of party identification has to be related, preferably strongly related, to such political factors as ideological affinity with the chosen party and positive evaluations of the party's policies on concrete issues.

Among Swedish voters, the strength component in party identification has a distinctly political flavor. People who locate themselves close to their preferred party on the left-right scale and who evaluate their party's policies favorably tend to have higher degrees of party identification than others. The strength of the relationship varies across the parties. The highest correlations were registered for the two largest Swedish parties, the Social Democrats and the Conservatives—about .40 for each party on the ideological, as well as on the policy evaluation, test (Holmberg 1992). The size of the correlations are on a medium level, but given the attenuating effect of measurement errors, they are quite impressive.

The fairly strong correlation between political factors and the strength of party identification in Sweden means that we would expect decreasing levels of party identification to go hand in hand with perceptions of increased distances between voters and their parties on the left-right scale, and that is exactly what we find. Comparing people's ideological distances between how they locate themselves and how they locate their preferred party on the left-right scale shows that most parties are perceived by their own voters to be farther away in 1991 than in 1979. Among Social Democratic voters, for example, 51 percent located the party and themselves on the same spot on the left-right scale in 1979. In 1991, the comparable result was only 42 percent.

The conclusion for the Swedish case is quite obvious. An increased political distance (ideological and policy-wise) between voters and parties in the last decade is one of the explanatory factors behind the fast decline in partisan ties.

The American case could be another example in support of the thesis that change in the aggregate level of the strength of party identification is related to factors having to do with varying degrees of political conflict. During the Reagan years, when partisanship increased again among American voters, more people perceived party differences than in previous years. According to results from the American National Election Studies, the percentage of Americans perceiving party differences was at its lowest in the 1970s, before the rise in the 1980s. The exact figures are the following: 1952, 50 percent; 1960, 50 percent; 1964, 51 percent; 1968, 49 percent; 1972, 46 percent; 1976, 47 percent; 1980, 58 percent; 1984, 63 percent; and 1988, 60 percent (Wattenberg 1990, 145).

Cohort Analysis of the Strength of Party Identification

Politics is important, but judging from the sizes of the relationships in the previous section, there is also room for other explanatory models. One which naturally suggests itself is the classic Michigan model, with very stable party identifications, low in political content and originating in childhood or adolescence. The Michigan model does not preclude change, but says that when it does happen, it happens only slowly, or under extraordinary circumstances (critical elections).

According to the Michigan group, the strength component in party identification changes with age. Converse puts it like this: "Identifications intensify as a function not of age per se, but rather as a function of the length of time that the individual has felt some generalized preference for a particular party and has repetitively voted for it" (Converse 1976, 12–13).

This aging or life cycle idea has been criticized by Paul Abramson, among others. Based on studies of American data, Abramson finds support for an alternative model (a generational model), which states that people's attitudes tend to be formed in their youth and remain fairly stable thereafter (Abramson 1983, 99–131). The strength of people's party identification does not increase with age, as the life cycle theory predicts, but remains at the level attained in the formative years.

A cohort analysis of Swedish data covering the period 1968–91 does not give unequivocal support to either model—not surprising, since with the data available, we cannot control all possible short-term effects. Table 3 contains a cohort matrix showing the proportion of party identifiers (strong and weak identifiers combined) for each election year and age cohort.

According to the pure life cycle model, the proportion of party identifiers should increase year by year in the table (row-wise), while the pure generational model predicts stable proportions.[10] The empirical results indicate decreasing levels of partisanship for all cohorts except one, where there is a small increase.

The downward trend in the strength of party identification was very tiny in most instances, however. The average linear slope coefficient, –.09, is close to zero for the five cohorts containing the longest time series, which is almost the same result as Abramson obtained in America for the period 1952–80. Abramson received a coefficient of –.04 (Abramson 1983, 114).

Given these results, it is difficult to keep arguing for the life cycle model. The data lend more support to a generational interpretation. One way of defending the age hypothesis, however, is to assume that different short-term effects prevent the strength component from increasing as it should, according to the life cycle theory. Converse talks of steady state periods in the United States (the years 1952–64) when the life cycle model worked, and crises periods (after 1964) when the natural aging process was disturbed by period effects (Converse 1976, 34, 67–117).

Converse's modified life cycle model finds some support in earlier Swedish data. In the years 1956–64, the strength of party identification (measured differently than in later years) increased in five out of seven age cohorts. Thus,

TABLE 3. Cohort Analysis: Party Identifiers among Eleven Age Cohorts in Nine Swedish Elections

Year of Birth	Election Year									Difference 1968–91	Slope (b)/time span
	1968	1970	1973	1976	1979	1982	1985	1988	1991		
1968–1975	—	—	—	—	—	—	—	—	30%		— / —
1960–1967	—	—	—	—	—	43%	39%	38%	28		−1.53 / 9 years
1952–1959	—	—	—	44%	44%	51	42	44	42		−0.18 / 15 years
1944–1951	44%	51%	45%	54	56	58	48	48	47	+3	+0.06 / 23 years
1936–1943	56	58	52	55	53	54	52	53	53	−3	−0.16 / 23 years
1928–1935	63	60	60	60	64	67	61	55	59	−4	−0.12 / 23 years
1920–1927	68	66	66	68	65	66	66	66	66	−2	−0.05 / 23 years
1912–1919	69	71	68	71	66	71	67	71	62	−7	−0.17 / 23 years
1904–1911	75	71	73	75	76	77	68	—	—		−0.07 / 17 years
1896–1903	75	73	74	71	—	—	—	—	—		−0.40 / 8 years
1888–1895	69	—	—	—	—	—	—	—	—		— / —
Total	65	63	60	61	59	60	53	51	47	−18	−0.70 / 23 years

Source: Swedish Election Studies.

Note: Party identifiers have been defined as strong and weak identifiers combined. The number of interview persons is at least 200 in each cell, except in 1991, where it is lower (between 80 and 150 persons per cell) because the 1991 data is only based on a preelection study. The slope coefficients are b-values in standard linear regression analyses treating the proportion of party identifiers as the dependent variable and election year as the independent variable. None of the b-values is statistically significant (p = .05), except the b-value for all respondents (−0.70).

to the extent that we are willing to view the years 1956–64 in Sweden as being more normal or steady state than later decades, Converse's new bellwether version of the life cycle theory is substantiated.

The most important conclusion from the cohort analyses, however, both in America and in Sweden, is that the life cycle model has not provided a true picture of how the strength component in party identification has changed over the last twenty years. Partisan ties have not become stronger with age. Today's politicians cannot rely on a life cycle process transforming young voters with weak or no partisan ties into full-blown party identifiers when they grow older.

The results clearly prove—at least for Sweden—that the parties in the past two decades have failed to recruit as many party identifiers among young people as they have previously. The decline in partisan ties among Swedish people is, to a large extent, a generational phenomenon. Older generations with stronger party attachments have been replaced with young generations with weaker partisan ties.[11] Evidently, the politically related downturn in partisan ties among Swedish voters in the last two decades has been most manifest among the young, incoming voters.

Parties and Party Identification, Something to Hold on to?

Looking at the downward trends in partisan ties in many countries—with Sweden as the most dramatic case—one cannot help but wonder whether we are witnessing a temporary phenomenon or a more permanent change. One effect of the decline in the strength of people's party identification, which has been felt already in many countries, is the increased levels of voter volatility. In Sweden, the change has been profound. In the calmer days of the 1950s, less than 10 percent of the voters switched parties at election times. In 1991, the percentage of Swedish voters who changed parties in comparison to their vote in 1988 was 30 percent. The downturn in partisan ties is one of the key factors behind this development. The panel results in table 4 clearly show the strong relationship between strength of party identification and party switching in Sweden.

Voters with a strong sense of party identification switch parties much less often than people with only party preferences or no party leanings. The probability of switching parties is about five times higher among people without any partisan ties than among persons with a strong party identification. Party identification is an important stabilizing force in a political system.

The young Warren Miller was quite aware of this when he, in his doctoral thesis, discussed the stability of American political behavior and the susceptibility of the American public to demagogic appeal. He saw parties and party identification as a stabilizing factor and a remedy against populistic dema-

TABLE 4.   Strength of Party Identification and Party Switching in Sweden

	Voters Switching Parties at the End of the Panel Three Years Later					
Party Identification at the	1973	1976	1979	1982	1985	1988
Start of the Panel	1976	1979	1982	1985	1988	1991
Strong party identification	6%	8%	9%	8%	10%	11%
Weak party identification	31	20	17	21	22	29
Party preference only	33	30	34	35	28	41
No party identification	43	28	31	41	40	57

Source: The analysis was first performed in Petersson 1977.

Note: The proportion of the four categories of attachment represented in each year's sample is for 1973: strong 31, weak 29, only preference 28, no identification 8; for 1976: 34, 27, 29, 10; for 1979: 36, 23, 31, 10; for 1982: 34, 26, 29, 11; for 1985: 30, 23, 36, 11; for 1988: 28, 24, 35, 13; for 1991: 24, 24, 37, 15.

gogues: "The maximum potential appeal of a Long, a Coughlin or a McCarthy may depend, essentially, upon the proportion of the population which reacts primarily to the individual politician rather than to the rational demands of national problems or to the emotional claims of party loyalty" (Miller 1954, 177).

Until now, all democracies have been built on political parties. In the wake of postmaterial theorizing, the necessity of parties has been questioned, however. The new independent and resourceful postmaterial citizen, according to the theory, is expected to be disloyal towards established authority and not in need of indirect representation through political parties. To the extent that collective efforts will still be required, alternative organizations and ad hoc groups will emerge. Political parties will, if not die out, at least be reduced to bare election vehicles or ritualistic antiquities.

Being very skeptical about sweeping theories of this kind, and faithful to the traditional maxims of political science, I will not attempt to foretell the future. I suspect, however, that political parties will prove to be far more tenacious than many postmaterial theorists expect.

However, if, despite all reservations, one wants to speculate about future developments, the results in figure 4 could prove useful. To broaden the scope, the data on the shift in the strength of party identification has been supplemented with information on the change in political interest. Following Barton (1955) and Petersson (1977), a typology was created based on intersecting political interest with strength of party identification.

Party identifiers with a considerable interest in politics are called *partisans*. *Independents* are persons with a strong political interest, but who do not identify with any party. *Habituals* are those who lack political interest, but who identify with a party. Finally, *apathetics* are people without party identification and no political interest (Granberg and Holmberg 1988, 185–89).

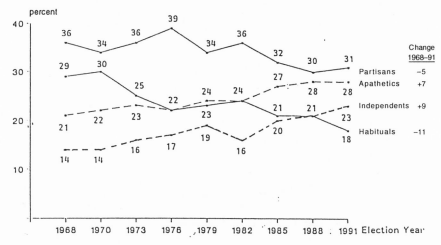

Fig. 4. The intersection of political interest and strength of party identification among Swedish people, 1968–91. *Partisans* are party identifiers
with a self-expressed political interest. *Habituals* are also party identifiers, but with a low political interest. *Apathetics* are people without political interest or party identification, although they may have a party preference. *Independents* are people with a political interest but no party
identification. (Data from Swedish Election Studies; analysis inspired by
Barton 1955 and Petersson 1977.)

No matter how one reads the results, they do not bode well for the stability
or permanence of Swedish parties. The proportion of partisans and habituals—
the nucleus of stability in any party system—is declining, while the two more
volatile groups, independents and apathetics, are on the rise.

From a normative standpoint, the different trends lead to mixed conclusions. While it is dismaying that the proportion of apathetics is growing, it is
also difficult not to welcome the decline of the habituals. The most crucial
result, however, is the pronounced increase of independents and the relatively
minor decrease of partisans, which give conflicting signals as to the future of
the party system.

The surge of independents (they are interested in politics but not loyal to
any particular party) spells trouble for the stability of the party system, while
the slow decline of the partisans encourages the parties to hope that they will
still be able to turn the tide. Furthermore, the change in the proportion of
independents and partisans is important from another, more theoretical, point
of view. Independents and partisans could be conceived as the ideal voters in
two different models of democracy—one collectively oriented model, where
citizens are provided indirect representation through parties and other perma-

nent organizations, and another, more individualistic model, where ad hoc groups, flash movements, referenda, and politically efficacious citizens constitute the basis for democratic processes of a less indirect kind.

Hence, the race between partisans and independents in the 1990s will not only decide the future of the Swedish party system; it will also have an impact on the kind of democracy we are heading for beyond the 1990s. And if the partisans and parties prevail, party identification will prevail and play a major role in future electoral research. The analyses in this chapter have proved, I think, how useful the concept of party identification is in comparative research, and that it could be used fruitfully in European multiparty systems. Not even the directional component of party identification was wasted. It proved very useful in analyzing what happened when the old, stable, Swedish party system fell apart and three new parties emerged. Consequently, as long as we have viable parties, the concept of party identification is something to hold on to, on both sides of the Atlantic.

APPENDIX

The Swedish party identification measurement is very similar to the American one, although not identical. The following four questions have been used to measure party identification in Sweden since 1968 (before that, slightly different questions were used):

QA Many People consider themselves adherents of a specific party. But there also are many others who don't have such an attachment to any of the parties. Do you usually think of yourself as, for instance, a folkpartist, socialdemokrat, moderat, centerpartist, vänsterpartist, miljöpartist, kds:are or nydemokrat or don't you have such an attachment to any of the parties?

1   yes, thinks of him/herself as adherent of specific party

2   doesn't know/hesitant

3   no, doesn't think of him/herself as an adherent of a specific party → QD

4   doesn't want to answer.

QB Which party do you like best?

1   Left Party

2   Social Democrats

3   Center Party

4   People's Party

5 Moderate Party

6 Christian Democrats

7 The Green Party

8 New Democrats

9 doesn't want to answer: → QE

x   other party: _____

QC Some People are strongly convinced adherents of their party. Others are not so strongly convinced. Do you yourself belong to the strongly convinced adherents of your party?

1 yes, strongly convinced

2 no, not strongly convinced → QE

x   other answers: _____

QD Still, is there any party that you consider yourself closer to than any of the other parties? (Which party?)

1 Left Party

2 Social Democrats

3 Center Party

4 People's Party

5 Moderate Party

6 Christian Democrats

7 The Green Party

8 New Democrats

9 doesn't know/doesn't want to answer/no party

x   other party: _____

Based on the answer to these questions, a fourfold strength of party identification variable is constructed in the following manner:

strong party identifiers . . . . .   1 on QA and QC
weak party identifiers . . . . . .   1 on QA and 2 on QC
party preference only . . . . . .   2, 3 or 4 on QA and party given on QD
no party identification . . . . .   2, 3 or 4 on QA and no party given on QD

The following short initials for the parties are sometimes used in Sweden: v = Left Party, s = Social Democrats, c = Center Party, fp = Liberals, m = Conservatives, kds = Christian Democrats, mp = Greens, and nyd = New Democrats.

NOTES

1. The unidimensionality of party identification has also been an issue in the American literature. The problem of the so-called leaners has been one of the bones of contention. See Petrocik 1974; Katz 1979; and Shively 1980.

2. For a critical and provocative analysis of the "decline of American political parties" thesis, see *The Myth of the Independent Voter* (Keith et al. 1992).

3. To facilitate the correlational analysis, the Swedish parties have been scored unidimensionally on a left-right scale based on how people (the entire sample) perceived the location of the parties on the left-right continuum. The perception data comes from the election studies in 1979 (for v, s, c, fp, m), 1988 (for mp), and 1991 (for kds, nyd). For the election years where it is possible, i.e., 1979–91, the analysis has also been done using perception data from the particular years. The results proved to be very similar, with differences of only .01 correlational units. The American results in figure 1 are based on data where the information on party identification was collected in a preelection survey and the vote information in a postelection survey. Hence, campaign volatility and measurement unreliabilities could lead to somewhat attenuated correlations. The Swedish results are based on merged pre- and postelection surveys for the years 1968 and 1973–91 (different samples were used, the pre-sample got a mail questionnaire after the election containing, among other things, a question on the final vote choice). The party identification data for 1956–64 stemmed from preelection studies only, while the 1970 data came from a postelection survey. The difference between results derived from pre- or postelection surveys was very small, maximum .01 correlational units, with post-surveys yielding the highest coefficients. In figure 1, in order to control for these design differences, the results for Sweden have been adjusted up .01 correlational unit for the election years of 1956, 1960, and 1964, and down .01 unit for 1970.

4. The results are based on postelection surveys only, in order to minimize the impact of election campaign induced party switching. Comparable results to the ones presented in the text, but for preelection surveys only, are the following: 1979, 8 percent; 1982, 9 percent; 1985, 12 percent; 1988, 12 percent; and 1991, 16 percent.

5. The analysis has been performed with the party variable scored in a left-right fashion, according to how the entire sample perceives the locations of the parties on the left-right dimension.

6. Kaase (1976, 99) reports on a German panel study done by Radtke that shows similar results to the Netherlands, i.e., slightly more people shifting their party identification while retaining their vote than the other way around. The quality of the study is in some doubt, however. Kaase writes: "Radtke's analysis . . . suffers from a change in question wording from wave 1 . . . to wave 2. In addition . . . only roughly one-third of his respondents identified with a political party at all."

7. Klingemann and Wattenberg 1991 and Converse and Pierce 1992 are two recent comparative studies of party identification; see also Jennings, van Deth, et al. 1990, especially chap. 8, "Partisanship and Electoral Behavior" by Samuel Barnes.

8. The full time series based on the Eurobarometer measurements of party attachments across the twelve member states is analyzed by Holmberg and Schmitt (1992). A

more thorough analysis of the strength of party identification variable in the seven Election Studies Programs is also performed in the same source.

9. The ideological conflict variable is based on left-right self-placement data. Distances between major parties have been used to construct an ideological left-right distance variable across time (Holmberg and Schmitt 1992).

10. The pure life cycle model does not predict indefinite yearly increases. Most models assume the increases to become smaller and smaller, until an asymptotic point is reached.

11. Westholm 1991 is an excellent study of political socialization in Sweden. Among other things, it contains a chapter on party identification (17–50).

REFERENCES

Abramson, P. 1983. *Political Attitudes in America: Formation and Change.* San Francisco: W. H. Freeman.

Barton, A. 1955. "The Concept of Property Space in Social Research." In *The Language of Social Research,* ed. P. Lazarsfeld and M. Rosenberg. New York: Free Press.

Borre, O., and D. Katz. 1973. "Party Identification and Its Motivational Base in a Multiparty System: A Study of the Danish General Election of 1971." *Scandinavian Political Studies.* 8:69–112.

Budge, I., I. Crewe, and D. Farlie, eds. 1976. *Party Identification and Beyond: Representations of Voting and Party Competition.* London: John Wiley and Sons.

Brody, R. 1977. "Stability and Change in Party Identification: Presidential to Off-Years." Paper presented at the annual meeting of the American Political Science Association, Washington, D.C.

Campbell, A., and H. Valen. 1961. "Party Identification in Norway and the United States." *Public Opinion Quarterly* 25:505–45.

Campbell, A., P. Converse, W. Miller, and D. Stokes. 1960. *The American Voter.* New York: Wiley.

Converse, P. E. 1976. *The Dynamics of Party Support: Cohort-Analyzing Party Identification.* Beverly Hills: Sage.

Converse, P. E., and R. Pierce. 1985. "Measuring Partisanship." *Political Methodology* 11:143–66.

———. 1992. "Partisanship and Party System." *Political Behavior* 14:239–59.

Dalton, R. 1991. "Responsiveness of Parties and Party Systems to the New Politics." In *Politische Klasse and Politische Institutionen: Probleme und Perspective der Elitenforschung,* ed. H.-D. Klingemann, R. Stöss, and B. Wessels. Wiesbaden: Westdeutscher Verlag.

Dalton, R., S. C. Flanagan, and P. A. Beck, eds. 1985. *Electoral Change in Advanced Industrial Democracies: Realignment or Dealignment?* Princeton, N. J.: Princeton University Press.

Fiorina, M. P. 1981. *Retrospective Voting in American Presidential Election.* New Haven, Conn.: Yale University Press.

Franklin C. H., and J. Jackson. 1981. "The Dynamics of Party Identification." Paper presented at the annual meeting of the American Political Science Association, New York.

Gilljam, M. 1990. "Sex förklaringar till valet av parti." In *Rött Blått Grönt. See* Gilljam and Holmberg 1990.

Gilljam, M., and S. Holmberg. 1990. *Rött Blått Grönt: En bok om 1988 års riksdagsval.* Stockholm: Bonniers.

———. 1993. *Väljarna inför 90-talet.* Stockholm: Norstedts.

Goldberg, A. S. 1969. "Social Determinism and Rationality as a Basis of Party Identification." *American Political Science Review* 63:5–25.

Granberg, D., and S. Holmberg. 1988. *The Political System Matters: Social Psychology and Voting Behavior in Sweden and the United States.* Cambridge, Mass.: Cambridge University Press.

Holmberg, S. 1992. "The Undermining of a Stable Party System." In *From Voters to Participants: Essays in Honour of Ole Borre,* ed. P. Gundelach and K. Siune. Aarhus: Politica.

Holmberg, S., and H. Schmitt. 1992. "Political Parties in Decline?" Paper presented at the ECPR Workshop, Limerick, April 1992.

Jennings, K., J. van Deth, et al. 1990. *Continuities in Political Action.* Berlin: de Gruyter.

Jennings, M. K., and R. Niemi. 1981. *Generations and Politics: A Panel Study of Young Adults and Their Parents.* Princeton, N. J.: Princeton University Press.

Kaase, M. 1976. "Party Identification and Voting Behavior in the West German Election of 1969." In *Party Identification and Beyond. See* Budge, Crewe and Farlie 1976.

Katz, R. S. 1979. "The Dimensionality of Party Identification in Cross-National Perspectives." *Comparative Politics* 11:147–64.

Keith, B., D. Magleby, C. Nelson, E. Orr, H. Westlye, and R. Wolfinger. 1992. *The Myth of the Independent Voter.* Berkeley: University of California Press.

Key, V. O. 1955. "A Theory of Critical Elections." *Journal of Politics:* 21:198–210.

———. 1966. *The Responsible Electorate.* Cambridge, Mass.: Harvard University Press.

Klingemann, H.-D., and M. Wattenberg. 1991. "Decaying versus Developing Party Systems: A Comparison of Party Images in the United States and Germany." *British Journal of Political Science* 22:131–49.

Lane, J.-E., and S. Ersson. 1991. *Politics and Society in Western Europe.* London: Sage.

Lawson, K., and P. M. Merkl, eds. 1988. *When Parties Fail: Emerging Alternative Organizations.* Princeton, N. J.: Princeton University Press.

LeDuc, L. 1981. "The Dynamic Properties of Party Identification: A Four-Nation Comparison." *European Journal of Political Research* 9:257–68.

Listhaug, O. 1989. *Citizens, Parties, and Norwegian Electoral Politics 1957–1985: An Empirical Study.* Trondheim: Tapir.

Markus, G. B. 1979. "The Political Environment and the Dynamics of Public Attitudes: A Panel Study." *American Journal of Political Science* 23:338–59.

Markus, G. B., and P. E. Converse. 1979. "A Dynamic Simultaneous Model of Electoral Choice." *American Political Science Review* 73:1055–70.

Miller, W. E. 1954. "Issue Orientation and Political Behavior." Ph.D. diss., Syracuse University.

———. 1991. "Party Identification, Realignment, and Party Voting: Back to the Basics." *American Political Science Review* 85:557–68.

Petersson, O. 1977. *Väljarna och valet 1976.* Stockholm: Statistiska centralbyrån.

Petrocik, J. R. 1974. "An Analysis of Intransitivities in the Index of Party Identification." *Political Methodology* 1:31–48.

Robertson, D. 1976. "Surrogates for Party Identification in the Rational Choice Framework." In *Party Identification and Beyond. See* Budge, Crewe, and Farlie 1976.

Särlvik, B. 1970. *Electoral Behavior in the Swedish Multiparty System.* Göteborg: Göteborgs universitet, Statsvetenskapliga institutionen.

Shafer, B. E., ed. 1991. *End of Realignment? Interpreting American Electoral Eras.* Madison: University of Wisconsin Press.

Shively, P. 1980. "The Nature of Party Identification: A Review of Recent Developments." In *The Electorate Reconsidered,* ed. J. Pierce and J. Sullivan. Beverly Hills: Sage.

Thomassen, J. 1976. "Party Identification as a Cross-National Concept: Its Meaning in The Netherlands." In *Party Identification and Beyond. See* Budge, Crewe, and Farlie 1976.

Visser, M. 1992. "The Role of Group Identifications in Dutch Politics." Paper presented at the ECPR Workshop, Limerick, April 1992.

Wattenberg, M. P. 1990. *The Decline of American Political Parties 1952–1988.* Cambridge, Mass.: Harvard University Press.

Westholm, A. 1991. *The Political Heritage: Testing Theories of Family Socialization and Generational Change.* Uppsala: Uppsala University, Department of Political Science.

CHAPTER 6

The Cumbersome Way to Partisan Orientations in a "New" Democracy: The Case of the Former GDR

Max Kaase and Hans-Dieter Klingemann

Prolegomenon

Political parties in Western Europe have traditionally been strong actors in the democratic political process. Historically, they assumed their importance in the context of political mass mobilization, the establishment of general suffrage, and the institutionalization of social cleavage systems that have characterized the European polities throughout the twentieth century. The linkages parties provided between individual citizens and the world of politics were firmly rooted in intermediary structures, such as trade unions, and were buffered by social milieus that, through various channels, integrated the citizens in an overarching system of political beliefs. These beliefs are quite rightfully called *political ideology,* a term coined to indicate the extent to which all elements of the political world—the events, issues, politicians, and corporate political actors—were seen and evaluated through a common ideational yardstick (Fuchs and Klingemann 1990).

The transformation of the European polities from predemocratic authoritarian regimes to democratic welfare states was a slow process. For instance, the establishment of general suffrage lasted at least until the 1920s and was not completed—with the exception of Switzerland in 1970—until the middle of this century. The time span of both this process and the linkage of political and social organizations through institutionalized conflict structures was probably the most important reason why Lipset and Rokkan (1967) in the mid-sixties could still rightfully speak of frozen party systems in Western Europe.

Keeping this gross scenario in mind, it cannot come as a surprise that Paul F. Lazarsfeld, as a European refugee, looked at American elections with a perspective that, when trying to understand the determinants of individual voting behavior, emphasized the links between political parties and social groups (Lazarsfeld et al. 1944; Berelson et al. 1954). By now, it is part of the common heritage in political sociology that Angus Campbell, Philip E. Converse, Warren E. Miller, and Donald E. Stokes, in many publications, starting in the early 1950s, began to challenge the validity of the European socio-structural voting model for the United States. In time, they successfully replaced it with a more *political* approach looking at issues, candidates, and, in particular, partisan orientations as those factors that were most relevant in understanding U.S. voting behavior.

The impact of macropolitical thinking by V. O. Key (1955) on the Michigan group surfaced very clearly in a piece by Angus Campbell (1966) published in the second large volume by that group (Campbell et al. 1966). The classification of elections derived from the dimensions of voting behavior and of party identification pointed to the 1932 and 1936 New Deal presidential elections as those where party identification, for the last time in the twentieth century, was substantially changed in order to remain, for a period of thirty years or so, consistently biased in favor of the Democrats: it had been realigning elections.

Of course, this approach at typologizing elections required the existence of a given party system for a substantial period of time *before* and *after* such specific elections. In addition, the overall institutional framework of the United States as a presidential system, plus its historical roots, has to be kept in mind in order to avoid unreflected transfer of such concepts as critical elections to other polities operating under very different institutional conditions. Nevertheless, these concepts automatically come to mind when discussing the situation of the East European polities, which are on their way to democratization, have all had at least one free general election, and, in this context, are beginning to set up party systems as core elements of their emerging institutional settings.

Many young European political scientists experienced a great deal of enthusiasm and intellectual stimulation in the 1960s, when they assembled at the Mecca of electoral sociology in the United States, the Survey Research Center of the Institute of Social Research at the University of Michigan in Ann Arbor (later to become even better known under the new label of the Center for Political Studies). One consequence of these intellectual encounters was broad, if not always tremendously successful, efforts to export core concepts of the analytical approach of the Michigan group to Europe, in particular the concept of party identification (for a documentation of such and related efforts, see Budge, Crewe, and Farlie 1976). In the (West) German case, these efforts, for one, finally resulted in the development of a functionally equivalent indicator for party identification. Since the late 1960s there has been an ongoing debate in Germany on the uses of the party identification concept for political analysis in the Federal Republic. One of the advantages of this debate has been the regular availability of data on various dimensions of partisanship. Usually, three such measurements are taken: vote intention (a question simulating a general election coming up next Sunday), a ranking of the major parties, and party identification (including an intensity measure for those who identify with a given party). Since early 1990, much of this information is also available for the GDR, after unification, for the five new Länder (states).

Another consequence of the Ann Arbor encounter has been the export of the concept of party image. Not so easy to handle in both measurement and data analysis, this approach to understanding attitudes toward political parties has become less widespread. However, systematic data gathering has taken place in West Germany in preelection surveys since 1969. In 1990, this type of data was collected for East Germany as well. We shall make use of this unique database for our analysis. Party images consist of characteristics people associate with political parties. Among the core image elements are beliefs about a party's ideology or policy position, group ties, its performance in government or opposition, and the efficiency and morality of its politicians. It is our key assumption that partisan attitudes reflected in the party image are good predictors of the individual voting decision. Stokes, Campbell, and Miller (1958, 368) put it this way: "The direction of a person's vote will depend in an immediate sense on his perceptions and evaluation of the things he sees in national politics." Thus, when it comes to the vote, parties and candidates will be judged by what people believe they do and stand for. This theoretical orientation assumes that citizens know something about political parties and that they use this information when they have to make political decisions. A large number of studies has demonstrated the explanatory potential of this approach.[1] This frame of reference might also help us to understand the emergence of partisan attitudes and their behavioral consequences in East Germany.

In the following, we shall first look at the development of the party system in East Germany in a historical perspective, in order to create a framework for the ensuing systematic analysis. We will then describe the development of partisan orientations on the dimensions of party identification, party rank order, and vote intention. In the next step, party images in East and West Germany will be scrutinized, before some systematic conclusions will be drawn from these analyses.

The Historical Roots of the Party System in East Germany

The road to democracy in Germany has been conflict-ridden and extremely bumpy. The foundation of the German Reich in 1871 happened at a time when feudalistic structures were still dominating society and politics. In the context of the lost First World War, the transformation from the Reich to the Weimar Republic was heavily burdened with the basic opposition to democracy by many elite strata (Dahrendorf 1965, 245–60; Stern 1961), the enormous inflation in 1919–24 (Eitner 1990, 11–20), the economic world crisis in 1929–32 and, related to it, the consequences of the reparations inflicted upon Germany in the Versailles Treaty (Schulze 1982, 46). This opposition culminated in the steep rise in electoral strength of the Nazi party and the eventual seizure of power by Adolf Hitler in January of 1933 (for an analysis of the social bases of Hitler's voters, see Falter 1991).

Looking across the nine Reichstag elections in the period of the Weimar Republic, it is the Social Democrats, the Center party, and, to a limited extent, the Liberals who can claim a certain amount of continuity in the German party system as it had developed since the middle of the nineteenth century. This continuity was, of course, completely broken with Hitler taking power and erecting what came to be known as the Third Reich.

When the Second World War came to an end in Europe in May of 1945, the German Reich, by Allied consensus, was split into four regions to be administered separately by the United States, Britain, France, and the Soviet Union. Not least, the cold war that alienated the West from the East resulted in the formation of two independent Germanies in 1949: the Federal Republic of Germany on the territory of the American, British, and French zones of occupation, and the German Democratic Republic on the territory of the Soviet zone.

The interruption from 1933 to 1945 seemed to come to an end in the Soviet zone when the Soviet military administration (SMAD) permitted the (re)establishment of the Communists (KPD), the Social Democrats (SPD), the Christian Democrats (CDU), and the Liberals (LDP) in July of 1945. As H. Weber (1992, 273) observes, it seemed for a while as if, with the exception of the historically discredited extreme right, continuity with the Weimar Republic party system had been maintained. This soon turned out, however, to be a severe misperception. The first step away from this was the KPD and SPD unification, enforced upon the SPD by the Communists and supported by the SMAD; the German Socialist Unity party (SED) was created. The second step was the dismantlement of the independence of the CDU and the LDP. The only two reasonably free elections in what in 1949 became the GDR were the September 1946 community elections and the October 1946 Länder (state) elections, both with rather disappointing outcomes for the Communists and the Soviets. The November 1932 Reichstag election was the last sufficiently free election in the Weimar Republic, while it is an open question whether one is willing to count or discount the 1946 state election as free. Thus, people living in the area of the GDR had witnessed at least forty-four and at most fifty-eight years without direct experience in free elections and exposure to a pluralist party system, when they were confronted with the first (and at the same time last) open election on the territory of the GDR, the Volkskammer election of March 18, 1990.

By contrast, the West German party system could, to a certain extent, take up from what had developed in the Weimar Republic (the large exception being the Christian Democrats, as a transdenominational conservative party replacing the catholic Center party). It developed without major interruptions from a (parliamentary) multiparty system (1949–57) into a three-party system (1957–83) and, since then, with the CDU/CSU, the SPD, the FDP, and the Greens, into a four-party system. Analyses by Converse (1969) and Gluchowski (1983) have shown that this continuity has resulted in an increasing attachment of the populace to parties within this system, at least until the early 1980s.

The Emerging Party System in East Germany: 1989–92

Whereas, in quite a few of the Socialist countries, traces of a counternotion to the monolithic socialist state and its mass organizations—the Civil Society— had begun to surface in the 1980s, East Germany remained what it always had been: the truest vassal of the Soviet Union and a state very strictly wedded to the Communist doctrine. The effects of *perestroika* finally caught up with the GDR, however, even if ever so indirectly, when Czechoslovakia and Hungary permitted refugees from the GDR to cross borders to Austria or to the Federal Republic freely. This exodus of tens of thousands of (mostly young) GDR citizens undoubtedly paved the way for the ousting of Erich Honecker in October of 1989 and for a first set of reconciliatory measures by GDR authorities, climaxing in the opening of the wall to West Germany for East German citizens on November 9, 1989.

It is, by now, history that the tone of the large demonstrations in the GDR, most notably in Leipzig, quickly changed in emphasis from relief from communist rule to German unification. Within the more limited scope of this chapter, we cannot analyze in detail the complex process leading to the abandonment of the independent state GDR (see Glaessner 1991 for an overview). What is important to keep in mind is that the new GDR government, under Hans Modrow, announced to the old GDR parliament, one week after the opening of the wall, that new and free elections would be held in the GDR in 1990. As it soon turned out, the delegitimization of the GDR mass organizations and the ruling elites had created a power vacuum that, fortunately, was filled, in part, by the Round Table, which came together for the first time on December 7, 1989. As a transitory intermediary organization, the Round Table channeled at least some of the new voices making themselves heard in the GDR in the process of transformation. When it became apparent to the GDR government, as well as to the Round Table, that social and political anomie might spread, both decided that the election to the Volkskammer should be moved ahead, from May 16 to March 18. This, of course, produced a great deal of pressure for all involved, in particular for the political parties interested in contesting that election (Boll and Poguntke 1992).

The many citizen groups that had blossomed since the autumn of 1989 were poorly prepared for the changes necessary to become operational political parties. To understand the party system in East Germany as it stands now, it is important to keep in mind that at least two former *block* parties—parties that were officially accepted in the GDR, but were under complete government control—had quasi sister parties in the West: the CDU and the LDP (with the FDP). On the one hand, these parties were associated by the public with the old regime and, therefore, lacked legitimacy. On the other hand, many members of these parties had kept away from official politics and had tried to establish civil rights in the East (like Lothar de Maizière, the new Minister President of the GDR, after the Volkskammer election). Rapid changes in the East CDU in terms of personnel and program were important conditions permitting the unification of the East and the West CDUs on October 1, just two days before unification. For the Liberals, this process proved much more cumbersome. The block Liberals (LDPD) renamed themselves the LDP, but at the same time an East German FDP had been founded, and in addition the liberal Forum party was also established. Efforts to unite the three parties after the Volkskammer election failed. As a consequence, the LDP fused with the old block party of the National Democrats (NDPD) to become the Union of Free Democrats (BFD). On August 11–12, the three East German liberal parties then existing united with the West German FDP. The one remaining block party, the Democratic Peasants party (DBDP), stayed independent for the Volkskammer election, but in June advised its members to join the CDU and then dissolved.

Of the new parties, the one that could rely most on tradition was, of course, the the Social Democratic party. Refounded in illegality in the GDR in the early autumn of 1989 as the Social Democratic party in the GDR, it renamed itself the SPD in January of 1990 and united with the West German SPD on September 27. Based in part on previous citizen groups, a wealth of other new parties also came into being. In February, three such groups formed the Alliance 90 (Bündnis 90). An East German Green party (jointly with a women's association) was also founded. One interesting additional feature in the emerging East German party system was the German Social Union (DSU), a party very much tailored after the Bavarian sister party of the CDU, the CSU. The DSU was correspondingly strongly supported by the CSU, probably with the expectation that its various efforts to extend beyond Bavaria, which, in the past, had failed time and again, could now meet with more success in the wake of German unification.

A particularly interesting question is what became of the previous system party, the SED. First renamed SED-PDS (Party of Democratic Socialism), the old party elites held this new party in firm grasp—too firm, in fact, in the eyes of many change-oriented socialists. Finally, in February 1990, the party had to alter its label to become just PDS. There is no question that the PDS attracted those disappointed with the failure in the GDR to find the "third way" between socialism and capitalism, as well as those who, for various reasons, were still instrumentally and/or emotionally attached to the old GDR.

This brief description can hardly do proper justice to the complexities, delicacies, problems, and rapidity of the process by which something superficially resembling a party system began to emerge in East Germany (a more detailed analysis of the first free election is offered by Volkens and Klingemann 1992). For the PDS and the old block parties, it is likely that, in terms of resources, they could build in part on what they had established in the GDR as block parties, although this still awaits detailed study (Boll and Poguntke 1992). It is ironic that at least the CDU and the liberal parties could, at the same time, also muster support from their West German sister parties. Obviously, for the other parties, it must have been much more difficult to develop the infrastructure necessary to compete in a national election on short notice; this is even true for the SPD and the DSU, who also profited from their West German sister parties. Very little support came from the West German Greens, who were emotionally opposed to unification and, for reasons of principle, were not organizationally oriented to start with.

In East Germany, in 1990 four elections were held altogether. These were the March 18 Volkskammer election and the May 16 community election before unification, and the October 14 Länder election, as well as the first all-German general election to the Bundestag on December 2, 1990, after unification.

As is usual in times of rapid political transitions, where new opportunities lurk, the number of parties and quasiparties participating in the Volkskammer election was well beyond thirty. Of those, quite a few availed themselves of the option offered by the electoral law to form coalition lists:

1. the Alliance for Germany (CDU, DA, DSU);
2. Union of Free Democrats (DFP, LDP, FDP);
3. Alliance 90 (NF, Democracy Now, Initiative Peace and Human Rights);
4. Greens (Greens, Independent Women's Union);
5. Left List-PDS

These coalition lists already foreshadowed what happened during 1990 in the process of the concentration of the East German party system.

Table 1 gives the results of the four elections held in 1990 in East Germany.

Of these four elections, the community election is something of a deviant case, as the 22.5 percent of votes for the "other parties" category indicate. The size of that category points to the phenomenon that in German community

TABLE 1.   Elections in East Germany in 1990

Turnout and Vote Distribution	Volkskammer Election, 3-18-90	Community Elections, 5-6-90	State[a] Elections, 10-14-90	General[b] Election, 12-2-90
Turnout	93.4%	75.0%	69.1%	74.7%
Vote distribution				
CDU/DA[c]	41.7%	30.4%	43.6%	41.8%
DSU	6.3	3.4	2.4	1.0
Liberals	5.7	6.3	7.8	12.9
SPD	21.9	21.0	25.2	24.3
Alliance 90	2.9	2.4	6.9	6.2
PDS	16.4	14.0	11.6	11.1
Other	5.1	22.5	2.5	2.7
Total	100.0	100.0	100.0	100.0

Source: For Volkskammer and community elections, *Statitisches Amt der DDR, ed., Statitisches Jahrbuch '90 der Deutschen Demokratischen Republik* (Berlin: Rudolf Haufe Verlag) 35:449, 450. For state election, Feist and Hoffmann 1991. For general election, Kaase 1993.

[a]Voting took place only in the five new Länder. After Berlin had been constituted as the 16th state of the Federal Republic (uniting East and West Berlin), the appropriate state election was held on December 2, 1990, jointly with the general election.

[b]Second ballot (Zweitstimme).

[c]The DA is added to the CDU just for the Volkskammer election.

elections there is a tradition for local groups independent of the national parties to compete for seats in the city councils. Apparently this tradition is also beginning in the East German communes, thereby rendering comparisons to the other three elections in the table difficult.

If, as a consequence, this election is excluded from further consideration, then a couple of observations regarding the outcome of the other three elections spring to attention. The first datum of interest is turnout. The very high participation in the March Volkskammer election speaks to the specific character of that election: a plebiscite in favor of German unification (Kaase 1993). Interestingly enough, the high stimulus general election in December produced a turnout rate substantially below that of the March election, and even below that for the first West German election in 1949. This low turnout seems to bespeak the ambivalence that East Germans, after forty years of uncontested elections, show towards the institution of popular elections. We shall return to this point later in the chapter.

The second result of considerable interest refers to the percentages for the two major parties, the CDU and the SPD. Considering the fact that almost all structural conditions making for a certain amount of gross stability of the vote were lacking in the former GDR, the consistency in the level of support across the three elections for these two parties comes as a great surprise. Of course, as usual, this gross stability masks a sizable amount of voter fluctuation between the parties (Forschungsgruppe Wahlen 1990, 54). Thus, it is plausible to assume that the continued high level of support for the CDU also reflects the decline of the DSU, as well as the disappearance of the Peasants Party (DBD), in that CDU losses to its liberal Bonn coalition partner were compensated by gains from previous DSU and DBD voters. A similar exchange process probably took place between the SPD and the Alliance 90/Greens, where SPD losses were made up for by gains from the PDS. Regarding the latter party, it is important to note that even after a substantial decline, this party—as the former system party—can still muster a good deal of support in East Germany.

In sum, the 1990 elections in East Germany seemed to hint at a process of party system consolidation, where the contours of the West German system, which to a large extent had been exported to the GDR in early 1990, were already clearly visible, with two exceptions. The first is the surprisingly low level of support for the Social Democrats (SPD), the only party with a succinct historical tradition and strong roots in the East German territory in the past. The second exception is the PDS. While this party had no electoral success whatsoever in West Germany (0.3 percent of the second ballot), because of the electoral law, which by a 1990 ruling of the constitutional court applied the existing 5 percent cutoff rule *separately* to the East and the West, this party is now represented with seventeen deputies in the German Bundestag, thereby increasing the number of parliamentary parties from four to five (counting CDU and CSU as one party).

When analyzing the political scene in East Germany, it has to be remembered that the political unification of the two German states did not join two polities on an equal footing. The GDR was integrated into the Federal Republic under article twenty-three of the West German constitution. This meant not only the loss of an independent political identity, but also the adoption, by East Germany, of the complete constitutional, legal, social, and economic framework of the old Federal Republic. We have just pointed out the extent to which this institutional setting in practice has influenced the development of the East German party system. On the other hand, unification beyond the set date of October 3, 1990, must be looked at as a process that is going to take time, and surely much more time than had been anticipated in mid-1990 when the detailed procedures for unification were set up.

Considering the time and structural bases the European party systems had to develop and consolidate, the East German 1990 elections took place almost in a void. An organizational infrastructure for the new parties was very much lacking; in 1992, even for the former block parties, it was an open question as to what extent this infrastructure had been established, especially in the communes. In addition, the strong linkages between political parties and interest groups, so typical for the intermediary structures in the European polities, were practically nonexistent in the East in 1990, after the proxy mass organizations erected by the Communists as part of their power structure were delegitimized and quickly vanishing. Again, as with the political parties, it is unclear to what extent the intricate and complex network of interest groups that evolved in West Germany over four decades has, by now, extended into the East. Finally, if one considers that the historical process of institutionalization of conflict structures has been interrupted to the point of nonexistence in East Germany, one has to wonder what the basis for the apparent continuity in voter preferences is that seemed so clearly visible in the election results in table 1.

We have mentioned before that practically all eligible East Germans had participated in the March Volkskammer election, and that the Democratic Alliance of CDU, DA, and DSU even came close to an absolute majority of the votes and seats (193 out of 400). Much of the enormous surprise this result produced in Germany can only be understood if one recollects that, practically up to the last week before the election, results from preelection surveys had unanimously seen the Social Democrats as the strongest party in the new East German parliament.

The plebiscitelike election raised the question for many observers whether this election could take up the function of an *aligning* election, to paraphrase Angus Campbell's terminology (see also Feist and Hoffmann 1991, 6). As the stability in election outcomes for the Bonn governing parties and the SPD across 1990 accumulated, the probability of that Volkskammer election serving as such an aligning election was substantially enhanced. It seemed that the overwhelming issue of unification might have become a functional equivalent to crises such as the Great Depression, which in the thirties installed the Democrats as the majority party in the United States. This could, then, provide the parties a firm baseline from which to start, and East Germany might even assume the role of an interesting paradox, in that networks of corporate actors would recreate the old West German conflict structures in the East from the top and would try to superimpose them on already-existing partisan orientations (Kaase and Gibowski 1990, 22–26).

Of course, the proof of the pudding rests with answering the questions of how long the stability of 1990 prevailed, what the background was for these developments, and what can be learned from these analyses in systematic terms.

Partisan Orientations in East Germany: 1990–92

In retrospect, one of the most astonishing features of the transformation process was the ease with which the East German citizenry was willing to accept the mostly unfamiliar labels of a pluralist party system and to choose from those parties. While it cannot come as a surprise that in December 1989 more than 50 percent did not give a party preference, by March 1990 this number had decreased to 11 percent; after the March election it was as low as 2 percent, and from then on it remained around that figure. If these results are valid indicators for at least a certain degree of familiarity not only with the party labels, but also with some content attached to the labels, then the question arises where this familiarity—which, as we shall show, did indeed exist—came from.

Clearly, part of the story is the early focus of attention on the unification issue, where, in particular, CDU and Liberals, on the one hand, and SPD, Greens, and PDS, on the other, had developed easily distinguishable policy positions. This is, however, only part of the story. Two young East German social scientists, Carsten Bluck and Henry Kreikenbom (1991), have proposed an interesting hypothesis that might help to explain another part of the puzzle. In the context of a series of small election studies conducted in 1990 in the city of Jena, they discovered that even before the opening of the wall in 1989, a substantial part of the Jena voters had developed some type of *virtual* identification with West German parties, in the sense of providing guidance for their own political orientations. They interpret this phenomenon with the well-known fact that in the GDR more than 80 percent of the households could (in technical terms) monitor the two major West German television networks (ARD and ZDF) and that, in the 1980s, at least half of those, with increasing tendency, regularly watched the West German TV programs (Dohlus 1991, 84; Bluck and Kreikenbom 1991, 497–98; Scheuch 1991, 268). Unfortunately, questions guided by the hypothesis of "virtual party identification" were, to the best of our knowledge, not asked in national surveys in that critical period, so that generalizable information along those lines seems not to exist.

Bluck and Kreikenbom (1991, 499) also mention the fact that this quasi-party identification favored the SPD, with 38 percent, above the CDU, with 24 percent, although in the city of Jena, where the surveys had been done, the SPD did not fare markedly above the national average in the East German elections. With the kind of weak database the authors command, it is difficult to tell whether this is a significant and reliable finding. It could, however, add to our understanding of why, in the pre-Volkskammer election surveys, the SPD did so much better than it finally did in the election itself.

If this turns out to be a stable result in future research, we will still not know where this prevalence for the SPD came from. We pointed out earlier that the GDR citizens had lived through a period of minimally forty-four and maximally fifty-eight years of lack of exposure to free democratic elections. If this time frame is projected on the individual chance of a GDR citizen having participated in any such election, then for the 1932 Reichstag election the individual had to be born in 1911, at the latest, to be eligible to vote; the respective group of citizens with Weimar voting experience were seventy-nine years and older in 1990. The same calculation, taking the 1946 state election as a vantage point, leads to a minimal birth year of 1925 to be eligible to participate in that election; the respective group in 1990 was at least sixty-five years of age, and made up about 18 percent of the 1990 electorate.

Since, for lack of data, cohort analyses are not possible, we decided to look at the relationship between age and voting preferences in both the Volks-kammer election and the general election, with a particular eye on SPD strength, because the SPD was the party with the highest continuity over time. With the coarse and extremely limited data at hand for this analysis, these data reveal just a very slight indication that there may still be a small residue of pretotalitarian political socialization. In sum, however, and in light of the large part of the electorate which was not directly exposed to the context of free elections before 1990, it can safely be assumed that these residues had no effect on the development of party preferences in the East and on the outcome of the elections.

The extent to which partisan orientations in the East have been shaped by political issues is probably most visible when looking at the occupational/class composition of the various party electorates. We have already noted the difficulties social research has had in designing a longitudinally valid measure of occupational position and status in a society in rapid transition from a "classless" to a "class" society. One finding, though, has been remarkably stable, independent of which concrete measure of occupational position was used: All through 1990, the strength of the CDU derived very much from the fact that it could attract a majority of workers, and this was true in a situation where, in the East (with about 6 percent Catholics), Catholicism did not support the kind of deviating worker vote away from the Social Democrats that is known from West Germany. Such a counterintuitive alignment would, of course, be subjected to strong pressures to change if issue agenda and competence attribution to the parties change, and if intermediary structures are beginning to develop that would support a reorientation of a specific social group integrated into that intermediary system.

The first indicator of partisanship to be analyzed is the party ranked first among the (five) major parties in the rank order question. It is an "easy" indicator, in that it, other than the vote, aims at present party preferences independent of any institutional or procedural background; one aspect of its easiness is that it is always just a small percentage of respondents (2–4 percent) who decline to answer the question. The curve in figure 1 depicts the distribution of rank one party preferences in East Germany, starting in March of 1990 and ending in May of 1992. Unfortunately, because of the October and December 1990 elections, measurements for those months are not available. Nevertheless, the data point clearly to the fact that the sense of doom and dissatisfaction that had begun to spread quickly after the December election in the East caught up with the CDU in March 1991 and has not eased its hold over that party since then. Whereas all other parties have remained more or less

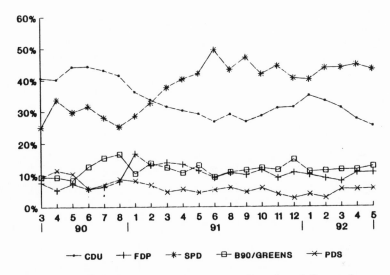

Fig. 1. First-ranked party in East Germany. (Data for all figures from monthly national Politbarometer surveys of the Forschungsgruppe Wahlen.)

stable over time, in a process of steady surge the SPD has now assumed a clear preponderance over the CDU, for a period of a year or so. If one looks at the political agenda of the East Germans before the December election, with its enormous downswing (Kaase 1993), this is not difficult to understand. A simple regression with time as the independent variable for the twenty-two time points and rank preference as the dependent variable gives a slope of -0.7 percent for the CDU and one of +0.9 percent for the SPD; this is, despite the statistical crudeness of the approach, a clear indication of the extent the two parties have switched positions.

Figure 2, which contains the comparable information on vote intention, is standardized to valid party answers only. The results closely parallel those of the ranking question (this is indicated by a correlation [Pearson's *r*] of .86 between the two measures), although a note of caution has to be introduced regarding the much higher number of nonvoters in the East than one has ever seen in comparable West German studies (usually between 3 and 5 percent) (see figure 3 for the East German data). If this is not a methodological artifact (adding up the nonvoters and the don't knows/refused produces about the same percentage of respondents not giving a voting preference in the East and in the West), then nonvoting in East Germany can be regarded as a clear indication of the exit option chosen by a quite sizable part of the populace. This could be a

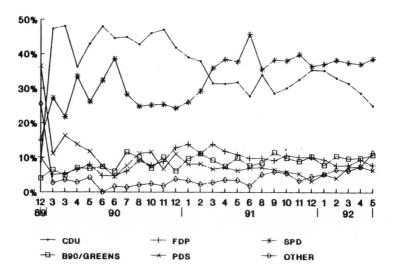

Fig. 2. Vote intention in East Germany

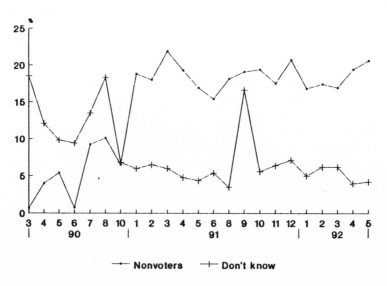

Fig. 3. Nonvoters and don't know, East Germany

hint that, indeed, the election as an institution continues to be burdened with recollections of a manipulated and choiceless ritual of a totalitarian regime. Even if this is true, though, it is, in addition to the large aggregate shift in party preferences, another indication also of a low level of identification with parties and the party system. In this sense, then, the aggregate stability of the 1990 election results would be misleading. Fortunately, we are in a position to test this proposition, at least for the time since April 1991, when party identification in the East was begun to be measured in exactly the same way that it has been measured for almost two decades now in the West.[2]

Before looking at these data, a few remarks on the development of party identification in West Germany and in Western Europe seem in order to put the East German data into perspective. In overall West European terms, there seems to be a certain amount of agreement that levels and intensity of partisanship over the last two decades or so have been slowly, but consistently, declining (Mair 1984; Holmberg and Schmitt 1994; Holmberg, this volume; there are exceptions, though, and these are stressed by Reiter 1989). In the West German case, between 1977 and 1992, there also was a small, but consistent decline in partisanship, which for forty-seven time points is reflected in a small negative slope of 0.15 percent. This result is very much in line with the analysis by Dalton and Rohrschneider (1990) that testifies to the decrease not only in level but also in strength of partisanship, and explains this decrease in the overall framework of the social cleavage dealignment model.

The party identification data, displayed from two angles in figures 4 and 5 (calculated once with the nonidentifiers—fig. 4—and once without—fig. 5) in terms of *partisanship* quite clearly reflect the distributions of partisan orientations already familiar from figures 1 and 2. This impression is statistically verified when computing the correlations between party identification share, party rank, and voting intention, as shown in table 2.

Under the reasonable assumption that party identification should be the measure least influenced by short-term political forces, one could have expected that the correlations between party identification and the two other party measures might be substantially below that between the rank and vote intention, which are equally subjected to short-term forces. This is, however, apparently not the case, as can also be seen when comparing figures 1, 2, and 5. Rather, it seems that the Kuechler (1990) criticism questioning the analytical independence of party identification in West Germany is also borne out for East Germany.

Probably the most important difference between East and West Germany is the level of nonidentification with any of the political parties. From the early stages of measurement in East Germany on, there has been, on the average, a ten percentage point difference between the East and the West; the lower level of identification in the East is certainly what one would have expected. Also

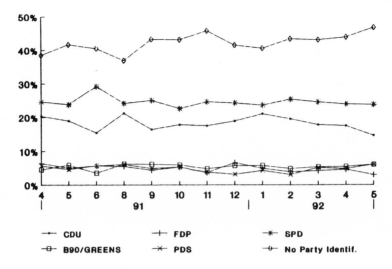

Fig. 4. Party identification in East Germany

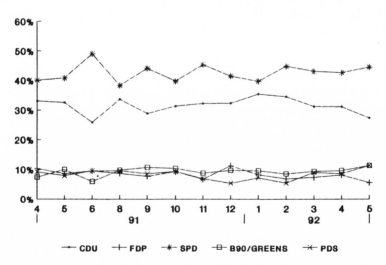

Fig. 5. Party identification in East Germany without "no party" identification

TABLE 2.   Correlations between Three Measures of Partisanship

Correlated Measures of Partisanship	Parties					Number[a] of Time Points
	CDU	SPD	FDP	Alliance 90	PDS	
Party ranked first/Voting intention	.86	.69	.74	.59	.89	13
Party ranked first/Party identification	.84	.80	.51	.63	.93	13
Voting intention/Party identification	.85	.81	.72	.70	.81	13

Source: See table 1.

[a]Because the party identification data are only available since April 1991, there are just thirteen data points in the analysis. One consequence of this limitation is that the data do not pertain to 1990. Entries are party shares for each point in time for which all three observations are present. Nonidentifiers and don't knows are excluded from the party identification measure, don't knows from the party rank measure, and nonvoters, refusals, and don't knows from the voting intention measure.

interesting, and in line with the way that party identification works in Germany, is the fact that present political dissatisfaction in Germany across the board has induced a rise in the level of nonidentification; however, it is stronger in the East than in the West. In sum, the data indicate that whatever partisanship orientations exist in the East, they are not yet firmly established and are very much subject to the political agenda prevailing in the country. In interpreting this instability, next to the political issues of the day, we certainly have to look at the insufficient buildup of intermediary structures linking the citizens with the parties. One important reason may also lie in the images East German citizens have developed of the parties during the short period of time they have been exposed to the normal democratic process in a pluralist democracy. This is the point we will turn to next.

Party Images: Theoretical and Methodological Considerations

How do East Germans perceive and evaluate the major parties in reunified Germany? In our attempt to answer this question, we use West Germany as a reference point. Thus, we compare the party images of East Germans with those of West Germans.

For the analysis of the responses to the open-ended questions on the good and bad points of the political parties, we have selected CDU (CDU/CSU), SPD, FDP, and the Greens (Alliance 90/The Greens). Detailed data which provide a good base for systematic comparison are available for both East and West Germany. Fieldwork was carried out in May/June (West Germany) and November (East Germany) of 1990.

What are our expectations? We start with the assumption that the major parties we look at were more or less new to the East German public in 1990. The SPD was refounded in January. The party labels of Christian Democrats and Liberals looked familiar to East Germans. However, as a consequence of the fusion with their West German sister parties, their programs were redefined and large parts of their political personnel exchanged. Not much remained of their block party days. Of all parties, Alliance 90/The Greens had the strongest roots in the short life of the democratic GDR, although it too had to readjust to the new situation.

By contrast, CDU/CSU, SPD, and FDP have been the major actors in the West German party system since shortly after the Second World War. Even the Greens (the youngest party, in the West German context) have participated in West German national politics for more than ten years. Thus, East Germans had been directly exposed to these parties and their competition for only about one year, whereas they had been part and parcel of West German political life for a much longer period of time. What does this fundamental fact mean for the development of party images? Obviously, this depends on the weight we assign to time as a variable in the formation of party images and on the impact that direct exposure to party politics has on the citizen's political choices.

Most theories postulate that time is positively related to the formation of partisan attitudes. The longer citizens are exposed to a set of political parties, the greater the chance to learn about them and ground perceptions and evaluations on long-term personal experience. That long-term personal experience leads to more firmly held political attitudes is also assumed. This long-term learning model would lead us to expect differences in the development of party images between West and East Germans: more West Germans than East Germans should hold well-developed party images.

In contrast to these assumptions, it is argued that the political orientations of citizens are strongly shaped by current events. This seems to be more rational than to rely on the impact of history. The logic of the current events model would imply that immediate circumstances dominate the party images. It would also imply either no or only small differences between East and West Germany in the explanatory power of image elements for the vote, a topic we cannot cover in this article. If current events are of different importance to East or West Germans, however, large differences may also be compatible with the current events model. To decide this will be a matter of plausible speculation.

There is, however, still a third possibility that would apply to East Germany. We have already mentioned that East Germans had a fair chance to learn about West German political parties through personal contacts with West German friends and relatives, as well as with West German mass media, television in particular. Instead of directly experiencing West German party politics, East Germans were exposed to it indirectly. Building on Weil (1993) and Dalton

(1994), Roller (1992) has aptly called this an outside learning situation, in contrast to inside learning. Research on media effects adds some plausibility to this indirect-exposure long-term learning model.

The ease with which the East Germans made their choice among the new parties in the elections of 1990 tends to support the direct-exposure current events model. The immediate situation, which, after all, was of historic dimensions, must—in this view—have had an overriding influence on party images. However, the differences in levels of party identification that we have found do point in the direction of the two variants of the long-term learning model. Before we explore whether open-ended material on party images contributes to further clarification, however, a few methodological considerations are in order.

Data for the analysis of party images have been generated in the Michigan tradition. Respondents were invited to discuss what they liked and disliked about the four parties under consideration. The interview transcript served as the base for quantitative content analysis of the responses. Such open-ended questions allow citizens to identify what is most important to them about the parties, regardless of whether such considerations might occur to the designers of the questionnaire. Unlike closed-ended questions that force people into boxes that may only partly reflect their thinking, open-ended questions allow respondents to say what, if anything, is on their minds. From their answers, we can determine how much attention people are paying to parties, as well as what specific images are most salient. Thus, open-ended questions provide an extraordinarily rich source of data regarding public attitudes towards parties.

In this analysis, we cannot present the full richness of the verbal material. For our purposes we have reduced the complexity of the arguments by classifying them into thirty-two categories, which can, in turn, be aggregated into a small number of higher order concepts. The most important distinctions are between types of image elements that are related to policies, social groups, and political actors. In addition, we report categoric and nonpolitical evaluations. "I like everything (nothing)" is classified as a categoric response. In addition to classification by type, each image element is also described by its evaluative content and its time frame. All image elements in a response are coded.

Party Images in East and West Germany: Salience, Similarities, and Differences

In the following analysis, we use this material to describe similarities and dissimilarities of the parties' images in East and West Germany.[3] To this end, we will first comment on the different saliency of political parties. Here we look at figures which show the proportion of East and West Germans which have answered the like/dislike questions.

Second, we present a systematic comparison of size of publics using major types of image elements and the positive or negative evaluation of the parties that results from its use.[4] This is of descriptive value. In addition, we try to relate the differences found to the three competing learning models. Large differences in usage of types of major image elements would be compatible with either a direct-exposure long-term learning or a current events explanation. While the first option is self-explanatory, the second alternative would apply when a current event is of much higher concern to the East Germans. Whether or not this is the case will be decided by informed speculation. Large differences, however, would hardly be in line with the indirect-exposure long-term learning model. Small differences, in turn, could be explained by the latter model, and, as above, by the current events model. Again, the first option is obvious. The second applies when a current event hits both parts of the country and affects a party's image similarly.

Third, to decide between the two possibilities, we take a quick look at changing saliency of major image elements in West Germany between 1987 and 1990. If size of image element publics changes drastically between the two points in time, we consider this an indication of current events. Combining results from the second and third step, we shall then come up with a rough classification of major types of image elements.

A comparison of the proportion of citizens who had nothing to say about the parties provides an initial estimate of the degree of differences we might expect between East and West Germans. These data are displayed in table 3. In West Germany, the likes/dislikes questions were first asked in 1969. At that time about one out of five respondents had nothing to say—positive or negative—about the CDU/CSU or the SPD. The proportion was even higher for the FDP (28 percent when first asked in 1972). Since then, the percentage of West Germans who had nothing to say about the political parties has fallen steadily. In 1987, the proportion hovered around 5 percent for CDU/CSU, SPD, and the Greens. It was 12 percent for the Liberals. Thus, although it took

TABLE 3. Proportion of the Electorate with Nothing to Say about the Political Parties, 1969–90

	East Germany	West Germany						
	1990	1990	1987	1983	1980	1976	1972	1969
CDU	8%	6%	5%	5%	9%	12%	14%	20%
SPD	13	6	6	5	7	9	13	22
FDP	28	13	12	9	17	19	28	—
Greens	12	7	5	7	—[a]	—[a]	—[a]	—[a]
N	959	1,476	1,953	1,197	1,519	2,076	1,588	939

Source: Various German Election Studies on Party Images, Hans-Dieter Klingeman, Principal Investigator.
[a]Not available.

some time, at the end of the 1980s, virtually all West Germans had something to say about the major political parties (Klingemann and Wattenberg 1992, 138–42). By 1990, the West German figures had not changed much. It seems as if, since 1983, a level has been reached that can hardly be expected to go down any further. If we take the West German finding as our point of reference, the proportion of East Germans who have nothing to say about the political parties is about twice the West German value for the SPD, FDP, and the Greens. In the case of the CDU, the difference is much smaller, but still 25 percent higher than in the West.

Thus, we do find a systematic difference between East and West Germans. More West Germans than East Germans have formed images about the major parties. This result supports the long-term learning model. But how do we rate the magnitude of the difference? The difference is certainly not small. However, the East German figures of 1990 correspond to West German figures of the seventies. One could say that the development of party images in East Germany is lagging about twelve to twenty years behind the current West German situation—but not longer. The proportion of West Germans who had nothing to say about the CDU or the SPD in 1969 was much larger than the proportion measured in 1990 for East Germans. This makes the lag look medium-sized, and probably speaks for the effects of indirect exposure.

Next, we will compare similarities and differences of East and West Germans with respect to the familiarity of image elements and the image elements' evaluative direction. Thus, we ask how many citizens mention a particular characteristic of a party and how that party is evaluated by the argument encapsulated in the image element. To make the task manageable, we concentrate on those image elements that are mentioned by at least 10 percent of the respondents.[5] This reduces the burden of description, although it still leaves us with a complex task.

Which are the image elements in East and West Germany which meet the 10 percent criterion? Table 4 presents an overview of the major characteristics people associate with the four parties available for comparison.

This initial comparison shows a great deal of similarity. East and West Germans are in complete agreement about the major image elements which characterize SPD and CDU. There is less agreement with respect to FDP and the Greens. In the case of the Greens, economic policy qualifies as a major image element in the East, but not in the West, and it is the other way around for categoric evaluation. The differences are largest for the FDP. East Germans associate a much greater number of major image elements with this party than West Germans. In general, however, the overall picture is one of similarity, not difference.

We have chosen party images of West Germans as our point of reference. If we summarize results from our *earlier* surveys, which we have conducted

TABLE 4.   Types of Image Elements Used by at Least 10 Percent of Respondents, 1990

Type of Image Element	SPD	CDU	FDP	Greens
Policies and Social Groups				
Liberal			E	
Economic policy	E/W	E/W		E
Social policy	E/W	E/W		
Environmental policy				E/W
Ost- and Deutschlandpolitik	E/W	E/W		
Foreign policy, other			W	
Lower class	E/W			
Middle class			E	
Upper class		E/W		W
Political Actors				
Efficiency	E/W	E/W	E/W	E/W
Morality	E/W	E/W	E/W	E/W
Coalition behavior			E/W	
Party program	E/W		E	E/W
Party organization	E/W	E/W	E	E/W
Politicians	E/W	E/W	E/W	
Categoric evaluation	E/W	E/W	W	W
Nonpolitical evaluation				E/W

Source: See table 3.

Note: E = East Germany; W = West Germany.

since 1969 in West Germany, we can list a small number of relatively stable major image elements which are characteristic for these parties (Klingemann 1983, 1986).

On the *image components related to policies and social groups,* the SPD is seen as competent in social policy, as representing the lower class, and as not too fit for economic policy. In addition, the SPD is perceived to have a positive record in the area of the pre-1989 Ost- and Deutschlandpolitik. For the CDU, it is the other way around. Its turf is economic policy, whereas its competence for social policy is rated low and its affinity to the upper class is not appreciated. In the long run, Ost- and Deutschlandpolitik does not meet the 10 percent criterion (average size of public 8 percent; evaluation 46 percent positive). The FDP is seen as liberal, and its record in foreign policy is regarded positively. Environmental policy is the positive trademark of the Greens. Their economic policy has received mixed evaluation.

Politicians and efficiency are the major *actor-related characteristics* for the SPD and the CDU. Evaluations differ. While efficiency is more attributed to the CDU, SPD politicians have, on the average, been perceived somewhat more positively than CDU politicians. Outstanding characteristics of the FDP are coalition behavior, morality, and politicians. This corresponds to political reality. In the past, the FDP's coalition preference has decided more than once which of the two big parties was able to govern. Most other voters don't like this situation, where the tail wags the dog. They react with a moral undertone. Thus, if the FDP is evaluated in terms of coalition behavior or morality, the evaluation is largely negative. Efficiency, party program, party organization, and morality are major actor-related image elements of the Greens. The state of the party organization, in particular, has never been a source of positive evaluation. But what, now, are the differences between East and West Germany?

A detailed analysis for the four parties (tables not shown) finds that similarities in the display of types of image elements prevail. This is also true, although less so, for the evaluative dimension. Subsequently, we point to types of image elements with large differences to find out whether a direct-exposure long-term learning explanation or a current events interpretation has more plausibility.

How many instances of large differences between East and West did we find?[6] The FDP's image is the most dissimilar among the four parties under consideration: five of eleven major types of image elements greatly differ in usage between East and West.

On the other hand, we have encountered a great deal of similarity regarding the images of the remaining three parties. Table 5 shows the major types of image elements that display large differences, according to our operational definition. Only one of ten image elements met the criterion for a large difference in case of the SPD. For the CDU, the relation was two of nine; for the Greens two of eight. Thus, differences there are, but they are small most of the time. On the one hand, the result is supportive of the indirect-exposure long-term learning model. It may mean that East Germans have learned from friends and relatives or the mass media about the major characteristics of West German political parties. On the other hand, differences may be small, but still compatible with a current events model. This would be the case if an event is perceived as equally relevant to a particular party's image in both parts of the country. To tell the two possible models apart, we need an outside criterion. Later on, we shall argue that image elements which show a large difference in saliency between 1987 and 1990 in West Germany may be candidates for a current events interpretation.

Is there a systematic pattern to the dissimilarities? Table 5 lists all types of major image elements which qualify for the large difference category. If there is a systematic pattern, it is the greater concern of East Germans with party-related characteristics. People are talking about the newly founded SPD's promising (or disappointing) program and about the West German CDU's and FDP's potential problems and prospects related to these parties' decision to fuse with the old GDR block parties. In this case, we tend to prefer the current

TABLE 5. Major Differences between East and West Germany Regarding Type of Image Elements

Type of Image Element	SPD	CDU	FDP	Greens
Image elements related to policies and social groups			Foreign policy (36)	
				Economic policy (183)
			Middle class (500)	
			Upper class (36)	
Image elements related to political actors	Party program (190)	Party org. (175)	Party org. (240)	
		Efficiency (158)	Party program (157)	
Categoric evaluation				Categ. (38)

Source: See table 3.

Note: Cell entries are image elements that differed by 50 percent or more between East and West Germany. Index values are given in parentheses.

events model for an explanation. After all, these issues were a direct conse-quence of the unification situation. One could also try to argue for the direct-exposure long-term learning model. In this case, we would have to stress the long-term direct experience with the old block parties. We would not deny that this is an important ingredient. However, on balance, we conclude that the issue could only arise in the unification situation. A similar argument may apply to the much higher use of efficiency as a characteristic of the CDU. After all, a CDU-led government had just demonstrated efficiency in bringing about unification.

Major differences in policies/social groups image elements only occur in the images of the FDP and Green parties. These differences are harder to explain than the actor-related differences. The FDP is a challenge. For the Greens we have no convincing explanation.

The FDP is associated with the upper class in West Germany and the middle class in East Germany. Upper class is coded when entrepreneurs, the rich, those with money, and so on, are mentioned. This species was relatively absent in the former GDR. Here, upper class was much more defined in terms of the ruling class, the *nomenclatura.* Thus, the term *middle class,* which refers to artisans, shopkeepers, small independent farmers, and related groups, may serve as a functional equivalent for *upper class* in the East German context to describe a group of higher economic status. Economically defined class relations as they exist in West German society have not been part of the direct experience of East Germans. Thus, we are prepared to explain the difference in terms of the direct-exposure long-term learning model. The more pronounced position of foreign policy in the FDP's image in West Germany may be due to the fact that East Germans associate foreign policy decisions more with the party of the chancellor and not with the FDP. West Germans, however, have experienced that the Free Democrats virtually owned the foreign policy domain since 1969. This would speak for the direct-experience long-term learning model.

When it comes to the Greens, we have no convincing explanation why economic policy is of greater importance in East than in West Germany. In both parts of the country, Greens normally try to discuss economic policies in terms of environmentalism. We speculate that the East German experience of economic policies that took considerations of environmental protection into account much less than in West Germany may have caused this difference. If this has some plausibility, we would classify the deviation as a hybrid caused by direct, as well as by indirect, long-term learning. Because we think that direct exposure is the more important criterion, we classify the instance accordingly. Finally, categoric evaluation is much more frequent in West Germany. Here, too, we need bold speculation to explain the difference. Considering the fact that in East Germany what we call the Greens (Alliance 90/The Greens) are broadly associated with the political forces that brought down the old Communist regime, it may be that categoric evaluations were that much more positive. Here, too, we have a borderline case between the direct-exposure long-term learning model and the current events model. In this instance, our scale tips in favor of the direct-exposure long-term learning model.

Summarizing major differences of the evaluative aspect of image elements between East and West Germany, we find a situation that is much less similar (table 6). For CDU, FDP, and the Greens, about half of their major image elements are evaluated differently by East and West Germans. Only for the SPD are there no large differences between East and West Germans at all. They agree on the evaluation of the SPD's image elements.

There is a common pattern to these findings. In all cases, the large differences are due to the fact that East Germans, relative to West Germans, have a more positive view of these image elements. This is in line with the general support pattern of the parties in East and West Germany in the 1990 election. There are plausible reasons to assume that the evaluation of image elements may be more different than their distribution. One explanation could be that while types of image elements are the same in East and West Germany, they are evaluated differently because of differences of interests in the two parts of the country.

TABLE 6. Major Differences between East and West Germany Regarding Evaluation of Image Elements

Type of Image Element	SPD	CDU	FDP	Greens
Image elements related to policies and social groups		Upper class (275) Ost- and Deutschl.-politik (163) Social pol. (156)	Upper class (213) Middle class (156)	
Image elements related to political actors			Morality (172) Party program (170)	Party org. (233) Party program (206) Morality (163)
Categoric evaluation		Categ. (152)	Categ. (169)	

Source: See table 3.

Note: Cell entries are image elements that differed by 50 percent or more between East and West Germany. Index values are given in parentheses.

For the record, we now summarize our best judgment regarding large differences in *types of image elements,* with special emphasis on East Germany. The preferred model is given in parentheses.

SPD: party program (current events).
CDU: party organization, efficiency (current events).
FDP: party organization, party program (current events), foreign policy, upper class, middle class (direct-exposure long-term learning).
Greens: economic policy, categoric evaluation (direct-exposure long-term learning).

Arguments for this classification seem plausible to us. For all other image elements with large differences, we need additional information to make classification possible and meaningful. We shall try to provide this information by considering stability and change of the major types of image elements in West Germany between 1987 and 1990. If the difference is large, we argue for a current events explanation.

Current Events: The Changing Saliency of Image Elements in West Germany, 1987–90

Similarity between party images of East and West Germans can be explained by the current events model or the long-term learning model, be it direct or indirect. A comparison of the 1987 and 1990 West German figures should help

TABLE 7. Changing Saliency of Types of Image Elements in West Germany, 1987–90

Type of Image Element	SPD	CDU	FDP	Greens
Image elements related to policies and social groups	Ost- and Deutschl.-politik (207)	Ost- and Deutschl.-politik (655)	Foreign, other (161)	Environment (35)
	Econ. pol. (45)	Social pol. (136)	Upper class (94)	
	Social pol. (121)	Econ. pol. (71)		
	Lower class (93)	Upper class (94)		
Image elements related to political actors	Part org. (128)	Morality (143)	Politicians (160)	Party org. (186)
	Efficiency (123)	Party org. (82)	Morality (58)	Party program (80)
	Politicians (116)	Politicians (116)	Coalition (111)	Nonpol. eval. (98)
	Morality (89) Party program (91)	Efficiency (97)	Efficiency (98)	Morality (101)
Categoric evaluation	Categ. (77)	Categ. (81)	Categ. (50)	Categ. (57)

Source: See table 3.

Note: Cell entries are image elements that differed by 50 percent or more between 1987 and 1990. Index values are given in parentheses.

us to sort out image elements that have undergone rapid change and become more prominent in 1990. Such image elements are our candidates for a current events explanation. In operational terms, we will stick to our definition of large difference. Thus, we select image elements when the 1990 value differs by 50 percent or more from the 1987 value. We will not attempt a detailed party-by-party description. For our purposes, it is sufficient just to present the index values for types of image elements and evaluation in table 7.

For policies and social group–related image elements, the message is clear and hardly surprising. The one and only image element rising to more prominence in 1990 was Ost- and Deutschlandpolitik. In the case of the FDP, the impact is visible in the rise of a general reference to foreign policy. People praised the FDP, and Genscher in particular, for a good foreign policy. Change between 1987 and 1990 is most distinct for the CDU. The proportion of West German respondents evaluating the party in this context rose from 5 percent in 1987 to 31 percent in 1990. The respective figure for the SPD doubled (1987: 10 percent, 1990: 21 percent).

Among the actor-related image elements, two meet our criterion. In 1990, politicians were mentioned much more frequently in connection with the FDP than in 1987. Closer inspection reveals that foreign policy and Genscher tend to co-occur. This makes a current events interpretation plausible. The largest change in the Greens' image relates to party organization. Party organization has been a negative characteristic of the Greens since 1983, when we asked the likes/dislikes question for this party for the first time. That the number of people evaluating the party by this image element could rise from 27 percent in 1987 to 43 percent in 1990 is hardly believable. However, the Green party's inability to find common ground with its sister parties in East Germany, which was added on to the normal fights between its realist and fundamental wings, must have made it possible. This, too, finds a reasonable current events explanation.

The Development of Party Images in East Germany

We have described the differences in party images between East and West Germany for 1990. As a result, we have singled out image elements which represent cases of large differences. We have discussed all of these cases and tried to locate them with respect to the current events explanation or to the direct-exposure long-term learning model. In the case of small differences between East and West Germany in 1990, we were unable to decide between the indirect-exposure long-term learning model and the current events model. Therefore we have, in addition, considered changes of major image elements from 1987 to 1990 in West Germany. Whenever large-scale differences between the two points in time occurred, we have assumed results to represent a current events situation. Thus, we are finally able to attempt an answer to the question of how we might explain the development of party images in East Germany.

In the beginning, we introduced three potential ways East Germans might have learned partisan attitudes, as reflected in party images: the current events model, the direct-exposure long-term learning model, and the indirect-exposure long-term learning model. How does the empirical evidence square with the logic of these models? Results are displayed in table 8.

Our findings support the current events model and the indirect-exposure long-term learning model. There are elements in the images of the FDP and the Greens that have the flavor of direct-exposure long-term learning, and we have classified them this way. Of course, even with our differentiated database, much of what we do remains guesswork, and in some cases boundaries are fuzzy. For example, if we had selected a lower threshold for our definition of large differences, we might have found some image elements fitting the models differently.

The proportion of image elements supporting the indirect-exposure long-term learning model is 80 percent for the SPD, 75 percent for the Greens, 67 percent for the CDU, and 45 percent for the FDP. For the FDP, 27 percent, and

TABLE 8.   Major Types of Image Elements and Models for Explanation of Image Formation in East Germany, 1990

| | Long-Term Learning Model | |
Current Events Model	Indirect Exposure	Direct Exposure
SPD	Party organization (138)	
Party program (190)	Efficiency (62)	
Ost- and Deutschlandpolitik (62)	Economic policy (80)	
	Politicians (89)	
	Categoric evaluation (111)	
	Social policy (110)	
	Lower class (90)	
	Morality (97)	
CDU	Morality (125)	
Party organization (175)	Social policy (76)	
Efficiency (158)	Upper class (77)	
Ost- and Deutschlandpolitik (123)	Categoric evaluation (78)	
	Economic policy (100)	
	Politicians (100)	
FDP	Liberal (144)	Middle class (500)
Party organization (240)	Coalition behavior (61)	Upper class (36)
Party program (157)	Morality (65)	Foreign policy, other (36)
Politicians (95)	Categoric evaluation (75)	
	Efficiency (92)	
Greens	Morality (130)	Categoric evaluation (38)
Economic policy (183)	Party organization (74)	
	Party program (119)	
	Nonpolitical evaluation (116)	
	Environmental policy (113)	
	Efficiency (109)	

Source: See table 4.
Note: Cell entries are major types of image elements. Index values are given in parentheses.

for the Greens, 13 percent, are in support of the direct-experience long-term learning model. What remains speaks for the current events model. Thus, outside learning was the modal way East Germans acquired partisan attitudes. To be sure, firsthand experience has come from current events, of which the unification issue was certainly the most important. We may have found some remnants from the past, in the case of the FDP and the Greens, but these will fade away.

Direct learning of the virtues and vices of party politics, however, has already begun for East Germans. We would be surprised if we did not find larger differences in party images in future studies. Results of the development of party attachment that we have reported earlier in the chapter clearly point in this direction.

Conclusions

Transformations in Eastern Europe have changed the global political land-scape, although in 1993 it is not at all clear what the long-term consequences of these changes will be. On a smaller scale, these transformations have also created a tremendous challenge and, at the same time, an opportunity for the social sciences. It is probably not too far-fetched to argue that we have been witnessing, and have been part of, a giant social experiment.

One of the most interesting questions to be tackled by political scientists in this context is what kind of political order will result from the transitions in Eastern Europe. Democracy is but one answer, and even there a lot of wishful thinking is involved. Of course, it will be some time before an answer can be given in a reliable fashion. Core elements of pluralist democracies are inter-mediary structures, interest groups and political parties among them most prominent. In this chapter, we have looked at the case of the emerging party system in East Germany, the former GDR.

It is unfortunate for comparative politics, though, that East Germany, for reasons specified above, is a very special case. Thus, our findings cannot be easily generalized. Nevertheless, we look at the political parties in the eastern part of Germany as a fascinating topic for political sociology.

The analyses have strongly supported the indirect-exposure long-term learning model, at least for the first phase of the East German party system. It is this model that best explains the ease with which most East Germans have adopted party labels exported to them from West Germany, along with a loose organizational infrastructure. Obviously, communication, and here mostly West German television, and personal contacts between West and East Ger-mans despite the "wall," over almost all of the period where two separate German states existed, is the prime explanatory factor in this type of learning model. This interpretation is well in line with the fact that it is the two major parties of CDU/CSU and SPD whose image structure can be best explained by that particular model. It is quite fitting to recall that analyses comparing democratic attitudes of East and West Germans (Bauer 1991; Dalton 1994; Weil 1992) were also puzzled by the convergence in these attitudes.

At the same time, our data on the temporal development of partisan attitudes point to the limits in this convergence interpretation. The enormous shift we have observed in party preferences after 1990 indicates that the current events model may have some virtue after all. It must be a relief for socialization theorists that, if our speculations hold, "virtual" learning of political orienta-tions is not quite equivalent to "doing it the hard way," over many years of direct exposure to political symbols, structures, and processes. Our tale signals that the road to democracy in Eastern Europe must indeed be traveled. There is no substitute for direct experience.

NOTES

The authors appreciate the technical support of Jürgen Hamberger, Bärbel Hoop, Jeffrey Huffman, and Martin Koczor in preparing the charts in this chapter.

1. Among the early Michigan studies which have made use of this approach are the following: Campbell, Gurin, and Miller 1954; Stokes 1958; Stokes, Campbell, and Miller 1958; Campbell, Converse, Miller, and Stokes 1960; and Stokes 1966.

2. The question wording runs as follows: (a) Direction: In Germany, many people adhere for some time to a specific political party although off and on they may vote for a different party. What about you: Generally speaking, do you adhere to a specific party? IF YES: Which one? (Interviewer: Note reply in questionnaire.) (b) Intensity (If party identification present): How strongly or weakly do you adhere—all in all—to that party: very strongly, quite strongly, moderately, quite weakly, very weakly?

3. West German results are presented by Klingemann (1983, 1986).

4. We have done some economizing in the presentation of the evaluation dimension. We need a simple indicator for the direction of the evaluative component of a particular type of image element used by the respective public. To derive it, we subtract the number of negative image elements from the number of positive image elements. In our analysis, we only use the figure that gives the proportion of respondents who, on balance, express a positive evaluation of the party. Thus, we neglect the fact that a low (high) positive value must not necessarily mean a high (low) negative value because of the third logical possibility that different respondents might evaluate the same type of image element differently. Our subtraction may not only yield a positive or negative sum, but it may also indicate that there had been an equal number of positive and negative image elements. The logic of comparison and reasoning will be the same as laid out above.

5. This criterion is nothing but a pragmatic decision about a plausible cutting point. A complete documentation of all data can be obtained from the authors.

6. As a guideline to operationalize a "large" difference, we decided to use an index based on dividing the percentage of the East German answers by the percentage of the West German answers in the respective category and multiplying this ratio by 100. All differences below the 50 or above the 150 ratio mark are regarded as "large." The 50× criterion, too, rests on a pragmatic decision and does not pretend to have any other quality.

REFERENCES

Bauer, Petra. 1991. "Freiheit und Demokratie in der Wahrnehmung der Bürger in der Bundesrepublik und der ehemaligen DDR." In *Nation und Demokratie: Politisch-Strukturelle Gestaltungsprobleme im neuen Deutschland,* ed. Rudolf Wildenmann. Baden-Baden: Nomos.
Berelson, Bernard R., Paul F. Lazarsfeld, and William N. McPhee. 1954. *Voting: A Study*

of Opinion Formation in a Presidential Campaign. Chicago and London: University of Chicago Press.

Bluck, Carsten, and Henry Kreikenbom. 1991. "Die Wähler in der DDR: Nur issueorientiert oder auch parteigebunden?" *Zeitschrift für Parlamentsfragen* 22:495–502.

Boll, Bernhard, and Thomas Poguntke. 1992. "The 1990 All-German Election Campaign." In *Electoral Strategies and Political Marketing,* ed. Shaun Bowler and David M. Farrel. London: Macmillan.

Budge, Ian, Ivor Crewe, and Dennis Farlie, eds. 1976. *Party Identification and Beyond.* London: John Wiley.

Campbell, Angus, Gerald Gurin, and Warren E. Miller. 1954. *The Voter Decides.* Evanston, Ill.: Row, Peterson.

Campbell, Angus, Philip E. Converse, Warren E. Miller, and Donald E. Stokes. 1960. *The American Voter.* New York: Wiley.

———. 1966. *Elections and the Political Order.* New York: Wiley.

Converse, Philip E. 1969. "On Time and Partisan Stability." *Comparative Political Studies* 2:139–71.

Dahrendorf, Ralf. 1965. *Gesellschaft und Demokratie in Deutschland.* München: Piper.

Dalton, Russell J. 1994. "Communists and Democrats: Democratic Attitudes in the Two Germanies." *British Journal of Political Science,* in press.

Dalton, Russell J., and Robert Rohrschneider. 1990. "Wählerwandel und Abschwächung der Parteineigung von 1972 bis 1987." In *Wahlen und Wähler: Analysen aus Anlaß der Bundestagswahl 1987,* ed. Max Kaase and Hans-Dieter Klingemann. Opladen: Westdeutscher Verlag.

Dohlus, Ernst. 1991. "Augen und Ohren nach Westen gerichtet? Zuschauer- und Hörerverhalten in den neuen Bundesländern." In *ARD-Jahrbuch 91.* Hamburg: Hans-Bredow-Institut.

Downs, Anthony. 1957. *An Economic Theory of Democracy.* New York: Harper and Row.

Eitner, Hans-Jürgen. 1990. *Hitlers Deutsche: Das Ende eines Tabus.* Gernsbach: Casimir Katz Verlag.

Falter, Jürgen W. 1991. *Hitlers Wähler.* Munich: C. H. Beck.

Feist, Ursula, and Hans-Jürgen Hoffmann. 1991. "Landtagswahlen in der ehemaligen DDR am 14. Oktober 1990; Föderalismus im wiedervereinigten Deutschland— Tradition und neue Konturen." *Zeitschrift für Parlamentsfragen* 22:5–34.

Forschungsgruppe Wahlen. 1990. *Bundestagswahl 1990. Eine Analyse der ersten gesamtdeutschen Bundestagswahl am 2. Dezember 1990.* Mannheim: Berichte der Forschungsgruppe Wahlen no. 61.

Fuchs, Dieter, and Hans-Dieter Klingemann. 1990. "The Left-Right-Scheme." In *Continuities in Political Action: A Longitudinal Study of Political Orientations in Three Western Democracies,* by M. Kent Jennings, Jan van Deth, et al. Berlin: Walter de Gruyter.

Glaessner, Gert-Joachim. 1991. *Der schwierige Weg zur Demokratie: Vom Ende der DDR zur Deutschen Einheit.* Opladen: Westdeutscher Verlag.

Holmberg, Sören, and Hermann Schmitt. 1994. "Political Parties in Decline?" Draft chapter for the Beliefs in Government Project, Mannheim and Colchester.

Kaase, Max. 1993. "Electoral Politics in the New Germany: Public Opinion and the Bundestag Election of December 2, 1990." In *The Domestic Politics of German Unification,* ed. Christopher Andersen, Karl Kaltenthaler, and Wolfgang Luthardt. Boulder, Colo.: Lynne Rienner Publishers.

Kaase, Max, and Wolfgang G. Gibowski. 1990. "Deutschland im Übergang: Die Parteien und Wähler vor der Bundestagswahl 1990." *Beilage zur Wochenzeitung "Das Parlament"* B37–38:14–26.

Key, V. O., Jr. 1955. "A Theory of Critical Elections." *Journal of Politics* 17:3–18.

Klingemann, Hans-Dieter. 1983. "Die Einstellungen zur SPD und CDU/CSU 1969–80." In *Wahlen und politisches System,* ed. Max Kaase and Hans-Dieter Klingemann. Opladen: Westdeutscher Verlag.

———. 1986. "Der vorsichtig abwägende Wähler: Einstellungen zu den politischen Parteien und Wahlabsicht: Eine Analyse anläßlich der Bundestagswahl 1983." In *Wahlen und politischer Prozeß: Analysen aus Anlaß der Bundestagswahl,* 1983, ed. Hans-Dieter Klingemann and Max Kaase, Opladen: Westdeutscher Verlag.

Klingemann, Hans-Dieter, and Martin P. Wattenberg. 1992. "Decaying Versus Developing Party Systems: A Comparison of Party Images in the United States and West Germany." *British Journal of Political Science* 22:131–49.

Kuechler, Manfred. 1990. "Ökologie statt Ökonomie: Wählerpräferenzen im Wandel?" In *Wahlen und Wähler: Analysen aus Anlaß der Bundestagswahl 1987,* ed. Max Kaase and Hans-Dieter Klingemann. Opladen: Westdeutscher Verlag.

Lazarsfeld, Paul F., Bernard R. Berelson, and Hazel Gaudet. 1944. *The People's Choice: How the Voter Makes up his Mind in a Presidential Campaign.* New York: Duell, Sloan and Pearce.

Lipset, Seymour M., and Stein Rokkan. 1967. "Cleavage Structures, Party Systems, and Voter Alignments: An Introduction." In *Party Systems and Voter Alignments,* ed. Seymour M. Lipset and Stein Rokkan. New York: Free Press.

Mair, Peter. 1984. "Party Politics in Contemporary Europe: A Challenge to Party?" In *Party Politics in Contemporary Western Europe,* ed. Stefano Bartolini and Peter Mair. London: Frank Cass and Co.

Reiter, Howard L. 1989. "Party Decline in the West: A Skeptic's View." *Journal of Theoretical Politics* 3:325–48.

Roller, Edeltraud. 1992. "Ideological Basis of the Market Economy: Attitudes Toward Distribution of Principles and the Role of Government in West and East Germany." Paper presented at the panel "Psychological Impediments to the Establishment of a Successful Market Economy," fifteenth annual scientific meeting of the International Society of Political Psychology (ISPP), San Francisco, Calif.

Scheuch, Erwin K. 1991. *Wie deutsch sind die Deutschen? Eine Nation wandelt ihr Gesicht.* Bergisch Gladbach: Gustav Lübke Verlag.

Schulze, Hagen. 1982. *Weimar, Deutschland 1917–1933.* 2d ed. Berlin: Siedler Verlag.

Stern, Fritz. 1961. *The Politics of Cultural Despair.* Berkeley: University of California Press.

Stokes, Donald E. 1958. "Partisan Attitudes and Electoral Decision." Ph.D. diss., Yale University.

———. 1966. Some Dynamic Elements of Contests for the Presidency. *American Political Science Review* 60:19–28.

Stokes, Donald E., Angus Campbell, and Warren E. Miller. 1958. "Components of Electoral Decision." *American Political Science Review* 52:367–70.

Volkens, Andrea, and Hans-Dieter Klingemann. 1992. "Die Entwicklung der deutschen Parteien im Prozeß der Vereinigung." In *Die Gestaltung der deutschen Einheit: Geschichte-Politik-Gesellschaft,* ed. Eckard Jesse and Armin Mitter. Bonn: Bouvier-Verlag.

Weber, Hermann. 1992. "Gab es eine demokratische Vorgeschichte in der DDR." *Gewerkschaftliche Monatshefte* 43:272–80.

Weil, Frederick D. 1993. "The Development of Democratic Attitudes in Eastern and Western Germany in a Comparative Perspective." In *Research on Democracy and Society,* vol. 1, eds. Frederick D. Weil, with Jeffrey Huffman and Mary Gautier. Greenwich, Conn.: JAI Press.

CHAPTER 7

Accounting for Divided Government: Generational Effects on Party and Split-Ticket Voting

Richard A. Brody, David W. Brady, and Valerie Heitshusen

The immediate source of divided government is obviously the political be-havior of the American voter. But acceptance of this fact has not given rise to an agreed upon account of the phenomenon: Martin Wattenberg, following the lead of Campbell and Miller (1957), tells us that "At the heart of the phenome-non of divided government is the decline of U.S. political parties. Divided government would not be possible without a substantial degree of split-ticket voting, and ticket splitting has only become prevalent in the recent period of weakened partisanship" (Wattenberg 1991, 39). Wattenberg's account assumes that weakened partisanship is a cause of ticket splitting and is not itself an effect of some set of forces giving rise both to ticket splitting and to weakened partisanship (Brody and Rothenberg 1988). Substantiation of this claim will require an investigation of the sources of split-ticket voting.

Paul Beck and his colleagues (Beck, Baum, Clausen, and Smith 1992) replicate the Campbell-Miller and Wattenberg findings in subpresidential elec-tions; weaker partisans are likely to vote for candidates of different political parties in elections for statewide constitutional officers. This research team also finds that Ohio voters are influenced by the visibility of the candidate—generally a matter of incumbency—in splitting their ballot between candidates of the major parties.

John Petrocik (1991) emphasizes differences in the sources of presidential and congressional elections; the two elections are simply about different things. In presidential elections, ties between issues and partisanship determine outcomes:

> Presidential elections are basically partisan affairs in which partisanship is reinforced and undermined (although most votes are reinforced) by the issues that provide the substantive discussion between the candidates. The weakly partisan and the nonpartisan are swayed by the issue agenda. . . . When the agenda of one party completely dominates . . . it will provoke high defection rates. (Petrocik 1991, 34)

Issues, according to Petrocik, are not the key to defection in congressional races:

> Congressional elections are also largely partisan affairs, but the intrusive element is not issues. Rather the intruding elements are quite stable structural features of U.S. politics [including] an electorate that is more Democratic than Republican, districts that are drawn to favor their Democratic incumbents, the relative homogeneity of a congressional district, [and] "better" Democratic candidates. (Petrocik 1991, 34)

Gary Jacobson (1990, 1991) agrees with Petrocik on the issue content of presidential elections, but he disputes the effects of "Democratic gerrymanders," and he argues that issues are important in congressional as well as presidential elections:

> The Democrats' continued dominance of the House . . . despite a string of Republican presidential victories is a consequence of electoral politics: of candidates, issues, electoral coalitions, and voters' reactions to them. . . . Republicans have made little progress in the House because they have fielded inferior candidates on the wrong side of issues that are important to voters in House elections. (Jacobson 1991, 59)

Jacobson proposes and tests separate models of presidential and House votes in the 1988 election. These models incorporate measures used to determine which political party is thought to be superior in handling issues of importance to the voter, voters' perceptions of the proximity of the parties on key issues, and voters' evaluations of President Reagan's performance as president. Jacobson uses his models to explain how voters choose among presidential and House candidates, to illuminate similarities and differences in the structure of choice in the two contexts, and, thus, to expand our understanding of ticket splitting and the origins of divided government (Jacobson 1991, 71).

These accounts of the origins of divided government have something to offer, but, individually and collectively, they leave room for further work. The most conspicuous shortcoming is a failure to provide a consistent explanation of the incidence of ticket splitting. For example, although he identifies changes in the strength of partisanship as a cause, Wattenberg recognizes that weakened partisanship is insufficient to account for much of the increase in ticket splitting. While there has been an increase in the proportion of Americans abjuring identification with the major parties, the change is insufficient to account for the trend in ticket splitting. Wattenberg suggests that:

> Party decline has . . . merely opened the door to the possibility of divided government, allowing other factors to guide outcomes for presidential and

congressional elections in opposite directions. Incumbency, for example, would not be as important a factor in maintaining Democratic control of the House if political parties were as strong as they used to be. Nor would it be possible for the party with the most identifiers in the electorate to routinely lose presidential elections in a strong party system. (Wattenberg 1991, 40)

Warren Miller's recent research suggests another factor that should be considered in investigating the comparative statics of the problem of divided government: in two recent papers, Warren has employed the concept of "political generation" in explanations of trends in turnout (Miller 1992a) and partisanship (Miller 1992b). He points out that

> the past three decades were filled with events that made the political involvement of the younger generation of voters distinctly different from that of their elders. . . . the relevant events began with the urban riots and Civil Rights demonstrations of the late 1960s and extended through the assassinations of the Kennedys and Reverend King. The events that molded the first post–New Deal generation included the evolution of political protest in a national counter culture movement; they extended into the triumphant protest and the tragic end of the Vietnam war, and the disillusioning fate of the Nixon presidency. (Miller 1992b, 334–35)

His basic approach in this research—one that should apply with equal force to the question of divided government—is "to compare citizens who differ primarily in the nature of the political epochs which shaped their identifications, perceptions, values and preferences on matters political" (Miller 1992b, 335).

Miller's notion of "political generation" directly connects to the issue of divided government via Wattenberg's hypotheses about weakened partisanship and Paul Abramson's contention that "the evidence strongly suggests that postwar [i.e., post–World War II] cohorts have been socialized to learn weak partisan loyalties . . ." (Abramson 1989, 256).

These studies point to the increased incidence of divided government, stemming from a number of sources: Increases in the number of pure independents would mean more ticket splitting, but this increase has not been large enough to account for the observed trend in the incidence of ticket splitting.[1] A general weakening of partisan identification among partisans can also be a source. However, as we will show, partisanship has not weakened for all age groups, so we will need to separate the weakening of partisanship from ticket splitting associated with population replacement. Beyond changes in partisanship and the composition of the electorate, we need to consider changes in the structure of American political institutions. Factors associated with the tendency to vote for incumbent members of Congress as individuals per se, rather than as representatives of political parties—the so-called *personal vote* (Alford and Brady 1989)—are likely to be sources of ticket splitting as well. Additionally, as Petrocik suggests, the patterns of issue and ideological homogeneity/heterogeneity for the major political parties are bound to produce marginal voters who cross the line and choose candidates of the other major party; some of these voters will be ticket splitters. It is to investigations of sources of votes for divided government in these broad areas that we now turn.

The research literatures on the origins of divided government and on political generations suggest that instead of comparing separate models of the vote for the presidency and the House and Senate, we should model ticket splitting, as such. These bodies of research also suggest that the ingredients of an explanation of ticket splitting include measures of the individual voter's partisanship, issues preferences (considered separately or clustered in ideologies), and political generation. Given the fact that voters respond to the proffered candidates, the research literatures also suggest that the importance of these explanatory elements will vary from election to election in ways that can be anticipated from the major party campaigns (Petrocik 1991).

In our investigations, we will distinguish between partisan defections and ticket splitting. Defections from partisanship and ticket splitting are related, but not identical, phenomena. A voter who retains her partisanship but votes for Senate, House, and presidential candidates of the other major party has surely defected from her partisanship, but has not contributed to divided government. Ticket splitting in American national elections is, ipso facto, a contribution to divided government. We do not require that one's congressional votes match and be cast for a party different than one's presidential vote; it is sufficient for our purposes that votes cast for one congressional office and the president are for candidates from different parties. Following the paths suggested in the research literature, we will begin by documenting the trends in ticket splitting and examining partisan and cohort differences in the likelihood of split-ticket voting.

Ticket Splitting, 1952–88

Figure 1 presents the trends in two measures of ticket splitting—presidential vs. House vote and presidential vs. Senate vote. Several features of these trends are noteworthy: Generally speaking, and despite differences in the composition of their respective electorates, the two measures trend together. It appears that the forces that produce a vote for the presidential candidate of one political party and a candidate for the House from the other political party also produce a split decision in presidential-Senate comparison. This is not to say that those

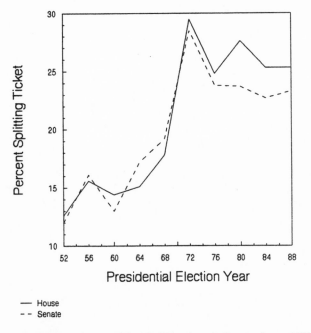

— House
- - Senate

Fig. 1. Split-ticket voting, 1952–88. (Data for all figures from 1952–90 Cumulative Date File of the National Election Study.)

who split their tickets invariably vote for the same party for the two congressional offices; plainly, they do not.[2] Rather, it means that explanations accounting for the actions of voters voting for different parties in House and presidential elections are also likely to be useful in explaining ticket splitting in Senate elections.

The similarity of the two trends is partly a product of the fact that the same presidential vote is used in both comparisons. To avoid this double counting and the redundancy in presentation it necessarily will entail, we have constructed a new variable that reflects the individual's contribution to divided government. If the individual's vote for either or both congressional offices is for the candidate of a party different than the party of the presidential candidate she or he supports, the vote will be coded as split; a nondivided vote will result if the individual voter supports the candidates of the same party for president, House, and Senate. Figure 2 displays the trend for this measure of ticket splitting.

The rate of split-ticket voting in the Eisenhower election in 1952 was less

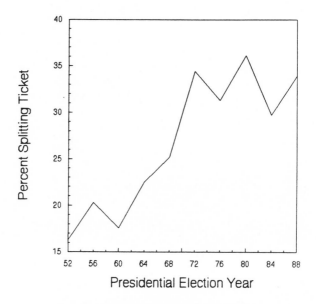

Fig. 2. Split-ticket voting, 1952–88

than half that for the Nixon reelection in 1972. Ticket splitting was on the rise
before the 1972 election—it rose in 1956, 1964, and again in 1968—but the
five most recent elections appear to be something entirely different. The step
change coincides with the McGovern candidacy, but, since ticket splitting has
not returned to its pre-1972 level, the reasons must go beyond the presence of a
particular candidate. Analytic problems arise from the fact that important
features of the American political system, in general, and the electoral system,
in particular, changed radically between 1968 and 1972— the list would include, in no particular order, changes in the nomination system, the turmoil
following the assassinations of the Kennedys and Martin Luther King, Vietnam, and the restructuring of party politics in the American South. We also
should consider the rise in the personal vote and turnover in the electorate. The
abruptness of the change is not compatible with simple population replacement, but if new generations have a different kind of partisanship than older
generations (Miller 1992b), we might expect a cohort effect to manifest itself.

We will begin with an examination of the contribution of party identification to the trend in ticket splitting. Figure 3 indicates that, aside from the
spectacular increase in ticket splitting in the years in which their party fielded
unpopular presidential candidates—1964 for Republicans, 1972 for Democrats—step increases in ticket splitting in the mid-1960s are evident for party
identifiers.[3] From 1976 on, Republicans have been slightly more likely than

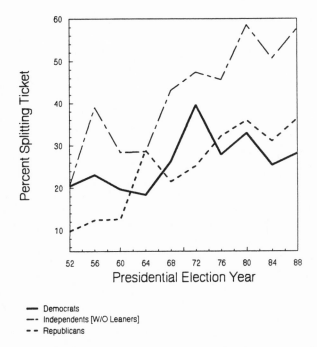

Fig. 3. Split-ticket voting: party identification groups, 1952–88

Democrats to cast divided ballots; this reverses the situation in the 1950s and coincides with the rise of the personal vote in congressional elections.

Pure independents are, not surprisingly, prone to cast divided ballots. Apart from the second Eisenhower election, their likelihood of splitting their tickets has increased steadily over the past forty years—the 1988 rate is nearly three times that of 1952. Since these voters are unanchored by partisanship, it is difficult to anticipate the sources of their divided ballots. If we were modeling election outcomes, we would feel responsible for investigating their behavior further, but in the context of the present essay, we will content ourselves with increasing our understanding of the contribution of partisans to divided government.

Turning from partisanship to age cohort, we can see that the idea of "political generation" offers potential for increasing our understanding of split-ticket voting and divided government. With one alteration, we adopt Miller's construction of the cohort variable. Warren groups the electorate into three generations: those who were age-eligible to cast their first presidential vote before 1932, the pre–New Deal cohort; those who became eligible between

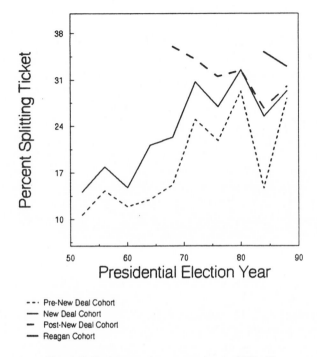

Fig. 4. Split-ticket voting: age cohorts, 1952–88

1932 and 1964, the New Deal cohort; and those who became eligible after 1964, the post–New Deal cohort (Miller 1992b). We subdivide the post–New Deal generation into those who came of age before 1980, for whom we will retain the designation post–New Deal, and those whose first opportunity to vote for president came in the 1980, 1984, or 1988 elections—the Reagan cohort.

Figure 4 indicates fairly reliable cohort differences. In every election, pre–New Dealers were less likely to split their ticket than were members of the New Deal cohort. Members of the post–New Deal cohort came into the electorate in 1968 about twice as likely to vote for candidates from different political parties in presidential and House elections as were the two older groups, but the difference disappeared during the Reagan and Bush elections. The Reagan cohort, in turn, was more willing than the next older group to vote for candidates of different parties in 1984[4] and 1988. But by 1988, cohort differences were substantially reduced.

With both party identification and political generation affecting ticket splitting, and given the shifts in the partisan composition of the electorate (Miller 1992b), further exploration will require multivariate analyses.

The Sources of Split-Ticket Voting

To assure ourselves that partisanship and age cohort are mutually independent sources of split-ticket votes and that the trend in ticket splitting is not simply a reflection of trends in partisanship and population replacement, we entered these factors, as an initial probe, in a multivariate analysis of straight and split-ticket votes. Table 1 presents this analysis for the ten presidential elections for which we have data.

Party identification includes "leaners" among the partisans; Democrats are coded "1," independents "2," and Republicans "3." The strength of partisanship is obtained by folding the seven-step measure of party identification; it ranges from "3" (strong identifiers) to "0" (pure independents). The age cohorts are coded as previously described, with the oldest group coded "1" and the youngest "4." Election years are scaled from 1952 to 1988.

The probit coefficients presented in table 1 indicate that three of the four of these variables affect the likelihood of dividing one's presidential and congressional votes between the two major parties. Over the ten elections, we find that Democrats are not significantly more likely to split their votes than are independents and Republicans. Wattenberg is correct; over these ten elections, stronger identifiers are less likely to split their tickets than are weaker partisans. Cohort also makes a difference; voters who most recently became eligible to vote are the most likely to cast a split ballot. However, these three individual attributes fail to detrend the data. After taking partisanship and age group into

TABLE 1. Sources of Ticket Splitting, 1952–88

Variables	Equation
Party identification	−0.021
	(0.024)
Strength of PID	0.253*
	(0.014)
Election year	0.013*
	(0.003)
Cohort	0.070*
	(0.022)
Constant	−25.639*
	(9.594)
% Correctly Predicted	72.952

Source: 1952–90 Cumulative Data File of the National Election Study.

Note: $N = 10,511$. Entries are probit coefficients; the dependent variable is coded "0" if candidate of the same party is supported for president, House, and Senate and "1" if the respondent votes for different parties for any of the three offices. Standard errors are in parentheses.

*$p \leq .05$.

account, we still find that more recent elections have more ticket splitting than do earlier elections.

The simplest way to detrend the data, in order to get a clearer view of the impact of the theoretical variables, is to analyze elections separately. Rather than present and discuss ten separate presidential elections, we have selected a few on which to concentrate. Before turning to a more intensive look at these elections, there is another consideration that needs to be discussed. To this point we have treated all split ballots equally—we have not distinguished voters who support their party's presidential candidate and split in their congressional vote from voters who defect to the opposition presidential candidate and remain loyal to the congressional candidates of the party with which they are identified. What is the justification for ignoring the direction of ticket splitting?

It is generally argued that Democratic identifiers split at the presidential level, while Republicans are loyal to their party's presidential candidate but defect, if they do so, in races for the House and Senate. Figure 5 presents the proportions of partisan ticket splitters defecting at the presidential level. It shows that the expected pattern generally holds: Democrats casting divided ballots are more likely to split at the presidential level than are Republican ticket splitters. In 1964, Republicans reversed the expected pattern and defected to the Johnson candidacy. However, 1964 is clearly an exception. Republicans nearly always split by defecting at the congressional level.

Democrats are more likely than Republicans to divide their votes at the presidential level. But, in recent elections, the interparty differences are smaller. In 1988, for example, four-fifths of the Democratic ticket splitters divided their ballots by supporting Republican candidates for congressional office. Even at the highest point of Democratic shunning of their presidential candidate, in 1972, a majority of Democratic ticket splitters supported McGovern for president. By and large, for partisans of both major parties, ticket splitting is produced by the attractiveness of the other party's candidates for the House and/or Senate.

These data should not cause us to lose sight of the fact that every voter in figure 5 is contributing to divided government. The candidates for national office that attract votes from the other party may vary by party and over time, but if and when we have divided government, these are the voters that make it happen, and it is their voting behavior that we need to explain.

To further carry out our explorations of ticket splitting, we will examine some cases in depth. In addition to age cohort and strength of partisanship, we will use measures of issue opinion and ideology to determine whether voters whose issue preferences and ideology are different from their fellow partisans are likely to divide their ballots. Accordingly, we expect conservative Republicans to be less likely than moderate and liberal Republicans to cast divided

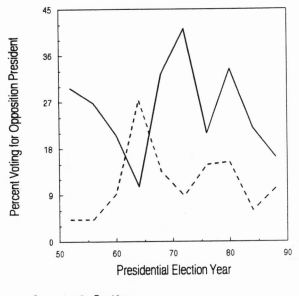

— Democrats voting Republican
- - Republicans voting Democratic

Fig. 5. Presidential vote among ticket splitters: partisan defections, 1952–88

ballots and conservative Democrats to be more likely than their fellow partisans who are liberal and moderate to find Republican candidates attractive. Initially, we will examine voting behavior in two elections that produced divided government: Democrats in 1972 and both Democrats and Republicans in 1988.

The issue opinion measures we used to index various types of conservatism clustered in the areas of race, foreign policy, New Deal liberalism, and gender politics. Three questions on civil rights and race relations were included.

The first of these asked:

[V0813] In the past few years we have heard a lot about civil rights groups working to improve the position of black people in this country. How much real change do you think there has been in the position of black people in the last few years: a lot, some, or not much at all?

The measure was scored from "1" (not much change) to "3" (a lot of change). The key phrase in the item was "real change," and apparently it registered with the electorate. Conservatives were likely to see "a lot" of real change as having taken place.

The second item in this domain asked:

[V0815] Are you in favor of desegregation, strict segregation or something in between?

The item was scored "1" (desegregation), "2" (in between), and "3" (strict segregation). There was no subtlety to the responses. Democrats favoring desegregation were expected to be less likely to split their ballots; segregation supporters were expected to vote a divided ballot. The expected relationship for Republicans was the mirror image of that for Democrats.[5]

The third race policy item was the seven-point scale on "aid to minorities." It read:

[V0831] Some people feel that the government in Washington should make every possible effort to improve the social and economic position of blacks and other minority groups. Others feel that the government should not make any special effort to help minorities because they should help themselves.

The measure was scored from "1" (belief in the idea that government should help blacks and other minorities) to "7" (belief that blacks and other minorities should help themselves). Our expectation was that self-help Democrats would be most likely to split their tickets in 1972. In 1988, we expected Republicans who believed in government aid to minorities and Democrats who favored self help would be most likely to split their tickets.

Given the prominence of Vietnam as an issue in the 1972 elections, we expected it to help us understand the voting behavior connected with divided government. Accordingly, we included the following item:

[V0826] Do you think we did the right thing in getting into the fighting in Vietnam or should we have stayed out?

The item was coded "1" (No, we should have stayed out), "2" "(it depends, not sure), and "3" "(yes, we did the right thing). Given this coding, we expected it to be positively related to defection from McGovern among Democrats in 1972. These expectations were tempered by previous research showing that, because of candidate actions, the direct impact of Vietnam was muted (Page and Brody 1972). The Vietnam item was irrelevant to, and therefore, not available for, use in 1988.

To expand our coverage of foreign policy issue opinions, we included a measure of isolationist sentiments. The following item was used:

[V0823] Do you agree or disagree with this statement: This country would be better off if we just stayed home and did not concern ourselves with problems in other parts of the world.

The item was coded "1" (agree), "2" (it depends), and "3" (disagree). It wasn't clear how preferences on this question would relate to split-ticket voting. In 1972, McGovern campaigned against the continuation of the war in Vietnam, but not against involvement in the world at large. In 1988, the responsibilities of the United States toward the "new world order" had not yet been articulated. While we could not anticipate the way that this belief would connect to ticket splitting, the importance of this sentiment (Peffley and Hurwitz 1992) argued for its inclusion.

To examine the effect of what has been called "New Deal liberalism," we included the following question:

[V0809] In general, some people feel that the government in Washington should see to it that every person has a job and a good standard of living. Others think the government should just let each person get ahead on his own. . . . Do you think the government . . .

The item was a seven-point scale. Given this response structure, we expected Republicans favoring a government guarantee would be more likely to split their tickets. We expected Democrats opposing government guarantees would be ticket splitters.

To explore the effects of gender politics, we examined two issues. The first of these determined preferences for abortion policy:

[V0837 and V0838] There has been some discussion of abortion during recent years. Which one of [these] opinions best agree with your views: [1972] 1. Abortion should never be permitted. 2. Abortion should be permitted only if the life or health of the women is in danger. 3. Abortion should be permitted if, due to personal reasons, the women would have difficulty in caring for the child. 4. Abortion should never be forbidden, since one should not require a woman to have a child she doesn't want. [1988] 1. By law, abortion should never be permitted. 2. The law should permit abortion only in case of rape, incest, or when the woman's life is in danger. 3. The law should permit abortion for reasons other than rape, incest, or danger to the woman's life, but only after the need for the abortion has been clearly established. 4. By law, a woman should always be able to obtain an abortion as a matter of personal choice.

In 1972 and 1988, we expected Democrats preferring restrictions or an outright ban on abortion would be more likely to cast a divided ballot. In 1988, we expected pro-choice Republicans would be more likely to split their tickets than pro-life Republicans.

We also included a measure of general views on women's rights and gender equality. The item read:

[V0835] Recently there has been a lot of talk about women's rights. Some people feel that women should have an equal role with men in running business, industry, and government. Others feel that a women's place is in the home.

The item was a collapsed seven-point scale coded "1" (women and men should have an equal role), "2" (neutral), and "3" (women's place is in the home). We

TABLE 2.   Sources of Ticket Splitting, Democrats, 1972

Variables	Equation
Strength of PID	−0.128*
	(0.089)
Age cohort	0.105
	(0.105)
Change in Blacks' position	0.016
	(0.106)
Government guaranteed job	0.066**
	(0.035)
Favor segregation	0.355**
	(0.104)
Should have stayed out of Vietnam	−0.007
	(0.067)
Abortion availability	−0.045
	(0.068)
Aid to minorities	−0.050
	(0.086)
Role for women	−0.072
	(0.079)
Isolationism	0.044
	(0.091)
Conservatism	0.265**
	(0.065)
Constant	−1.631**
	(0.585)
% Correctly predicted	65.870

Source: See table 1.

Note: $N = 460$. Party groups include "leaners." Entries are probit coefficients; the depenent variable is coded "0" if candidate of the same party is supported for president, House, and Senate and "1" if the respondent votes for different paties for any of the three offices. Standard errors are in parentheses.

*$.05 \leq p \leq .10$. **$p \leq .05$.

expected Democrats preferring gender equality to be less likely to split their ticket in 1972 and 1988 and Republicans preferring gender equality to be more likely to cast a split ballot in 1988.[6]

To get at the impact of the personal vote for incumbent members of Congress, we used a collapsed version of V1004, coded "0" if the incumbent was a Republican and "1" if the incumbent was a Democrat.[7] We also employed a general measure of ideology—V0801—drawn from thermometer measures of opinions of liberals and conservatives.

With these measures of issue preference and ideology, we can proceed with the exploration of ticket splitting in the three case studies.

Table 2 details the analyses of ticket splitting among Democrats in 1972, and table 3 presents the analyses for Democrats and Republicans in 1988. We will begin with the Democrats in 1972.

TABLE 3. Sources of Ticket Splitting, 1988

Variables	Equation for Democrats	Equation for Republicans
Strength of PID	−0.172**	−0.007
	(0.093)	(0.094)
Age cohort	0.013	0.029
	(0.110)	(0.110)
Change in Blacks' position	−0.091	0.008
	(0.107)	(0.112)
Government guaranteed job	0.75**	−0.029
	(0.036)	(0.042)
Abortion availability	0.029	0.154**
	(0.074)	(0.078)
Aid to minorities	0.175**	−0.145*
	(0.091)	(0.103)
Role for women	0.192**	0.144*
	(0.112)	(0.106)
Isolationism	0.057	−0.043
	(0.082)	(0.094)
Conservatism	0.132**	−0.301**
	(0.079)	(0.110)
Incumbent running	−0.738**	0.792**
	(0.165)	(0.150)
Constant	−1.036*	0.314
	(0.660)	(0.687)
% Correctly predicted	71.240	64.458

Source: See table 1.

Note: N for Democrats = 379. N for Republicans = 332. Party groups include "leaners." Entries are probit coefficients; the dependent variable is coded "0" if candidate of the same party is supported for president, House, and Senate and "1" if the respondent votes for different parties for any of the three offices. Standard errors are in parentheses.

*.05 ≤ *p* ≤ .10. **p ≤ .05.

Considered as a whole, this analysis supports the expectation that conservative Democrats would be more likely to cast a divided ballot in 1972 than would liberal or moderate Democrats. More specifically, Democrats who said that each person should get ahead on her or his own, who favored strict segregation, and who rated conservatives more positively than liberals were those most likely to be ticket splitters in 1972. The other measures of issue opinion were not significantly related to the likelihood of casting a divided ballot; these included some issues that were very prominent in 1972. Vietnam opinion and attitudes toward abortion and gender equality did not help us to understand ticket splitting in 1972. Abortion and gender equality were not prominent issues in the election campaigns. Vietnam certainly was a major theme, but it did not help us explain defection by Democrats. This may be an artifact of the relationship of Vietnam to liberalism/conservatism, and not a substantive finding.[8]

Age cohort failed to achieve statistical significance in this case. It appears that, in 1972, age cohort was a surrogate for issue positions. When issue preferences were entered directly into the analyses, cohort no longer played an explanatory role.

As expected, weaker Democrats and Democrats who were conservative on racial and New Deal policy issues were the likely ticket splitters in 1972. The McGovern candidacy crystallized the policy concerns of Democratic conservatives, and they expressed these concerns at the polls.

Like 1972, the 1988 presidential and congressional elections also led to divided government. About a third of the Republican and a quarter of the Democratic voters cast their ballot for the candidates of different parties at the presidential and congressional levels (see fig. 3 above). Figure 5 shows that, although Democrats were twice as likely as Republicans to vote for the other major party's presidential candidate, the overwhelming majority of ticket splitters in both parties voted for the other party's candidate in the House and/or Senate.

The analysis of split-ticket voting in 1988 is presented in table 3. The variables entered into these two equations were, by and large, those we used in our analysis of ticket splitting in 1972.[9] To capture the effect of factors associated with the personal vote, we added a dummy for the partisanship of the member of Congress if the incumbent was seeking reelection. In the Democratic equation, the incumbency variable was scored "0" if the incumbent was a Republican seeking reelection; in the Republican equation, the incumbency variable was scored "1" if the incumbent seeking reelection was a Democrat; otherwise it was scored "0."

These two cases indicate that ticket splitting is a matter of odd person out. Party identifiers who are ideologically different from the majority of their fellow partisans and/or those who express issue preferences different than those held by a majority of those identified with the same political party are the ones likely to split their ticket. The issues primed by a particular election campaign are the ones most likely to distinguish ticket-splitting partisans from those voting a straight party ticket.

Republicans who cast a divided ballot in 1988—primarily by voting for Democrats at the congressional level—were more liberal than their fellow Republicans. As expected, Republicans casting divided ballots were attracted to incumbent congressional Democrats. But they were also likely to be pro-choice, to believe that the government should aid minorities, and to feel more positive toward liberals and less positive toward conservatives than Republicans who did not split their tickets. Clearly, these Republicans appeared, to a greater degree than other Republicans, to share the policy preferences and ideology of Democrats in Congress. It is interesting that neither strength of Republican partisanship nor the age cohort to which the voter belonged helped us to understand ticket splitting in 1988. In this analysis, it appears that both strength of identification and age cohort were surrogates for issue opinions.

In most respects, Democratic ticket splitters were the mirror image of Republican ticket splitters in 1988. They were more conservative than their fellow Democrats. Democrats casting divided ballots were more likely to express the opinion that Americans in general, and African Americans in particular, should get ahead on their own and without assistance from the federal government. They were more likely to express the view that "a women's place is in the home" than were Democrats who voted for their party's candidates for president, House, and Senate. They were more likely to rate conservatives more positively than liberals and to find attractive the Republican member of the House of Representatives in their district.

The one difference between Democrats and Republicans in the 1988 elections appeared in the effect of the strength of identification of ticket splitting. As we have seen, issue opinion and ideology reduce to insignificance the impact of strength of partisanship on Republican ticket splitting. Taking these matters into account does not exhaust the effect of strength of partisanship for Democrats; weaker Democrats, irrespective of ideology and issue preferences, were more likely than stronger Democrats to cast a divided ballot in 1988.

Discussion

The 1972 and 1988 elections are not unique; other elections which produced divided government show results essentially similar to 1972 and 1988.[10] These case studies point to the conclusion that split-ticket voting and, when it occurs, divided government are grounded in the issue opinions and ideology of individual voters. Partisans who cast a divided ballot are likely to hold issue positions different from their party's median voter—more conservative than the median Democrat and more liberal than the median Republican. Our findings are generally consistent with the notion that specific issue and ideological differences matter to the extent that the issues are primed by the presidential campaigns and/or by the events of the recent past. Campaigns do not only activate partisanship; they can also increase the relevance of differences between the individual and his or her political party.[11]

We have considered ticket splitting in national elections irrespective of the direction in which voters vote away from their partisanship. But, most of the time, the direction of the split is toward the incumbent member of Congress of the other major party. However, taking account of the attractiveness of the incumbent does not reduce the effects of issue opinions and ideology—partisans who prefer policies or who take ideological stands different from the center of gravity of their political party are those most likely to cast divided ballots. In other words, issue and ideological distance from the party's median voter matters. In 1972, it led conservative Democrats to support the Nixon candidacy. In 1988, it led voters in both parties to vote in favor of the other party's congressional incumbents. And in 1964, it led moderate and liberal Republicans to favor Johnson over Goldwater.[12]

Taking into account strength of identification, issue opinions, ideology, and the attractiveness of incumbent members of Congress eliminates the direct effect of age cohort on ticket splitting. However, as figure 6 suggests, the relationship between age cohort and strength of identification means that the absence of cohort as a significant factor in our case studies does not fairly represent its indirect effect on ticket splitting. Over this period of electoral history, younger cohorts came into the electorate with a weaker average strength of identification than that of older cohorts. Population replacement has led to more ticket splitting, because younger voters are less partisan than were older voters when they were young.

The link between age cohort and weakened partisanship does not come with a ready explanation, but Warren Miller's (1992b) conclusion that the circumstances in which an age cohort receives its political socialization affects its partisanship must be near the mark. Strength of partisanship appears to be stable among the members of a cohort; only the post–New Deal cohort exhibits consistent change over the period, but even after these increases it is still weaker than the two older cohorts.[13]

Population processes have tended to replace older, stronger identifiers with younger, weaker partisans. This means an electorate more vulnerable to campaign appeals and/or more willing to put issue preferences and ideology ahead of party in its voting decisions. These developments have increased the likelihood of divided government, but the 1992 elections show that increased likelihood is not certainty. In advance of the arrival of data from the 1992 National Election Study, we cannot know with certainty what led to the

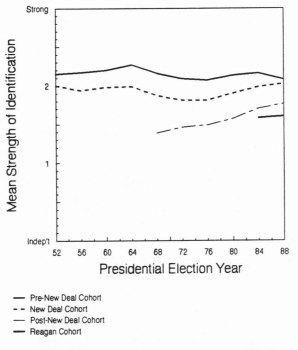

Fig. 6. Strength of partisanship: age cohorts, 1952–88

Democratic victory. But we will not be surprised to find that socially moderate, weaker—perhaps younger—Republicans were an important part of the Clinton coalition. Whether or not they were also split-ticket voters will depend on the home style of the incumbent representative and senator and his or her ideological distance from the voter.

N O T E S

Thanks are due to R. Douglas Rivers for invaluable assistance with this project. The data used in this paper are drawn from the 1952–1990 Cumulative Data File of the National Election Study and were made available through the Inter-University Consortium for Political and Social Research; neither the NES, the ICPSR, nor Doug are responsible for our use of the data or the conclusions we reach.

1. Between 1952 and 1988, the proportion of pure independents increased from 6 percent of identifiers to 10.8 percent; among ticket splitters it increased from 6.7 percent to 11 percent.

2. Over the ten elections, about a third (35 percent) of those who split their tickets voted for the same party for House and Senate and a different party for president;

another third (34 percent) voted for the presidential and senatorial candidates of the same party and a different party for the House; the balance (31 percent) matched their House and presidential vote and voted for a senator of the other party. There is some variation in these proportions from election to election, but there is no obvious pattern or trend.

3. Here we use the definition of party identification proposed by Wolfinger and his colleagues (Keith et al. 1991) and include "leaners" among the partisans.

4. With only seven members of this cohort in the 1980 sample, we are reluctant to present the 1980 percentage.

5. This item was not used in 1988, but where it is available we will use it.

6. Ethel Kline (1984) would lead us to expect a more complex relationship between gender issues and the vote. She finds, inter alia, that male support of feminist issues is an expression of liberalism. By contrast, women's support of feminist issues is more than liberalism—it has an experiential component as well. This would argue for an interaction term combining gender and issue opinion. Tests of this possibility fail to produce a statistically significant interaction term.

7. This measure is unavailable in 1972.

8. Among Democrats in 1972, Vietnam opinion and conservatism were correlated. As we move from most liberal (coded 1) to most conservative (coded 5), the proportion expressing the opinion that it was a mistake to get involved in Vietnam in the first place decreased monotonically from 76.3 percent to 44.4 percent, and the percentages expressing the view that it was not a mistake increased monotonically from 15.1 percent to 45.7 percent.

9. The NES did not ask the segregation question [V0815] in 1988, and by 1988, Vietnam was no longer relevant.

10. Analyses of the 1980 and 1984 elections, despite differences in detail, indicate that ticket-splitting Democrats were more conservative and pro-life than Democrats casting a straight party ballot and Republicans were the mirror image of the Democrats.

11. It would not surprise us to find that, inter alia, experienced and well-financed congressional incumbents are skilled at crafting messages that appeal to identifiers with the opposition party whose policy positions fall on their party's side of the median.

12. In 1964, 26.6 percent of identified Republicans chose Johnson over Goldwater. Sixty percent of these voted a split ballot; 40 percent voted a straight Democratic ticket. Taking account of ticket splitting, we find that Johnson supporters among Republican identifiers tended to be weaker identifiers and to be more liberal on New Deal issues and opposed to segregation.

13. Over the twenty years for which we have a sufficient number of observations, the post–New Deal cohort's average strength of partisanship has strengthened nearly four-tenths of a scale point (from 1.39 to 1.76); the t-ratio for this change in means is 4.18.

REFERENCES

Abramson, Paul R. 1989. "Generations and Political Change in the United States." *Research in Political Sociology* 4:235–80.

Abramson, Paul R., and Ronald Inglehart. 1992. "Generational Replacement and Value Change in Eight West European Societies." *British Journal of Political Science* 22:183–228.

Alford, John, and David Brady. 1989. "Personal and Partisan Advantage in U.S. Congressional Elections, 1846–1986." In *Congress Reconsidered,* 4th ed., ed. Lawrence Dodd and Bruce Oppenheimer. Washington, D.C.: Congressional Quarterly Press.

Beck, Paul A., Lawrence Baum, Aage R. Clausen, and Charles E. Smith, Jr. 1992. "Patterns and Sources of Ticket-Splitting in Subpresidential Voting." *American Political Science Review* 86:916–28.

Brody, Richard A., and Lawrence Rothenberg. 1988. "The Instability of Partisanship: An Analysis of the 1980 Election." *British Journal of Political Science* 18:445–65.

Campbell, Angus, and Warren E. Miller. 1957. "The Motivational Basis of Straight and Split-Ticket Voting." *American Political Science Review* 51:293–312.

Jacobson, Gary C. 1990. *The Electoral Origins of Divided Government: Competition in U.S. House Races, 1946–1988.* Boulder, Colo.: Westview Press.

———. 1991. "The Persistence of Democratic House Majorities." In *The Politics of Divided Government,* ed. Gary W. Cox and Samuel Kernell. Boulder, Colo.: Westview Press.

Keith, Bruce E., David B. Magleby, Candice J. Nelson, Elizabeth Orr, Mark C. Westley, and Raymond E. Wolfinger. 1991. *The Myth of the Independent Voter.* Berkeley, Calif.: University of California Press.

Klein, Ethel. 1984. *Gender Politics.* Cambridge, Mass.: Harvard University Press.

Klingemann, Hans-D., and Martin P. Wattenberg. 1992. "Decaying versus Developing Party Systems: A Comparison of Party Images in the United States and West Germany." *British Journal of Political Science* 22:131–49.

Miller, Warren E. 1991. "Party Identification, Realignment, and Party Voting: Back to Basics." American Political Science Review 85:557–68.

———. 1992a. "The Puzzle Transformed: Explaining Declining Turnout." *Political Behavior* 14:1–43.

———. 1992b. "Generational Changes and Party Identification." *Political Behavior* 14:335–52.

Page, Benjamin I., and Richard A. Brody. 1972. "Policy Voting and the Electoral Process: The Vietnam War Issue." *American Political Science Review* 66:979–95.

Peffley, Mark, and Jon Hurwitz. 1992. "International Events and Foreign Policy Belief Systems: Public Responses to Changing Soviet-American Relations." *American Journal of Political Science* 36:431–61.

Petrocik, John R. 1991. "Divided Government: Is It All in the Campaigns?" In *The Politics of Divided Government,* ed. Gary W. Cox and Samuel Kernell. Boulder, Colo.: Westview Press.

Wattenberg, Martin P. 1991. "The Republican Presidential Advantage in the Age of Party Disunity." In *The Politics of Divided Government,* ed. Gary W. Cox and Samuel Kernell. Boulder, Colo.: Westview Press.

The Context of Voting

CHAPTER 8

Are British Elections Becoming
More "Presidential"?

Ivor Crewe and Anthony King

Almost every American, confronted with the phenomenon of a British general election, is tempted to turn it in his or her mind into an American presidential election—that is, to personalize it, to see it as a contest between two political leaders rather than one between two political parties. The British question "Which party will win?" becomes the American question "Which candidate will win?" The Conservatives versus Labour becomes, in most Americans' minds, Churchill versus Attlee, Heath versus Wilson, or Major versus Kinnock.

The temptation to turn British general elections into American presidential elections is understandable. It is always tempting to construe another country's politics in terms of one's own, and it is always tempting, too, to take the innumerable complicated phenomena of modern politics—electoral systems, party systems, the political parties' programs, their images, their records in office—and reduce them to the personalities of individuals and the clashes and contests between them. The British, in considering their own elections, are far from immune to this temptation. On the one hand, they solemnly insist on the primacy of parties and policies over personalities in British electoral politics; on the other, they themselves frequently discuss British elections in personality terms. In view of the importance of individual leaders in the electoral politics of other countries, and in view of the fact that the personalities and styles of British party leaders must play *some* part, however small, in influencing the electoral fortunes of the British parties, it is odd that very little scholarly attention has been paid to attempting to assess just how important the party leaders in Britain are. There is a small body of relevant literature, and we shall refer to it as we go along, but, remarkably, there exists no book on the subject, or even a journal article that seeks to address the main issues in a general way. This chapter tentatively undertakes that task.

Before we proceed, however, one important point needs to be made. In a party-centered political system like the British, a party leader can influence the electoral fortunes of his party in either or both of two ways. First, he can influence the political party he leads—its ideology, its policies, its image—in such a way that the party as a whole, including himself as leader, is made more or less attractive to voters; that is, he can influence voters indirectly via his influence within his party. Second, he can influence voters directly, via the effects that his own personality, characteristics, and style have on them, irrespective of the image of his party as a whole. To be sure, personality images and party images are bound to affect one another, and the leaders' so-called direct effects on voters are largely mediated in practice by television and the press. Nevertheless, it is perfectly possible to imagine a leader doing wonders for his party indirectly, while at the same time being a considerable handicap to it in terms of his direct relationship with the electorate.

Neil Kinnock, the Labour leader between 1983 and 1992, appears, on the face of it, to be a case in point. During the nine years he was leader, especially during the period following Labour's 1987 election defeat, Labour transformed its policies and image in a way that undoubtedly enhanced its standing with voters; and Kinnock is widely given the major part of the credit for bringing about this transformation (Hughes and Wintour 1990; Seyd 1992). Kinnock, in this sense, was an electoral plus for his party. But at the same time, Kinnock, during most of his period as leader and certainly during the 1987 and 1992 election campaigns, was not held in high esteem by the great majority of the British public. In this sense, Kinnock was almost certainly an electoral minus for Labour.

In this chapter, we focus on the party leaders' direct effects on voters, via their personalities and personal styles; but the possibility that leaders may also have indirect effects, and that these indirect effects may actually outweigh the direct effects, should not be lost sight of. Any account that, like this one, focuses solely on personality and style is bound to be somewhat partial.

Setting and History

Leaders matter in British electoral politics. Leaders do not matter in British electoral politics. Both statements have a certain surface plausibility; there is much to be said a priori for both of them.

The view that leaders' personalities can have—or might be expected to have—a direct bearing on British electoral outcomes has been most succinctly stated by Butler and Stokes (1974, chap. 17). They point out that party leaders are likely to fulfill all the requirements that have to be fulfilled before any political issue can affect voters' decisions. Voters are aware of the party leaders. They know something about them. They correctly associate them with their parties. Voters also typically have views, often quite strongly held views, about the various leaders (not surprisingly, in view of the fact that most British party leaders have been conspicuous public figures for a considerable number of years). In addition, it seems reasonable to suppose that voters' opinions about the party leaders are liable on some occasions to be skewed, with a substantial majority of voters preferring the leader of one major party to that of the other. If they do, then judgments about the two leaders could influence not merely individual voters' decisions, but the outcome of whole elections. Butler and Stokes conclude that Harold Wilson, for instance, was a net asset to the Labour party throughout the period of their studies.

The contrary view—that the personal qualities of leaders are typically of little importance in British elections—has never been stated in quite such a straightforward way. Rather, it is implicit in the great bulk of the British voting behavior literature. Most of the major writings on voting in Britain focus on such phenomena as party identification, the links between partisanship and social location, the parties' perceived competence, and their stands on current issues. In sharp contrast to the equivalent literature on the United States, the British literature does not focus on the leaders' personalities and styles and has very little to say about them. For example, the latest volume emanating from the British Election Studies, *Understanding Political Change* (Heath et al. 1991) contains only three references to Margaret Thatcher, despite the fact that it covers the years 1979–87, and it makes no attempt to assess her impact on the Conservative party's electoral fortunes during those years. The implication is that the party leaders are best understood as merely parts, and usually small parts, of competing political packages that have party-political labels firmly attached to them. The parties, not the leaders, are what matter.

The historical record, taken at face value, tends to support this second view: that the party leader's role in elections in Britain is quite limited. There have been thirteen general elections in Britain since the war. In connection with eleven of them, we have not merely the record of how people actually voted, but also a body of opinion poll evidence relating to the relative standings of the leaders of the two major parties. As table 1 shows, in eight of the eleven cases, the party of the leader whom the public held in higher esteem duly won; but in three of the cases, 1945, 1970, and 1979, the party led by the person whom people said they preferred to see as prime minister in fact lost. The record thus gives the impression that British voters, confronted with a choice between voting on the basis of which party they prefer and voting on the basis of which party leader they prefer, are inclined to put their party preference ahead of their leadership preference.

It would be tempting, on this basis, to conclude that British elections are not presidential elections and simply to leave it at that. But of course such a conclusion, while possibly correct, would be egregiously superficial. We need to dig deeper in order to discover how far British party leaders' personalities

TABLE 1.   Leader Preferences and Election Outcomes, 1945–92

General Election	Leader Preferred by Voters	Party Gaining Plurality of Votes	Leader Preferences, Votes Consistent?
1945	Churchill, Con.[a]	Labour	no
1950	—	—	—
1951	—	—	—
1955	Eden, Con.[b]	Conservative	yes
1959	Macmillan, Con.[c]	Conservative	yes
1964	Wilson, Lab.[d]	Labour	yes
1966	Wilson, Lab.[e]	Labour	yes
1970	Wilson, Lab.	Conservative	no
Feb. 1974	Heath, Con.	Conservative	yes
Oct. 1974	Wilson, Lab.	Labour	yes
1979	Callaghan, Lab.	Conservative	no
1983	Thatcher, Con.	Conservative	yes
1987	Thatcher, Con.	Conservative	yes
1992	Major, Con.	Conservative	yes

Source: Gallup 1976; *Gallup Political Index.*

Note: Except where indicated below, leader preferences are measured by the responses to the question "Who would make the better prime minister— . . . or . . . ?" In the case of the elections from 1970 onward, polling organizations other than Gallup, notably NOP, have reported the responses to identical or similar questions, and their findings have been broadly in line with Gallup's.

[a]In 1945, the Gallup Poll did not include any questions asking voters to compare Winston Churchill and Clement Attlee, the Labour leader, directly; but a few weeks before the election, which his party lost, Churchill had an approval rating of 83 percent (Gallup 1976, 109), while fewer than half of Gallup's sample thought that, if Labour were returned to power, Attlee should be prime minister (1976, 112).

[b]As in 1945, no question asking voters to compare the two major party leaders directly was posed, but Sir Anthony Eden's approval rating as prime minister was 73 percent (Gallup 1976, 347), and, asked who would be the best man to lead Britain in any high-level talks between the West and Russia, a mere 20 percent cited Attlee (1976, 347).

[c]Again, Gallup's respondents were not asked to make a direct comparison between the two main party leaders, but they were asked, separately, "How strongly do you feel about having Mr. Macmillan/Mr. Gaitskell as Prime Minister?" The proportion saying they were "very favorable" or "favorable" to a Harold Macmillan premiership was 67 percent. The proportion responding in the same way about Hugh Gaitskell was only 48 percent.

[d]Gallup did not ask the "best prime minister" question in 1964, but NOP did—and consistently gave Harold Wilson a narrow lead.

[e]No polling organization asked respondents to choose directly between Harold Wilson and Edward Heath, but Gallup asked respondents to rate each of the two leaders on a number of items, and Wilson came out well ahead of Heath on all of the favorable ones (*Gallup Political Index* no. 71, March 1966, 33).

and styles influence both individual British voters' decisions and the overall outcomes of British elections. After all, the Conservatives in 1945 might have fared even worse if Winston Churchill had not been their leader, and the Conservatives in 1979, 1983, and 1987 might have done even better (or worse) if their leader had been someone other than the formidable Margaret Thatcher. The historical record by itself is not sufficient.

Analytic Strategies and Data

The political science literature on the role that leaders and candidates play in influencing voters' decisions—most of it relating to the United States, but some of it relating to Britain and other countries—adopts one or the other of two broad analytic strategies. The two are complementary, rather than conflictual (and it is hard to see how any other could be devised). For purposes of shorthand, we will call one the improved prediction strategy and the other the thought experiment strategy.

The improved prediction strategy is the one used by Shanks and Miller in their pathbreaking articles in the *British Journal of Political Science* in 1982, 1990, and 1991. This approach asks, in effect, the following question. Suppose that we know a great deal about an individual, about his or her social location, ideological and partisan predispositions, policy preferences, and evaluations of current conditions. What does it add to our ability to predict how the individual will vote to know something about his or her judgments about the personalities and styles of the major parties' leaders (or, as in the United States, their presidential candidates)? In other words, in this approach the predictive capacity of voters' views about leaders' and candidates' characteristics is weighed against the predictive capacity of their social location and their other political predispositions and attitudes.

Shanks and Miller distinguish sharply between the prediction of the votes of individuals and the contribution that perceived candidate personality traits may, or may not, make to determining the overall outcomes of elections. They conclude that favorable evaluations of Ronald Reagan, as compared with Jimmy Carter and Walter Mondale, had a considerable bearing on individual voters' decisions in 1980 and 1984, but that, perhaps surprisingly, they contributed little to the overall outcomes of the presidential elections in those two years. With regard to the 1988 election, some of the perceived candidate traits of George Bush and Michael Dukakis likewise appear to have had some bearing on individual voters' decisions, but very little in determining the overall election outcome.

The alternative strategy, the thought experiment strategy, approaches the problem from a different angle. It weighs the appeals of individual party leaders (negative or positive) not against other aspects of their party's appeal (or lack of it) to individual voters, but against the appeal that their party would have had if it had been led by someone else. That "someone else" could be some idealized party leader, or another leader drawn from the same political party, or even the leader of one of the other parties. The phrase "thought experiment" is appropriate in this context for the obvious reason that the party in question, at the election in question, *was* led by its then leader and was *not* led by someone else. In an even more straightforward way than the other one, this approach takes the analyst into the realm of counterfactuals.

This second approach is implicit in the "trial heat" questions that American polling organizations frequently ask during presidential primary campaigns; and the British polls similarly ask people from time to time how they would vote (or would have voted) if, say, John Smith had replaced Neil Kinnock as Labour leader, or Margaret Thatcher, rather than John Major, had been Conservative leader in April 1992. A good example of this approach, as used by political scientists, can be found in Bean and Mughan's 1989 article in the *American Political Science Review*. Bean and Mughan compared voters' assessments of the two major party leaders at each of two parliamentary elections—Margaret Thatcher (Conservative) and Michael Foot (Labour) in Britain in 1983, and Bob Hawke (Labor) and John Howard (Liberal) in Australia in 1987—and asked themselves what the results of the two elections would have been if each of the two main parties in each of the two countries had been led, not by its actual leader, but by the leader of the other main party in the country.

Contrary to the findings of most studies of parliamentary elections conducted on the improved prediction principle (for example, Graetz and McAllister 1987), Bean and Mughan conclude that the two pairs of party leaders in Britain and Australia made a substantial difference to the 1983 and 1987 election outcomes. They suggest that, if British voters in 1983 had ascribed the same personal qualities to Michael Foot as they in fact ascribed to Margaret Thatcher (in other words, if Michael Foot had *been,* in effect, Margaret Thatcher), the Conservatives would still have beaten Labour, but the gap between the two parties would have been narrowed by some six percentage points. In the Australian case, they go so far as to suggest that the 1987 result might actually have been reversed: that if the Liberal party had been led by a leader who was a clone of Bob Hawke in terms of his personality traits, it might actually have defeated Labor instead of itself being heavily defeated.

The advantages and disadvantages of these two analytic approaches are readily apparent. The improved prediction approach is more firmly rooted in the data. It says no more than that voters who, other things being equal, hold a high opinion of a party's leader or candidate are more likely to vote for that party than voters who do not hold such a view (assuming that there is any kind of party leader effect). The improved prediction approach, in this sense, is a relatively safe one; those who use it seldom venture predictions about how the elections they analyze would have turned out on alternative party leader or candidate scenarios. On the other hand, the thought experiment approach, while analytically riskier (and not, ultimately, subject to having its findings proved or disproved one way or the other), has the advantage of directly addressing a class of political questions that most people are interested in, namely, "How would election X have turned out if A or B, rather than C, had been the party leader or the presidential candidate at the time?" It is this strategy that will mainly be employed in the analysis later in this chapter.

The data themselves, however, present considerable problems. The main problem is simply that there are so few of them. Because students of British voting behavior have been so little interested in the impact of party leaders on voters and elections, most of them have chosen not to ask more than a very small number of survey questions about them. In the eight British election studies that have been conducted in the direct line of succession from the original Butler-Stokes survey of 1964 (Butler and Stokes 1974), there have been only two, those of 1983 and 1987 (Heath, Jowell, and Curtice 1985; Heath et al. 1991) in which more than one question has been asked about each of the major party leaders. In most cases, one question, and only one, has been thought sufficient.

Partly as a consequence, the questions that have been asked have tended to yield simple evaluative scores, with little in the way of supporting evidence showing why people evaluate the leaders in the way they do. Only the 1983 and 1987 studies, already mentioned, seek to explore the sources of voter evaluations. The result is that, although matters have improved somewhat in recent years, what Miller and Levitin said a number of years ago about the United States (1976, 41) remains broadly true of Great Britain: "Although issues, candidates, and parties are all familiar rubrics for classifying the determinants of the vote, little attention—either conceptual or empirical—has been given to assessing public response to the attributes of the candidates." The only partial exceptions in the British case are Bean and Mughan (1989) and Stewart and Clarke (1992).

The final problem is that the data yielded by the various British studies are not easily comparable over time. As table 2 shows, the same leader-related sequence of questions was asked in 1964, 1966, and 1970; but then a different sequence was asked in February 1974, October 1974, and 1979. Although more detailed questions were asked in 1983 and 1987, they were not, in fact, the same questions. Shanks and Miller, in their analyses of the American studies of the 1980s, had to contend with a number of changes in the relevant parts of the NES interview schedule, but the U.S. NES studies are a model of stability compared with their British counterparts.

The Concept of "Presidentialization"

The fact that the available data are hard to compare over time is particularly frustrating, because if strictly comparable data were available, we would be in a better position to address a question that invariably arises in connection with

TABLE 2. Leader-related Questions Asked in Butler-Stokes and Subsequent Election Studies

1964–70

"Is there anything in particular that you like about Sir Alec Douglas-Home [Edward Heath, Harold Wilson]? Anything else?"

"Is there anything in particular that you don't like about Sir Alec Douglas-Home [Heath, etc]? Anything else?"

[Overall net evaluation scores for each leader consist of the number of positive mentions (up to five) minus the number of negative mentions (up to five). Preferred party leader is the one with the largest positive net evaluation score.]

February 1974–1979

"Let us say that you gave each of the parties a mark out of ten points—a mark according to how much or little you like it. You can give each party any mark from 0 out of 10 for least liked to 10 out of 10 for most liked."

[Interviewer proceeds to ask about the three parties (and also SNP/Plaid Cymru in Scotland/Wales).]

"Now lets turn to how much you *personally like* some leading politicians."

"What mark out of 10 would you give Mr. Edward Heath? And what mark out of 10 would you give Mr. Harold Wilson?" [also asked about Jeremy Thorpe and Enoch Powell].

1983

"Looking at this card, on the whole how effective or ineffective do you think Mrs. Thatcher is as a *prime minister?*"

"And on the whole how effective do you think Mr. Foot would have been as a prime minister?" [also asked about Jenkins and Steel].

"Still think of these four party leaders: at the time of the general election, which one do you think would have been the prime minister most able to unite the nation / most likely to get things done / most likely to improve Britain's standing abroad / with most concern for all groups in society / would get most out of a team / most in touch with ordinary people's problems?"

"Which of the qualities on this card would you say Mrs. Thatcher has? (caring / determined / shrewd / likeable as a person / tough / listens to reason / sticks to principles)" [also asked about Foot, Jenkins, and Steel].

[The 1983 survey was not analyzed for this chapter.]

1987

"Now some similar questions, but this time about some of the main party *leaders*. Would you describe Mrs. Thatcher as good at getting things done / extreme or moderate / looks after one class or all classes / capable or not capable of being a strong leader / caring or uncaring / likely to unite or divide the nation / likeable or not likeable as a person?" [also asked of Kinnock, Steel, and Owen]

[The number of positive attributes (out of a maximum of seven) attributed by the respondent was weighted by 1.4285 ($10 \div 7$) to produce a score ranging from 0 to 10.]

the role of party leaders in British elections: Have British elections in recent years become more "presidential"?

The view that they have is very widely held. The parties, it is said, build their campaigns around their leaders to a far greater extent than they once did; and the media's focus on the leaders during campaigns is nowadays intense. At a time, moreover, when the bonds of party loyalty are loosening in Britain, as they are in the United States, the leaders' individual personalities and styles might be expected to make a greater impact than in the past on voters' final decisions. The Thatcher years certainly reinforced the idea that British electoral politics was becoming more presidential, with Margaret Thatcher, both in government and during election campaigns, functioning as a kind of super president. Kavanagh, in his survey of changes in electioneering methods in Britain, says that "elections are more leader-centred" (Kavanagh 1992, 84), and Denver, in his textbook on voting behavior in Britain, notes that British general elections are increasingly "portrayed as contests between candidates for Prime Minister rather than between political parties competing for control of government" (Denver 1989, 88–89).

The notion of presidentialization is thus in the air. Newspaper columnists and television commentators more or less take it for granted. But what exactly does "presidentialization" in this context mean? A few moments' reflection suggests that it could mean at least five different things.

In the first place, presidentialization could refer to an increased tendency on the political parties' part to focus their campaigning efforts on their leaders, and likewise to an increased tendency on the media's part to present the events of the campaign in a leader-centered way. It is almost universally assumed in Britain that both the parties' campaigns and the media's coverage of them have become more presidential in this sense, but in fact there is precious little evidence that this is so. On the contrary, a content analysis of the campaign coverage in the main television news bulletins since the 1964 general election (see table 3) suggests that television coverage of British campaigns is not significantly more leader-centered now than it was in the 1960s, and that, if anything (despite Thatcher), there was a decline in leader-centeredness during the 1980s compared with the previous decade. A content analysis of the parties' own election broadcasts would almost certainly point in the same direction. The notion that, at the campaigning level, British electoral politics have become more presidential is, at best, not proven.

Presidentialization could refer, secondly, to any presidentialization of the parties' images that may have occurred—that is, to any tendency for voters, thinking about the parties, to do so increasingly in terms of their leaders' personal attributes and styles. Klingemann and Wattenberg (1992) found in West Germany, for example, that between 1972 and 1987 an increasing proportion of voters asked what they liked and disliked about the main parties

TABLE 3.   Leaders' Prominence in Television News Bulletins

	1964	1966	1970	Feb. 1974	Oct. 1974	1979	1983	1987
	Percentage of Quotations of All Conservative and Labour Politicians on News Bulletins Devoted to Quotations of the Two Parties' Leaders							
Conservative	35.0	59.4	51.2	—	50.4	43.6	46.7	44.4
Labour	47.4	46.2	53.3	—	55.1	39.7	32.6	54.3
	Percentage of Total Air Time Given to All Conservative and Labour Politicians Devoted to the Two Parties' Leaders							
Conservative	—	70	60	60	51	62	48	47
Labour	—	56	56	59	51	64	43	57

Source: Harrison 1965, 170; Harrison 1966, 130; Harrison 1971, 207–8; Harrison 1974, 149; Harrison 1975, 142–43; Pilsworth 1980, 209; Harrison 1984, 160–61; Harrison 1988, 144–45.

Note: Data are for news bulletins on main BBC1 and ITV.

responded in terms that included mentions of the parties' leaders. Such identifications between the parties and their leaders might be purely nominal (in the way, say, that the British Conservative party is associated with the color blue); but they might also represent an increasing tendency to judge the parties as a whole in terms of the personal traits, both positive and negative, of their leaders. Unfortunately, no data bearing on this point with regard to Great Britain are available for recent elections.

A third possible meaning of presidentialization might be that voters do not increasingly perceive parties in terms of their leaders, but, rather, come increasingly to form two separate sets of political judgments: one relating to the parties, the other to their leaders. Far from the parties and leaders becoming more associated in people's minds, they might become less associated. If this were to happen, individual voters' judgments of the parties and their leaders might, by accident, tend to fluctuate together; but, much more probably, there would be a secular increase in the proportion of voters who said they identified with one party (or supported it, or preferred it, or whatever) but who at the same time said they preferred the leaders of one or more of the other parties. Presidentialization in this case would mean an increasing tendency of voters to see leaders as discrete political objects, separate from the parties. Klingemann and Wattenberg have shown that this bifurcation has in fact taken place in the minds of American voters, largely at the parties' expense.

A fourth possible meaning of presidentialization is consistent with this separation-of-judgments possibility. Indeed, it arises directly out of it. Suppose that more and more voters distinguish in their political thinking between their judgments of the parties and their judgments of the parties' leaders. Under these circumstances, they might continue to give primacy in deciding how to cast their ballots to their partisan judgments; or, alternatively, they might attach increasing importance to their judgments of the leaders. If more and more voters put their leader preferences ahead of their party preferences, then the elections in question could indeed be reasonably described as having become increasingly "presidential" elections. What we would require in order to explore this possibility would be data bearing on the net effect of leader preferences on the vote—that is, the effect of leaders' personalities and styles independent of such other considerations as partisan predispositions and policy preferences.

Measuring the net effect of evaluations of presidential candidates' traits is, of course, one of the concerns of Shanks and Miller in their recent articles, and their analytic strategy is a variant of the improved prediction type of strategy referred to earlier. In their articles, Shanks and Miller list a number of independent variables or "explanatory themes"; and they list them in a presumed causal sequence, with each theme conceived of as being, to some extent, causally dependent on the themes higher on the list, and also as being at least partly responsible in a causal sense for the themes lower on the list. In their 1990 article, relating to the 1984 U.S. presidential election, they place perceived candidate traits seventh on their list of eight explanatory themes (1990, 170–71); and in their 1991 article, relating to the 1988 election, they place them ninth on their list of nine explanatory themes (1991, 134–35). Shanks and Miller make clear their assumptions in placing candidate traits so far along in the analytic sequence:

> Comparative evaluations of candidates in terms of such characteristics as leadership or empathy should be sharply related to the actual vote *because of their causal proximity to that choice.* Our analysis is designed to remove the confounding influence of other prior variables from our estimate of the impact of such candidate traits, and to assess the degree to which those traits add to our explanation of electoral decisions—instead of merely transmitting sentiments that have their origin in prior dispositions, policy preferences or performance evaluations. (Shanks and Miller 1991, 136; emphasis added)

Fifth, and finally, the presidentialization of British elections could also refer to any increase in voting based on party leader evaluations that materially affected the outcomes of general elections. After all, there could be an increase in the number of individual voters who were influenced by leaders' personalities and styles without that increase being reflected in any way in the formation of Her Majesty's Government. The increase might be on too small a scale. Alternatively, opinion might be distributed in such a way that the favorable or unfavorable effects of one leader's perceived traits on his or her party were offset by the favorable or unfavorable effects of the other party leader's perceived traits on that party. Only in a close election, with opinion heavily skewed in one party leader's favor, would one expect the election outcome to be determined by the relative standings of the leaders; and, even then, the true determinants of the election's outcome might still lie elsewhere (in, say, voters' policy preferences or their performance evaluations).

In the next section, we examine the available British data to see whether voters in Britain seem to differentiate more clearly than in the past between parties and leaders, to see whether the party leaders seem to be having a greater influence on individual voters' decisions than in the past, and, finally, to try to determine whether the outcome of any recent British election has, in fact, been decided by voters' differential perceptions of the leaders. In this section, we confine our detailed analysis to five elections held at approximately four- to eight-year intervals, those of 1964, 1970, February 1974, 1979, and 1987. These five include two of the three postwar elections in which the person apparently preferred as prime minister was not the leader of the party that eventually won.

Presidentialization or Not?

We first ask: Is there evidence that British voters are increasingly disposed to evaluate the party leaders separately from their parties? In other words, is American-style bifurcation increasingly taking place in Britain? If it is, we would expect to find an increase over time in the proportion of each party's identifiers who, despite their identification, prefer another party leader to their own or, at the very least, regard one or more of the other party leaders as being on a par with their own.

The data need to be interpreted with a little caution, since the questions asked in the relevant studies were changed in February 1974, and again in 1987 (see table 2). Moreover, the original Butler-Stokes studies of 1964 and 1970 did not ask respondents to say what they liked and disliked about the leader of the Liberal party (not surprisingly, since the Liberals then attracted only about 10 percent of the vote). This failure to ask about the Liberal leader accounts for the gaps in the tables below. Nevertheless, despite the gaps, the data do have a story to tell—and it is not the one called for by the presidentialization hypothesis.

Table 4 looks at Conservative party identifiers across the five elections. Probably the most significant rows, because the most complete, are the two at the top of the table, showing the proportion of Conservative identifiers at each election who preferred their own party leader and the proportion who preferred the leader of the Labour party. As can be seen, the largest percentage of Conservative identifiers who clearly did make a distinction in their minds between the parties and their leaders—and who preferred the leader of another

TABLE 4.   Preferred Party Leaders of Conservative Identifiers, 1964–87

Preference	1964	1970	Feb. 1974	1979	1987
Own party leader	47%	69%	70%	68%	61%
Labour leader	31	16	4	8	5
Liberal leader	—	—	16	10	24
Own and other leader equally	22	15	10	14	10

Source: British Election Studies for 1964, 1970, February 1974, 1979, and 1987—cross-sectional samples.

party to their own—comes not in the most recent election of the series, that of 1987, but in the most distant, that of 1964, when Harold Wilson was held in higher esteem than Sir Alec Douglas-Home by nearly one-third of the Conservative party's natural supporters. Many Conservatives still preferred Wilson to Edward Heath in 1970, but the proportion preferring the Labour leader to their own has never again been so high. To be sure, the proportion of Conservative identifiers preferring the leader of some other party was high in 1987, but the total of those who in 1987 preferred the Labour leader or one of the two Alliance leaders, 29 percent, was still smaller than the 31 percent who preferred the Labour leader alone nearly a quarter of a century before.

In connection with the Conservatives, the observed pattern is almost certainly explained not in terms of some long-term trend toward greater presidentialization, but in terms of Harold Wilson's attraction for considerable numbers of Conservative identifiers in the specific circumstances of the 1960s and 1970. No Labour leader since then (including Wilson in February 1974) has been nearly so attractive. Insofar as Conservative identifiers were tempted away from their natural party by the leader of another party in the 1970s and 1980s, the pull was exerted (probably mainly on weak Conservative identifiers) not by Labour, but by the Liberal leaders, Jeremy Thorpe and David Steel, in February 1974 and 1979, and by the two Liberal-SDP Alliance leaders, David Owen and David Steel, in 1987. Thus, the proportion of Conservatives preferring the leader of another party appears to have fluctuated since the mid-1970s partly as a function of Liberal or center party strength.

Table 5 repeats the same exercise in connection with Labour identifiers. The pattern here does seem to be one of a long-term tendency, at least as

TABLE 5.   Preferred Party Leaders of Labour Identifiers, 1964–87

Preference	1964	1970	Feb. 1974	1979	1987
Own party leader	82%	77%	76%	69%	69%
Conservative leader	5	8	3	6	5
Liberal leader	—	—	8	6	16
Own and other leader equally	13	15	13	19	10

Source: See table 4.

TABLE 6.   Preferred Party Leaders of Liberal Identifiers, 1964–87

Preference	1964	1970	Feb. 1974	1979	1987
Own party leader	—	—	73%	53%	67%
Conservative or Labour leader	—	—	11	23	24
Own and other leader equally	—	—	16	24	9

Source: See table 4.

regards Labour identifiers' apparently increasing reluctance to back their own party leader and their apparently increasing readiness to prefer the leader of another party (so long as that party is not the Conservatives). Such a pattern is obviously consistent with the idea that Labour identifiers are becoming more prepared to make separate judgments about the parties and their leaders. The data are, however, open to another—and, in our view, more plausible— interpretation, namely, that Labour identifiers have always had a certain capacity to distinguish between the parties and their leaders and that what has happened since the mid-1970s has not been an *increase* in that capacity, but rather a greater willingness on the part of voters to *exercise* that capacity. In the early period, Labour was led by the highly esteemed Harold Wilson. In subsequent elections, it has been led by the somewhat less highly esteemed James Callaghan and by the much less highly esteemed Neil Kinnock. It is this decline in Labour identifiers' confidence in their own leaders—combined with their growing preference for Liberal and Liberal-SDP leaders—that accounts for the apparent increase in the party-leader bifurcation in Labour identifiers' minds. Since the apparent trend in the table is, in fact, almost certainly not a trend, it could easily be reversed (if in the late 1990s, for example, Labour had a Wilson-like leader while the Conservatives had a Home-like leader). The fact that the proportion of Labour identifiers preferring the Conservative leader has not increased since 1964 tends to support this interpretation.

The data in table 6, relating to the Liberals and, in 1987, to the Liberal-SDP Alliance, are harder to interpret, since data for 1964 and 1970 are missing and since the number of Liberal and center-party identifiers in the British Election Study samples has always been small. Even so, the few data in the table point to a leader-specific interpretation, rather than one dependent on a long-term trend over time. The proportion of Liberal identifiers preferring their own party leader fell in 1979, then rose in 1987. The proportion preferring the leader of another party rose sharply between February 1974 and 1979, but then stabilized between 1979 and 1987. The figures for February 1974 probably reflect the high esteem in which Jeremy Thorpe was held among the small number of Liberal party identifiers at that time.

Table 7 seeks to draw these threads together, presenting our findings first, in the top four rows, for Conservative and Labour identifiers taken together,

TABLE 7. Preferred Party Leaders, 1964–87: Summary Table

Preference	1964	1970	Feb. 1974	1979	1987
Conservative and Labour identifiers (combined)					
Own party leader	65%	73%	73%	67%	64%
Opposition party leader	17	8	3	7	6
Liberal leader	—	—	12	8	20
Own and other leader equally	18	19	12	18	10
All identifiers					
Own party leader	—	—	73	66	65
Another party leader	—	—	15	17	26
Own and other leader equally	—	—	12	17	9

Source: See table 4.

and then, in the bottom three rows, for all identifiers. Two elections stand out from this table. One is that of 1964, when a record number of major-party identifiers distinguished between the two main party leaders and preferred the leader of the opposite party. (It is only a pity that data on evaluations of the Liberal leader in the 1964 election are not available.) The other election that stands out is that of 1987. The data for 1987, with the large numbers of all party identifiers preferring the leader of another party, almost certainly reflects the high level of Alliance strength at that election (it secured 22.6 percent of the United Kingdom vote) and the high esteem in which both David Owen and David Steel were held. If 1987 were not included in the table, there would be little temptation to identify a trend.

This conclusion is reinforced when we approach the problem from another angle. Table 8 assumes that at each of our five elections, voters evaluated the major parties and the major parties' leaders on a scale running from 0 to 10. It further assumes that the pair of scales—the party scale and the leader scale—is strictly comparable at any one election and is roughly comparable across the series of elections. If voters are more and more disposed to evaluate each party's leader independently of his or her party, then we would expect the gap between the evaluation of the party and the evaluation of the leader among each group of party identifiers to grow over time (irrespective of whether the leader scored higher or lower than the party). The data in table 8 refer to Conservative identifiers, then Labour identifiers, and then the two together. As can be seen, there is, in fact, no tendency for the gap in evaluations to grow over time. Again, it is only the 1987 election that contrives to give that appearance. Neil Kinnock, we know from other evidence, was less well regarded by Labour identifiers than was their party.

The fact that evaluations of parties and leaders do not seem to be diverging more and more over time leads to the expectation that leaders will not be having any increasing effects on the votes of individuals. After all, if leaders

TABLE 8. Party versus Party Leader Evaluations, 1964–87: Mean Differences

Preference	1964	1970	Feb. 1974	1979	1987
Conservative identifiers: mean difference in evaluation of Conservative party and Conservative leader	0.20	0.28	0.44	0.20	0.25
Labour identifiers: mean difference in evaluation of Labour party and Labour leader	0.61	0.56	0.29	0.02	1.33
Conservative and Labour identifiers combined: mean difference in their evaluation of their party and their party leader	0.41	0.43	0.36	0.11	0.73

Source: See table 4.

are still seen merely as part of larger partisan packages, or, alternatively, if voters' views of leaders remain largely derivatives of their other political attitudes, as suggested by the Shanks-Miller analysis, then it would be surprising (and puzzling) if leader evaluations were coming to have a greater and greater impact on the vote.

But it is at this point that the limitations of our data begin to pose serious problems. One obvious way of measuring any increase in leader effects over time is to see whether there is, over time, any increase in the probability of those who identify with a particular party defecting from that party and refusing to vote for it if they happen for any reason to prefer the leader of another party. Unfortunately, whereas the questions asked by the British Election Studies after February 1974 invited respondents to express their views about the Liberal and Social Democrat leaders as well as the Conservative and Labour leaders, the earlier studies did not. Thus, for example, whereas we know with regard to the 1979 election what proportion of Conservative identifiers preferred David Steel, as well as James Callaghan, to Margaret Thatcher, we know with regard to the 1964 election only what proportion of Conservative identifiers preferred Harold Wilson. Jo Grimond, the then Liberal leader, is simply left out of the frame. The consequence, of course, is that comparisons between the 1964–70 data and the post-February 1974 data are extremely hazardous.

The degree of hazard is increased by the fact that in the mid-1970s, Britain entered a phase of something approaching three-party politics, with roughly 20 percent of the voters backing the Liberals or the two Alliance parties at most general elections, and with many voters, including many Conservative and Labour identifiers, being attracted to the center parties and their leaders. Genuine leader effects under these circumstances are in danger—even more than usual—of being confounded with other effects, in this case with the center parties' increased, but highly diffuse, appeal.

Table 9 needs to be read against this background—and therefore, to a considerable extent, to be read in two parts, on either side of the vertical line

TABLE 9. Vote Defection Rates of Party Identifiers, 1964–87

Preference	1964	1970	Feb. 1974	1979	1987
Conservative identifiers					
Rank own leader first	3%	4%	4%	2%	3%
Rank own leader equal with another	7	7	16	10	7
Rank another leader first[a]	10	12	37	18	24
Increased defection probability	3.3	3.0	9.3	9.0	8.0
Labour identifiers					
Rank own leader first	3%	7%	7%	6%	7%
Rank own leader equal with another	11	11	17	18	12
Rank another leader first[a]	18	29	34	40	37
Increased defection probability	6.0	4.1	4.9	6.7	5.3
Liberal/Alliance identifiers					
Rank own leader first			16%	18%	12%
Rank own leader equal with another			19	37	26
Rank another leader first[a]			50	56	35
Increased defection probability			3.1	3.1	2.9
Conservative and Labour identifiers					
Rank own leader first	3%	5%	6%	4%	5%
Rank own leader equal with another	9	9	17	15	10
Rank another leader first[a]	14	18	36	27	28
Increased defection probability	4.7	3.6	6.0	6.8	5.6
All identifiers					
Rank own leader first			7%	5%	6%
Rank own leader equal with another			17	18	13
Rank another leader first[a]			36	32	30
Increased defection probability			5.1	6.4	5.0

Source: See table 4.

[a]In the 1964 and 1970 British Election Studies, respondents were not asked to evaluate the Liberal party leader. In these two years, 'another party leader' therefore means the Conservative or Labour leader.

separating the earlier of the two periods from the later. The table sets out for the different parties' identifiers the proportions at each election who defected to another party, among those who ranked their own party leader first, among those who ranked their own party leader equal to the leader of another party, and among those who actually ranked the leader of another party first. In every case, not surprisingly, the proportions of defectors are higher among those who failed to rank their own party leader first; we have calculated an "increased defection probability" simply by dividing the proportions of defectors among those who ranked another party's leader first by the proportion of defectors among those who ranked their own party's leader first. An increased defection probability of five simply means that a party identifier who preferred another party's leader to his or her own was five times as likely to defect as an identifier with the same party who preferred that party's leader. (We say nothing about the absolute numbers of defectors at this stage).

As the table makes clear, there was no tendency for these increased defection probabilities to grow in size, either in the 1964–70 period or in the February 1974–1987 period. Among Labour identifiers, there was not even any tendency for the defection probabilities to increase between the two time periods; the 1987 probability, 5.3, is actually lower than that for 1964, 6.0. The Conservative identifiers' probabilities do, however, increase from the earlier period to the later. Indeed, they are between two and three times larger after February 1974. Our surmise, however, is that these increased probabilities are not the result of some greatly increased pulling power on the part of non-Conservative leaders, but are an artifact of the changed question wording and the changed political climate referred to above. In our view, many weak Conservative identifiers and Conservatives temporarily disaffected from the party would have deserted it in the polling booth in any case; their preference for other parties' leaders was merely another sign of their disaffection.

Another possible measure of the importance that individual voters attach to the party leaders in making their voting decisions is the degree to which they rate the leader of the party they vote for higher than the party itself. A person who voted for, say, the Conservative party at a particular election might be supposed to have done so out of admiration for the Conservative party's leader, if he or she rated the leader significantly above the party. By the same token, leader effects on voters' decisions might be supposed to have increased over time if voters' judgments of the parties they voted for consistently ran ahead of their judgments of the parties themselves. Similarly, if British elections really were becoming more presidential in this sense, we might expect voters for one party to take an increasingly disparaging view of the leader of the main opposing party, as compared with the party itself.

Table 10 explores this possibility. It records for each of the five elections, and for each main category of voters, the mean of the difference between the score for the party leader in question and the score at the same election for his or her party. (The figures in the table are the means of the differences between the leader score and the party score recorded for each individual respondent, not the differences between the mean party scores and the mean leaders' scores across respondents.) A plus sign indicates that the leader in question is rated higher than his or her party. A minus sign indicates that he or she is rated lower. The problems of question wording encountered above are still present in this table—for example, the nearly complete set of plus signs, with relatively high values, in the 1987 column is probably an artifact of the specific survey questions used in that year—but the problems are probably not as serious as those in table 9.

TABLE 10. Mean Difference between Voters' Evaluation of Their Party and Their Party Leader, 1964 to 1987

	1964	1970	Feb. 1974	1979	1987
Conservative voters					
Con leader-Con party gap	−0.20	−0.27	−0.37	−0.14	−0.29
Lab leader-Lab party gap	+0.97	+0.51	+0.03	+1.16	+1.54
Labour voters					
Lab leader-Lab party gap	+0.64	+0.58	−0.28	+0.01	+1.27
Con leader-Con party gap	−0.09	−0.08	−0.55	+0.52	+0.16
Liberal/Alliance voters					
Lib party-Lib leader gap	n.a.	n.a.	+0.18	+0.59	+1.50
Con leader-Con party gap	−0.14	+0.09	−0.63	+0.36	+0.20
Lab leader-Lab party gap	+1.02	+0.90	−0.12	+0.66	+2.16

Source: See table 4.

Note: Cell entries are the mean of the difference between the score for leader and score for party recorded for each individual respondent, *not* the difference between the mean score for the party and the mean score for the leader. A '+' means that the leader is rated higher than the paty. A '−' means that the leader is rated lower than the party.

Table 10, whatever the limitations of the data, offers no support whatever to the idea that party leaders are increasingly attracting support to, or alienating support from, the parties they lead. Not only are most of the values in the table quite small, but there are few signs of the values increasing in the expected direction over time. Conservative leaders since 1964 seem consistently to have run behind their party in the eyes of Conservative voters (including when Margaret Thatcher was leader); and, far from giving Labour leaders lower and lower ratings compared with the Labour party, Conservative supporters appear, if anything, to have done the opposite. Labour leaders over the years have likewise not consistently improved their position vis-à-vis their party in the eyes of Labour voters—who, in addition, have not taken an increasingly dim view of Conservative leaders, compared with the Conservative party. The findings relating to the Liberals and the 1987 Liberal-SDP Alliance are equally unhelpful to this version of the presidentialization hypothesis.

In short, our data, although far from ideal, leave us skeptical of the idea that, in determining how individual voters will cast their ballots, British general elections have become more leader-dominated in recent years. Moreover, we suspect that, if we were in a position to adopt, election by election, the Shanks-Miller version of the improved prediction strategy, we would find that many of the leader effects we do appear to observe would turn out to have been caused by some logically prior political predispositions and attitudes.

Be that as it may, what matters in the end, politically, is not whether the voting decisions of individuals are influenced by political leaders' styles and personalities, but whether, if they are so influenced, the influence is on a sufficient scale and is sufficiently skewed to affect the outcomes of whole elections. Do individuals' private decisions have broader systemic effects?

To try to establish whether they do, we conducted a heroic (possibly rash) thought experiment. The experiment cannot distinguish between genuine leader effects and effects that manifest themselves in the leaders but are, in fact, rooted in prior dispositions and attitudes; but what it can do, if successful, is establish the outer limits to possible leader effects on election outcomes. The genuine leader effects are almost certainly less—possibly substantially less— than the ones we detect in our experiment; but they are unlikely to be greater.

From the data previously presented, we know the proportions of each party's identifiers who, at each of our five elections, preferred the leader of another party to their own, or who rated their own leader equally with that of another party (tables 4, 5, and 6). We also know the proportions of each of those categories of party identifiers who, when they finally came to cast their ballots at each of the five elections, deserted their own party for another (table 9). We can, in addition, obtain from the British Election Studies data two further pieces of information in connection with each election: first, the proportions that those who identified with each of the three main parties constituted of all those who went to the polls; and, second, the proportions in which the minority of Liberal identifiers who went to the polls but did not vote Liberal divided their vote between the Conservative and Labour parties. From these data, we can easily calculate, for example, the proportion of all voters in 1964 who were Conservative identifiers but who preferred Harold Wilson to Sir Alec Douglas-Home and also (for whatever reason) defected from the Conservative ranks. (The proportion, as it happens, was 3.1 percent.)

Our experiment, using these data, falls into two parts. The first is concerned with estimating the actual effects of expressed leader preferences on the actual outcomes of each of our five elections. What difference may voters' preferences for leaders have made?

To do so, we took all the party identifiers who turned out to vote, separated out those who positively preferred another leader or who preferred another leader equally, noted the latter groups' actual defection rates at each election, and calculated the increment or decrement to the winning party's margin produced by these considerable numbers of defector-recruits. In the case of Conservative and Labour identifiers, our estimate does not identify the actual proportions in which the defectors split between voting Liberal and voting for the opposite major party. We assume instead, we think realistically, that a substantial majority of defectors switched to the Liberals, and that the Liberal/opposite party split was the same for both Conservative and Labour identifiers. In the case of Liberal identifiers, it is not wise to make any similar assumption about their behavior, and our estimate therefore does include the precise Conservative/Labour split of those Liberals who defected, according to whether they ranked the Conservative leader first, the Labour leader first, or both equal first. Nonidentifiers are excluded from the estimates altogether: in the period under investigation, there were very few of them, and most of them did not vote. All our estimates take all voters as the base and not either all respondents or merely identifiers.

Table 11 sets out the results of this first part of our experiment. It comprises, to repeat, actual estimates of the effect of expressed leader preferences on the winning party's actual margin of victory at each of the five elections. (We are, so far, taking the data as we find them.) As can be seen from the second row of the table, the effect of expressed leader preferences in four of the five elections was to boost the winning party's margin of victory. In three cases, 1964, 1970, and 1987, the boost was quite small, less than one percentage point, but in the other case, that of 1979, it was quite substantial, 2.1 percent. The striking election, however, is that of February 1974. In February 1974, the Conservatives outpolled Labour by a tiny margin of 0.8 percent, but because of the geographical spread of the major parties' vote and the workings of the electoral system, Labour "won" the election in the sense of winning the largest number of seats in the House of Commons; Harold Wilson returned to Number Ten. But, according to our estimate, the net effect of expressed leader preferences in February 1974 was not in favor of the Conservatives, but in favor of Labour; and, had it not been for the boost that Harold Wilson gave to the Labour party, and the potential support that Edward Heath cost the Conservatives, the Conservatives' victory margin in terms of votes might have been not the 0.8 percent that it actually was, but 1.8 percent—probably enough to have enabled the Conservatives to remain the single largest party in Parliament. The numbers in our data are small, the margins in our estimates are also small, and the expressed leader preferences on which we rely certainly do not comprise the only motives that impelled voters at the five elections to defect from their normal party in favor of another one. Even so, the findings in table 11 are, at the very least, intriguing.

TABLE 11. Actual Impact of Expressed Leader Preferences

	1964	1970	Feb. 1974	1979	1987
Winning party's actual margin in the election	1.9%	2.3%	0.8%	7.1%	11.8%
(national vote, Great Britain only)	Lab.	Con.	Con.	Con.	Con.
Impact of expressed leader preferences	0.6	0.9	1.0	2.1	0.2
	to Lab.	to Con.	to Lab.	to Con.	to Con.
Winning party's margin without effects of	1.3	1.4	1.8	5.0	11.6
expressed leader preferences	Lab.	Con.	Con.	Con.	Con.

Source: See table 4.

Apart from February 1974, the other two columns in the table that deserve attention are those relating to 1970 and 1979. The received wisdom about British politics—substantially reinforced by the contemporary opinion poll findings (see table 3)—is that voters' preferences for Harold Wilson over Edward Heath boosted Labour in 1970, and that voters' preferences for James Callaghan over Margaret Thatcher boosted Labour, despite Labour's defeat, in 1979. Our findings suggest the opposite: that leader effects on balance aided the Conservatives, rather than Labour, in both 1970 and 1979. The explanation, according to our data, is that, while at both elections fewer Labour identifiers than Conservative identifiers preferred the leader of another party (hence, in part, the initial opinion poll findings), a larger proportion of the Labour identifiers actually defected. Our analysis thus draws attention to the importance of distinguishing between mere preferences and the disposition to act, or not act, on the basis of (or at least consistently with) those preferences.

We now move to the second (and even more heroic) part of our experiment. In this part, we try to imagine, not what the actual effects of expressed leader preferences were, but what they would have been if each of the two major political parties had been led at each election, not by the person who actually led it, but by the leader of the other major party. In other words, although the method we employ is different, our broad analytic strategy is that of Bean and Mughan (1989).

Our method is to hold the rates of defection of the various categories of party identifier constant, but to impute to Conservative identifiers Labour identifiers' distributions of leader preferences and to Labour identifiers Conservative identifiers' distributions of preferences. In the case of Liberal identifiers, we simply transpose their preferences for the Conservative leader at each election and their preferences for the Labour leader. Those who rated their own party leader equally with that of another party's leader are treated in the same way as in the first part of our experiment. Similarly, the calculations of the presumed effect of these (transposed) expressed leader preferences are made in exactly the same way as before. Our reason for holding constant the propensity to defect (it could have been varied between the parties in the same way) is that we are wary of engaging in a form of double-counting. We hypothesize that, in so far as we are correctly identifying genuine leader effects at all, we are locating them by means of voters' expressed leader preferences. To add to the analysis the rates at which the identifiers of different parties defect from their party would be to increase the already considerable risk that expressed leader preferences are, in any case, a result of other short-term forces (perceptions of national and personal conditions, agreement with current policies, etc.).

Table 12 sets out the results of our calculations of the impact that transposing the various groups of party identifiers' expressed leader preferences had on each winning party's margin of victory. Wilson is now leader of the Conser-

TABLE 12.   Impact of Expressed Leader Preferences with Leaders Reversed

	1964	1970	Feb. 1974	1979	1987
Winning party's actual margin in the election	1.9%	2.3%	0.8%	7.1%	11.8%
(national vote, Great Britain only)	Lab.	Con.	Con.	Con.	Con.
Impact of expressed leader preferences	0.6	0.9	1.0	2.1	0.2
	to Lab.	to Con.	to Lab.	to Con.	to Con.
Hypothesized impact if major party leaders	3.9	1.3	2.6	0.8	0.9
reversed	to Con.	to Con.	to Con.	to Lab.	to Con.
Winning party's hypothesized margin with	2.0	3.6	3.4	6.3	12.7
leaders reversed	Con.	Con.	Con.	Con.	Con.

Source: See table 4.

vative party and Home the leader of the Labour party in 1964, Wilson and Heath change places in 1970 and February 1974, and so on. And the voters respond accordingly. The second row from the bottom of the table offers estimates of how the five election outcomes would have been changed if the five pairs of leaders had all changed places. The entries in this row measure, as seems appropriate, the impact of our leader reversals, not on the actual election result in each case, but on what the result would have been in the absence of the leader effects we identified in the course of the first part of the experiment (see table 11). The bottom row goes on to suggest which party would have won, and what its winning margin would have been, if the party leaders had indeed been swapped.

As Bean and Mughan found, in the case of Australia in 1987, this part of our experiment suggests that had this, in fact, happened, the results of two of our five elections might have been significantly different. In 1964 a Wilson-led Conservative party might possibly have defeated a Home-led Labour party, and in February 1974, a Wilson-led Conservative party might well have beaten a Heath-led Labour party quite comfortably and succeeded in retaining its overall majority. (The one highly counterintuitive result in the table—the one for 1987 suggesting that a Kinnock-led Conservative party might have done better against a Thatcher-led Labour party—is entirely an artifact of the large proportion of Conservative identifiers who preferred the Liberal-SDP Alliance leaders, especially David Owen, to their own.)

It goes without saying that the results of our two-part experiment should be treated with considerable caution. We need to emphasize again our awareness of the limitations of our data and our consciousness that what we have called leader effects may well be reducible—indeed, in many cases, probably are reducible—to other attitudinal effects that are not captured in our analyses. That said, the effect of our experiment is almost certainly to place a ceiling on any genuine leader effects that may be present—and the ceiling is just high enough to suggest that the potential impact of British party leaders' personalities and styles on voting and elections ought in future to be taken somewhat more seriously by students of British electoral politics. At the very least, if genuine leader effects do not exist, or are wholly insignificant, that fact should be demonstrated, rather than merely assumed.

Conclusions

The main thesis that we have been testing in this chapter is the suggestion that British electoral politics have become more presidential in recent years. Our main finding is that there is very little evidence to suggest that this is so. Television coverage of elections is not more presidential. Voters display little or no long-term tendency to distinguish more sharply in their minds between parties and leaders. Likewise, they show no signs of increasingly evaluating the party leaders separately from their parties. Their votes as individuals do not seem to be more influenced than in the past by their evaluations of the leaders. And leaders' characteristics do not seem more likely now than in the past to determine election outcomes. Almost any way the term is defined, the 1964 general election seems to have been at least as "presidential" as any of its more recent successors. But for the fortuitous juxtaposition of Harold Wilson and Sir Alec Douglas-Home as party leaders, the outcome of that election might well have been different. Equally presidential elections probably took place in the even more distant past.

This conclusion raises, however, another question: If British elections have always been, at least to some extent, presidential, exactly how presidential have they been? Very? Or only slightly? This question we have only begun to explore in this chapter. Our evidence suggests the possibility that the impact of leaders' personalities and styles may have been enough to sway the outcome of at least two closely fought elections of recent years, those of 1964 and February 1974; but, as we have said repeatedly, we have not, thus far, been in a position to disentangle rigorously the possible effects of leaders from other effects, notably those identified by Shanks and Miller. A replication of the Shanks-Miller analysis for any recent British election, insofar as one is practicable, would advance our understanding considerably.

One final thought. Our belief is that under some circumstances, party leaders in Britain can have an effect on individual voters' decisions and the outcomes of general elections, but that this effect is likely to be small in comparison with, for example, their perceptions of national and personal conditions and their evaluations of the competence of the governing party and the putative competence of currently available alternatives. But, of course, this is precisely the conclusion toward which many American researchers, including Shanks and Miller, also appear to be moving. May it turn out that even American presidential elections are not, in fact, so very "presidential" after all?

REFERENCES

Bean, Clive, and Anthony Mughan. 1989. "Leadership Effects in Parliamentary Elections in Australia and Britain." *American Political Science Review* 83:1165–79.

Butler, David, and Donald Stokes. 1974. *Political Change in Britain: The Evolution of Electoral Choice.* 2d ed. London: Macmillan.

Denver, David. 1989. *Elections and Voting Behaviour in Britain.* Hemel Hempstead: Philip Allan.

Gallup, George H. 1976. *The Gallup International Public Opinion Polls: Great Britain, 1937–1975.* New York: Random House.

Graetz, Brian, and Ian McAllister. 1987. "Party Leaders and Election Outcomes in Britain, 1974–1983." *Comparative Political Studies* 19:484–507.

Harrison, Martin. 1965. "Television and Radio." In *The British General Election of 1964,* by D. E. Butler and Anthony King. London: Macmillan.

———. 1966. "Television and Radio." In *The British General Election of 1966,* by D. E. Butler and Anthony King. London: Macmillan.

———. 1971. "Broadcasting." In *The British General Election of 1970,* by David Butler and Michael Pinto-Duschinsky. London: Macmillan.

———. 1974. "Television and Radio." In *The British General Election of February 1974,* by David Butler and Dennis Kavanagh. London: Macmillan.

———. 1975. "On the Air." In *The British General Election of October 1974,* by David Butler and Dennis Kavanagh. London: Macmillan.

———. 1984. "Broadcasting." In *The British General Election of 1987,* by David Butler and Dennis Kavanagh. London: Macmillan.

———. 1988. "Broadcasting." In *The British General Election of 1987,* by David Butler and Dennis Kavanagh. London: Macmillan.

Heath, Anthony, Roger Jowell, and John Curtice. 1985. *How Britain Votes.* Oxford: Pergamon.

Hughes, Colin, and Patrick Wintour. 1990. *Labour Rebuilt: The New Model Party.* London: Fourth Estate.

Kavanagh, Dennis. 1992. "The United Kingdom." In *Electioneering: A Comparative Study of Continuity and Change,* ed. David Butler and Austin Ranney. Oxford: Clarendon.

Klingemann, Hans-Dieter, and Martin P. Wattenberg. 1992. "Decaying Versus Developing Party Systems: A Comparison of Party Images in the United States and West Germany." *British Journal of Political Science* 22:131–49.

Miller, Warren E., and J. Merrill Shanks. 1982. "Policy Directions and Presidential Leadership: Alternative Explanations of the 1980 Presidential Election." *British Journal of Political Science* 12:299–356.

Miller, Warren E., and Teresa E. Levitin. 1976. *Leadership and Change: The New Politics and the American Electorate.* Cambridge, Mass.: Winthrop.

Miller, William L., Harold D. Clarke, Martin Harrop, Lawrence LeDuc, and Paul F. Whiteley. 1990. *How Voters Change: The 1987 British Election Campaign in Perspective.* Oxford: Clarendon.

Pilsworth, Michael. 1980. "Balanced Broadcasting." In *The British General Election of 1979,* by David Butler and Dennis Kavanagh, London: Macmillan.

Seyd, Patrick. 1992. "Labour: The Great Transformation." In *Britain at the Polls, 1992,* ed. Anthony King. Chatham, N.J.: Chatham House.

Shanks, J. Merrill, and Warren E. Miller. 1990. "Policy Direction and Performance Evaluation: Complementary Explanations of the Reagan Election." *British Journal of Political Science* 20:143–235.

———. 1991. "Partisanship, Policy, and Performance: The Reagan Legacy in the 1988 Election." *British Journal of Political Science* 21:129–97.

Stewart, Marianne C., and Harold D. Clarke. 1992. "The (Un)Importance of Party Leaders: Leader Images and Party Choice in the 1987 British Election." *Journal of Politics* 54:447–70.

CHAPTER 9

On Warren Miller's Longest Footnote:
The Vote in Context

John Sprague

Origins

My subscription to the *American Political Science Review* began with the issue of December 1956, and hence I missed, by one issue, reading Warren Miller's article "One-Party Politics and the Voter" immediately on its publication. It was about five years later that Heinz Eulau put the article in my hands, and since then the content of this particular scientific work has influenced, mightily, my allocation of intellectual effort over the past three decades. The article is a signal contribution to the science of politics, and I am deeply pleased to be offered this chance to develop some themes initiated in that work, and at the same time to honor its author.

The strategy of my effort in this paper is to emphasize the durability of the empirical results reported by Miller, to generalize his arguments about partisan environments by extending them in a natural way to the social environment (a subject addressed in the closing pages of Miller's article), and finally, to illustrate the extensions by applying them to ancient surveys taken very close in time to those that Miller originally analyzed. On the one hand, I wish to show the contemporary relevance of Miller's classic analysis, while on the other hand, I attempt to construct related analyses of a paradigmatic variety with materials available shortly after his work was published. Intellectual history in the discipline went a different route, but some different mix of circumstance might have tilted the direction of scientific development. Thus, the empirical work reported here can be interpreted as partially an exercise in counterfactual argument.

What This Essay Is About

The paper that follows provides an example of a strategy for combining aggregate data from whatever appropriate source with sample survey information to obtain an elaborated, perhaps richer, analysis of voting behavior. Although statistics are invoked not at all, there is certainly a strong Bayesian flavor, or at least spirit, in the strategy outlined.

In principle, any additional information could be used. By and large in political science, at least in our data analysis modes, once we have learned basic econometric strategies for incorporating prior information in the course of our graduate education, we find ways to never use such strategies in our day-to-day work. This chapter provides an (I believe relatively rare) example to the contrary, substantively motivated by social class voting, and theoretically motivated by appeal to hypotheses of contextual effects on voting arising from social structure.

If what follows is Bayesian in spirit, it most emphatically is not Bayesian statistics. The focus is on the logic of a persistent problem of parameter under-identification in modeling contextual effects with aggregate data, and on how sample survey information and aggregate data might be jointly brought to bear on the attendant technical difficulties.

At times in the narrative it is necessary to pay attention, for the argument is close. The algebra is entirely elementary, for sure, but it does display a representation of the qualitative theoretical argument in informal mathematics. Thus, the equations are an important part of the argument, and I therefore apologize up front for both their number and their centrality to the present effort. Miller's original article, and especially footnote 6 in that article, also demands some close attention.

Durable Conclusions

In order to discuss the significance of Miller's results, the basic design strategy should be kept in mind. His article stratifies respondents by four categories of counties, varying from weakly Democratic to strongly Democratic, based on the aggregate reported election results in the 1952 presidential election. Thus, the design seeks to investigate the effects of partisan context on political behavior. After establishing that the sample plausibly reflects the aggregate election results and that partisanship, issue orientations, and candidate orientations plausibly march with the county partisan context, Miller presents and discusses two tables—one controlling motivational factors and assessing vote variation as a function of partisan county context, and one controlling motivational factors and further assessing motivational variation as a function of variation in partisan county context. The tables are complex, rich in content, and comprehensively interpreted in the original article.

From the analyses and discussion, three particularly hardy conclusions emerge in "One-Party Politics and the Voter." Of considerable interest, though not the central thrust of the original article nor my focus in the present paper, is the independence of partisan identification from variation in the partisan milieu or context. Second, one-party dominance of politics produces heterogeneity of candidate and issue orientations for the minority party. Third, and of continuing relevance for understanding national politics as locally mediated, minor parties suffer in votes, and major parties get a bonus, from the partisan context—them that has, gets, or, put another way, those rich in votes get richer and those poor in votes get poorer in response to the county partisan context.

Along with only a handful of other studies, "One-Party Politics and the Voter" provides a contextual analysis of political behavior based on a national sample. Few scholars have pursued this strategy with national samples since Miller's early effort, and one area rich with promise for contemporary analyses of a related nature would be analyses of the political consequences of racial distribution densities. But that moves us into the generalization of the argument to social contexts taken up below.

A Long Footnote

A striking feature of Miller's argument is its qualitatively rich discussion and its implicit, and sometimes explicit, quantitative backbone. Indeed, the quantitative theme is inescapable, essential for the developments offered here, and it is most forcefully illustrated in a long footnote where the critical theoretical issue being examined turns on the matter of functional form.

Early in his article, Miller chose to deal with a breaking point or marked discontinuity in response effect in the very long footnote 6. (I claim that this is Warren Miller's longest footnote, although Paul Beck demurs). The footnote is reproduced here as an appendix. The note in the original consumes the better part of each of two pages and includes, central to the themes developed here, two figures. The figures plot variable X as a theoretical display against the percentage Democratic of the two-party vote (Miller 1956, 709–10). The first figure displays a trace that is constant at the extremes and for some interval from the extremes of percentage Democratic (with opposite effects on X), with a short interval of rapid transition around the center of the Democratic contextual percentage. Perhaps the pattern might be described as two step functions at the extremes wedded to a linear transition of sharp gradient in the center. This theoretical figure of Miller's illustrates the discontinuous, or sudden break, possibility of responsiveness to variation in Democratic voting context.

By contrast, the second figure displays a modest gradient for a continuous straight line, as one moves from low to high concentrations of Democratic percentage of the two-party vote. After setting forth the possibilities which might lead to a sharp break, Miller concludes:

> In all the analyses . . . there was no indication that a real breaking point did in fact exist near either end of the dominance continuum. Conse-

quently, the use of the concept of a continuum of relative dominance not only provides *a* needed solution to the methodological problem involved, but also appears to provide *the* solution most compatible with the relevant data. (Miller 1956, 710; emphases in the original)

This is a straightforward quantitative argument about functional form, and the analyses reported below do not contradict this fundamental proposition.

It turns out, however, that when aggregation of individual level data is considered, or when the concept of context is extended from the political environment to the social or economic environment as well, the fabric of formal considerations, even for elementary models, leads to new insight into the issue of linear versus nonlinear effects. Indeed, linear contrasted with nonlinear effects provides one key perspective on issues of cross-level inference, especially where some data are aggregated, as I hope to show.

Linear and Nonlinear Contextual Effects

Just as the partisan vote probability may vary as the partisan context varies, the vote may also vary as a function of the social or economic context. In keeping with my pledge to use ancient data, a demonstration of the linear and nonlinear phenomena, based on Swedish electoral data reported by Herbert Tingsten in *Political Behavior* (1937), is instructive. Tingsten provides two tables based on elections in Stockholm reporting vote aggregated to precincts. These data can be used to illustrate Miller's principal of continuous change as manifested in the power of a social context, as well as to show the appearance of nonlinear effects when the data are aggregated. I use the Tingsten data because the patterns are so pronounced that recourse to statistical fitting procedures appears not to be necessary. With the empirical examples displayed, we can then turn to a systematic development of the simplest social context models and illustrate them further with SRC (not NES) data for the 1960 election. The key to the entire argument is the following proposition: *contextual effects at the individual level are manifested as linear marginal effects that, when aggregated (integrated) over numbers of individuals, will typically exhibit nonlinear patterns of effects.* A systematic development of the idea of individual marginal effects (not all linear) integrated to group aggregate effects, typically nonlinear, is given by Przeworski (1974). The modeling strategy followed here is more directly constructive and descriptive.

The tactic is to show the two kinds of effects empirically, and then to show the logical individual-level model construction that leads to the different functional forms. It is possible to compute, from Tingsten's data for these Stockholm precincts, the proportion of the Social Democratic party vote relative to the eligible adults, and the proportion of the working class (Social Class

III) relative to the eligible adults. These measures provide a classic ecological model possibility when the Social Democratic vote proportion is plotted against the working-class proportion. This plot is set out in figure 1, along with the line of constant return, $Y = X$. The data points clearly would accommodate a marked S-curve, and, in fact, a logistic curve fits these data with extraordinary accuracy (Huckfeldt and Sprague 1993). Curve fitting is relevant, but is not the purpose of displaying figure 1, which shows what may be typical—an aggregate (social) context (here, working-class density in voting precincts) displaying a marked political response nonlinearity. In figure 2, the least squares line is imposed and the interpretive conclusion persists—an S-curve would fit more adequately. These data, aggregate data, show a breaking point or nonlinear change at both ends of the class distribution similar to Miller's first theoretical figure in footnote 6. The hypothesis that these aggregate data point toward is that individual members of Social Class III do not have a constant probability of supporting the Social Democrats with their votes, as social class densities vary over the precincts.

But Tingsten, along with Swedish electoral bureaucrats, provides an additional comparison. The electoral officials also collected information on voting participation by social class. Thus, it is possible to make a similar plot for voting turnout by the working class expressed as a proportion of the working class in Stockholm precincts scattered on the proportion of adults who are members of the working class. Once more, the line of constant return, $Y = X$, is also plotted for reference. These data are displayed in figure 3.

It is crucial to recognize that the plot in figure 3 contains no ecological error—that is, it contains no compositional error in the dependent behavior. Thus, figure 3 displays the probability that a member of the working class participates politically by voting, as the concentration of working-class persons varies in the precinct environment. There is clearly some form of social reinforcement phenomenon at work, but the crucial point is that the scatter displays an essentially linear relationship. (See figure 4, which imposes the least squares line.) That linear relationship is precisely what Miller's argument in footnote 6 predicts (the second figure in footnote 6), since here there is no compositional error from aggregation. For figure 1, where compositional error on Y is present, there is also a reinforcement effect, but the plot is nonlinear. This also is what Miller predicts for social context effects by fair inference from his discussion (Miller 1956, 722–25) of the probability model in *Voting* (Berelson, Lazarsfeld, and McPhee 1954, 126–27).

This essential result can be summarized as follows. In the absence of compositional measurement error arising from aggregation, a social context effect on voting is evidenced by a systematic linear functional relationship (figure 4). When, however, a compositional measurement error is present arising from aggregation, a social context effect on voting is evidenced by a

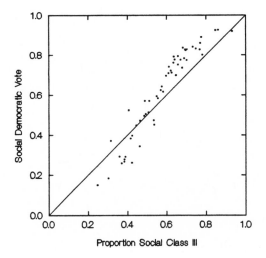

Fig. 1. Vote on class with line $Y = X$. (Data for all figures from Tingsten 1937.)

nonlinear functional relationship (figure 2). Tingsten's data allow an empirical illustration of both effects.

Can the nonlinear pattern for aggregate contextual effects be recovered from first principles (that is, from behavioral assumptions at the individual level suitably aggregated)? This is the fundamental question that this paper addresses and elaborates.

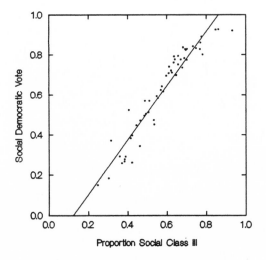

Fig. 2. Vote on class with OLS line

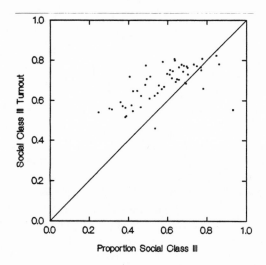

Fig. 3. Turnout on class with line $Y = X$

The task at hand, then, is to systematize these empirical results, consistent with Miller's predictions, findings, and arguments, as well as to further elaborate the argument of footnote 6. What individual level elementary modeling premises are both consistent with Miller's arguments and findings and also consistent with the observed nonlinearity in the aggregate Tingsten data? My solution to this is a brief recapitulation of a model due to Raymond Boudon

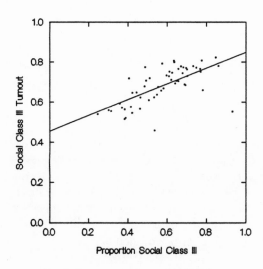

Fig. 4. Turnout on class with OLS line

(1963). This is then followed by an application of the model to 1960 SRC data, showing the continuous effect predicted by Miller and also showing the aggregate effect predicted by an elaborated (and aggregated) model. A parameter identification problem arises from the development, and the final part of the argument proposes a solution that ameliorates, although does not eliminate, the problem.

The words that follow combine some algebraic logic capturing the qualitative argument with data illustrating the principles advanced. My object, to repeat, is to show how survey data, aggregate data, and an elementary, but perhaps useful, model of social context effects can be combined to provide an enriched analytic strategy for investigating social influences on voting behavior. The analyses are designed only to illustrate the strategy, and should be taken in that spirit. Put another way, I ask the reader to suspend disbelief long enough to follow the argument. My attempt is to develop the argument with great care, justifying each step, both algebraically and empirically, so at the end, the reader has some chance of being both persuaded and also of knowing the premises, the logical foundation, of the argument.

The Logic of Contextual Composition

The general form of an argument that appeals to a contextual effect hypothesis for explanation may be characterized in a simple functional notation as follows. A behavior, B, can be explained or accounted for by a theory, T, which takes arguments, A_i. If any of the A_i constitute predicates positing an explanatory role for political contexts, P, then this scheme represents Miller's theorizing. If any of the A_i attribute an explanatory role to the social context, S, then, similarly, the scheme characterizes theoretical appeal to social contexts.

The critical logical structure of a contextual argument, whether the appeal is to political context, social context, or both, is that the contextual arguments are used nontrivially in deductions to the behavior, B. The scheme can thus be written as

$$B = T(A_i, \ldots, P_i, \ldots, S_i, \ldots A_i).$$

Most frequently in the literature, contexts are constructed based on geographical areas. That is natural in the voting context, but by no means necessary, since schools, work places, or the softball team might, in principle, constitute relevant contexts partially shaping political behavior. A theorist commits to a contextual hypothesis, abstractly considered, if his or her explanation of behavior requires measurement on political or social contexts in order to make specific predictions. This characterization of contextual theories is, I believe, completely within the spirit of "One-Party Politics and the Voter."

Now we turn to one particular example of a contextual model; one that posits a role for social context and that lends itself to manipulation of voting survey data, as well as aggregate demographic (census) data. The purpose is to display the bare bones logic of one version of a social context model of political behavior and to apply it to some, of course ancient, SRC voting survey data. The model is designed to study political behavior as a function of social class and the formulation is for an aggregate data model, which can then be used to exploit individual-level survey data. Parameter identification is severe in the pure version of the aggregate model, and attempts to deal with this difficulty provide a plot that may sustain the reader's interest. The model is developed from ideas first proposed, to my knowledge, by Boudon (1963); and the particular form set forth adapts, adopts, and relies on, for social context arguments, Miller's principle of continuous gradual response to context, as argued in footnote 6 of "One-Party Politics and the Voter."

An Aggregate Data Model of Social Context Effects

Consider a qualitative political behavior and qualitative social property that occur dichotomously (that is, an individual exhibits the behavior or property or does not, unambiguously). Designate these as B and S. Contingency tables based on sample surveys are still used to study the joint dependencies between two such properties, although today, the usual form is a more or less elaborate multivariate statistical model. Whether the tactic is a table or a multivariate model, a characteristic result is extracted, in the end, that gives the conditional probability that an average individual exhibits B given that he or she has the property S. For concreteness, suppose the behavior is voting for the Democratic party and the social property is being a member of the working, or blue-collar, class.

(It can be noted in passing that any individual either does or does not exhibit the behavior, so that the conditional probability either conceals ignorance about the true basis of behavior or, alternatively, characterizes a probability parameter for a class of individuals as a whole, say blue-collar workers, that assumes the individual mechanism is probabilistic at bottom. A third view is that the conditions of observation impose these alternative interpretations, which has the methodological and theoretical implication that observation will seldom appear decisive, as between the first two interpretations, when adherents of both points of view contend.)

In this probabilistic interpretation, a social context hypothesis is advanced to partition individual probabilities into idiosyncratic (individual) and contextual (environmental) components. Thus, a social context thesis, just as Miller's political context argument, emphasizes the jointness of individual and contextual contributions in explanation, and it is also inherently quantitative, in that it seeks to apportion probability magnitudes to different sources. The critical apportionment is between the contextual sources and the individual property sources and, perhaps, their joint effect.

The initial modeling contemplates aggregate measurement on some spatial units, for example, SRC sample counties. The contextual thesis asserts that the rate at which B is observed to occur in the units of observation is systematically dependent on the occurrence of the social characteristic in an appropriately chosen (theoretically dictated) social aggregate. Almost always, the aggregate unit of observation is an imperfect model of the theoretical social aggregate, and frequently in contextual investigations a legally supplied aggregate unit, such as the county or township, is used when the appropriate theoretical unit is very likely the neighborhood, or perhaps the political ward in a city. "One-Party Politics and the Voter" did use the county as the unit of political context measurement. From a social context measurement perspective, it is forcefully true that census takers do not necessarily organize their data for the convenience of social scientists. This is a troublesome problem precisely because it is almost always the case, hence, the probability of detecting contextual effects is lessened by the usual conditions of observation—that is, by the way cheap data are available. There are exceptions to this in the literature, usually arising from designs that set out to investigate contexts from the first (Katz and Eldersveld 1961; Foladare 1968; Segal and Meyer 1974; Huckfeldt and Sprague 1992), but the county is used as the unit of contextual observation in the empirical work reported below. The convenient fiction may be maintained, perhaps supported by Miller's success with the county unit, that the county unit is the unit dictated by theory. This is much more plausible for political contexts, of course, than it is for social contexts. The literature on politics in context has been comprehensively reviewed by Books and Prysby (1991), and an expository development of the status of contextual investigations is given by Huckfeldt and Sprague (1993).

For an aggregate model of social class contextual effects, the social context hypothesis can be formalized in its simplest form by writing a specification for the components of the probability that a member of the class S behaves in the fashion B. Designate this as $PROB(B|S)$. The quantity $PROB(B|S)$, following Miller's principle by analogy for social context effects, is composed of three components—first, that of the individual (idiosyncratic); second, that of the social category of interest (here, working class membership); and third, the context of other social categories (treated here as residual non–working class or non–peer memberships). A standard interpretation is that they represent the effects of social influence arising from social interaction and some law of behavior determining social influence. The residual category can be ignored, but it is useful to include it since its inclusion provides a complete mapping of the behavior of the population in terms of sources in the social structure. Thus, following Miller's principle in the spirit of Occam's razor, the simplest algebraic rendering of the probability might be given as

$$PROB(B|S) = p_1 + p_2 S + p_3(1 - S), \tag{1}$$

where S measures the density of the social characteristics in the theoretical aggregate unit as a proportion of adults, and the p_i are fixed parameters.

There is a feature of this elementary form for an aggregate model probability that may be subtle and is important to emphasize. Nothing in the form (1) exhibits nonlinearity, in keeping with Miller's thesis. At the same time, and certainly true of Miller's argument as well, there is no such thing as a fixed probability in this contextual world. All probabilities of behavioral events are contingent on the context in which they occur. The form (1) vividly points this out. To specify the probability, $PROB(B|S)$, also requires the specification of a context—a measure of S and a particular value of S. The important point, conceptually, is that a statement concerning the probability of B among the S willy nilly requires simultaneously a statement about the probability of S among the units of observation. Put more bluntly, the form (1) denies the possibility of a fixed probability for behaving in the fashion B, given property S, provided that p_2 or p_3 is nonzero. And note further that the form (1) is a model of Miller's analogous display procedures and argument for political contexts.

If the form (1) is taken as a model for a contingency table analysis, then it is clear that, even after controlling for all other relevant individual determinants of behavior, the appropriate analytic strategy is that taken by Miller—vary the context and watch the contingent probabilities vary. On the other hand, if (1) is taken as a model for aggregate data analysis, not only will the parameters be unidentified, but also the equation (1) cannot be the appropriate model for aggregate data analysis, for it denies the contextual thesis, that is, the fixed coefficient on S implied by the linear form contradicts the density dependence on behavior. It is the Tingsten data pattern for the Social Democratic vote displayed in figure 1 that cannot be recovered. For an aggregate model, there is no provision for the amplification arising from the dependence of behavior on social densities. What can be done?

One strategy for repairing the aggregate data model is to appeal once more to Miller's principle of the uniformity of contextual effects at the individual level, combined with Boudon's strategy for recovering nonlinear behavior (figure 1) at the aggregate level. We do this in stages. Miller's hypothesis is captured by the form (1). Boudon's strategy is to treat this form as a probability operator on the population of the aggregate units of observation. The combination of strategies leads to a straightforward, if unidentified, aggregate model.

For completeness, an equation symmetric with (1) can be written for the probability that non-working-class citizens exhibit the behavior of interest. The formulation assumes that the behavior of an average individual in an average aggregate context is the object of interest, and that the social context is measured by the density of class as a proportion, say, of all adults. This leads, in analogy to (1), to

$$PROB(B|1 - S) = p_4 + p_5(1 - S) + p_6S, \tag{2}$$

which partitions the probability $PROB(B|1 - S)$ into individual, peer context, and non–peer context components.

Boudon's ingenious solution was to treat equations (1) and (2) as probability operators on the population of aggregate units of observation by invoking a substitution procedure. Thus write

$$B = PROB(B|S)[S] + PROB(B|1 - S)[1 - S] \tag{3}$$

and substitute (1) and (2). Both (1) and (2) describe Miller's uniform individual-level response to (social) context, and the substitution incorporates that hypothesis into an aggregate model. Keeping with our interpretation of simple dichotomous qualitative behavior, say the vote, the quantity B in a unit of observation is the aggregate rate at which the individual-level behavior occurs measured, say, as a proportion of adults in a unit. The quantities S and $(1 - S)$ on the right-hand side of (3) measure social class densities in a unit of observation as a proportion of adults. Thus, we have an aggregate (Boudon) contextual model resting on individual-level (Miller) probability component premises. It is easy to see from (3) that the aggregate model maps a mutually exclusive and exhaustive partitioning of the social structure of the population to a mutually exclusive and exhaustive partitioning of the same population in terms of partisan voting behavior, B, and implicitly $(1 - B)$. A generalization of both behavior and social structure could be obtained by increasing the fineness of the partitioning.

The descriptive model implied by (1), (2), and (3) is not algebraically rich enough to produce the logistic pattern of figure 1, but it is rich enough to allow for amplification of context in nonlinear fashion—Boudon's original goal. And it is also rich enough for simulating aggregate models with survey data in the spirit of the dependent measure displayed for Tingsten's Stockholm turnout data in figure 2, but using recent ancient data—the 1960 SRC voting survey.

Making the appropriate substitutions of (1) and (2) into (3) and rearranging the result algebraically yields

$$B = [p_4 + p_5] + [p_1 + p_3 - p_4 - 2p_5 + p_6]S + [p_2 - p_3 + p_5 - p_6]S^2. \tag{4}$$

The nonlinearity is revealed by the presence of the S^2 term, which also reveals a fundamental weakness of this aggregate model, and one difficult to avoid in aggregate contextual models. That weakness is a random mixing assumption. In "One-Party Politics and the Voter" Miller provides a criticism of this random mixing notion, although not necessarily as manifested in an aggregate data model (Miller 1956, 722–24). If equation (4) were to be estimated by least squares for a typical set of aggregate units, it is clear that the theoretical parameters are not identified, since (4) will yield only three coefficients, including the intercept, and there are six theoretical parameters to be estimated. Now, if we join some survey data with some aggregate census social information for the same population, in the spirit of Miller's political county contexts, some amelioration of the identification problem may be achieved, while at the same time, the contextual logic can perhaps be rendered empirically clear by example. That is the next part of the program.

Social Context and Survey Observations

Employing the 1960 SRC election study, equation (1) may be (almost) directly evaluated. The equation remains unidentified in parameters, but this is not crucial. What is to be shown is, first, that the rate at which blue-collar workers identify with the Democratic party and the rate at which blue-collar workers express an intention to vote Democratic is dependent on blue-collar densities in the expected direction when controlling for class and, second, that the estimated parameters for individual and contextual probability effects can be recovered from a truncated Boudon aggregate model with relatively high accuracy, using the survey to construct surrogate aggregate units in which true parameters are known, thus partially justifying the random mixing interaction hypothesis necessary to the aggregate data application. Equation (1) is rewritten here for reference as

$$PROB(B|S) = p_1 + p_2 S + p_3(1 - S). \tag{5}$$

Combining the 1960 SRC election respondents by county (yes, the N will be small for many counties), it is possible to obtain an estimate of the proportion of the adults in a county that are in the blue-collar class and, furthermore, the proportion of the blue-collar workers who identify or vote with the Democratic party. These latter measures do not contain compositional error from aggregation; they are similar to the Tingsten data in figure 2. For a given aggregate unit, a county constructed from the survey respondents, a direct estimate of $PROB(B|S)$ is thus determined. This number varies across counties, as does the proportion of blue-collar workers, and hence, the dependence of the rate of Democratic identification or intended Democratic voting among the blue-collar workers may be studied as a function of blue-collar density. Equation (5) may be rearranged for estimation as

$$PROB(B|S) = [p_1 + p_3] + [p_2 - p_3]S. \tag{6}$$

Provided it is not the case that $p_2 = p_3$, which must occur with probability zero, then, if p_2 or p_3 is different from zero, a contextual effect may be demonstrated.

For Democratic vote or identification and blue-collar worker density, the signs of the coefficients $[p_2 - p_3]$ and $[p_1 + p_3]$ may be anticipated systematically. The logic of parameter identification for this model is similar to that in Goodman's model of aggregate regression (Goodman 1953). Prior empirical work (prior to 1960) shows that blue-collar workers have substantial probability of favoring, with sentiment or behavior, the Democratic party. This is consistent with most interpretations of the New Deal and its aftermath, as well as with the systematic analysis of voting by survey techniques—the central tendency of workers' behavior and feeling lies on the Democratic side. This implies that $PROB(B|S)$ is larger for the Democratic than the Republican party, which is true for these 1960 data. Furthermore, p_1, the individual level component, may be assumed positive on similar grounds. It is reasonable to expect the interaction with one's peers will reinforce the existing propensity in the peer group, hence p_2 may be assumed positive. This mechanism of reinforcement makes common sense and is systematically discussed theoretically by Coleman (1964). The parameter p_3 estimates the effect on the members of S, in the present instance blue-collar workers, of residual interaction with all remaining adults. It seems plausible that, in the average, this effect of the residual population will be smaller in magnitude than either the individual or peer context effects. Thus, even if the sign of p_3 is negative, it will not overwhelm p_1, and the net effect on the coefficient will be such that the coefficient remains positive. Thus, given these arguments, the intercept should be positive and the slope on blue-collar worker density should be positive for both Democratic identification and intended voting among the blue-collar workers, provided only that social class contextual effects are operative.

The argument is more intricate for this simplest of all models than is required with a more general model. If the estimated model characterized a more complex partitioning, say four occupational groups, then the residual group's effect, equivalent to p_3 in the present formulation, would tend to irrelevancy, and all that would be required of theory is systematic anticipation of signs for coefficients on groups.

The results of performing the appropriate regressions are set forth in table 1. The results are consistent with the argument. The intercepts are positive, as anticipated, and so are the slopes. What is perhaps surprising is the magnitude of the slopes, and more so when it is realized that the slopes are systematically

TABLE 1. Regressions of Democratic Vote Intention and Partisan Identification on Blue-Collar Worker Densities

Coefficient	Democratic Intended Vote	Democratic Partisan Identification
Intercept $(p_1 + p_3)$	+0.24	+0.33
	(3.58)	(4.68)
Slope $(p_2 - p_3)$	+0.37	+0.39
	(2.55)	(2.59)

Source: SRC Voting Study (1960).

Note: County $N = 96$. The dependent behaviors are measured by forming the ratio of blue-collar workers exhibiting the property in a county to the total number of blue-collar workers in that county (in the sample). The independent social density, blue-collar workers, is formed by the ratio of the number of blue-collar workers in the sample for a county to the total sample for that county. In the identification measure, strong and weak Democrats are included, but not independent leaners. The intended Democratic vote includes those Democratic with qualifications. Blue-collar workers combines those who are skilled, unskilled, or live with heads of household so classified.

Parentheses enclose t-tests for the overall coefficients.

Total variance accounted for by the regression for each independent behavior is 5 percent for intended vote and 6 percent for partisan identification.

smaller in magnitude than the true slopes because of the measurement procedure. Furthermore, the t-tests reported in table 1 are systematically low, for the data points were not single observations, but rather means.

The 1960 survey included 1,181 respondents spread over 97 counties, although one county was excluded for technical reasons. The average sample size for each county is of the order twelve. A rough estimate of the corrected t-tests can be obtained by multiplying the reported test by the square root of twelve to take advantage of the knowledge that each data point was a subsample mean. Even if the reported t-values are used, however, the slopes reach the .01 significance level for a one-tailed test.

The measured variables for the 96 counties frequently had a very small number of respondents, thus introducing random error in the measurement of the county proportions in addition to random error arising from sampling. This error will not affect the covariation between behavior and social density on average—it is as likely to increase as decrease a term, since it is random—but it will systematically increase the variance of the social density term. This variance occurs in the denominator of the least squares slope estimate and, thus, systematically depresses the magnitude of the estimated slope.

In summary, for the 1960 SRC election survey data, the distribution of the rate of individual Democratic political behavior in counties for the occupational class blue-collar worker apparently depends on blue-collar worker concentrations in those same counties. Note in particular that the effect of class membership is not all found on the intercept (individual effects). This dependence on blue-collar densities is consistent with a reinforcement of behavior through social interaction interpretation. Furthermore, for technical reasons, the reported estimates and t-tests of contextual effects are probably conservative.

With aggregate data, the direct measurement of the behavior of an occupational group, unlike the controlled dependent measure in table 1, is confounded with the behavior of other groups—the ecological inference problem. By making some strong simplifying assumptions, that is, by doing what must be done in all regression applications to secure identification by setting some coefficients to zero, it is possible to illustrate the potential success of the aggregate model in recovering the true parameters by simulating aggregate observations with the survey counties. The simulation is strictly a logical simulation with real data. No dice are thrown, except the original dice that determined the sample actually drawn by the Survey Research Center. Assume that cross-group effects are not operative and that the residual class of non-blue-collar workers is not subject to peer group context effects. It seems especially reasonable to reject measurable peer group effects on the residual class, for it includes both professionals and the poverty stricken. This points up the potential gains to be obtained from a more complex partitioning. These suppositions may be summarized by

$$p_3 = p_5 = p_6 = 0. \tag{7}$$

The resulting model then appears as

$$PROB(B|S) = p_1 + p_2 S$$

$$PROB(B|1 - S) = p_4 \tag{8}$$

$$B = PROB(B|S)[S] + PROB(B|1 - S)[1 - S],$$

which becomes, after substitution and rearrangement,

$$B = p_4 + (p_1 - p_4)S + p_2 S^2. \tag{9}$$

The equation (9) may be estimated by least squares and the theoretical parameters estimated from the least squares coefficients. Now, however, the dependent behavior, B, is not measured among the blue-collar workers, but among the aggregate adult (sample) county populations. This situation simulates the typical aggregate data problem, but, under the hypothesis that p_3 is zero, the estimates of table 1 now identify the parameters for individual and contextual effects, and these estimates may be compared with those recovered from the least squares coefficients of (9). The comparison is presented in table 2, for party identification.

TABLE 2. Class Controlled and Class Uncontrolled Parameter Estimates for Democratic Party Identification

Parameters	Class Controlled in Partisan Identification	Class Not Controlled in Partisan Identification
Individual effect for blue-collar workers (p_1)	+0.33	+0.35
Contextual effect of peers for blue-collar workers (p_2)	+0.39	+0.28
Individual effect for non-blue-collar workers (p_4)	—	+0.51

Source: SRC Election Study (1960).

Note: County $N = 96$. The measures employed in regression were blue-collar proportions of county samples, strong and weak identifiers among the blue-collar workers for the class-controlled regression, and strong and weak identifiers among the entire county sample for the class-not-controlled condition. See notes to table 1 for more detail.

Table 2 shows that the aggregate model defends itself reasonably well. The parameters estimated from the survey-constructed aggregate data are close to those estimated when class was directly controlled by measurement in the dependent variable (when partisan identification was expressed as a known rate among the blue-collar workers).

A final comparison can be made that indicates the crude central tendency of the observations are quite well estimated by the regression procedures. The parameter p_1 estimates the individual level effect and p_2 the peer context effect. To estimate the total Democratic identification among blue-collar workers, the quantity p_2 must be multiplied by the proportion of the total sample blue-collar—the average context—and then this result added to p_1 to obtain the total average probability. Results obtained from following this procedure for both regression estimates are given in table 3, which compares the estimates to the known gross count among blue-collar workers. As might be expected, the aggregate simulation is off by more, 6 percent, than the class-controlled esti-

TABLE 3. Democratic Partisan Identification among Blue-Collar Workers, in Proportions

Source	Democratic Identification
Total survey count estimate	0.52
Regressions for data organized by county	
Class controlled in dependent variable	0.48
Class not controlled in dependent variable	0.46

Source: SRC Election Study (1960).

Note: Sample $N = 1,181$. County $N = 96$. See notes to tables 1 and 2 for measurement of variables and definition of class-controlled and not-controlled measurements.

mate, 4 percent. However, both are very close to the direct count estimate, and perhaps surprisingly close.

Two results seem plausible in light of the analyses surrounding tables 1, 2, and 3. First, partisan voting and identification exhibit contextual effects. Second, parameter estimates of contextual effects arising from aggregate analysis are not necessarily wildly off the mark. It would be cowardly, in light of this defense of the aggregate model, not to make an application to genuine aggregate data, an enterprise which is taken up next.

A Contextual Model for Aggregate Observations

Proceeding now with some additional confidence in the aggregate analysis possibilities, the truncated contextual model specified in (8) can be estimated for fully aggregate county data. Sample information is temporarily abandoned, and the data employed in the estimation are for the 1960 election county election results, along with demographic information taken from the 1960 census. The counties analyzed are just those counties included in the 1960 SRC election study. Once more, it is assumed that cross-group effects are zero and that no peer context effects are present for the residual non-blue-collar group. The blue-collar workers are conceptualized as blue-collar workers plus spouses, and are estimated by combining the census of population categories for construction, durable and nondurable manufacturing, and transportation, and then expressing this sum relative to the total nonfarm workforce. Thus, the proportion of adults who are blue-collar worker class members is represented by the proportion of the workforce in the specified categories. The Democratic proportion for the nation as a whole is 2 percent larger than the number estimated from the 1960 election study. Furthermore, a few comparisons for those counties with larger numbers of respondents in the 1960 survey indicate that the blue-collar measures are roughly comparable, as should be true for a representative sample. No obvious errors arise from lack of representativeness of the aggregate county units of observation.

The results of performing the appropriate regressions and solving for the theoretical parameters from the least squares coefficients are given in table 4. The estimated parameters from the survey regressions for vote intention are also included in table 4, to facilitate comparisons. For this particular set of estimates, the aggregate analysis attributes roughly three times as much importance to individual components, when compared with contextual component class effects. This ratio is obtained by expressing p_1 relative to the product of p_2 and the average blue-collar worker density. The direct survey estimate, from the regression with class controlled by measuring the vote intention among the blue-collar workers in each county sample, yields a ratio of less than two. These quantitative estimates indicate that, on the average, perhaps one-fourth

TABLE 4. Aggregate Model Parameter Estimates for 1960 Democratic Vote among Blue-Collar Workers Compared with Survey Estimates for Intended Democratic Vote

Parameters	Aggregate Data Regression	Survey Data with Class Controlled	Survey Data with Class not Controlled
p_1	0.34	0.24	0.35
p_2	0.19	0.37	0.28
p_4	0.25	—	0.36

Source: Voting data from files compiled by Louis P. Westefield.

Note: The data for the aggregate regression are taken from the *City, County Data Book* based on the 1960 census of population. For the survey measures see notes to table 1 and 2. Blue-collar definition for the census measure is given in text.

Total variance accounted for by the aggregate data county (census based information) regression is 6 percent.

to one-third of the observed rate of Democratic voting among blue-collar workers is appropriately attributed to the occupational class context in which the behavior takes place. The occupational environment is not politically neutral, given an areally nonuniform distribution of blue-collar occupations.

It is possible to extract quantitative estimates of the relative importance of individual and social context effects from the tables reported by Segal and Meyer (1974). When this is done, it appears that the influence of the social context is greater than the influence of the individual-level social context control effects. To reach that conclusion with firmness, however, requires both analyses and a model I have not yet seen.

From the 1960 election survey, the proportion of blue-collar workers intending to vote Democratic is known. The proportion of all others intending to vote Democratic is also known. Using these proportions, an expected Democratic vote can be computed for any given unit of observation, once the occupational structure is known (i.e., once the proportion of blue-collar workers is known). Such a prediction is independent of context, and is termed here the survey independent individual model. By contrast, the contextual model includes a term that varies nonlinearly with variation in occupational density. The significance of the difference in model predictions is illustrated in table 5, which gives the expected Democratic vote for hypothetical counties of zero, 50, and 100 percent blue-collar worker density. The range of prediction obtained from the independent individual model is 6 percent, while for the contextual model the range is 28 percent. Of course, the rate of change is distributed nonlinearly over this range for the contextual model (concentrations become important the more concentrated they become). The voting behavior of Iowa farm communities and Boston industrial suburbs ought to be more accurately anticipated by the contextual model than the independent individual model.

TABLE 5. Democratic Vote Expressed as a Proportion of Adults as Blue-Collar Worker Density Varies

Blue-Collar County Density	Survey Independent Individual Model	Aggregate Data Contextual Model
0.00	0.33	0.25
0.50	0.36	0.34
1.00	0.39	0.53

Source: Parameters from table 1 and table 4.

Note: Prediction for independent individual model is formed as

$$0.39S + 0.33 (1 - S).$$

Prediction for contextual model is formed as

$$0.34S + 0.19S^2 + 0.25 (1 - S).$$

In "One-Party Politics and the Voter," Miller reports ranges for political context voting effects of 30 percent for Democratic Identifiers and 18 percent for Republican Identifiers. The social class effects reported in table 5 are of comparable possible ranges. But what happens for real counties?

Comparisons of observed and predicted values for an arbitrary handful of counties are presented in table 6. Table 6 shows that in the high range of Democratic voting, the contextual model and independent individual model do not differ, while at the low end of Democratic voting, the contextual model is somewhat better. Why is the contextual model not markedly better at the high end of Democratic voting, and why is it somewhat better at the low end?

The answer probably lies in the distribution of blue-collar workers, which at their most dense concentration in these data reach only to 55 percent of the population (Worcester, Massachusetts). By contrast, Tingsten's Stockholm precinct data include some precincts which reach 95 percent Social Class III densities. On the other hand, the low Democratic voting counties have about one-half as many blue-collar workers as the high Democratic voting counties (27 percent in Taylor, Texas). If areas of behaviorally meaningful worker

TABLE 6. Two-Model Comparison of Predictions of Democratic Vote

County	Observed	Independent Individual Model	Contextual Model
Muhlenberg, Kentucky	0.27	0.37	0.29
Wayne, Michigan	0.47	0.33	0.34
Worcester, Massachusetts	0.47	0.36	0.36
Taylor, Texas	0.16	0.35	0.29

Source: City, County Data Book based on the 1960 census of population.

Note: Counties are arbitrarily selected and should not be thought of as typical.

Prediction equations are given in the notes to table 5. Both models require the same single observation on social structure, i.e., the proportion of blue-collar workers, in order to calculate predicted values.

concentrations much larger than one-half the population could be obtained, presumably the contextual model would yield better predictions in such areas than the individual model. With the county level data at hand, no further evaluation can be made. A natural extension would be to isolate communities with known extreme demography from 1960 census materials or other sources and compare model performances. Modern practice has been to move toward smaller contextual units of observation—which tend to exhibit the required within homogeneity—but that moves us away from our ancient data sources (see Huckfeldt and Sprague 1992).

In the final section of this paper, some amelioration of the identification constraints is sought by means of a strategy that combines the results from surveys with the results from aggregate data within the same formalization. It turns out that some relief can be achieved, but the problem of complete identification of the theoretical parameters remains only softened, not solved.

Ameliorating the Identification Problem

The contextual model for aggregate data analysis specified by equations (1), (2), and (3) takes the form, repeating (4),

$$B = [p_4 + p_5] + [p_1 + p_3 - p_4 - 2p_5 + p_6]S + [p_2 - p_3 + p_5 - p_6]S^2 \quad (10)$$

after substitution and algebraic rearrangement. The equation (10) may be associated in the natural way to the linear form

$$Y = m_0 + m_1 X + m_2 Z. \quad (11)$$

When the m_i are estimated by least squares, the identification problem can be summarized in the matrix system

$$\begin{pmatrix} 0 & 0 & 0 & 1 & 1 & 0 \\ 1 & 0 & 1 & -1 & -2 & 1 \\ 0 & 1 & -1 & 0 & 1 & -1 \end{pmatrix} \begin{pmatrix} p_1 \\ p_2 \\ p_3 \\ p_4 \\ p_5 \\ p_6 \end{pmatrix} = \begin{pmatrix} m_0 \\ m_1 \\ m_2 \end{pmatrix} \quad (12)$$

Where may additional constraints be obtained? From theory is the correct answer, of course, but absent theory, how can survey information be utilized? The answer to that question is by interpretation of equations (1) and (2) or (3) in terms of survey information—an answer already anticipated in earlier discussions.

The proportion of blue-collar workers intending to vote Democratic in 1960 is estimated as .391 from the survey count. If the contextual thesis is correct, this number must be made up of individual, peer context, and non-peer context effects. Hence, it is equivalent to equation (1). Designate this number as $PROB(B|S)^*$ and write the additional constraint as

$$PROB(B|S)^* = p_1 + p_2 S^* + p_3(1 - S^*).\tag{13}$$

The symbol S^*, rather than S, is employed to emphasize the dependency of the mean observed behavior rate on mean social density.

A symmetric constraint for the nonmembers of S may be written, $PROB(B|1 - S)^*$, presumably giving five constraints on the six unknown p_i. Then, with an additional ad hoc assumption (for example, cross-group effects are equal), the necessary identification would be accomplished. However, it turns out that we must be satisfied with the addition of (13) to the system (12), for the addition of the symmetric constraint for the nonmembers of S, when embedded in (12) along with (13) and *any* other constraint, does not provide independent information.

Proceed then to estimation with the identifying hypothesis

$$p_3 = p_6 = 0,\tag{14}$$

where S and non-S do not influence each other, and by invoking survey information taken from the same county populations with the interpretation (13). The resulting matrix system is

$$\begin{pmatrix} 0 & 0 \\ 1 & 0 \\ 0 & 1 \\ 1 & S^* \end{pmatrix} \begin{pmatrix} 1 & 1 \\ -1 & -2 \\ 0 & 1 \\ 0 & 0 \end{pmatrix} \begin{pmatrix} p_1 & m_0 \\ p_2 & m_1 \\ p_4 = m_2 \\ p_5 & PROB(B|S)^* \end{pmatrix}\tag{15}$$

The system (15) gives the moderate amelioration of the identification problem promised earlier.

Applying (15) to the results of earlier analyses produces the parameter estimates given in table 7. The results seem reasonable. Individual-level effect parameters are marginally larger than peer context parameters for blue-collar workers. The same is much more markedly true for the residual non-blue-collar worker class, as might have been anticipated.

Is the negative sign for peer context effect on non-blue-collar workers reasonable? Yes. The 1960 survey shows that the residual class favored the Republican party over the Democratic party in vote intention by a ratio of

TABLE 7. Parameter Estimates for the Augmented Yet Still Truncated Contextual Model (Based on Aggregate Regression Results Combined with One Constraint from Survey Information)

Parameter and Description	Parameter Value
p_1 Individual effect for blue-collar workers	+0.31
p_2 Peer contextual effect for blue-collar workers	+0.22
p_4 Individual effect for non-blue-collar workers	+0.28
p_5 Peer contextual effect for non-blue-collar workers	−0.03

Source: City, County Data Book based on the 1960 census of population. Voting from files compiled by Louis P. Westefield. SRC Voting Study 1960.

Note: The model is augmented, since four, rather than three, parameters are estimated. The model is still truncated, since only four, rather than the full six, theoretical parameters are estimated. The truncation is accomplished by the hypothesis, not totally unreasonable, that there are no cross-group effects, implying the quantitative requirements $p_3 = p_6 = 0$.

about four to three. Hence, when nonworkers talk to nonworkers, if there is reinforcement of individual propensities, it should be at the expense of Democratic voting—which is what the negative coefficient for p_5 shows. It very well may be that p_5 is zero, which is, again, not unreasonable for this crude residual category.

The estimates of table 7 do not do gross injustice to intuition, and thus, they suggest that interpreting and combining the two kinds of information in the same formalization may be a constructive research strategy.

Contexts and Functional Forms

This paper has developed an elementary model for the analysis of social context effects with aggregate data. The intent has been to make the logic of social context models clear with a model unencumbered by the usual substantive controls and statistical worries. Substantive variable controls and most statistical issues have largely been ignored in order to focus on the logical structure of one quantitative version of the social context effect thesis designed for aggregate data analysis.

The social context hypothesis and the political context hypothesis share an important feature: both posit (quantitative) interaction effects. The results for the aggregate social context estimates reported here (for those ancient SRC data) exhibit this interaction as nonlinearity in response *at the aggregate level,* in a manner analogous to the breaking point effects sketched by Miller in footnote 6. However, the underlying premises are linear and continuous, precisely analogous to Miller's arguments in footnote 6. It is the cross-level aggregation that apparently produces the (expected?) nonlinearities in the effects of context. It may be, of course, that social context has more inherent nonlinear response embedded within it than does the political context. This is indeed what Miller argues, in criticizing the probability model of voting advanced by the authors of *Voting*. As Miller puts it, in turning the random mixing argument of Berelson and his associates against them, "the Elmira data repeatedly demonstrate that interaction in matters political is anything but random" (Miller 1956, 722–23). The residual point that I wish to emphasize here, however, is that the aggregate social context effect model I have constructed is on all fours with Miller's thesis about the linear response to variation in the political context at the individual level. In the formulation I have presented, social context effects share this uniform (linear) response, so forcefully demonstrated for the effects of political context in "One-Party Politics and the Voter."

This paper has also developed a possible strategy for combining aggregate and survey data within the same formalization, in order to further the identification of parameters in an elementary aggregate data contextual model. Along the path of this ameliorative strategy, an investigation of context in terms of survey data aggregated by county units was conducted. The results of analysis suggest that both partisan intended vote and partisan identification may be peer context-dependent for reasonable social categories. Furthermore, the aggregate data results for voting behavior are not highly discrepant from the survey results for intended vote. I conclude that further investigation of the possibility of combining survey with aggregate analysis, along the lines of the last section of this paper, is justified.

There are some obvious opportunities for developing strategies combining different information sets. The National Election Studies and the General Social Survey both provide comprehensive databases, extended in time, that have been exploited by many sociologists and political scientists. The sampling frames can be isolated and the respondents matched to geographic contexts for which a rich demographic and economic record is available. Three particularly rich possibilities stand out: racial and ethnic densities; religious affiliation concentrations; and economic structure, including employment patterns.

As noted, statistical issues have been largely ignored here. The colinearity between the S and S^2 term is the most troublesome statistical problem for the particular contextual model that has been studied here. This produces great uncertainty with respect to the location of coefficient values. A potential strategy for dealing with this problem might be to add control variables to the aggregate regression in a frank attempt to simply increase fit. If the fit increased sufficiently, and in a convenient way, it might sharpen the t-tests and thus provide more confidence in the quantitative statements concerning the relative importance of individual and contextual effects and the shape of the aggregate curves reflecting such effects. Presumably, the control variables that would be entered would reflect the conditions of individuals likely to affect their private calculations. Thus, the effect of class membership, p_1, should be markedly reduced, while the effect of peer context, p_2, should be relatively unaffected.

More important by far than the colinearity problem is the careful development of the social categories to be used in the analysis. Blue-collar workers have been used in the present paper largely because the units of aggregation—counties—are so crude. Nevertheless, a much more careful reconstruction of this category than was used here is both possible and appropriate. If finer aggregates were used, such as minor civil divisions, greater care in constructing the social category measures would be even more important. Additionally, with finer aggregates, it is likely that greater variance across the social categories could be obtained, coupled with greater homogeneity within units, producing a stronger design overall.

The major substantive implication of the contextual thesis at the theoretical level is the doubt it casts on the meaning of contingent probabilities based only on sorting individual level properties. If the contextual components are substantial, as I believe, then a serious empirical and theoretical challenge emerges for the reanalysis and modeling of some large portion of our elementary factual knowledge concerning political behavior.

Finally, the value of true quantitative theory is underscored by the identification problem in the aggregate model of social context effects. Matters of functional form, of a quantitative science, cannot be ignored. If the quantitative law governing direction of influence between different occupational groups were known, the mindless and equally quantitative practice of setting parameters to zero could be avoided. If the mechanism by which peers influence each other were known in quantitative form, then the effect of peer context would not require separate estimation. These are issues of specific functional form in an appropriate formal language, and require moving beyond assertions of general substantive causation to explicit formal and quantitative characterizations of the laws determining observed behavior, including the effects of social and political context.

APPENDIX

FOOTNOTE 6

The next page reproduces footnote 6 from Warren Miller's "One-Party Politics and the Voter." The note runs across two pages, and I have patched the two together with a copy machine to facilitate presentation. As the text notes, my collection of *American Political Science Reviews* does not quite extend back to September of 1956. I am indebted to my colleague John Kautsky, Professor Emeritus, Washington University, for allowing access to his extensive collection of *Reviews* in order to produce this facsimile.

* This is an important consideration which governs the categorization of counties. As can be seen in Table I, the "most Republican" counties were in 1952 more extremely pro-Republican than the "most Democratic" counties were comparably pro-Democratic. If the 1936–1948 average were used, instead of the data for 1952, the situation would be reversed (without seriously rearranging the counties), with few or no counties being as extremely pro-Republican as their most pro-Democratic opposite numbers. The difficulty of attempting to decide what *absolute* standards are sufficient to define "extremely Republican" or "extremely Democratic" under two such different situations as represented by the 1936–1948 period and the one year 1952 is avoided, without adjusting or otherwise violating the data, by the use of the *relative* "most Republican" and "most Democratic" designations.

Tables II, III, and IV, and the exploratory analyses on which they are based, provide an empirical justification for talking about counties as being distributed on a continuum of greater-to-lesser Democratic (or Republican) dominance. Adoption of a fixed breaking point to define one-party control would seem to imply a discontinuity, or at least curvilin-

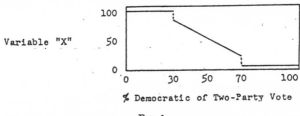

Fig. 1

earity, in relationships which, in fact, has not been observed in these data. One might assume, for example, that a partisan division as extreme as 70–30 would indicate a qualitatively different situation from that indicated by any more evenly balanced division, such as 65–35, 58–42, 51–49. One might assume further that once the 70–30 point was reached, more extreme divisions would not alter the essentially "one-party" nature of the situation. If this set of assumptions were to be verified, one would then expect a general case of relationships involving party dominance and any other related factor to be something like that in Figure 1. In Figure 1, of course, co-variation between party dominance and Factor "X" is found only in the middle of the two-party vote range and disappears when either party gains complete control. In all relevant instances in the analysis with which this discussion is concerned, the observed relationships were of the general type where co-variation extended in an apparently linear fashion from one extreme of partisan dominance to the

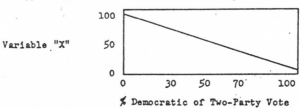

Fig. 2

other as in Figure 2. There was no indication that a real breaking point did in fact exist near either end of the dominance continuum. Consequently, the use of the concept of a continuum of relative dominance not only provides *a* needed solution to the methodological problem involved, but also appears to provide *the* solution most compatible with the relevant data. This is not, of course, intended to constitute an argument that all relationships involving party dominance are linear, nor that they are necessarily continuous.

NOTE

Portions of the data utilized in this paper were made available by the Inter-University Consortium for Political and Social Research. The data were originally collected by Angus Campbell, Phillip Converse, Warren Miller, and Donald Stokes, Survey Research Center, University of Michigan. Neither the original collectors of these data nor the Consortium bear any responsibility for the analysis or interpretations presented here.

REFERENCES

Berelson, Bernard R., Paul Lazarsfeld, and William N. McPhee. 1954. *Voting: A Study of Opinion Formation in a Presidential Election.* Chicago: University of Chicago Press.
Books, John W., and Charles L. Prysby. 1991. *Political Behavior and the Local Context.* New York: Praeger.
Boudon, Raymond. 1963. "Propriétés Individuelles et Propriétés Collectives: Une Problème d'Analyse Ecologique." *Revue Française de Sociologie* 4:275–99.
Coleman, James S. 1964. *Introduction to Mathematical Sociology.* New York: Free Press.
Foladare, Irving S. 1968. "The Effect of Neighborhood on Voting Behavior." *Political Science Quarterly* 83:516–29.
Goodman, Leo A. 1953. "Ecological Regression and Behavior of Individuals." *American Sociological Review* 18:663–64.
Huckfeldt, Robert, and John Sprague. 1992. "Political Parties and Electoral Mobilization: Political Structure, Social Structure, and the Party Canvass." *American Political Science Review* 86:70–86.
———. 1993. "Citizens, Contexts, and the Multiple Levels of Democratic Politics." In *The State of the Discipline II*, ed. Ada W. Finifter. Washington, D.C.: American Political Science Association.
Katz, Daniel, and Samuel J. Eldersveld. 1961. "The Impact of Local Party Activity Upon the Electorate." *Public Opinion Quarterly* 25:1–24.
Miller, Warren. 1956. "One-Party Politics and the Voter." *American Political Science Review* 50:707–25.
Przeworski, Adam. 1974. "Contextual Models of Political Behavior." *Political Methodology* 1:27–61.
Segal, David R., and Marshall W. Meyer. 1974. "The Social Context of Political Partisanship." In *Social Ecology*, ed. Mattei Dogan and Stein Rokkan. Cambridge, Mass.: MIT Press.
Tingsten, Herbert. [1937] 1963. *Political Behavior: Studies in Election Statistics.* Trans. Vilgot Hammarling. Reprint. Totowa, N. J.: Bedminster.

Elites and Representation

CHAPTER 10

Empirical Research into Political Representation: Failing Democracy or Failing Models?

Jacques Thomassen

Introduction

The results of empirical research into the process of political representation are
not very reassuring for stern believers in democratic government. Members of
representative bodies are more inclined to follow their own conscience than to
follow the lead of their constituency. The extent to which the electorate coerces
legislative bodies to act according to its will is very limited, because most
voters don't know the record of political parties and individual candidates, let
alone whether they would vote according to their judgment on this record. In
many respects, the political attitudes and opinions of members of representative bodies hardly reflect the attitudes and opinions of the electorate.

The organizing principle of most studies of representation is political
linkage. This refers to "any means by which the political leaders act in accordance with the wants, needs, and demands of the public in making government
policy" (Luttbeg 1974, 3). The different means or mechanisms by which this
can be achieved are also referred to as models of representation. The most
widely recognized models are the delegate model, the political parties model,
and the consensus, or belief sharing, model. What these models have in common is that they refer to an empirical model of political representation that is
deduced from a normative theory of democracy. Therefore, the purpose of
most studies of political representation, is *not* to develop a causal model of
political representation that can explain as much as possible of the empirical
reality of the process of political representation, but to assess to what extent
political reality is consistent with the normative ideal. Therefore, by criticizing
models of political representation because of their poor explanatory power, one
would be missing the point. A more logical interpretation of a poor fit of
models of political representation would be that there is a wide discrepancy
between the normative ideal and empirical reality, and therefore, that there is
something wrong with representative democracy.

However, this is only a legitimate conclusion when the model of political representation involved is an impeccable translation of a viable normative theory of political representation. In this paper, I will try to evaluate the delegate model and the political parties model from this perspective. The consensus, or belief sharing, model will only be referred to in the context of the political parties model.

By accepting Luttbeg's definition of political linkage as the essential issue in the study of political representation, one has implicitly accepted a populist view on representative democracy (see also Dahl 1956). According to this definition "the policies passed by government must reflect both the preferences of the governed and, most desirably, the public's interest" (Luttbeg 1984, 1). In this view, a representative democracy is only "a sorry substitute for the real thing" (Dahl 1982, 13), whereas the "real thing" is a direct democracy. Therefore, the ideal of a representative democracy is the identity between the will of the people and government policy. Ideally, parliament should make the decisions that the people themselves would have made had they been able to decide themselves.

However, one should be aware of the fact that this view on representative democracy is not the only legitimate one. In the liberal theory of democracy, there is a division of labor between voters and their representatives that yields a less rigid view of the relationship between the opinions of the voters and the behavior of their representatives (Herzog 1989; Kielmansegg 1988; Riker 1982).

The Mandate-Independence Controversy: Spellbound by Edmund Burke

The most famous ideal types of representation are the two sides of the mandate-independence controversy: should deputies act according to the will of their constituencies, or according to their own mature judgment? The intellectual source of this controversy is Edmund Burke's famous speech to the electors of Bristol in 1774, and in particular this quote:

> Parliament is not a *congress* of ambassadors from different and hostile interests, which interests each must maintain, as an agent and advocate, against other agents and advocates; but Parliament is a *deliberative* assembly of *one* nation, with *one* interest, that of the whole—where not local purposes, not local prejudices, ought to guide, but the general good, resulting from the general reason of the whole. (as quoted in Birch 1972, 39)

I'm not sure when Burke's thoughts began to dominate political representation research, but I suppose it was in 1959, when Eulau and his associates published

Fig. 1. Style and focus of the representative's role

"The Role of the Representative: Some Empirical Observations on the Theory of Edmund Burke." Much more than Burke himself, Eulau et al. made a distinction between two variables: the *focus* and the *style* of political representation. These two perspectives can be presented simply (see fig. 1). The figure does not exhaust all possibilities mentioned by Eulau et al. There is a third role conception with regard to the style of representation (politico), and the focus of representation can logically refer to an almost infinite number of entities. But figure 1 is sufficient as a frame of reference to illustrate Burke's conception of political representation and its persistent influence on discussions about political representation.

The focus of representation refers to the interest representatives must defend: local interests of their constituencies, or those of the *one* nation. Burke's position is clear: he chooses for the national interest. The style of representation refers to the question of whether representatives should act as agents who take instructions from their constituents, or act according to their own "mature judgement." Burke chooses for the latter role conception. Therefore, Burke's position is represented by cell D in figure 1.[1] The conception he opposes is in cell A: the role conception of deputies who defend the *interests of their districts* according to the *instructions* from their constituencies. The two logically remaining possibilities are those of deputies who defend the interests of their constituencies without following the instructions from their constituents (B) and deputies who defend the general interest, but according to the views of their constituents (C).

Only the role conception of a delegate (cells A and C) can be considered as a model of linkage. A pure Burkean role conception of deputies, who think that the will of their constituents should not be decisive for their behavior, cannot, by definition, be an instrument to implement the people's will. This does not necessarily mean that such deputies do not, in reality, express the will of their constituents. It only means that their role conception in this respect is irrelevant, because it cannot explain a possible correlation between their roll call behavior and their districts' will.

It is my feeling that the scientific interest in the mandate-independence controversy is inversely proportional to its relevance in a modern representative democracy, in particular in the parliamentary democracies of Western Europe. It is hard to see how the role conception of an instructed delegate can be reconciled with the mechanisms of modern parliamentary democracy.

One might even argue that it was already becoming obsolete in Burke's days. The idea of instructed delegates, taking their instructions from their districts, comes from another time, with different ideas about the role of the state. Political theories are, more often than not, formulated after a certain political practice. Theories of political representation are no exception to this rule. Modern parliaments descend from a practice of representation that has little to do with modern mass democracy. The institutions that preceded modern parliaments, and the first stage in the history of representative government, began in several European kingdoms in the thirteenth and fourteenth centuries, when representatives of the different estates or communities within society were invited to give consent to measures by the king, in particular, measures of taxation. These institutions emerged in feudal societies where rights, powers, and privileges depended on the ownership of land. Therefore, they are a heritage of feudalism, in which the power of the king was ultimately limited and very much dependent upon the consent and the financial support of his vassals, who were reigning in their own estates. These early representative bodies were formed by the representatives of the different regions (however defined) of the country. They were there less to deliberate on national policy than to defend the local interests vis-à-vis the king. They were representatives just as a diplomat is a representative of his country. It is also clear that the first task of a diplomat is to defend the interests of his country. An important function of parliament was also the possibility and the duty of the members to present the grievances of their constituents in parliament. As such, parliament was a part of the judicial system. No principal change in the theory of representation was needed, as long as political representatives could be viewed as agents, sent to the national parliament by the estates or communities within society to give or withhold their consent to measures of taxation or legislation proposed by the executive (Birch 1972, 24–37).

However, the development of the relationship between king and parliament, especially in Britain, made this theory of representation gradually obsolete. The more parliament succeeded in placing the sovereignty of parliament above that of the king, the less parliament became the body of agents of district interests opposite the king. The more parliament became the center of power, the more responsible it became for the national interest, and the less welcome pure geographical interests became. In Britain, the Tory attitude in the eighteenth century "was the traditional one that the function of MP's was to represent local interests and to seek redress for particular grievances, it being assumed that the king and his ministers had the main responsibility for interpreting the national interest. In contrast, Whig spokesmen insisted that parliament was a deliberative body, representing the whole nation, whose decisions should be more than a mere aggregate of sectional demands" (Birch 1972, 38).

Therefore, Edmund Burke was following in a long tradition when he made his famous speech to the electors of Bristol in 1774. His conception was nothing less than the logical requirement of a modern nation state. And yet, it would be a surprising thought to consider Edmund Burke as the father of modern democracy. Of course, he was not. But even a pure populist view of democracy does not necessarily lead to a different conclusion. The radical Rousseauistic view on democracy that was dominant during a short period of the French Revolution was extremely hostile to the possible influence of regional interests in the national assembly. In this view, the general interest and the will of the people are indivisible, and can most certainly not be considered as the resultant of different interests. Accordingly, the new constitutions on the European continent demanded of members of parliament that they represent the general interest, and forbade them to take instructions from anybody. Therefore, it is at least disputable to argue that a Burkean role conception can hardly be considered democratic, whereas the role conception of an instructed delegate would portray the real democrat (Farah 1980, 251).

The objections against the instructed delegate model, therefore, can hardly be seen as an infringement of modern democracy. It is fairer to say that it prepared the road for modern democracy. The idea of representing geographically defined collectivities to the throne had to yield to a modern conception of popular rule, where general individual enfranchisement enabled individual citizens to participate in the rule of the nation.

The argument so far can be summarized on the basis of figure 1. The role conception of an instructed delegate is to be found in the first column. Cell A represents the role conception of deputies who defend the interests of their constituencies and, at the same time, follow the will of their constituents in doing so. I have argued that this combination of roles portrays a conception of representative government that is completely obsolete. The representatives' role is no longer to defend the interests of their local districts with central government, but to participate in the national policy-making and legislative process. A more differentiated conclusion might be that the task of members of parliament to defend local interests, acting as delegates or as trustees, has become marginal, compared to their role in general policy making, where *specific* local interests are hardly at issue.

But once one accepts the argument that representatives should serve the general interest of the nation, rather than the interests of their constituents, how can one at the same time persist in a delegate role with respect to one's own constituency? This role conception means that one is willing to serve the general interest, but is guided by the vision on this of one's own constituency.

For Burke, this was undoubtedly a strange position. Living in the age of the enlightenment, he believed in a parliament as "a *deliberative* assembly of *one* nation, with *one* interest, that of the whole—where not local purposes, not local prejudices, ought to guide, but the general good, resulting from the general reason of the whole" (as quoted in Birch 1972, 39). In his view, parliamentary debate was an essential stage in parliamentary decision making among representatives who were free to act according to their "own mature judgment." Therefore, he rejected a system "in which the determination precedes the discussion; in which one set of men deliberate, and another decides; and where those who form the conclusion are perhaps three hundred miles distant from those who hear the arguments" (as quoted in Pitkin 1967, 147).

Of course, Burke was not the greatest friend of populist democracy. But, as argued above, even from the point of view of populist democracy, the instructed delegate model is not the most logical alternative in a modern representative democracy. Once one accepts that the major content of a modern conception of political representation refers to matters of general policy, the fruitfulness of an approach of political representation in which the representation of geographical districts is essential becomes very doubtful. Purely regional issues have, over the past century, undergone a secular decline in intensity through the progressive nationalization of most political controversies.

In modern states, the lines of political dispute cut across purely geographic boundaries (Converse and Pierce 1986, 517–18). There are few reasons to believe that people living within the same district will have common views on matters of general policy such as "censorship, capital punishment or the merits of the divorce laws" (Birch 1972, 89). Electoral districts tend to be "so diverse in the kinds of values and beliefs held, that whatever measures of central tendency are used to classify a district are more likely to conceal than to reveal its real character" (Eulau and Wahlke 1979, 115–16). Policy preferences tend to be related to interests and interest groups that must, of necessity, cut across a purely geographically defined division (Weissberg 1978, 537). In these circumstances, it is difficult to see how a single deputy would be able to act according to *the* district sentiment. Therefore, if the purpose of representative democracy is to translate the policy views of the electorate into public policy, it is very dubious whether one should lay such an emphasis on the relationship between individual members of parliament and their constituencies. The modern mechanisms to express different views on matters of national policy are political parties, not individual deputies. By focusing on the relationship between individual deputies and their districts, one tends to neglect a major element in modern representative democracy—that is, the overriding importance of political parties and interest groups.

Summarizing, there are three reasons to doubt whether the delegate model, in the sense of an individual relationship between members of parliament and their districts, is consistent with the normative view underlying a modern conception of representative democracy. First, it is contradictory to the dominant Burkean view of political representation that is inserted in the constitution of most continental parliamentary democracies. Second, modern politics are dominated by national controversies on which electoral districts tend to be heterogeneous. Third, it neglects the overwhelming importance of political parties in modern representative democracy.

This does not necessarily mean that it should fail as an empirical model of representation. It only means that a possible failure as an empirical model cannot easily be interpreted as a failure of representative democracy. In the next section, it will be seen to what extent the model is fruitful as an empirical model of political representation in comparative research.

The Delegate Model as a Model of Linkage

The mandate-independence controversy has been introduced into empirical research by Eulau and Wahlke (see above). But its prominent position in the comparative research on political representation is due to the fact that it is incorporated in the Miller-Stokes model that was introduced in the 1960s (Miller and Stokes 1963; Stokes and Miller 1962; Miller 1964). This model was the source of inspiration for a major comparative research project that was initiated by Warren E. Miller of the University of Michigan in the late 1960s and early 1970s. Book-length reports were published on the studies in France, Italy, the Netherlands, Sweden, and West Germany (Barnes 1977; Converse and Pierce 1986; Farah 1980; Holmberg 1974; Thomassen 1976).

Miller and Stokes presented their model as a simple, but ingenious, causal scheme (see fig. 2). It is an ingenious scheme because this paradigm makes it possible to test the empirical validity of the two sides of the mandate-independence controversy. The lower path of the model (ACD) presents deputies who are willing to behave according to their districts' will. This role conception is only an effective instrument to enact the will of the district when their perception is at least correlated with the actual will (AC). Above, it has been argued that a pure Burkean role conception of deputies, who think that the will of their constituents should not be decisive for their behavior, cannot, by definition, be an instrument to implement the people's will. However, this does not necessarily mean that such a deputy does not, in reality, express the will of his constituents. It only means that the role conception, in this respect, is irrelevant, because whether the deputy concerned will vote according to his district's will or not depends on the correlation between his own opinion and the district's will (AB). However, the explanation of such a correlation lies outside the mandate model, because in these circumstances, the deputy is a representative *malgré lui* (Converse and Pierce 1986, 502).

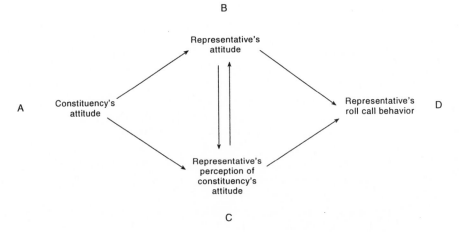

Fig. 2. Connections between a constituency's attitude and its representative's roll call behavior. (Adapted from Miller and Stokes, o.c., 361.)

Miller and Stokes report that the results of their analysis are different for different policy domains. In the domain of foreign policy, there was hardly a correlation between the roll call behavior of the deputies and their districts' will. In the case of social welfare and civil rights, there was a substantial correlation between voters' opinions and the roll call behavior of their representatives. The explanation in these two cases was different, however. In the case of social welfare, influence ran via the upper path of the model, whereas in the case of civil rights, the lower path was involved. Miller and Stokes conclude that it would be wrong to choose just one model of representation. The strength of the different models depends on the kind of issue. In the case of foreign policy, members of the House themselves have hardly enough information to make a sound judgment, let alone allow their constituency to judge them on their record on these issues. The situation with respect to the civil rights issue was completely different. Representatives from the southern states, in particular, could not afford to take a wrong stand on this issue, on pain of an electoral defeat (Miller and Stokes 1963, 55).

Miller and Stokes' pioneering study was followed by a great number of publications challenging or refining the initial approach. A large part of this literature is devoted to methodological problems, such as the use of a correlation coefficient as a measure of congruence (Achen 1977, 1978) and the problem of small sample size within congressional districts (Cnudde and McCrone 1966; Erikson 1978). Several authors have tried to develop a more refined model to explain roll call votes by introducing possible explanatory factors, like the relative importance of constituency characteristics versus party membership (Page et al. 1984), the accuracy of congressional perceptions of constituency views (Clausen 1977; Friesema and Hedlund 1974; Hedlund and Friesema 1972), and role orientations (Friesema and Hedlund 1974; Kuklinski and Elling 1977; McCrone and Kuklinski 1979).

However diverse these different approaches are, they have one thing in common: the conceptualization of the representational relationship as dyadic (Hurley 1982). A notable exception to this rule is Weissberg's challenge of the dyadic perspective. He argues that, according to an equally valid tradition, the central question should be "whether Congress as an institution represented the American people, not whether each member of Congress represented his or her particular district" (Weissberg 1978, 535). Weissberg's approach has not gathered much of a following in the United States. In general, the dyadic perspective of the Miller-Stokes model, as such, has hardly been disputed.

Therefore, it is no wonder that this model became the source of inspiration for a number of studies in different countries. In some of these studies, however, it became immediately clear that the Miller-Stokes model was not fully applicable. Barnes, in his study on representation in Italy, decided against a precise replication of the Miller-Stokes design, mainly for two reasons: first, because of Italy's system of proportional representation; and second, because of the overriding importance of political parties in explaining deputies' political behavior. Because of the fact that on most votes almost all deputies accept party discipline, it hardly made sense to study roll call votes as a dependent variable. It made even less sense because roll call voting is secret when a substantial minority requests it. As a consequence, most of the important and controversial votes are secret. Members sometimes vote against their parties on these ballots, but individual deviations cannot be documented. Italian members of parliament are elected in multimember districts. However, Barnes found that constituency explained very little of the variation in representatives' opinions, once political party was taken into account. Party differences, rather than constituency differences, could explain the impressively strong relationship between the opinions of elites and masses (Barnes 1977). Therefore, one can conclude that implementation of the Miller-Stokes model in the Italian context was neither feasible nor fruitful.

For more or less similar reasons, the Miller-Stokes model has never been applied in the Dutch and Swedish studies. In the Netherlands, use of the model was out of the question because of the electoral system of proportional representation, which uses the whole country as one single constituency. Members of parliament are elected according to a list system and have no special relationship with a particular district (Thomassen 1976). In Sweden, it was decided in advance that the Miller-Stokes model was hardly applicable, because of the overwhelming influence of party compared to constituency (Holmberg 1974, 1989).

In the two remaining countries, France and West Germany, the full Miller-

Stokes model was applied by Converse and Pierce, and Farah, respectively. The difficulties that had to be met in these two studies illustrate, in addition to the theoretical considerations above, the limited feasibility of the delegate model, or of any model based on the relationship of individual members of parliament and their constituencies, in the context of a parliamentary system. In addition to the heterogeneity of geographically defined districts in any modern state, the two major problems are the dominance of party discipline and the role conceptions of members of parliament, topics to which I shall now turn.

The Problem of Party Discipline

The dependent variable in the Miller-Stokes model is the roll call vote of the individual deputy. A first requirement for the fruitfulness of the model is that there is something to be explained, that is to say, that there is a certain amount of variance in the dependent variable that can be measured. In the parliamentary democracies of Western Europe, contrary to the United States, it is very questionable whether much variance will be left after political party membership has been taken into account. As Converse and Pierce correctly observe, "substantial party discipline in voting is a standard feature of most of the world's legislative bodies, and therefore the U.S. Congress, with its relatively weak party discipline, is more to be remarked upon than the French situation" (Converse and Pierce 1986, 552). Knowing the strength of party discipline in European legislatures is a major a priori reason for being somewhat doubtful about the fruitfulness of the Miller-Stokes model. Therefore, it is not much of a surprise that the measurement of individual roll call behavior was very difficult, if not impossible, both in France and in Germany.

In France, in the time period of the study, between the beginning of the Third Legislature in May 1967 and the termination of the Fourth Legislature in December 1972, in more than 96 percent of all roll call votes, there was no substantive defection in the roll call vote from the party position (Converse and Pierce 1986, 552–54). This means, of course, that in all those cases, knowledge of a deputy's district does not add anything to the explanation of his roll call behavior, once we have established his party group membership. Therefore, it seems to be a legitimate conclusion that direct constituency influence has only a marginal impact above the influence of political parties. This, of course, does not mean that in all other cases deputies would be deviating from their district's opinion. Insofar as a deputy votes according to his party line, and the majority of the district agrees with that line, he acts according to the will of at least the majority of the district, without any deliberate act. However, if that is the case, it only confirms the general point to be made—that in cases of general policy, it is ideology and political parties that count first, and districts only second.

In Germany, it was even more difficult to use individual roll call votes as a dependent variable. Farah observes that in Germany "there are three kinds of roll-call votes: the secret ballot, used only in cases of elections of parliamentary officials; the show-of-hands ballot, the most common form of voting; and *namentliche Abstimmungen,* the only vote which has the deputy's name affixed to it. For the purpose of testing the Miller-Stokes model of representation the latter voting form is the only one that is directly applicable because it is the only one that can be linked to the district" (Farah 1980, 148).

However, during the sixth session of the Bundestag, the period of Farah's study, no *namentliche Abstimmungen* were recorded. This made it impossible to distinguish the actions of the individual MPs from that of their party. Therefore, Farah draws the obvious conclusion: "At this stage district-level representation loses its meaning" (Farah 1980, 218). To solve the problem that individual roll call votes were not registered, she decided to construct a surrogate measure for the roll call vote. Because most issues are party specific, it was decided to treat the roll call voting of the elites as party specific. All CDU members were assigned a score of "0," and the SPD members a score of "1." The FDP elites were given a score midway between the two other parties, ".5" (Farah 1980, 148–52). Because of this procedure, individual deviations from the party's position are, by definition, impossible. In the case of the French study, there was at least a theoretical possibility of a district's influence over and above the parties' positions in about 4 percent of all votes. In the German case, even this marginal influence was, by definition, impossible.

Therefore, as far as a constituency influence can be measured, this is nothing more than the correlation between district sentiments and the positions taken in parliament by the party whose candidate was chosen in a particular district. A positive correlation indicates that CDU-oriented districts tend to agree more with CDU policy than SPD-oriented districts. This is not to say that such correlations tend to be high by definition. Quite the contrary, both the French and the German study prove that this is not the case at all. In the German case, there is no trace of such a correlation. Farah, therefore, concludes that "the mandate version of representation does not seem to be operative in Germany" (Farah 1980, 182). At the same time, she is puzzled by the findings that emerge with respect to the responsible party model. "On the one hand party voting dominates the legislative process while on the other hand there is nothing in our initial findings to suggest that the German parties act in an accountable or responsible way vis-à-vis the district. The concept of the responsible party system, after all, assumes that there is at least some basic level of congruence between voter attitude and deputy behavior. Our results indicate that there is essentially no relationship between these two terms" (Farah 1980, 185).

A similar comment is made by Converse and Pierce. District positions on specific issues have hardly any predictive meaning for roll call behavior in France. However, the model seems to be saved by the fact that there is a substantial correlation between left-right position of districts and roll call behavior.

The authors explain this "ironic" fact by the supposition that, on the one hand, relative to judgments about district sentiments on specific issues, the perceptions of left-right district coloration are heavily constrained by reality, while, on the other hand, "the deputy is also more like his district, seemingly because elections winnow along left-right lines much more clearly than they do along lines of more specific issues" (Converse and Pierce 1980, 719). I cannot think of any better explanation. But is not the very fact that in both cases the left-right position is much more important than the position on specific issues another indication of the overriding importance of national conflict dimensions instead of district-specific factors? Does not the dominant influence of the left-right dimension simply mean that left-oriented people vote for candidates of left parties and that, therefore, districts with a majority of left-oriented voters will elect a candidate of a left party?

Farah finally finds that, as far as there is any congruence between district sentiments and roll call behavior, it is between partisan supporters and the roll call behavior of their party. She then concludes that this congruence is primarily caused by the fact that citizens are inclined to identify with a party label and, by their votes, exert some control over the actions of the political parties. Finally, she rightly concludes that, in this instance, the representational relationship is not linked to a particular geographical area, but is defined in terms of a national constituency (Farah 1980, 212).

This is precisely the point. Once one takes the high level of party discipline as given, a completely different kind of model, the responsible party model, in which, not trusteeship, but rather a delegate role with respect to party, is an essential characteristic, seems to be more indicated. This is not to say that the Responsible Party Model is a valid model of political representation. This is still to be seen, but at least in the context of the Western European parliamentary democracies, with their high degree of party discipline, it has more a priori validity than any model that is based on the relationship between individual deputies and their districts.

The Problem of Role Conceptions

A second reason to be somewhat skeptical about the fruitfulness of the Miller-Stokes model is the available empirical evidence with respect to role conceptions of members of parliament. The lower path of the Miller-Stokes model assumes an influence of constituencies on deputies' roll call behavior by way of their perception of the district's will. Two conditions have to be met for this part of the model to work. First, deputies must behave in accordance with their perception of the district's will, and second, this perception must be correct. If both conditions are met, at least the data are consistent with an instructed delegate model. However, the explanation of the correspondence between a deputy's behavior and his district's sentiment is by way of his role conception, the conception of an instructed delegate. If such a role conception is not present, it is hard to see how this explanation can be maintained.[2]

The conclusion of all empirical research of role conceptions that I know of is unambiguous. Members of parliament who consider themselves as instructed delegates of their constituents or voters are a small minority. The verdict of Converse and Pierce, after having compared data from France, the United States, and the Netherlands, is perfectly clear: "The only thing the three legislatures have in common is that their members appear to give rather short shrift in their legislative decision making to the majority opinion of voters in their districts" (Converse and Pierce 1986, 675). In Germany, only 3 percent of the members of the Bundestag regarded themselves as instructed delegates (Farah 1980, 238). Above, it has been argued that in a European context, these results are not surprising. In most continental European countries, a Burkean role conception is demanded by the constitution. But the essential message is that the available empirical evidence does not support the hypothesis that role conceptions belong to the "means by which political leaders act in accordance with the wants, needs and demands of the public in making government policy" (Luttbeg 1974, 3).

However, the poor explanatory power of the Miller-Stokes model, and of the delegate model in particular, is not a sufficient reason to argue that it is not a fruitful approach to study the process of political representation. The explicit objective of the model is to assess to what extent political reality is consistent with the normative theory of political representation. If it is not consistent, the explanation might be that the process of political representation is less democratic than it should be. However, such a conclusion is only justified if the normative theory of political representation on which the model is based is beyond dispute. I have argued that it is not. The instructed delegate model can hardly be regarded as a viable theory of representative democracy in the context of the parliamentary democracies in Western Europe. In the United States, the mandate-independence controversy is not irrelevant. In a presidential system, the president has his own electoral mandate. It is not vitally important that he is supported by a majority in parliament. Therefore, party discipline can be lenient and individual members of Congress can be more sensitive to the feelings of their home district. However, in a parliamentary system, the executive has no other basis than its majority in parliament. This makes party discipline essential for the survival of the government. In this situation, political parties, and not individual members of parliament, are the key actors in the system of political representation. Therefore, models of political representation, like the responsible party model, that take the key position of political parties into account have a higher prima facie validity than any model that is based on the relationship between an individual member of parliament and his constituency. However, it still remains to be seen to what extent the political parties model is based on a viable normative theory of democracy that can be translated into a model that is consistent with political reality.

The Political Parties Model

Originally, political parties, in addition to regional interests, were considered inimical to democracy. Theories of political representation had difficulty in dealing with political parties. No doubt, this is partly because the major theories of political parties were formulated and established before modern political parties came to exist. But even the much-praised book of Hannah Pitkin (1967) comes close to neglecting the existence of political parties. Parties, for a long time, had a negative image. They were seen as threatening the common interest of the one nation. Also, party discipline was hard to reconcile with the prevailing theories of political representation.

It seems to be a strange paradox that it was Burke, again, who recognized the function of political parties, not as evil factions which threatened the unity of the nation, but as instruments to model modern government where traditional concepts were no longer satisfying. Again, this breakthrough was related to the changing relationship between king and parliament. With the increasing power of parliament, the opposition between king and parliament as an institution lost much of its relevance, yielding to the different outlooks within parliament with respect to government policy (Sartori 1976, 10). Burke defined a political party as "a body of men united, for promoting by their joint endeavors the national interest, upon some particular principle in which they are all agreed" (as quoted in Sartori 1976, 9). By recognizing a particular principle as the basis for a political party, Burke seems to recognize ideology as the basis of a political party. But, of course, Burke was all but a populist, and it is most unlikely he would be flattered to be considered as the inventor of the political parties model in the sense of a model of linkage. It was not before the twentieth century that the essential function of political parties in the political representation process was recognized.

Once more, it was the development of political reality, rather than the development of political thinking, as such, that forced the recognition of political parties. The extension of the suffrage forced members of parliament to compete for electoral votes. To do so effectively, a certain organization was needed. This organization could be provided by political parties. It has been argued time and again that political parties are the only modern possibility to give any real meaning to the traditional concept of popular government.

A radical view on the democratic function of political parties can be found in the writings of Leibholz (1966, 226). In his opinion, liberal representative democracy has yielded to the *Parteienstaat*. He considers these two forms of government incompatible. This, however, is no reason to reject the role of political parties. Quite the contrary, in his view the existence of political parties can solve the classic contrast between representation and identity. He considers the *Parteienstaat* as a modern version of populist democracy, in which the will of the majority of the political parties is identical with the will of the people. Parliament is no longer a place of deliberation. Its only function is to register decisions that are taken outside parliament by the political parties.

Certainly, in its original form, the Anglo-Saxon concept of *party government* was based on a less radical democratic view. Precisely by dismissing the existence of a *volonté générale,* Schumpeter gave the initial impetus to the theory of party government. In his view, the competition between political parties for the votes of the electorate is the essential characteristic of modern democracy. Accordingly, he defines a political party as "a group whose members propose to act in concert in the competitive struggle for political power" (Schumpeter 1976, 83).

Schumpeter's theory of democracy is far removed from a model of linkage. For the very reason that he didn't think much of public opinion, he considered the concept of populist democracy as purely utopian. Therefore, it is remarkable that the basic idea of a competition between political parties was gradually transformed into a populist model of linkage. This model was systematically expounded in the report *Toward a More Responsible Two-Party System* (American Political Science Association 1950; see also Birch 1972; Dahl 1956; Downs 1957; Kirkpatrick 1971; Schattschneider 1942). The essential characteristic of the model is that there are only two relevant actors in the process of political representation: voters and political parties. Political parties are seen as unitary actors. Party discipline within and outside parliament is such that individual politicians play second fiddle, at most.

The more specific requirements of the model are all logical deductions from the assumption that the popular will must be reflected in government policy. These requirements are:

1. Political parties must present different policy alternatives to the voters. In other words, there must be different parties with different programs.
2. The internal cohesion, or party discipline, of political parties must be sufficient to enable them to implement their policy program.

3. Voters must vote rationally, that is to say, they must vote for the party whose program is closest to their own policy preferences. This last requirement implies two other ones:
   a. Voters must have policy preferences.
   b. Voters must know the difference between the policy programs of different political parties.

The criticism of this model has been no less than that devoted to the delegate model. There are at least three kinds of arguments that can be distinguished within the extensive literature on the subject. First, there is the *normative* argument, usually dismissing the populist philosophy of the model; second there is the argument—mainly from the public choice literature—that a policy mandate from the electorate via the mechanism of the political parties model is a *logical* impossibility. And, last but not least, there is the persistent argument that the model is *empirically invalid,* because neither political parties nor voters are behaving according to the assumptions of the model.

In most writings, there is no clear distinction between these three basic arguments. The rejection of the political parties model as a viable normative theory is very often based on empirical and logical arguments. I will follow the same procedure. I will go into the empirical and logical merits of the model in order to assess the viability of the normative theory on which the political parties model is based.

Of the requirements of the responsible party model, those referring to political parties seem to be least troublesome, certainly in the parliamentary systems of Western Europe. It has already been observed that party discipline, in general, is extremely high and also the requirement that voters should have a choice between different political parties with different platforms is easily met. But the model can only operate when all requirements are met, because "the logical structure of the model is such as to suggest that if one of its several requirements is not met, then the whole structure collapses as a rationale; the chain is no stronger than its weakest link" (Converse and Pierce 1986, 698).

That weakest link is obviously the requirement that voters should vote according to their policy preferences. The results of the relevant empirical research seem to be unequivocal. Stokes and Miller were among the first to test to what extent American voters met the requirements of the model. They found that American party voting does not fit the model. The electorate's perceptions of the parties betrayed very little information about current policy issues (Stokes and Miller 1962, 198). Perhaps even more striking is the fact that only 47 percent correctly attributed control of the Eighty-fifth Congress to the Republicans (Stokes and Miller 1962, 199). Under these conditions, it becomes impossible to vote according to one's issue positions or one's evaluation of the parties' legislative record. Kirkpatrick, in a long comment on the report of the

Committee on Political Parties, of which he himself had been a member, gives short shrift to the empirical validity of the model: "The cumulative impact of voting studies on the committee model of the responsible party doctrine is, quite simply, devastating" (1971, 972). This conclusion seems to be well established by empirical research in several countries. Converse and Pierce, for instance, after having tested to what extent the French electorate met the requirements of the model, concluded that "our findings on the mass side of the interaction certainly cast the most severe doubt on the truth and utility of characterizing representation in France in such terms" (Converse and Pierce 1986, 705).

And yet, time and again, it has been argued that such a verdict might be too harsh. More recently, it has been observed that in the advanced industrial democracies, a process of *cognitive mobilization* has occurred (Dalton 1988; Inglehart 1990). As a consequence, more citizens than ever are said to be capable of behaving according to the requirements of classic democratic theory. It is beyond the scope of this paper to evaluate the extensive literature on the subject of (the increase of) issue voting. In fact, we don't have to in order to assess the empirical validity of the Responsible Party Model.

Bearing in mind that the validity of the model will be made or broken by its weakest chain, and for the sake of the argument, let us start from the most optimistic position to be found in the literature, with respect to the extent to which voters meet the requirements of the Responsible Party Model. If that position still cannot save the model, there is no reason to take less optimistic views into consideration.

A more or less random example of the optimistic view is Dalton's statement that

> "More citizens now possess the political resources to follow the complexities of politics; they have the potential to act as the independent issue voters described in classic democratic theory but seldom observed in practice. . . . Greater issue voting may make candidates and parties more responsive to public opinion. Thus the democratic process may move closer to the democratic ideal." (Dalton 1988, 200–201)

Do independent issue voters indeed move the democratic process closer to the democratic ideal? If the democratic ideal is populist democracy, this conclusion might be founded on quicksand. Even when all voters vote according to their issue positions, the election outcome does not necessarily convey an electoral mandate on whatever policy position. Without further assumptions, a single vote does not convey a mandate with respect to any policy domain at all. Political parties offer a package deal to the voter. By voting for a particular party, voters are forced to vote for the whole package. The voter who is in favor of party A with respect to policy domain 1, but of party B with respect to domain 2, has no alternative but to choose for one of the two on the basis of his own idiosyncratic weights given to the different policy domains.

This may be an acceptable solution for the individual voter, but for the political system, it means that there is no logical relationship between the electoral majority and the policy majority on any specific issue. This phenomenon is known as the Ostrogorski paradox (Rae and Daudt 1976). As a consequence, as Dahl puts it, "all an election reveals is the first preferences of some citizens among the candidates standing for office," for "we can rarely interpret a majority of first choices among candidates in a national election as being equivalent to a majority of first choices for a specific policy" (Dahl 1956, 125–27).

The only solution to this paradox that I can think of is the assumption that both political parties, in the composition of their programs, and voters, when they decide which party they will vote for, are constrained by the same unidimensional ideology—that is, conforming the basic elements of the Downsian model.[3] Only then it is absolutely clear where the electoral majority stands in policy matters.

This, however, is a very severe requirement. Thanks to the pioneering work by Converse in the early sixties, it is common knowledge that the ideological constraint of issue positions among the mass public is limited, if existent at all (Converse 1964). However, more recent work with respect to the electorate in West European countries might lead to a difference in nuance. Granberg and Holmberg (1988, 67) argue that it is to be expected that in a country with a strong, disciplined party system, such as that in Sweden, issue positions will be more constrained than in a more loosely structured system, such as the United States. They demonstrate that this is indeed the case. Also, the relationship between issue positions and the position on a left-right continuum is stronger in Sweden than in the United States (Granberg and Holmberg 1988, 67–71). Fuchs and Klingemann (1990) report that a great majority of the Dutch and German electorates are capable of attributing a substantive meaning to the concepts of "Left" and "Right." The electorates in the West European democracies seem to be well aware of the relative positions of the political parties on the left-right continuum (Converse and Pierce 1986; Granberg and Holmberg 1988; Thomassen and Jennings 1989).[4] A majority of the voters in both the Netherlands and Sweden were found to behave according to Downsian theory by voting for the party that was closest to their own position on a left-right scale (Van der Eijk and Niemöller 1983, 278; Granberg and Holmberg 1988, chapter 6).

If voters' issue positions are defined by a single ideological dimension, and if they vote according to their position on that dimension, the conditions for a coercive system of representation are met. Hence, one should expect a high level of congruence between parties' policy positions and the policy preferences of their voters. To assess to what extent this is the case was one of the explicit objectives of all the studies of political representation mentioned above.

With respect to left-right positions, an interesting phenomenon seems to occur in many European countries. Political elites tend to place themselves more to the left than the voters of their parties (Barnes 1977; Converse and Pierce 1986; Dalton 1985; Holmberg 1989; Thomassen and Zielonka 1992). It is hard to explain this discrepancy. The most likely explanation is a cultural one: for a long time, being a conservative was not very fashionable in Europe. Even people with outright conservative policy views would not easily call themselves conservative. Whatever the cause of this phenomenon, the consequence of it is that the *absolute* congruence between the political elite and the rank and file is low, whereas the *relative* congruence is high, which is to say that the rank order of the parties is about the same on both levels. Whether one wants to consider this combination of a low absolute and a high relative congruence good or bad depends on the view of political representation one prefers to take (see Achen 1977, 1978; Converse and Pierce 1986, 599). In the case of the left-right scale, it might be argued that positions on the scale have only a relative meaning, and therefore cannot be used to establish an absolute substantive difference between the political parties and their voters. Therefore, one might conclude that, in general, the congruence between representatives and their voters, in this respect, is not bad at all.

For at least two reasons, it is hard to draw general conclusions with respect to the congruence on specific issues. First, the variety of measurement techniques and policy domains is such that comparisons between different studies are hardly possible. Second, conclusions are usually drawn in terms of absolute congruence, which leads to the problem that it is a matter of interpretation whether or not a difference of .50 on a five-point scale is really small (Dalton 1985, 277) or whether an average difference between percent distributions of fifteen percentage points is really large (Holmberg 1989, 14). For the purpose of this paper, it is sufficient to know that the degree of congruence seems to be different for different issues. In general, political parties' elites seem to be fairly representative of their voters on social-economic issues, such as income policy, codetermination of workers, and the relationship between the public and private sector, and on moral issues, like abortion. Representativeness is less on foreign policy, and nonexistent on issues like aid to third world countries and law and order. With respect to these kind of issues, and, in general, with respect to libertarian values, there is a world of difference between party elites and their rank and file, certainly within the traditional parties on the left (Dalton 1985; Hoffmann-Lange 1987; Holmberg 1989; Thomassen 1976).

These results should raise suspicion against the claim that left-right place-ment acts as a summary of the contemporary issues orientations of both the elites and the mass public (Dalton 1985, 283; Inglehart 1984). The differences in the level of congruence between different issue domains suggest that among the political elite, the left-right dimension has a more abstract meaning than among the mass, and can, therefore, encompass a greater variety of issues. This would explain that with respect to those issues that fall outside the limited left-right framework that is shared by mass and elite, a mechanism of political representation tends to be weak, or even absent.

The results of a more detailed analysis of the constraint of issues among members of parliament and voters in several countries are consistent with this explanation. The difference in constraint between the two groups is tremen-dous (Converse and Pierce 1986, chapter 7; Granberg and Holmberg 1988, 73; Thomassen 1976, 166). The correlation between issue positions and left-right position among the electorate is, in general, dramatically low (Converse and Pierce 1986, 236–37).

As far as traces of issue constraints can be found, these seem to be limited to those issues that are related to the traditional cleavage structure, in which religion and class played a dominant role. The less related an issue is to this cleavage structure, the less constrained it will be among the mass public by the ideological dimensions that are related to these cleavages, and the lower the consensus between the political elites and the mass public on that issue will be.

If this is a valid interpretation, one might argue that the process of *cogni-tive mobilization* will increase the level of conceptualization of the mass public and, hence, make policy representativeness easier. This prospect might turn out to be poor comfort. Although it is true that the constraints among the better educated and involved part of the electorate are higher than among the elector-ate at large, even among this group, the constraints are much lower than among members of parliament, certainly when it comes to the relationship between issue domains (Thomassen 1976, chapter 8). Converse and Pierce found that, at the most, among 15 percent of the French electorate, a leftist vote could be interpreted in terms of specific issues.

This, however, is still the most benign interpretation of the future validity of the responsible party model. According to a different scenario, we might as well be faced with a devilish paradox. How certain can one be that the decline of the traditional cleavage structure will be succeeded by alternative coherent ideological and value systems that may serve to constrain both party and voting behavior (Van der Eijk et al. 1992, 427)? Is it not just as likely that the new citizen that is so enthusiastically welcomed by Dalton will be competent enough to vote according to his most individual mix of policy preferences? In that case, the more citizens "act as the independent issue voters described in classic democratic theory" (Dalton 1988, 200), the less likely it is that the election outcome conveys a clear policy mandate.

Above, it was argued that the complicated chain of the responsible party model is no stronger than its weakest link. That weakest link is, without any doubt, the requirement that the election outcome be interpreted as a policy mandate. It is quite obvious that, for logical and empirical reasons, such a mandate is hardly possible.

Riker takes even one more step by arguing that the decision-making process that is assumed by the model is essentially not democratic at all. According to his judgment, the notion of responsible parties might make sense if policy decisions can be reduced to binary decisions. But because in the real world there are almost always more than two alternatives, the most that responsible parties can do is select two of them. Reducing policy alternatives to binary alternatives "requires some social embodiment of Procustes, who chopped off the legs of his guests to fit them into the bed in his inn" (Riker 1982, 65). In order to reduce the number of alternatives to exactly two, some Procrustean leader or elite is needed to do the chopping. Once this is recognized, it should be obvious that any populist theory of democracy, assuming that policy decisions are backed by an electoral majority, is not feasible, because there is no particular decision method for three or more alternatives that is unequivocally consistent with the idea of democratic government (Riker 1982, 60–65).

Political Representation: A Research Agenda

The argument so far leads to the conclusion that neither the instructed delegate model nor the political parties model is based upon a viable theory of democracy. Nor is either one of them very successful as an empirical model. Does this mean that we should give up empirical research along these lines? It most certainly does not. It only means that these two models, in their present form, should get less emphasis in future research. Miller and Stokes, in their seminal article on political representation in America, observed that "no single tradition of representation fully accords with the realities of American legislative politics." Instead "the American system is a mixture, to which the Burkean, instructed delegate, and responsible party models all can be said to have contributed elements" (Miller and Stokes 1963, 56).

It seems to me that it is still a wise policy not to get caught in the idea that either this or that model should be alone and fully applicable. Different models can be applicable in different circumstances.

Both the instructed delegate and the political parties model are rather rigid models. Both models reflect a populist view on political representation, according to which the ideal of a representative democracy is the identity between the will of the people and government policy. However, as has been argued in the introduction to this chapter, one should be aware of the fact that this view on representative democracy is not the only legitimate one. According to a less rigid view, representatives and political parties should not necessarily reflect the will of the majority of the electorate on each and every single issue, but should at least be responsive, that is to say, should take the opinions and interests of the people into account. Such a more relaxed view on political representation is less demanding and will yield partly different research questions that might be more relevant for the real world of politics.

Above, it has been argued that the instructed delegate model does not reflect a viable theory of democracy because it is based on an old-fashioned view of representation. The task of members of parliament to defend local interests has become marginal, compared to their role in general policy making. And, because electoral districts tend to be heterogeneous with respect to matters of general policy, it is difficult to see how a single deputy would be able to act according to *the* district sentiment. In addition to this a priori argument, it was argued that because of both the extent of party discipline and the role conceptions of members of parliament in the parliamentary systems of Western Europe, the delegate model was doomed to fail as an empirical model.

However, this is not to say that the relationship between an individual member of parliament and his or her constituency is irrelevant for the process of political representation. First, the relevance of the relationship depends on the constitutional setting. In the American presidential system, a strict party discipline is less essential for the survival of the incumbent government than in the parliamentary systems of Europe. Therefore, it can be more lenient. The civil rights domain in the Miller-Stokes study is a perfect illustration of the fact that, at least in the United States, the electorate is quite capable of imposing its will on representatives, once it takes a passionate position on a particular issue. But even in parliamentary systems, there might be some variation in the extent of party discipline. The larger the majority of the governing party or coalition, the more lenient it can be with deviations from the party line (see Converse and Pierce 1986, 558). In that case, there might be more room for individual members of parliament to respond to the opinions on particular issues in their home districts. To what extent this is the case is a question that deserves more comparative research.

Secondly, studies of political representation tend to underestimate the importance of the relationship between an individual member of parliament and his constituency by focusing almost exclusively on *policy responsiveness* and roll call behavior. But the representative role of a member of parliament implies more than representing policy views. *Service responsiveness,* or ombudsman activities, and *allocation responsiveness* are also important aspects of the role of the representative (Eulau and Karps 1977; Cain et al. 1987; Weissberg 1978). A high level of party discipline is not necessarily prohibitive to such activities.

Although Converse and Pierce found very few defections from party discipline in the French Assembly, a disproportional number of the defections that did occur referred to a single issue where the interest of the Paris region was involved, and delegates from this region decided to put the region's interest before the party line (Converse and Pierce 1986, 560). However, these activities seldom result in direct legislative action. Therefore, to trace such activities on the side of the MP, studying the issues raised during the question hour and the extent to which officials are directly approached by MPs on behalf of their constituents might be more appropriate.

The relationship between an individual member of parliament and both his or her constituents and interest groups might also be underestimated because of the traditional focus on roll call behavior. In the first part of this paper, it was argued that trying to explain the roll call vote behavior of individual MPs by characteristics of their constituencies is not a very fruitful approach in West European parliamentary democracies, because there is not much left to be explained after party membership has been taken into account. Party discipline is such that very few deviating votes can be registered. But this does not necessarily mean that MPs don't take the attitudes or interests of their constituency, however defined, into account. It only means that it won't show on the floor of parliament. If one is really interested in the *process* of parliamentary decision making in a parliamentary system, with its disciplined parties, roll calls are hardly informative. The relevant processes occur behind closed doors *within* the parliamentary parties. Observing these processes might reveal much more of the possible influence of group interests—but also constituency influences—than the plenary debate and the final roll call. Therefore, the real challenge for future political representation research is to get behind those closed doors.

All these nuances, however, cannot change the conclusion that certainly in the parliamentary democracies of Western Europe political parties, rather than individual members of parliament, are the principal actors in matters of general policy. Therefore, despite all possible objections, the political parties model still seems to be the most fruitful point of departure to study the process of political representation in these systems. But sticking to the exact wording of the model as presented above will obstruct, rather than stimulate, relevant research into the process of political representation.

The essential requirement of the model is that the election outcome be interpreted as a clear policy mandate. In the real world, this will hardly ever be the case, mainly because it is close to impossible for the electorate to meet the severe requirements of the model that can logically be deduced from this essential requirement. The model expects of voters that they vote not only prospectively, but also according to an ideological position that constrains their issue positions. Therefore, if the quality of representative democracy is measured with the yardstick of this model, retrospective voting will not qualify (Fiorina 1981, 196). And whatever the conclusions of recent publications on the rationality of the mass public may be (Erikson et al. 1991; Page and Shapiro 1992; Heath et al. 1991), these cannot change the negative conclusions with respect to the political parties model, as long as different issue positions are not constrained by a single ideology. However, from a more realistic view on political representation, one of the most important challenges for future research is to explain why political parties are representative of their voters on some issues, but not on others.

N O T E S

An earlier version of this paper was presented at a conference on political representation, Wissenschafszentrum für Sozialforschung, Berlin, April 12–14, 1991. Parts of it were published in Thomassen 1991.

1. Of course, one should avoid falling into the trap of too rigidly separated categories. Even though Burke's preference was clear, he felt at the same time that "it ought to be the happiness and glory of a representative to live in the strictest union, the closest correspondence, and the most unreserved communication with his constituents" (as quoted in Eulau et al. 1959, 747).

2. The significance of empirical research of role conceptions in this connection has been the subject of a long debate. According to Eulau and Wahlke (1978, 17), measurements of role conceptions were never meant to predict legislative behavior. But I must confess it is beyond my understanding how the role conception of an instructed delegate can explain the lower path in the Miller-Stokes model, either when this role conception is absent or when it makes no difference as far as legislative behavior is concerned (see Friesema and Hedlund 1974; Kuklinski and Elling 1977; McCrone and Kuklinski 1979).

3. One might object that this is not the only solution possible. In a multidimensional cleavage structure and a multiparty system, each combination of policy positions might be represented by a different party. But in almost every multiparty system, the government will consist of a coalition of political parties. The policy program of the government will be defined by negotiations among the coalition partners after the elections. This makes the translation of an electoral mandate into government policy in a multiparty system virtually impossible. On the (im)possibility of rational voting under coalition governments, see Downs 1957, 147.

4. One should realize, though, that in most studies the *aggregate* perception of the position of the parties is used as a measurement to indicate how voters perceive the parties. Converse and Pierce (1986, 114) correctly observe that these aggregate measurements can conceal individual perceptions that are all wrong.

REFERENCES

Achen, Christopher H. 1977. "Measuring Representation: Perils of the Correlation Coefficient." *American Political Science Review* 21:805–15.
———. 1978. "Measuring Representation." *American Journal of Political Science* 22:475–510.
American Political Science Association. 1950. *Toward a More Responsible Two-Party System.* Washington: American Political Science Association.
Barnes, Samuel H. 1977. *Representation in Italy: Institutionalized Tradition and Electoral Choice.* Chicago: University of Chicago Press.
Birch, A. H. 1972. *Representation.* London: Macmillan.
Cain, Bruce F., John Ferejohn, and Morris P. Fiorina. 1987. *The Personal Vote: Constituency Service and Electorate Independence.* Cambridge: Harvard University Press.
Clausen, Aage. 1977. "The Accuracy of Leader Perceptions of Constituency Views." *Legislative Studies Quarterly* 2:361–84.
Cnudde, Charles F., and Donald J. McCrone. 1966. "The Linkage between Constituency Attitudes and Congressional Voting Behavior: A Causal Model." *American Political Science Review* 60:66–72.
Converse, Philip E. 1964. "The Nature of Belief Systems in Mass Publics." In *Ideology and Discontent,* ed. David E. Apter. New York: Free Press.
Converse, Philip E., and Roy Pierce. 1986. *Political Representation in France.* Cambridge: Harvard University Press.
Dahl, Robert A. 1956. *A Preface to Democratic Theory.* Chicago: University of Chicago Press.
———. 1982. *Dilemmas of Pluralist Democracy, Autonomy vs. Control.* New Haven and London: Yale University Press.
Dalton, Russell J. 1985. "Political Parties and Political Representation: Party Supporters and Party Elites in Nine Nations." *Comparative Political Studies* 18:267–99.
———. 1988. *Citizen Politics in Western Democracies: Public Opinion and Political Parties in the United States, Great Britain, West Germany, and France.* Chatham, N. J.: Chatham House.
Downs, Anthony. 1957. *An Economic Theory of Democracy.* New York: Harper and Row.
Eijk, C. van der, and B. Niemöller. 1983. *Electoral Change in the Netherlands, Empirical Results and Methods of Measurement.* Amsterdam: CT-Press.
Eijk, C. van der, Mark Franklin, Tom Mackie, and Henry Valen. 1992. "Cleavages, Conflict Resolution, and Democracy." In *Electoral Change: Responses to Evolving Social and Attitudinal Structures in Western Countries,* ed. Mark Franklin, Tom Mackie, and Henry Valen. Cambridge, Mass.: Cambridge University Press.
Erikson, Robert S. 1978. "Constituency Opinion and Congressional Behavior: A Reexamination of the Miller-Stokes Representation Data." *American Journal of Political Science* 22:511–35.
Erikson, Robert S., Norman R. Luttbeg, and Kent L. Tedin. 1991. *American Public Opinion.* New York: Macmillan.

Eulau, Heinz. 1987. "The Congruence Model Revisited." *Legislative Studies Quarterly* 12:171–214.

Eulau, Heinz, John C. Wahlke, William Buchanan, and LeRoy C. Ferguson. 1959. "The Role of the Representative: Some Empirical Observations on the Theory of Edmund Burke." *American Political Science Review* 53:742–56.

Eulau, Heinz, and John Wahlke 1978. *The Politics of Representation: Continuities in Theory and Research.* London: Sage.

Eulau, Heinz, and Paul D. Karps. 1978. "The Puzzle of Representation: Specifying Components of Responsiveness." In *The Politics of Representation: Continuities in Theory and Research,* by Heinz Eulau and John Wahlke. London: Sage.

Farah, Barbara G. 1980. *Political Representation in West Germany: The Institution and Maintenance of Mass-Elite Linkages.* Ph.D. diss., University of Michigan, Ann Arbor.

Fenno, Richard E. 1978. *Home Style: House Members in Their Districts.* Boston: Little, Brown.

Friesema, H. Paul, and Ronald D. Hedlund. 1974. "The Reality of Representational Roles." In *Public Opinion and Public Policy,* ed. Norman R. Luttbeg. Homewood, Ill.: Dorsey Press.

Fuchs, Dieter, and Hans-Dieter Klingemann. 1990. "The Left-Right Schema." In *Continuities in Political Action: A Longitudinal Study of Political Orientations in Three Western Democracies,* by M. Kent Jennings, Jan W. van Deth, et al. Berlin: Walter de Gruyter.

Granberg, Donald, and Sören Holmberg. 1988. *The Political System Matters: Social Psychology and Voting Behavior in Sweden and the United States.* Cambridge, Mass.: Cambridge University Press.

Heath, Anthony, Roger Jowell, John Curtice, George Evans, Julia Field, and Sharon Witherspoon. 1991. *Understanding Political Change: The British Voter 1964–1987.* Oxford: Pergamon.

Hedlund, Ronald D., and H. Paul Friesema. 1972. "Representatives' Perceptions of Constituency Opinion." *Journal of Politics* 34:730–52.

Herzog, Dietrich. 1989. "Was heisst und zu welchem Ende studiert man Repräsentation?" In *Konfliktpotentiale und Konsensstrategien: Beiträge zur politischen Soziologie der Bundesrepublik,* ed. Dietrich Herzog and Bernhard Wessels. Opladen: Westdeutscher Verlag.

Hoffmann-Lange, Ursula. 1987. "Eliten als Hüter der Demokratie?" In *Politische Kultur in Deutschland,* ed. Dirk Berg-Schlosser and Jakob Schissler. Opladen: Westdeutscher Verlag.

Holmberg, Sören. 1974. *Riksdagen Representerar Svenska Folket: Empiriska Studier i Representativ Demokrati.* Lund: Studentlitteratur.

———. 1989. "Political Representation in Sweden." *Scandinavian Political Studies* 12:1–35.

Hurley, Patricia A. 1982. "Collective Representation Reappraised." *Legislative Studies Quarterly* 7:119–36.

Inglehart, Ronald. 1984. "The Changing Structure of Cleavages in Western Society." In *Electoral Change in Advanced Industrial Democracies: Realignment or Dealign-*

ment? ed. Russell J. Dalton, Scott Flanagan, and Paul Allen Beck. Princeton: Princeton University Press.

————. 1990. *Culture Shift in Advanced Industrial Societies.* Princeton: Princeton University Press.

Kielmansegg, Peter Graf. 1988. *Das Experiment der Freiheit: Zur gegenwärtigen Lage des demokratischen Verfassungsstaates.* Stuttgart: Klett-Cotta.

Kirkpatrick, Evron M. 1971. " 'Toward A More Responsible Two-Party System': Political Science, Policy Science, or Pseudo-Science?" *American Political Science Review* 65:965–90.

Kuklinsky, James H. 1978. "Representatives and Elections: A Policy Analysis." *American Political Science Review* 72:165–77.

Kuklinsky, James H., and Richard C. Elling. 1977. "Representational Role, Constituency Opinion, and Legislative Roll-Call Behavior." *American Journal of Political Science* 23:278–300.

Leibholz, G. 1966. *Das Wesen der Repräsentation und der Gestaltwandel der Demokratie im 20. Jahrhundert.* 3d ed. Berlin: Walter de Gruyter.

Luttbeg, Norman R., ed. 1974. *Public Opinion and Public Policy: Models of Political Linkage.* 3d ed. Ithaca, N.Y.: F. E. Peacock.

McCrone, Donald J., and James H. Kuklinski. 1979. "The Delegate Theory of Representation." *American Political Science Review* 23:278–300.

Miller, Warren E. 1964. "Majority Rule and the Representative System of Government." In *Cleavages, Ideologies, and Party Systems: Contributions to Comparative Political Sociology,* ed. Erik Allardt and Yrö Littunen. Helsinki: Transactions of the Westermarck Society.

Miller, Warren E., and Donald E. Stokes. 1963. "Constituency Influence in Congress." *American Political Science Review* 57:45–56.

Page, Benjamin I., and Robert Y. Shapiro. 1992. *The Rational Public: Fifty Years of Trends in Americans' Policy Preferences.* Chicago: University of Chicago Press.

Page, Benjamin I., Robert Y. Shapiro, and Paul W. Gronke. 1984. "Constituency, Party, and Representation in Congress." *Public Opinion Quarterly* 48:741–56.

Pitkin, Hanna. 1967. *The Concept of Representation.* Berkeley and Los Angeles: University of California Press.

Rae, Douglas W., and Hans Daudt. 1976. "The Ostrogorski Paradox: A Peculiarity of Compound Majority Decision." *European Journal of Political Research* 4:391–98.

Riker, William H. 1982. *Liberalism versus Populism: A Confrontation Between the Theory of Democracy and the Theory of Social Choice.* San Francisco: W. H. Freeman.

Sartori, Giovanni. 1976. *Parties and Party Systems: A Framework for Analysis.* London: Cambridge University Press.

Schattschneider, E. E. 1942. *Party Government.* New York: Rinehart.

Schumpeter, Joseph A. 1976. *Capitalism, Socialism, and Democracy.* 5th ed. London: George Allen and Unwin.

Stokes, Donald E., and Warren E. Miller. 1962. "Party Government and the Saliency of Congress." *Public Opinion Quarterly* 26:531–46.

Stone, Walter J. 1979. "Measuring Constituency-Representative Linkages: Problems and Prospects." *Legislative Studies Quarterly* 4.

Thomassen, Jacques J. 1976. *Kiezers en Gekozenen in een Representatieve Demokratie.* Alphen aan den Rijn: Samsom.

———. 1991. "Empirical Research into Political Representation: A Critical Reappraisal." In *Politische Klasse und Politische Institutionen: Probleme und Perspektiven der Elitenforschung,* ed. Hans-Dieter Klingemann, Richard Stöss, and Bernard Wessels. Opladen: Westdeutscher Verlag.

Thomassen, Jacques, and M. Kent Jennings. 1989. "Party Systems, Party Differences, and Homogeneity." Paper presented at the first annual Workgroup on Elections and Parties, International Political Science Association/International Studies Association, Paris.

Thomassen, Jacques, and Mei Lan Zielonka. 1992. "Het Parlement als Volksvertegenwoordiging." In *De Geachte Afgevaardigde,* ed. Jacques Thomassen, Marinus van Schendelen, and Mei Lan Zielonka. Muiderberg: Coutinho.

Weissberg, Robert. 1978. "Collective vs. Dyadic Representation in Congress." *American Political Science Review* 72:535–47.

CHAPTER 11

National Party Conventions: Changing Functions, New Research Strategies

Leon D. Epstein

In helping to celebrate Warren Miller's splendid career, I hope to enhance our appreciation of his recent studies of convention delegates by placing those studies in the intellectual context of our discipline's scholarship concerning national party conventions. I shall discuss how the conventions have changed over the last several decades, and how political scientists have studied them as they changed. The history reveals what I regard as the understandable development, in accord with twentieth-century American political culture, of popular, rather than leadership, selection of presidential nominees, and thus, of conventions shorn of their traditionally crucial decision making. I do not join the chorus that so deplores the contemporary presidential nominating process as to urge a restoration of something like the old system. Imperfect though the process may be, and surely subject to continued modification, it is unlikely to be superseded by autonomous convention choices of presidential nominees.

Understandable too, I shall contend, has been the response of political scientists to the institutional development. Their greater concentration on the characteristics of delegates than on the activities of delegates at conventions is consonant with the now-limited power of conventions. Yet, as I shall suggest, especially in my conclusion, the conventions still play important enough roles, as well as some new ones, to justify field work whose findings can add to the impressive knowledge that Miller and others provide from their quantitative analysis of convention delegates.

A Changing Institution

Political scientists, like everyone else, long perceived national party conventions as effectively selecting presidential nominees. So it was in the middle of this century, when members of our profession began systematically to study conventions. Entering the profession at about that time, I recollect how much it was taken for granted that conventions actually decided presidential nominations. My generation observed the decisive role of conventions both in historical accounts and in newspaper and radio coverage of contemporary events. In 1932, at age thirteen, I was impressed by the Democratic convention's nomination of Franklin Roosevelt on the fourth ballot, after a deal had been struck to achieve the two-thirds majority the Democrats then required. Nor did the convention look less crucial in the Republican contests of 1940 and 1948, or in the Democratic contest of 1952; all three required more than one ballot, and two of the three produced a nominee who had not been the front-runner on the first ballot. Current observations of this sort complemented what was taught in college courses about more spectacular, but fairly recent, historical instances of convention decision making: 103 ballots at the Democratic convention of 1924, the negotiated arrangements (supposedly in a smoke-filled room) that led Republicans to the tenth-ballot nomination of Warren Harding in 1920, and the dramatic convention speech by William Jennings Bryan that made him a serious Democratic contender and the eventual nominee on the fifth ballot in 1896.

We were aware that first-ballot nominations were common when incumbent presidents sought reelection, and that they also occurred on occasions when nonincumbents established themselves as overwhelmingly popular choices. Yet, these uncontentious nominations, while frequent, were hardly so pervasive as to diminish the nominating authority of the convention. Significantly, no trend toward first-ballot nominations of nonincumbents was readily discernible at midcentury; five such nominations had been made in the twenty-two major-party conventions from 1912 through 1952, in comparison to eight in the twenty-two major-party conventions from 1868 through 1908. Presidential primaries, whose numbers waxed and waned between 1912 and 1952, did not yet coincide with a material change in convention decision making.

The midcentury view of convention nominations persisted for a decade or two after 1952, despite new dissents. The 1964 edition of V. O. Key's widely accepted textbook retained the language of an earlier edition: "The convention, diverse in its composition and unpatterned in its ways, remains free to choose presidential candidates from a range of alternatives" (Key 1964, 436). On other pages, Key decidedly approved of the exercise of discretion by delegates, and of leadership roles in negotiating convention agreements. These were, he thought, the practices that made parties capable of governing through the presidential system. Many political scientists shared Key's belief in the usefulness of brokered nominations. Indeed, they continued to do so in later decades, when no brokered nominations occurred.

From one standpoint, it is anomalous that the brokered national convention, as well as its admiration by political scientists, should have survived to the middle of the twentieth century. By then, the direct primary was well established in most states as the means to select party nominees for Congress and for state offices. Only a few states (not many more than today) retained convention nomination for major offices. Elsewhere, despite the continuing influence of state party organizations in determining primary outcomes, the direct primary looked like a durable product of progressivism. States had not retreated from its use after 1920, as they had from presidential preference primaries. The latter had a curious history. Adopted by many states in the same pre-1917 reform era during which the direct primary had been adopted for congressional and state nominations, presidential primaries at first spread almost as far and fast as the direct primaries themselves. In at least one of each major party's conventions of 1912, 1916, and 1920, over half of the delegates were selected in presidential primaries (Ceaser 1979, 222–23). In 1913, President Woodrow Wilson regarded their growth so favorably that he urged Congress to enact "legislation which will provide for primary elections throughout the country at which the voters of the several parties may choose their nominees for the Presidency without the intervention of nominating conventions" (Israel 1966, 2548). But even at the high tide of progressivism, Congress did not heed Wilson's call. Then, after 1920, several states either abandoned presidential primaries altogether, or employed various practices to make them less salient as registers of popular choice (Ceaser 1979, 227). Delegates chosen in presidential primaries became a distinct minority at each convention during the next half century. At most, primaries could be influential, but not decisive.

Political scientists might advance good reasons for national conventions to have retained their nominating power, though state conventions had lost theirs, but those reasons do not reduce the significant untypicality of presidential nominations in midcentury America. In that light, it should be easy to understand that when national conventions finally did lose decision-making authority, in the 1970s and 1980s, presidential nominations were thus brought in line with prevailing practices for other offices. And it should also help us to understand that it is now unlikely, if not impossible, for a convention to reassert its old power against the leading survivor of presidential primaries.

Common though it is to think of convention power having been lost mainly between 1968 and 1972, earlier dates can be suggested for the process of change to have begun. Even at midcentury, analysts unknown to me may have discerned a decline. If so, their impact was limited. For in 1952, when the American Political Science Association sponsored the first systematic study of conventions (David, Moos, and Goldman 1954), the undertaking assumed that conventions made the nominating decisions. Indeed, both major-party conventions actually made these decisions in 1952. The Democrats needed three ballots to settle on Adlai Stevenson, who had campaigned in no primaries, and the Republicans reached a first-ballot nomination of Dwight Eisenhower only after switches from original roll call responses and, more significantly, after crucial negotiations and floor fights over credentials.

In 1956, however, the situation was different. Although President

Eisenhower's routine renomination represented nothing new, this time Stevenson also won a first-ballot nomination that followed from his victory in important presidential primaries. We could not then have known that these first-ballot nominations marked the beginning of a continuous string down to the present day. Generally, too, most of our profession did not, in my recollection, yet conclude that conventions, with or without multiballots, were ceasing to be the effective nominators. Doubts, however, were not uncommon, and at least one political scientist went much farther. In a well-known journal article, William G. Carleton argued that a major change in convention decision making had occurred and that the first-ballot nominations of 1956 verified what he saw as a thirty-year trend to choose preconvention favorites (Carleton 1957, 225).

Carleton's article, published in a widely read professional journal, is remarkable for its virtually exact prediction: "It is probable that by 1976 or 1980 all that a nominating convention will do will be to meet to ratify the nomination for president of *the* national favorite already determined by the agencies, formal and informal, of mass democracy . . . " (1957, 237). Carleton's prescience followed from his assessment that broad social forces had subjected the presidential nominating process to the ways of mass democracy (1957, 237, 240). Accordingly, after 1924, each major-party convention had nominated "a national favorite—usually *the* national favorite . . . " (1957, 227). The development occurred without any increase in the number of primaries and without any other substantial change in the machinery of delegate selection. What happened was that more attention was given to existing primaries, as well as to other indications of popular support, including public opinion polls from the 1930s. Consequently, Carleton contended, conventions no longer nominated favorite sons or dark horses. Even when more than one ballot was still required, the nominee was demonstrably popular.

Note that in Carleton's argument, the shift to single-ballot nominations is a less crucial measure of change than the increased acceptance of preconvention favorites. Thus, the old order gives way after 1924, rather than after 1952. We might dispute the early date on the ground that not all of the post-1924 nominees, like Wendell Willkie in 1940, had been established preconvention favorites. Even so, Carleton's criterion is appealing. Multiballot nominations, whose likelihood was reduced after the Democrats abolished their two-thirds rule in 1936, are not the only indicators of decision making at the convention. Single-ballot nominations may also be preceded by negotiations among delegates. The truly important question is whether delegates in convention make the nominating decision, or merely ratify the popular choice, as determined by one means or another before the convention.

In fixing the time when conventions shifted to ratification of the popular choice, in the virtually automatic manner of the last two decades, we can see at least a trend in that direction after 1924. It now appears to have been confirmed both in 1956 and in 1960, when John F. Kennedy used a few well-publicized primary victories and a national public relations campaign to establish himself as the popular preconvention favorite, and then the Democratic nominee. Needing many more delegates than could then have been won in primaries, Kennedy had demonstrated sufficient vote-getting ability to convince a majority of delegates, more specifically their leaders, that he should be nominated. Whether the Republican convention of 1964 was similarly influenced to nominate Barry Goldwater is more debatable. His popular mandate from primaries looked less impressive than Kennedy's, and he almost certainly struck established Republican leaders as less electable than Kennedy had seemed to Democratic leaders in 1960. Yet, efforts to deny Goldwater's bid by convention brokerage failed dismally. Indeed, no truly brokered choice was made at any convention during the 1960s, unless we count the Democratic nomination of Hubert Humphrey in 1968. But Humphrey, while entering no primaries, was probably as close to a popular choice among Democratic voters as could have been made after the late withdrawal of President Lyndon Johnson and the assassination of Robert Kennedy.

Nevertheless, conventions during the 1960s could still be perceived as exerting actual nominating authority. Even though they uniformly chose the popular preconvention favorites, the process of determining that favorite was not so regularized as to establish the hard and fast public expectations evident in the next few decades. As Key wrote in 1964, "While the primary has modified nominating practices, it has not produced conventions of automata that mechanically record the preferences expressed by the voters at home" (Key 1964, 411). In the 1960s, it was not usual to treat presidential primary victories as so essential to nomination as Davis (1967) regarded them in his then-controversial book on the subject. Commonly, presidential nominations were still assigned to what we call the "mixed system," in which certain crucial delegates, themselves uncommitted by primaries, decided how much weight to give to the results of presidential primaries and other expressions of popular preference. Characterizing the period beginning in 1912, the mixed system was distinct, but not wholly different, from the national convention nominations of the preprimary era that had lasted from the 1830s through 1908.

In retrospect, the conventions of the 1960s appear transitional. For example, Byron Shafer recently acknowledged that by 1956, "the nomination had effectively departed from the convention" (Shafer 1988, 17–18). The departure was then, he said, institutionalized in the post-1968 reforms of delegate selection (1988, 39). For Shafer, as for the rest of us, the institutionalization remains important, even as we now see the limited role of the national conventions of the 1970s and 1980s as the product of a long-term development begun after 1952, or even after 1924 or 1912. Though the post-1968 changes appear as culminating events in a fairly long historical process, rather than as an entirely novel departure from an established order, they were nevertheless rapid, broad, and durable enough to have remained in force for the two decades since their establishment.

The essence of the post-1968 system, it seems to me, is a convention composed largely of delegates selected to record the presidential candidate preferences of voters in primaries and, to a lesser extent, in open caucuses. The percentage of each major party's delegates chosen in primaries has varied, and so has the percentage committed to candidates by those primaries (Polsby 1983, 64), but beginning in 1972 the numbers have been sufficient to lead to the nomination of the candidate who had won the most delegates in primaries, even if a few more delegates were needed to reach a majority at the convention. In this vital respect, Republican and Democratic practices have been similar. Presidential primaries have been used in about the same number of states by one party as by the other, and voter preferences in those primaries determined Republican, as well as Democratic, nominations in the 1970s and 1980s. Republicans, in effect, adapted to the increased emphasis on primaries that followed, unintentionally, from the Democratic reforms initiated by the McGovern-Fraser Commission. On the other hand, Republicans did not accept anything like the new Democratic rules imposing strict national party guidelines for delegate selection, including affirmative-action standards and proportional representation of candidate preferences. Nor did Republicans create, as did the Democrats in 1984, a substantial minority of superdelegates to attend the convention, by virtue of their public or party offices and without having to be pledged to any candidate. But so far, the superdelegates have done no more than help nominate an apparent winner of primaries. For Democrats, as for Republicans, the post-1968 system has produced a preconvention choice. The closest call was on the Republican side in 1976, when the nomination contest between Gerald Ford and Ronald Reagan extended to the convention itself. So, too, did the Democratic contests of 1972 and 1980 continue at the conventions, but without much doubt that the clear winners in the primary process would be confirmed (Shafer 1988, 74).

As the convention itself ceased to be the arena in which nominations were brokered, it changed in other ways. Each convention became considerably larger. From about 1,200 delegates in 1952, the Republican total for 1992 was about 2,200, having increased sharply to around that level in 1976. The rise in Democratic delegates is more spectacular. Also at about 1,200 in 1952, it was near 4,300 in 1992, after an almost continuous rise, especially from 1964. These new numbers alone might make it harder to broker a presidential nomination, but even the old conventions of 1,200 were so large that brokerage presumably depended on relatively few delegation leaders. Many more delegates would not alone preclude such bargaining. Certain other changes, however, make brokering more difficult. State delegations, again especially on the

Democratic side, are now much more often divided according to candidate preferences, and almost always these preferences are for national candidates. Practically gone are favorite-son delegations following a governor or another state politician who seeks influence in determining the nomination, rather than the nomination itself.

Whether the contemporary convention is actually so fragmented as to be unsuited to brokering a presidential nomination remains a moot point, as long as the preconvention process regularly produces a nominee. Several times, however, the emergence of a preconvention winner looked uncertain at some stage of the process. Not only was the Republican nomination of 1976 a close-run contest, but the Democratic party's proportional representation, when first established, and then again when made much stricter, was expected to be an obstacle for a candidate seeking a majority of delegates in a multicandidate field. But so far, proportional representation has merely prolonged the process of gathering that majority. When a majority has not been achieved before the convention, a candidate has been so close as to be treated as the winner certain to attract the requisite additions. Nevertheless, such preconvention successes over two decades may not have been entirely inevitable results of the process, but partly the consequences of fortuitous circumstances.

Uncertainty about the emergence of preconvention winners is increased by the frequency of changes in the post-1968 system. The Democrats' shifting use of proportional representation, sometimes with large exceptions and sometimes not, is only one example. Others, chiefly initiated by Democrats, but affecting Republicans too, include shortening the delegate selection season; holding southern primaries on a single early "super Tuesday"; front-loading, as other states (like those in the South) move primaries to early dates, in order to increase their influence; and switching of states and parties between caucus and primary methods, so that the latter were less predominant in 1984 than they had been in 1980 and as they became again in 1988 and 1992.

Still the changes during the twenty years of the post-1968 system were consistent with the maintenance of a basic pattern of determining popular preferences through a fairly long series of events scheduled state-by-state, rather than centrally. Moreover, throughout this period, the pattern was distinguished by the same disproportionately influential first primary in New Hampshire. Therefore, if we still regard the system as essentially unsettled, it is probably less because of the changes I have noted than because of great dissatisfaction that leads to hopes for a drastic transformation of the systems. Familiar complaints are that the process is too long and arduous, that personal campaigning as though one were running for sheriff is demeaning for a presidential aspirant, that the financial cost is too high, and that the news media play too large and too destructive a role.

These objections, it is argued, keep worthy candidates from seeking presidential nominations that they would welcome, if obtainable from their peers at a convention. Therefore, many political scientists, journalists, and public figures now advocate what they regard as a return to peer-review nominations by a convention dominated, in one way or another, by public office holders, party officials, and other organizationally chosen delegates. That a major party would now contrive so drastic a challenge to popularly determined nomination strikes me as politically too hazardous to be more than a remote possibility. Less appealing to political scientists, but potentially more popular for the broader public, is the adoption of a national primary, or perhaps four regional primaries, so as fully to regularize the process of popular choice. National conventions might thus be deprived of even their formal presidential nominating ballots, but otherwise left with the roles performed under current arrangements.

Those existing convention roles, while less commanding than the actual selection of presidential nominees, are nonetheless substantial. Delegates, even when committed by primary results to a prospective nominee, may have opportunities to influence platform provisions, rules, and perhaps vice-presidential selection. Such opportunities clearly arise when a nominee's power is constrained by a perceived need to conciliate supporters or a dissident minority.

Changing Research Interests

Most of my review of how political scientists have studied national conventions will cover only about one-fourth of the history of those conventions, since I have little concern with any work preceding the systematic research that began in 1952. Even that date, however, allows the inclusion of studies based on the assumption that conventions still decided nominations. Thus, I can discuss the relationship of the loss of nominating power to discerned changes in research interests, affecting subject matter, style, and method.

Although I am unaware of much pre-1952 research on conventions, I know that general books on parties always recognized the importance of conventions. Certain authors of these books drew on observations of conventions and on conversations with participants, along with documentary sources. The leading example is Bryce (1891); he has two chapters on national nominating conventions, one providing a fairly detailed description of procedures based on observations of the 1884 conventions (Bryce 1891, 2:187). Ostrogorski, first publishing in 1902, wrote more briefly about national conventions, but he certainly recognized their import (Ostrogorski 1964, 2:133–43). So did parties textbooks that became popular in the early twentieth century. For instance, Sait devoted two full chapters to a detailed presentation of the composition and proceedings of the national conventions (Sait 1939, 529–96). He cited each party's official report of its proceedings and the accounts of historians and journalists. Neither in Sait nor elsewhere, however, have I found references to *systematic* studies by political scientists. Certainly, political scientists, like journalists and historians, wrote about conventions. Peel and Donnelly (1935) did so in their book on the 1932 campaign; they have a chapter on the two major party conventions, which they attended and about which they comment from personal observation to supplement documentary sources.

Personal reports by political scientists received less attention than those of journalists. Mencken's opinionated coverage became famous. His 1932 dispatches, published in book form, now seem odd in regarding Franklin Roosevelt as "a feeble and dubious candidate" (1932, 183), but Mencken supplies considerable information of interest to a political scientist. He writes about the high proportion of professional politicians among delegates, their successful search for the still legally prohibited alcoholic beverages, and their difficulties in paying their expenses during a prolonged convention (like that of the Democrats in 1924). We may have no better source about many aspects of past conventions. Anyway, no source is more entertaining.

Turning from my short historical detour to the promised review of the last forty years of political science research on conventions, I should stress that the review is meant to be sufficient only to illustrate three lines of inquiry. The first is field observation of convention activities, the second is roll call analysis, and the third is quantitative analysis of delegate characteristics.

Field Observation at Conventions

My subject here is work mainly undertaken at conventions themselves. The studies often include data on delegate characteristics, but these data, which may or may not have been collected at the convention, are not the sole or principal focus, as they are in studies that I put in my third category. The point is illustrated in the first major political science study of national political conventions. Its initially published five volumes (David, Moos, and Goldman 1954) certainly concentrated on the activities of convention delegates, both in the nominating process and in such matters as platform making. Four of the five volumes were devoted to reports on each state's delegations, Republican and Democratic. Political scientists, or occasionally other knowledgeable persons from a given state, wrote about each particular party delegation, describing what the delegates did at the convention, as well as something about the preconvention politics of their state. More than 100 political scientists participated in what was described as "by far the most ambitious attempt undertaken to apply the case method of research in the field of politics" (1954, 1:viii).

Although the 1952 study undoubtedly emphasized nominating activities, the directors of the project also collected data on the characteristics of delegates. These data, along with similar, but more limited, information from 1948 and 1956, were subsequently published in a synthesizing work (David, Goldman, and Bain 1960). Even here, however, the characteristics of delegates were discussed in only one chapter of thirty pages in a book of about six hundred pages. For this volume, like the five-volume work published six years earlier, is concerned with the determination of presidential nominations and thus with convention activities. Allowing that even some contested nominations had been effectively decided before conventions, the authors believed that "More often, the period of active contest, if it has occurred at all, extends into the opening days of the convention, with general uncertainty over the outcome" (1960, 6).

Since that belief persisted in the 1960s, it could have provided the basis for the field work that continued, though on a smaller scale than that of 1952. An excellent example is the study of the 1960 conventions sponsored by the Eagleton Institute (Tillett 1963). It contains twenty-two short chapters, mostly on particular state delegations. Chapters are written by political science instructors or assistant professors selected as Eagleton Fellows—fourteen Democrats and ten Republicans—to attend one or another of the two conventions. The study directors were Professors Austin Ranney and Ivan Hinderaker, and the Fellows included later luminaries like Lucius Barker, David Derge, Charles Jones, John Kessel, and Aaron Wildavsky. Their chapters are rich in detail about the behavior of delegates, and they reflect close observation at the conventions.

Again in 1964, Eagleton Fellows attended the national conventions, and Tillett (1966) drew on their several unpublished papers to write a sophisticated and well-informed chapter in a book on the 1964 elections. Moreover, several of the contributors to the Eagleton study of 1960 continued to do fieldwork at later conventions. John Kessel, attending the 1964 Republican convention as a party staff member, subsequently wrote a chapter about how that convention confirmed, against a still-reluctant minority, the nomination that Barry Goldwater had won in primaries and caucuses (Kessel 1968, 91–119). Similarly classifiable as observational reports of convention activities are Wildavsky's studies of 1964 Republicans and 1968 Democrats. The two studies drew mainly on unquantified, unstructured interviews to learn about the nature of ongoing conventions, along with delegate characteristics. They are conveniently published in a collection of the author's work (Wildavsky 1971) that includes the earlier 1960 study already cited. In 1964, the research involved "some 150 interviews" with Goldwater delegates from California, New Jersey, and Illinois, all of which were conducted by Wildavsky and four helpers in the lobby of the San Francisco hotel where those delegates were staying (Wildavsky 1971, 269). The probing, unstructured interviews yielded illustrative quotations for Wildavsky's well-known distinction between "purists" and "politicians" (1971, 252) and for his discussion of the impact of an influx of purists on convention outcomes. Similar methods at the 1968 Democratic convention yielded similar findings about purists of the left as the 1964 study had for purists of the right; this time, however, Wildavsky and a larger number of colleagues and graduate students conducted "approximately 500 interviews," again in hotel lobbies, but covering all major delegations, plus some smaller delegations (1971, 287). Wildavsky argues that "The advantage of this type of interviewing is that it is possible to get answers on the spot and delve more deeply than is ordinarily possible in mail questionnaires or the usual sample surveys. We have no way of knowing how representative our responses are but the large number of interviews and the consistency of responses augurs well on that score" (1971, 287).

Extensive field research at conventions was undertaken in the 1970s by Denis Sullivan and various associates. Their publications do include significant quantitative tabulations of delegate characteristics, but they are even more notable for their reported observations of convention activities. Begun just as conventions were coming to be viewed as mere ratifiers of nominating results determined elsewhere, research at conventions themselves was nonetheless justified by reference to the importance of convention legitimation along with ratification. Legitimation can involve a nominee's concessions on platform issues or party rules in order to obtain more than nominal consensual support from the minority of delegates who had supported other candidates; arrangements for such concessions are subjects for observational research at conventions.

Sullivan and his colleagues published a volume devoted to the 1972 Democratic convention (Sullivan, Pressman, Page, and Lyons 1974). It drew on the work of a large group of Dartmouth faculty and students who attended the convention in Miami. Besides structured interviews of a randomly selected sample of 234 delegates and the use of a preconvention CBS poll of all delegates, the research team engaged in firsthand observation of caucuses, state delegation meetings, and convention proceedings (1974, 9). An impressive analytical product is a sharp comparison of the roles of interest group caucuses and state delegations. The latter, it was found, retained advantages that the caucuses did not have, as candidate organizations communicated chiefly through state delegations (1974, 62–68). Reports of what occurred in caucus sessions are often detailed and revealing. Equally so is the account of the politics of platform writing, especially descriptions of McGovern organization efforts to keep out certain radical proposals favored by many McGovern supporters, and of the revolt against a drafting subcommittee (1974, 71–115). Altogether, the volume is richly rewarding in its explanations of what happened at the convention, and also for its finding that while "purist" McGovern delegates did not become more pragmatic after their convention victory, the party "regulars" became purists, of a non-McGovern persuasion, after their loss (1974, 125–27).

A partially changed group of authors extended the research of 1972 to two later conventions. The first was the Democratic midterm convention of 1974, findings from which appear in a volume by Sullivan, Pressman, and Arterton (1976). Preconvention and postconvention questionnaires supplement interviews and observations at the 1974 convention. Again, however, I concentrate on what is learned about convention proceedings. Most striking, in contrast to the nominating convention of 1972, is the absence of delegates organized by competing candidate organizations (1976, 34–35). Another contrast related to the 1972 findings is the increased activity of group caucuses, attributed in part to the absence of candidate-organization power (1976, 73, 116). The second post-1972 convention similarly studied was the Republican convention of 1976. It was the subject of five articles published in a single issue of a journal (Sullivan, Nakamura, Weinberg, Arterton, and Pressman 1977–78). This time, as expected, candidate organizations are again dominant, and they are observed to influence delegates directly (1977–78, 637, 663–64). State delegations thereby become important channels of information. Interest-group caucuses were less consequential at the Republican convention (1977–78, 682).

Since the studies by Sullivan and his colleagues in the 1970s, I have not found any large-scale systematic field study of a national convention. What I have encountered are occasional efforts by individual scholars. For example, Jo Freeman drew on her considerable experience as an interviewer and observer at conventions to compare Republican and Democratic elites (1986). Lucius Barker, who had earlier contributed to the 1960 Democratic convention study, now recorded his impressions of the 1984 convention in a chapter of a book about his participation in Jesse Jackson's presidential nominating campaign (Barker 1988, 141–74). Serving as a Jackson delegate from Missouri, Barker provides a day-to-day account, in diary form, of his activities and of his observations of the divided Missouri delegation and of the frustrated efforts of Jackson delegates to obtain acceptance of their platform proposals. Though it is a political scientist's insightful report on a convention, the chapter attracted much less attention than did the book's compelling description of the significance of Jackson's campaign.

Other individual political scientists continued to report their observations of conventions in the 1980s. Nelson Polsby did so in his book on party reform (1983, 76–77), and also more fully on the Democratic nominations of 1980 and 1984 in his chapters in multiauthored volumes devoted to the elections of those years (Polsby 1981, 37–60; Polsby 1985, 36–65). The same two volumes have parallel chapters on the Republican nominations by Charles Jones (1981, 61–98; 1985, 66–99). Conventions were merely parts of the nominating process about which Polsby and Jones wrote, but those parts include personal observations at the conventions. For instance, Jones states that in 1984, he attended eight caucuses, sampling a state delegation from each region (Jones 1985, 95). Both Polsby and Jones are also among the several political scientists whose personal observations are drawn upon by Byron Shafer (1988) in his broad major work on national conventions. In 1980 and 1984, Shafer and three to five disciplinary colleagues attended each convention. How systematically they operated is not clear, but each of Shafer's colleagues kept notes for submission to Shafer each day, and also for later reflections sent to Shafer after the convention (Shafer 1988, 379, 381).

No doubt, Shafer drew on his colleagues' field observations, along with his own, for his four chapters on the conventions. But these chapters, constituting about half of Shafer's book, are not meant to give detailed accounts of what happened in either 1980 or 1984. Rather, they supply evidence to bolster Shafer's persuasive thesis that conventions have been significantly changed by recent delegate selection practices. Thus, the convention is, for him, a "window on a changing national politics" (Shafer 1988, 298). Through the window, Shafer observes such phenomena as decreased television coverage and greater party concern with using convention time for events designed to appeal to a general election audience, instead of accommodating convention participants. Shafer's study also includes data on delegate characteristics and on many other matters. The field observations I have stressed are by no means his dominant source of information.

Nor, I should now note, were field observations dominant, generally, in research on conventions in the 1980s. In particular, as I indicated earlier, no later systematic team study like that of Sullivan and his colleagues has come to my attention. Interest in field research at conventions surely remains, however. It is demonstrated in the more or less individual inquiries I have described and I suspect in other efforts unknown to me. Furthermore, "The Working Group for the Study of Political Party Conventions," organized chiefly by David Bositis, encouraged political scientists to attend the 1992 conventions, with particular reference to observing organized groups. At least one close study of Democratic and Republican platform making is forthcoming from L. Sandy Maisel.

Roll Call Analysis

Given the increased use of roll call analysis in congressional research as political scientists have become trained in statistical methods, its extension to national conventions is understandable. To my knowledge, however, the number of studies is limited. One reason is that conventions may have few roll calls, and even fewer of consequence, when presidential nominations are determined in advance. Before they were thought to be so determined, roll call analysis probably looked more promising. The four studies I know of deal mainly with pre-1972 conventions. The first is an article by Munger and Blackhurst (1965) that analyzes how state delegations, in voting on nominations, were aligned with some consistency in ideological factions at each party's conventions between 1940 and 1964. A few years later, Gerald Pomper (1971) used similar analytical methods in studying the two 1968 conventions, but found that the 1940–64 patterns did not hold. Neither Nixon's support nor Humphrey's was consistent with earlier ideological alignments. "A shift of power within the parties," Pomper declared, "is clearly evident" (1971, 829). A differently focused study by Johnson and Hahn (1973) uses roll call data to show how the number of conventions that delegates attended (1944–68) related to their votes for particular presidential candidates for nomination (Johnson and Hahn 1973, 160). Finally, there is a study by Howard Reiter (1980) that does include conventions in the late 1970s, even though its scope is largely historical. Reiter carefully tabulates the voting of state delegations on a single roll call, either a nominating ballot or a platform resolution, at each convention since 1896, through 1976 for the Republicans and 1978 for the Democrats. He impressively confirms his hypothesis that with the decline in power of state and local party leaders to control delegations, ideology and constituency characteristics result in greater factional stability at conventions.

Quantitative Studies of Delegate Characteristics

"Delegate characteristics" include much more than demographic data, and the scholarly findings yield significant political implications. Hence, the research category is hardly narrow, despite my exclusion from it of studies requiring actual observation of convention activities. To be sure, scholars conducting quantitative studies may themselves attend conventions, and even gather data there. But, as I shall note, the largest of such studies depend heavily on questionnaires completed elsewhere. Given the knowledge sought, work is not adversely affected by an absence of convention observation. Nor is its importance diminished by the convention's loss of power to make presidential nominations; delegates can be worth studying, regardless of their roles at conventions. They remain a widely acknowledged national party elite, conveniently identified every four years. Having at hand the names and addresses of several thousand political participants is an advantage that might well be envied, for example, by scholars searching for lists of county-level leaders of presidential campaigns (Clark, Bruce, Kessel, and Jacoby 1991, 581).

First among well-known, large-scale studies concerned only with the characteristics of delegates is the work by McClosky, Hoffmann, and O'Hara (1960). It was conducted in 1957–58 through mail questionnaires to delegates and alternates who had attended the Republican and Democratic conventions of 1956. Obtaining data from over three thousand participants, McClosky and his colleagues compared what they found with data from Gallup's sampling of Republican and Democratic voters. Explicitly, they treated each convention's delegates and alternates as party leaders, while Republican and Democratic electoral identifiers served as party followers. Asking about views on twenty-four issues, they found not only that significant differences existed between Republican and Democratic leaders, but also that the greater progressivism of the Democratic leaders was closer to the views of Democratic followers than the relative conservatism of Republican leaders was to Republican followers. Indeed, the views of Republican followers were closer to the views of Democratic leaders than of Republican leaders (McClosky, Hoffmann, and O'Hara 1960, 411, 422). In a later publication, McClosky (1964) used the same delegate and alternate questionnaire returns to compare the pro-Democratic ideological values of what he now called "political influentials" with the expressed values of the electorate.

Even while McClosky and his colleagues employed thousands of mail questionnaires to reach delegates, others effectively used structured interviews at conventions. For example, Marvick and Eldersveld (1961) obtained interviews with thirty-two Democratic and thirty-eight Republican delegation chairpersons at conventions in both 1952 and 1956. Their tabulated findings are not about issue positions or ideology, but about the respondents' background, prior political experience, and actual convention procedure. The last of these research subjects reflects an interest in decision making like that of the research I classified as field observation, but I choose (not unreasonably, I hope) to list the study here because of its emphasis on tabulated data from structured interviews. That Marvick and Eldersveld should have had a decision-making interest in the 1950s is, after all, to be expected, given the still-prevailing assumption that conventions made presidential nominating decisions. At that time, McClosky and his colleagues seemed exceptional in concentrating so exclusively on the characteristics of delegates.

Soon, however, that concentration was evident in other studies using structured interviews at conventions. Soule and Clarke (1970, 1971) provide a good example in two journal articles on delegates to the Democratic and Republican conventions of 1968. Employing teams of interviewers, they collected information from 187 Democrats and 171 Republicans. In addition to casting more light on distinctions between professionals and amateurs at the Democratic convention (1970, 893), Soule and Clarke specifically confirm McClosky's earlier finding about the issue differences between Democratic and Republican delegates (1971, 77, 89).

Study on a larger scale resumes for the 1972 conventions. Here, Warren Miller plays a major role in initiating the research that leads eventually to his own published contributions. The first product of the new effort, however, was a large volume on the 1972 conventions by Jeane Kirkpatrick (1976). Assisted in data gathering and analysis by Miller and others at the Center for Political Studies, Kirkpatrick used 1,336 interviews and 2,449 mail questionnaires to develop findings about delegates and, to some extent, about what they did at the conventions. She stressed changes already evident, especially on the Democratic side. Although the convention remained, for her, an important decision maker, even in presidential nominations, the study's treatment of the delegates as a significant political elite does not rest on the now-doubtful assumption about a convention's decision-making power. Borrowing her terms from Mosca (1939, 404–5), Kirkpatrick identified the delegates as the "second stratum" of the ruling class, as distinguished from a much smaller top ruling class (Kirkpatrick 1971, 13). Two of her many findings are especially well known and controversial. She concluded that new kinds of delegates, supporting George McGovern or George Wallace, were less attached to party than were supporters of Richard Nixon, Hubert Humphrey, or Edmund Muskie (1971, 103, 150–53), and that Democratic delegates, especially McGovern delegates, were less representative of the views and values of voters than were Republican delegates (1971, 331)—thus reversing McClosky's finding for 1956.

From Kirkpatrick's study, I skip over the work of others during the next decade, in order to move directly to Miller and Jennings (1986) and Miller (1988), since they draw upon, as well as extend significantly, the database available to Kirkpatrick. Careful and sophisticated longitudinal analysis, partly from panel responses, is a striking feature. Relying on mail questionnaires for delegates after 1972, the first work adds data on 1976 and 1980 convention delegates, and the second work adds data on 1984 delegates. Both books compare the characteristics, notably issue preferences and ideological attributes, not only of Republican with Democratic delegates, but also of each party's delegates with each party's voters (as sampled in surveys for the Center for Political Studies). Unlike Kirkpatrick, Miller and Jennings explicitly put aside the study of convention decision making by delegates. Now, if not in 1972, scholars might well be expected to assume that conventions have lost their power to decide nominations. They may still acknowledge, as do Miller and Jennings, that conventions make other important decisions. But Miller and Jennings are not concerned with those decisions. They are "almost exclusively" interested in the role of delegates "as campaign activists" (Miller and Jennings 1986, 4). In fact, their elite consists of convention delegates who also actively participate in the presidential campaign (1986, 22–23, 239), as current delegates (but not all former delegates) are assumed to do. Focusing thus on a presumably significant element of presidential party leadership,

Miller and Jennings consider the extent to which delegate-activists are representative of voters.

Merely illustrative of their rich findings are the following: Despite many new delegates at each convention, delegate members of the campaign elites of 1972, 1976, and 1980 were largely repeaters (1986, 35, 240). Liberal strength declined among Democratic activists, as did support for moderate leadership among Republicans, but much less as a consequence of individual-level change and much more as a consequence of conversion (1986, 60, 156). Campaign activists of both wings of both parties continued to be an economically advantaged and a well-educated elite (1986, 75). For the full period from 1972 to 1980, the contrast between professional politicians, in the center, and amateurs, on the left, in the Democratic party was not as great, or as different from the Republican pattern, as it had appeared in the 1972 study (1986, 78). Similarly, the longitudinal data made it clear that new Democratic personnel had not diluted overall commitments to party (1986, 85). Again at odds with what had been discerned in 1972, the data now revealed a growing issue distance between Republican elites and Republican voters (1986, 207, 219); by 1980, Republican delegates were, on average, "even further removed from their party base than were the Democratic delegates from theirs" (1986, 248).

Miller's own book (1988), besides its addition of data on 1984 convention delegates, contains new, insightful analysis of the representational links of party elites and party voters. For example, Miller asks whether voters, in choosing delegates to represent their candidate preference, have consented to any other kind of representation, at conventions or elsewhere, and whether even the candidate preferences, as expressed in the winter and early spring, remain the same in the summer (1988, 110–11). Representativeness is also explored by comparing the issue positions of delegates elected in primaries, delegates elected in caucuses, and superdelegates in relation to the issue positions of party voters (1988, 125–30). Findings are more firmly established in certain other areas: From 1980 to 1984, intraparty factionalism declined among Republican and Democratic elites, while interparty differentiation increased on measures of policy-relevant attitudes (1988, 28–30). The partisan elites can "fairly be described as ideologically polarized" (1988, 54). Though party voters remain less polarized, Republican elites and voters, by 1984, were about as much like each other on policy preferences as were Democratic elites and voters (1988, 38–39). This rough balance of 1984 differs not only from what Miller and Jennings reported in 1980, but also from what Kirkpatrick had found in 1972 and from the contrasting pattern McClosky had found in 1956. No doubt, each of the four different pictures accurately portrays the elite-mass relationship for its particular election year. The lesson from the longitudinal data is that the relationship is time bound. An evidently more durable characteristic among both Republican and Democratic elites is that party regulars, not issue-oriented reformers, are closer to the policy preferences of party voters (Miller 1988, 81). How durable this, or any other characteristic, remains is something that we shall be able to learn from data to become available from already-conducted surveys of 1988 delegates and voters, and probably from work undertaken in 1992 and later.

I should not give the impression that Miller and Jennings are the only scholars concerned with quantitative studies of delegates during the last decade or so. Other work includes interesting comparisons of national convention delegates with differently defined party elites. Jackson, Brown, and Bositis (1982), noting a study of county chairs in 1972 (Montjoy, Shaffer, and Weber 1980) at odds with Kirkpatrick's findings for national convention delegates in the same year, sought in 1980 to compare the ideologies and issue positions of national convention delegates, county chairs, state party chairs, national party committee members, and party voters. Perhaps the sharpest finding is that Democratic county chairs, but not Republican county chairs, are closer than other elite categories to their party voters (Jackson, Brown, and Bositis 1982, 174). A similar observation is made by Baer and Bositis (1988, 182). Here and elsewhere in the 1980s, scholars tend to find an ideological distinction between Republican and Democratic elites resembling that reported by Miller and Jennings. A recent example is in a study of county presidential campaign chairs in 1988 (Bruce, Clark, and Kessel 1991, 1102). Similarly, Rapoport, Abramowitz, and McGlennon, studying state-level delegates chosen in eleven caucus-convention states in 1980, show a consistent liberalism among Democrats and a consistent conservatism among Republicans (Rapoport, Abramowitz, and McGlennon 1986, 50). In the same book, various authors also make the point that these delegates, like the national convention delegates studied by Miller and Jennings, were attached to party, and specifically to party victory, rather than only to ideological purity.

Conclusion

As projected at the start of this essay, quantitative studies of delegate characteristics have indeed become more prominent than field observations of conventions, as the decision-making powers of the conventions appear to have significantly diminished. Arguably, scholars see less point in observing convention decision-making processes when those processes no longer settle presidential nominations. Thus, one could account for a diminished interest in undertaking expensive, large-scale field observations, like the APSA-sponsored study of 1952. On the other hand, quantitative studies of delegate characteristics are not merely responses to changes in the power of conventions. They began in the 1950s, before that power was assumed to have diminished, and their continued development reflects our discipline's increasing emphasis on quantitative work in general, and on systematically gathered survey and questionnaire data in particular. The relationship is apparent in Warren Miller's extension to convention delegates of the analytical methods he had helped pioneer in voting-behavior research. No doubt, quantitative studies of delegate characteristics will continue to thrive. National convention delegates, whatever their powers, remain a party elite well worth learning more about, and especially as Miller and Jennings define that elite.

Field observation of conventions, however, has never disappeared, and there may now, for good reason, be a modest revival. Increasingly salient are the activities of interest groups in securing representation among convention delegates and in thus promoting their causes in platform drafting and in speech making. In 1992, the Christian Coalition at the Republican convention attracted special attention, but labor unions, teacher associations, and other organized groups have also been actively represented at Democratic conventions. Delegates, it seems, may be committed by voters to help nominate a particular candidate, but at the same time devoted to promoting policies different from those of the candidate. Thus, one suspects that some of President Bush's delegates in 1992 were his only for the nomination. If so, it is not merely fieldwork at conventions that is in order, but also fieldwork during the delegate selection process. How, in each state, are delegates actually chosen to fill the slots won by presidential candidates? Even if candidates or their agents fill the slots, are they effectively pressed to include certain activists? Or, to turn the question around, how do organized interest groups secure delegate positions for their members?

Related to such inquiries is the question of financial sponsorship of delegates. Attending national conventions is expensive, and traditionally most delegates have paid their own way. As late as 1964, over 90 percent did so, according to the only exploration I have seen (McKeough and Bibby 1968, 95). Later, impressions of increased labor union support for delegates suggest that the percentage covering their own travel and hotel costs may have declined somewhat, at least among Democrats. Perhaps various nonunion groups now also provide support. Would such help have consequences for delegate behavior at conventions? And would more widespread financial support reduce the relatively high income levels of each party's national convention delegates, compared particularly with those reported for the same party's county chairs and county leaders of presidential campaigns (Kessel 1991, 80)? Income levels indicate self-selection by the prosperous and suggest useful inquiries about the influence of campaign contributions in winning delegate slots. Such inquiries, however, assume that delegates have sought their selection, rather than being persuaded to serve. This assumption, itself, could be investigated by fieldwork, as well as by mail questionnaire.

The case for preconvention field research concerning the selection of delegates rests on the continued importance of the convention, even when we expect primary voters, rather than convening delegates, to choose presidential nominees. The convention remains a significant defining event for a party, both to mobilize its activists and to appeal publicly on behalf of its presidential ticket. How well each party convention succeeds in achieving these objectives, and especially how it mobilizes its activists without offending a less committed public, is a critical part of the presidential campaign. Experience in 1992, when the Democratic convention succeeded as the Republican did not, is only the latest example of a phenomenon more often illustrated in recent years by greater Republican than Democratic success. Managerial skill is, no doubt, an explanatory factor in each instance, but so, too, one can reasonably hypothesize, is the composition of the convention. Not only can that composition influence a party's platform, but also the content of the television drama and news package that the convention conveys.

Although no revival of convention power to nominate presidents is thus necessary in order to justify field observations along with quantitative studies of delegate characteristics, I am careful not to exclude absolutely the revival of the old power. The possibility, as I have argued, is remote, and I am not persuaded that it is even desirable. But prediction in political science is an uncertain endeavor. One can at least imagine circumstances in which a party, not daring to contrive a return to a brokered convention, might, nevertheless, stumble into it. Suppose a convention, chosen under present rules, had to choose a presidential nominee, either because no preconvention winner emerged or because a winner suffered a disqualifying calamity between the primaries and the convention. Then, if the convention's choice were elected president, subsequent convention decision making might become popular and feasible. However imaginary, that type of change would be in accord with the unplanned and episodic development of national conventions, along with much else, in American politics.

REFERENCES

Baer, Denise L., and David A. Bositis. 1988. *Elite Cadres and Party Coalitions: Representing the Public in Party Politics.* Westport, Conn.: Greenwood.

Barker, Lucius J. 1988. *Our Time Has Come: A Delegate's Diary of Jesse Jackson's 1984 Presidential Campaign.* Urbana: University of Illinois Press.

Bruce, John M., John A. Clark, and John H. Kessel. 1991. "Advocacy Politics in Presidential Parties." *American Political Science Review* 85:1089–1106.

Bryce, James. 1891. *The American Commonwealth.* Chicago: Sergel.

Carleton, William G. 1957. "The Revolution in the Presidential Nominating Convention." *Political Science Quarterly* 72:224–40.

Ceaser, James W. 1979. *Presidential Selection: Theory and Development.* Princeton, N.J.: Princeton University Press.

Clark, John A., John M. Bruce, John H. Kessel, and William G. Jacoby. 1991. "I'd Rather Switch than Fight: Lifelong Democrats and Converts to Republicanism Among Campaign Activists." *American Journal of Political Science* 35:577–97.

David, Paul T., Malcolm Moos, and Ralph M. Goldman, eds. 1954. *Presidential Nominating Politics in 1952.* Baltimore: Johns Hopkins University Press.

David, Paul T., Ralph H. Goldman, and Richard C. Bain. 1960. *The Politics of National Party Conventions.* Washington, D.C.: Brookings Institution.

Davis, James W. 1967. *Springboard to the White House: Presidential Primaries.* New York: Crowell.

Freeman, Jo. 1986. "The Political Culture of the Democratic and Republican Parties." *Political Science Quarterly* 101:337–56.

Israel, Fred L., ed. 1966. *The State of the Union Messages of the Presidents: 1790–1960.* New York: Chelsea House.

Jackson, John S., III, Barbara Leavitt Brown, and David A. Bositis. 1982. "Herbert McClosky and Friends Revisited: 1980 Democratic and Republican Party Elites Compared to the Mass Public." *American Politics Quarterly* 10:158–80.

Johnson, Loch K., and Harlan Hahn. 1973. "Delegate Turnover at National Party Conventions, 1944–68." In *Perspectives on Presidential Selection,* ed. Donald R. Matthews. Washington, D.C.: Brookings Institution.

Jones, Charles O. 1981. "Nominating Carter's Favorite Opponent: The Republicans in 1980." In *The American Elections of 1980,* ed. Austin Ranney. Washington, D.C.: American Enterprise Institute.

———. 1985. "Renominating Ronald Reagan: The Compleat Politician at Work." In *The American Elections of 1984,* ed. Austin Ranney. Durham, N.C.: Duke University Press.

Kessel, John H. 1968. *The Goldwater Coalition: Republican Strategies in 1964.* Indianapolis: Bobbs-Merrill.

Key, V. O., Jr. 1964. *Politics, Parties, and Pressure Groups.* New York: Crowell.

Kirkpatrick, Jeane. 1976. *The New Presidential Elite: Men and Women in National Politics.* New York: Russell Sage Foundation and The Twentieth Century Fund.

McClosky, Herbert. 1964. "Consensus and Ideology in American Culture." *American Political Science Review* 57:361–82.

McClosky, Herbert, Paul J. Hoffmann, and Rosemary O'Hara. 1960. "Issue Conflict and Consensus Among Party Leaders and Followers." *American Political Science Review* 54:406–27.

McKeough, Kevin L., and John F. Bibby. 1968. *The Costs of Political Participation: A Study of National Convention Delegates.* Princeton, N.J.: Citizens' Research Foundation.

Marvick, Dwaine, and Samuel J. Eldersveld. 1961. "National Convention Leadership: 1952 and 1956." *Western Political Quarterly* 14:176–94.

Mencken, H. L. 1932. *Making A President: A Footnote to the Saga of Democracy.* New York: Knopf.

Miller, Warren E. 1988. *Without Consent: Mass-Elite Linkages in Presidential Politics.* Lexington: University Press of Kentucky.

Miller, Warren E., and M. Kent Jennings. 1986. *Parties in Transition: A Longitudinal Study of Party Elites and Party Supporters.* New York: Russell Sage Foundation.

Montjoy, Robert S., William R. Shaffer, and Ronald E. Weber. 1980. "Policy Preferences of Party Elites and Masses: Conflict or Consensus?" *American Politics Quarterly* 8:319–44.

Mosca, Gaetano. 1939. *The Ruling Class.* New York: McGraw-Hill.

Munger, Frank, and James Blackhurst. 1965. "Factionalism in the National Conventions, 1940–1964: An Analysis of Ideological Consistency in State Delegation Voting." *Journal of Politics* 27:375–94.

Ostrogorski, M. 1964. *Democracy and the Organization of Political Parties.* Garden City, N.Y.: Anchor Doubleday.

Peel, Roy V., and Thomas C. Donnelly. 1935. *The 1932 Campaign: An Analysis.* New York: Farrar and Rinehart.

Polsby, Nelson W. 1981. "The Democratic Nomination." In *The American Elections of 1980,* ed. Austin Ranney. Washington, D.C.: American Enterprise Institute.

———. 1983. *Consequences of Party Reform.* New York: Oxford University Press.

———. 1985. "The Democratic Nomination and the Evolution of the Party System." In *The American Elections of 1984,* ed. Austin Ranney. Durham, N.C.: Duke University Press.

Pomper, Gerald M. 1971. "Factionalism in the 1968 National Conventions: An Extension of Research Findings." *Journal of Politics* 33:826–30.

Rapoport, Ronald B., Alan I. Abramowitz, and John McGlennon, eds. 1986. *The Life of the Parties: Activists in Presidential Politics.* Lexington: University Press of Kentucky.

Reiter, Howard L. 1980. "Party Factionalism: National Conventions in a New Era." *American Politics Quarterly* 8:303–18.

Sait, Edward H. 1939. *American Parties and Elections.* New York: Appleton Century.

Shafer, Byron E. 1988. *Bifurcated Politics: Evolution and Reform in the National Party Convention.* Cambridge, Mass.: Harvard University Press.

Soule, John W., and James W. Clarke. 1970. "Amateurs and Professionals: A Study of Delegates to the 1968 Democratic National Convention." *American Political Science Review* 64:888–98.

———. 1971. "Issue Conflict and Consensus: A Comparative Study of Democratic and Republican Delegates to the 1968 National Conventions." *Journal of Politics* 33:72–91.

Sullivan, Denis G., Jeffrey L. Pressman, Benjamin I. Page, and John J. Lyons. 1974. *The Politics of Representation: The Democratic Convention of 1972.* New York: St. Martin's.

Sullivan, Denis G., Jeffrey L. Pressman, and F. Christopher Arterton. 1976. *Explorations in Convention Decision Making: The Democratic Party in the 1970s.* San Francisco: W. H. Freeman.

Sullivan, Denis G., Robert T. Nakamura, Martha Wagner Weinberg, F. Christopher Arterton, and Jeffrey L. Pressman. 1977–78. "Exploring the 1976 Republican Convention." *Political Science Quarterly* 92:633–82.

Tillett, Paul, ed. 1963. *Inside Politics: The National Conventions, 1960.* Dobbs Ferry, N.Y.: Oceana Publications.

Tillett, Paul. 1966. "The National Conventions." In *The National Election of 1964,* ed. Milton C. Cummings, Jr. Washington, D.C.: Brookings Institution.

Wildavsky, Aaron. 1971. *The Revolt Against the Masses and Other Essays on Politics and Public Policy.* New York: Basic Books.

CHAPTER 12

List Alliances: An Experiment in Political Representation

Henry Valen

This chapter deals with list alliances in proportional representation (PR) systems. A system of list alliances (*listeforbund*), which was introduced in Norway by an electoral reform of 1985, will be presented as a case study. Electoral statistics, as well as a nationwide voter survey at the Storting election the same year, made it possible to study the impact of the reform. Before presenting the analysis, a few general remarks are required about electoral alliances.

The Quest for Equity

The purpose of electoral alliances is to improve the representation of the parties involved. Such alliances date back to the emergence of political parties. The activities and character of alliances are conditioned by the electoral system. A well-known example is alliances in majority election systems, with runoffs or reelections. All parties may run candidates and gauge their strength at the first election. If the system also permits all parties to run candidates at reelections, cooperating parties may agree to withdraw from the contest in specific constituencies and support one another's candidates. As a result, the parties involved may be overrepresented in relation to their share of the votes.[1] This strategy has been observed at numerous elections in European countries applying majority election systems, of which France is an outstanding case (Duverger 1951, 325–51; Tsebelis 1990). When Norway applied a majority system from 1906 to 1918, bourgeois parties cooperating at runoff elections managed to strengthen their joint representation greatly at the cost of the Labor Party (Valen 1991).

Conditions for alliances in PR systems are different. The PR method implies that seats will be distributed among competing parties proportionally to their strength at the polls. In practice, however, it is extremely difficult to achieve full proportionality (Rokkan 1968; Taagepera and Shugart 1989). Distortion in favor of some specific party/parties may partly result from the representation formula applied; partly it is due to the fact that some minor parties do not reach the threshold of representation, either nationally or in

289

specific constituencies. In the latter case, larger parties will, more or less automatically, be overrepresented.

The easiest way of obtaining proportionality seems to be by organizing the whole country as a single constituency. The Netherlands is an interesting example. During World War I, the parties were bitterly divided over two major issues: the financial position of religious schools, and the introduction of universal suffrage. Both issues were resolved in "the historical compromise" of 1917. The reform included the introduction of proportional representation in combination with a list system and the treatment of the entire country as a single electoral district, which allowed the Liberal party to survive. The new system was also advantageous for the Catholics, whose electoral support was heavily concentrated in the southern provinces. The excess of Catholic votes in the South and the votes of Catholic minorities in northern districts were no longer wasted under nationwide proportional representation (Andeweg 1989, 45). However, except for Israel, which, like the Netherlands, occupies a relatively small territory, PR countries tend to be divided into a number of constituencies. Due to geographical variations within the country, elected representatives are required to relate directly to the electorate of their respective constituencies.

In practically all PR countries, there is an almost eternal cry for more equity of representation among competing parties, and numerous reforms have been attempted to improve proportionality (Taagepera and Shugart 1989; Dodd et al. 1987). List alliances have been a hot topic in this discussion. The main argument is that by pooling their votes minor parties may reach the threshold of representation and thus reduce or eliminate the overrepresentation of larger parties.[2] It may be objected that electoral alliances are not restricted to small parties. Indeed, a reform allowing for alliances has to be universally applicable, and larger as well as minor parties may find the system beneficial for their interests. Nonetheless, the demand for improvement of proportionality seems normally to be the legitimation for such reforms.

Alliance Strategies

Broadly speaking, we may distinguish between two types of alliances, "joint lists" and "list alliances." Two or more parties may decide to run joint lists either nationally or in specific constituencies. By joining forces, they will improve their chances at the allocation of seats. The disadvantage is that the cooperating parties are unable to present themselves as independent alternatives in the competition for the vote. This disadvantage is avoided when list alliances are applied. In this case, the cooperating parties run separate lists, but they have agreed to pool their votes in the final count. The two types of alliances differ with regard to legal status. Whereas joint lists between several parties can normally be established without interference by electoral law, list alliances require explicit permission, since they imply alternative voting and the transference of votes from one party to another.

Costs and Benefits of Alliances

Advantages of forming electoral alliances can easily be appreciated. Small parties that separately are below the threshold of representation may jointly reach the magic level. Even larger parties can profit from being part of an alliance. Surplus votes for a given party, not enough to capture another seat, may be credited to some other party, which may thus obtain representation. When the method is applied in a number of constituencies with differing vote distributions, all participating parties have some probability of gaining extra seats.

However, electoral alliances are not only a matter of arithmetic. If alliances could be formed exclusively on the basis of calculated gains, alliances would shift from one constituency to another, depending partly upon distributions of votes at preceding elections, partly upon public opinion polls. Consequently, a great variety of alliances would appear throughout the nation, involving all parties in the system. But, as a result, the electorate would be unable to identify political alternatives. In the real world of politics, options for competing parties are restricted.

The question is: how do we identify such options? Is there some theory available according to which alliances might be predicted? Coalition theory, which is concerned with conditions for establishing government alliances, seems to be relevant in this regard. Early students of coalitions (Gamson 1961; Riker 1962) tried to explain party behavior in terms of office-seeking motivations. Coalitions were analyzed by applying mathematical models drawn from the theory of n-person games, in which various solutions were proposed as a way of determining which coalition(s) would be formed or which pay off configuration(s) would prevail. Political parties were seen as unconstrained actors seeking to maximize their share of the spoils of office. To put it somewhat simply, Riker (1962) and Gamson (1961) based their predictions on a size principle (the principle of minimum winning coalitions) and did not take into account party platforms or ideology.

The second model of party behavior put policy objectives at the center of party motivation, in the sense that parties enter coalitions for the purpose of promoting specific policies. Policy-based theories emerged as a response to office-based theories (Leiserson 1966; Axelrod 1970). Theoretically, there will be a great number of possible coalitions after an election. In reality, however, combinations of possibilities are limited, taking into account political similarities and differences between parties. As put by von Beyme (1985, 323):

"Where there is strong opposition between parties of conflicting ideologies, many coalitions which might be arithmetically possible would be politically impossible right from the start" (see also Sjöblom 1968, 269). Thus, the incorporation of "political distance" drastically improved the predictive power of the theories, since a number of combinations could be eliminated. Most of the recent studies of policy-based theories refer to European multiparty systems (de Swaan 1973; Lijphart 1984; Pridham 1986; Laver and Schofield 1990; Strøm 1990).

A third objective of party behavior is predicted by vote-seeking models. So far, this motivation has not been much elaborated in empirical research, although some theoretical attempts have been made by Austen-Smith and Banks (1988) and Laver (1989) to explore the interaction between electoral competition and coalition bargaining. In doing so, they apply the rational choice theory of party competition elaborated by Anthony Downs (1957), which states that parties are seeking to maximize their share of the votes in order to control government. Downs's theory assumes that a dynamic relationship exists between parties and their supporters. Voters react on government policy, and, in turn, parties are responsive to the electorate because they are dependent on their votes to obtain office. Indirectly, therefore, the electorate has an impact upon the decisions of parties, since leaders are always calculating the reactions of possible supporters.

In current studies of coalition behavior, the three models—all within the rational choice tradition—are regarded as independent and mutually conflicting forms of behavior in which parties can engage. But, obviously, it is no easy task to assess empirically the relative significance of the three types of party motivations. The parties may face a conflict between vote-seeking on the one hand and more immediate policy and office-seeking on the other. Thus, Strøm argues: "the conflict between present office (and policy) seeking and the future vote-seeking boils down to a trade-off between short term and longer term benefits" (Strøm 1990a, 573).

Types of motivations applied by students of government coalitions are also relevant in the study of electoral alliances, although with varying force. Evidently, the least applicable models are those based on office-motivations, since these kinds of alliances are not designed for governmental office-seeking, except in cases where they coincide with existing or prospective government coalitions. Vote-seeking is the main purpose of electoral alliances, but considerations of policy will also be involved indirectly. Let us illuminate this point by presenting an example from France, which, under the Fourth Republic, practiced a PR electoral system. At the 1956 national elections, list alliances played a predominant role. Three sets of alliances occurred in numerous constituencies throughout the country: (1) Socialist-Radical alliances, which in a few places were called *Republican Front;* (2) MRP-Conservative alliances;

and (3) Poujadist alliances (Pierce 1956, 391–422; Williams 1964). Parties included varied to some extent from one region to another, but basically, the respective alliances consisted of parties that were close neighbors along the left-right continuum. Behind each of the three blocs, we find parties that were not only concerned with maximizing their representation, but were also promoting specific policies.

Thus, coalition theory may give a clue to understanding conditions under which parties enter into electoral alliances. Such alliances have important political consequences for the parties concerned, as well as for their voters. Since the parties involved are basically interested in maximizing their joint vote, they have to support one another in the campaign, or at least abstain from mutual attacks. The implication is that participating parties will be held more or less responsible for the policies of one another. As a consequence, only parties that are rather similar in policies and ideology are likely to gain from joining an electoral alliance. If policy differences are too big, a given party may be faced with liabilities for the policies or behavior of some coalition partner. Thus, potential gains in terms of seats may be outweighed by losses at the polls resulting from unpopular policies.

List alliances may also create problems for the individual voter. Again, let us lean on the theory of Anthony Downs (1957) to give some theoretical "body" to our empirical assumptions. The idea of interdependence between parties and electorate assumes that voters prefer specific parties because they are interested in policy outcomes. Rational voters, informed about party policies, will choose a party indicating a position close to their own views. In other words, the voter acts instrumentally by choosing the party that he expects will benefit his own interests (Downs 1957, 36).

A competing theory has been proposed by Macdonald, Listhaug, and Rabinowitz (1991). They argue that it is the policy direction, rather than policy distances, that is the motivating force for the individual voter. This debate does not affect our analysis, however. Our main point is that individual voters are faced with a choice among several parties that, in their perception, may differ widely regarding policy positions. If their preferred party is involved in a list alliance, they are forced into a kind of alternative voting, without being able to control the alternatives. Provided they are informed about the alliance, they cast their votes for their preferred party, knowing that their votes may be transferred to some other party that they may like or dislike. In case of conflicting feelings, the question is how strongly they identify with their own party, and how much they dislike the respective alternative parties. Obviously, information about possible alliances is of crucial significance for the behavior of individual voters.

In studying the impact of electoral alliances it is appropriate to address two levels in the system, political parties and the electorate. We assume that both sets of actors behave rationally; both parties and voters weigh the costs and benefits involved in their choices and make the decision which produces the greatest net benefits, Thus, two hypotheses may be proposed:

1. Only parties which are similar with regard to policies and ideological outlook are able to engage in list alliances.
2. Voters who are directly affected by list alliances are inclined to shift party if they dislike some party in the alliance, provided they are informed about the alliance.

The Norwegian Reform

When Norway shifted from majority elections to a PR system in 1919, a proposal to permit list alliances (listeforbund) was rejected on ethical grounds.[3] The new electoral system, which applied the d'Hondt formula of representation, resulted in considerable distortion among the parties in seat allocation (Valen 1991). In 1930, the proposal of listeforbund reappeared and was accepted by a majority in the Storting. By applying this method at the election of 1930, and at the three subsequent Storting elections, bourgeois parties gained a number of extra seats at the cost of Labor (Kristvik and Rokkan 1964). In 1949, when Labor held a majority in the Storting, the liste-forbund was revoked. By a major electoral reform of 1953 (Valen 1993), the d'Hondt formula of representation was replaced by a modified version of the Sainte Laguë formula.[4] This reform greatly improved proportionality. However, distortion again increased in the 1970s (Valen 1991), due to the emergence of new miniparties that fell below the threshold of representation.[5] The larger parties were correspondingly overrepresented. To some extent, the partisan distortion was contained by joint lists among middle-sized parties, almost exclusively parties at the center, the Christian People's party, the Center party, and, to a lesser extent, the Liberals. At the 1981 election, joint lists appeared in seven out of nineteen constituencies.

The size of the various parties may be described in terms of seats obtained in 1981: the Socialist Left party, four; Labor, sixty-five; the Liberals, two; the Christian People's party, fifteen; the Center party, eleven; the Conservative party, fifty-four; and the Progress party, four. The Marxist-Leninists, as well as the Liberal People's party, did not obtain representation.

In 1985, the Christian People's party and the Center party made a proposal to reintroduce the listeforbund system, in order to improve proportionality. The proposal was supported by the Conservatives, who at this time shared government power with the two former parties, and by the right-wing Progress party. The reform implied that the listeforbund would only come into effect if it resulted in extra seats for the participating parties.

The listeforbund system had not been applied since the election of 1945. Thus, the reform provided entirely new opportunities for leaders, as well as for voters, of the postwar generation. In this paper, an attempt is made to study, on the one hand, to what extent and with what effect the parties applied the listeforbund at the 1985 Storting election and, on the other hand, the reactions of the electorate. To what extent did the voters know about the reform? How did the reform affect their electoral choice? And how did they like the reform?

Perception of Party Space and Political Distances

As stated above, our hypothesis is that only parties that are similar with regard to policies and ideological outlook are able to engage in list alliances. As a measure of similarities and differences among parties, we shall present voter perceptions of the political space and party distances. Our measurements are drawn from a nationwide voter survey at the 1985 election (Aardal and Valen 1989). It should be noted, however, that the distances reported have remained remarkably stable over time. Three types of data will be applied:

1. Left-right position
2. Second choice
3. Sympathy thermometers for political parties

Left-Right Position

The respondents were asked, "We have here a scale running from 1 on the left-hand side—i.e., those who stand on the far left politically—to 10 on the right-hand side—i.e., those who stand on the far right politically. Where would you place yourself on such a scale?" Figure 1 shows how voters placed themselves, from left to right, in 1985.

Evidently, an overwhelming majority prefer to place themselves close to the midpoint of the scale. The average value for voters of each individual party marked along the x-axis demonstrates that nearly all parties have the majority of their supporters near the center point. Most interesting is the location of the two biggest parties, Labor and the Conservatives, with Labor a little to the left of the center and the Conservatives a short way out to the right. Indeed, the distance between these major contenders in the system is not very big. Thus, the parties at the center which are located between the two big parties are confined to a limited area in the left-right spectrum. It should be observed that voters of the Christian People's party and the Center party are slightly closer to the Conservatives than to Labor, while Liberal voters tend to be closer to Labor. Even the extreme parties, Socialist Left and Progress, are not located very far out on the respective wings.

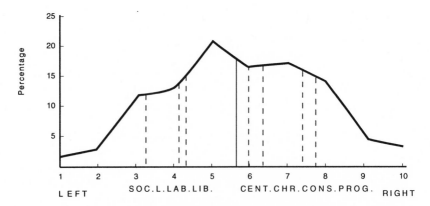

Fig. 1. Self-location of voters along the left-right scale, 1985. (Data for all figures from Norwegian Election Study of 1985.)

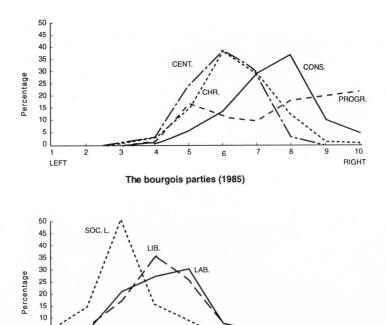

The bourgois parties (1985)

The socialist parties and Liberal party (1985)

Fig. 2. Self-location of voters from left to right

Figure 2 presents the distribution for each individual party.

Most voters tend to be found within a limited area. In the Socialist Left Party, for example, an overwhelming majority have scale values from 1 to 4, while most Laborites are located from 3 to 5, and the Conservatives from 6 to 9. The exception is, however, provided by the Progress party, whose voters are spread over a wide area from 5 to 10, although most concentration is on the right wing. The profiles of the Center and Christian People's parties are remarkably similar.

This description of the left-right profiles of the parties coincides with major government alternatives. At the time of the 1985 election, a coalition government formed by the Conservatives, the Christian People's party, and the Center was in power. The three coalition parties are rather close. It should be observed that left-right position is not the only conflict dimension separating Norwegian parties. In their work on directional theory, in which Norwegian data are applied, Macdonald, Listhaug, and Rabinowitz (1991) have demonstrated how Norwegian parties differ along several issue dimensions. Their observations are consistent with previous spatial analyses of the system (Converse and Valen 1971; Valen and Rokkan 1974; Valen 1990).

Second Preferences

Once we know the ideal position of an individual, defined by voting, the second choice will mark the shortest distance to the nearest neighbor in the party system. It is not known how great this distance is for the individual voter (Converse and Valen 1971, 126–33). Theoretically, however, second preference provides an interesting opening into a study of the form of the party system. From a purely practical point of view, it may be interpreted as an alternative voting preference.

Table 1 presents voters' second preferences in relation to voting in the 1985 election. The parties are ranked approximately from left to right in the table (see fig. 2). The material shows that voters have a tendency to indicate their nearest neighbor in the party spectrum as their party of second preference. This tendency is most obvious for the parties on the outermost right and left. Over 70 percent of those voting for the Socialist Left party and the Progress party indicate the Labor party and the Conservative party, respectively, as their second preference. The Socialist Left is the most attractive party with Labor voters, and almost half of all Labor voters mentioned this party. The other half are distributed to the nonsocialist parties, with the Liberal party and the Conservative party as the most frequent choices. The second preferences of Conservative party voters are more diffuse: the majority tend to go for the Center party, after which comes the Progress party, with the Christian People's party and the Labor party sharing third place. The picture is less clear regarding the

TABLE 1. Vote Preference and Second Choice, 1985

	Voted in 1985						
Second-Choice Party	Socialist Left	Labor	Liberal	Christian People's	Center	Conservative	Progress
Socialist Left	—	45%	35%	2%	2%	3%	5%
Labor	71%	—	28	9	9	16	8
Liberal	10	12	—	2	5	3	2
Christian People's	2	4	7	—	31	16	—
Center	1	5	6	39	31	26	3
Conservative	1	9	4	33	31	—	77
Progress	3	3	4	1	1	20	—
Other answers[a]	4	2	3	3	2	4	—
Don't know, no answer	7	20	12	10	19	24	6
Total[b]	99	100	99	99	100	100	101
N	105	706	68	180	129	561	66

Source: Norwegian Election Study of 1985. Principal Investigators: Henry Valen and Bernt Aardal.

[a]Includes Red Election Alliance, Liberal People's party, Norwegian Communist party, and other small parties.

[b]Percentages do not always total 100 due to rounding.

parties at the center. The Liberal party's supporters prefer the socialist parties by a large majority. The two governing parties in 1985—the Christian People's party and the Center party—prefer one another, as well as their coalition partner, the Conservative party. Even so, nine percent of voters in both parties put the Labor party in second place.

The pattern in table 1 indicates that the distance between the parties, measured in terms of second preference, follows the parties' location along the left-right axis. Such pictures are far from being unambiguous, however. The most interesting deviation concerns the relationship between the parties at the center and those on the wings. We hardly ever find the Christian People's party and Center party voters putting the Progress party in second place, and these two parties are correspondingly unpopular among the Progress party's voters. Likewise, there is a tremendous distance between the Socialist Left party, on the one hand, and the Christian People's party and the Center party, on the other. The third among the parties at the center, the Liberal party, does, however, stand quite close to the socialist parties.

Party Sympathy

Our third measuring instrument, the "sympathy thermometer," has been adopted in order to register voters' feelings in relation to each of the parties in the system. The sample was shown a scale running from 0 (least sympathy) to 100 (most sympathy), and respondents were asked to rank each of the parties in relation to the scale. The results are shown in table 2.

As we might reasonably expect, voters ranked their own party highest, and in this respect there are only small variations to be found from one party to the next. The question of how voters rate parties other than their own deserves greater attention.

If we consider the sympathy scores in table 2 in relation to the existing government alternatives, we can begin to make out the contours of two blocks of parties: on the one hand, the two socialist parties and the Liberal party, and, on the other, the four nonsocialist parties.[6] These are not homogeneous groups, however. Supporters of both the Labor party and the Liberal party show considerable sympathy for the Center party. Within the nonsocialist group, there is considerable mutual sympathy between the three government parties—the Conservative party, the Christian People's party, and the Center party. The Conservative party also enjoys much favor from the Progress party, although sympathy for the Progress party is far weaker among Conservative voters. However, the most important divergence concerns the rating of the Progress party by supporters of the Christian People's party and the Center party, who rank the Progress party lower than nearly every other party. As pointed out by Valen (1990) and Macdonald, Listhaug, and Rabinowitz (1991), this

TABLE 2. Party Sympathy and Electoral Behavior: Mean Value on the Sympathy Thermometer

Party Assessed	All Voters	Voter Identification						
		Socialist Left	Labor	Liberal	Christian People's	Center	Conservative	Progress
Socialist Left	42.0	84.5	52.7	57.9	25.4	29.1	23.7	27.9
Labor	61.0	66.3	87.4	55.8	43.1	44.0	40.1	44.9
Liberal	42.8	52.0	47.4	81.7	42.9	38.4	33.8	34.4
Christian People's	46.6	21.8	38.8	36.5	86.5	58.7	51.7	44.2
Center	51.5	37.5	44.1	48.7	66.1	82.9	54.8	43.7
Conservative	54.6	22.0	32.5	38.2	63.1	60.4	84.8	71.7
Progress	29.0	8.0	18.1	15.4	27.2	22.4	43.9	83.2

Source: Norwegian Election Study of 1985.

divergence does not only stem from left-right variations. The two parties at the center are also strongly opposed to the Progress party along cultural and urban-rural dimensions.

But, by and large, our three measurements of political distance produce similar results. Voters tend to structure the parties along the left-right axis, and their perception of distance in relation to different parties is determined by their own self-location within the system. If we assume that party leaders tend to share the spatial perceptions of the electorate, they are not likely to frustrate their own voters by entering into unpopular alliances.[7] We may now turn to the question of how the actual list alliances fit the perceptions described above.

The Application of Listeforbund

List alliances were established in fourteen of the nineteen constituencies (provinces). In one of them (Telemark), two alliances occurred. According to electoral law, separate lists are prepared and administered by the province branches of the respective parties. We may safely assume, however, that regarding questions of electoral alliances, national party headquarters are involved.[8] For one thing, the parties have to decide whether list alliances in given constituencies are likely to result in gains of additional seats. For each constituency, electoral statistics will inform about seat allocations at the preceding election, provided given list alliances were then applied. It can also be estimated on the basis of electoral statistics how much change in vote distributions is required in order to win new seats. Public opinion polls provide information about changes since the last election. Second, parties have to decide which alliances are politically desirable.

As table 3 indicates, nearly all alliances in 1985 were constituted by parties at the center: the Christian People's party, the Center party, and also the tiny Liberal People's party. One may wonder why the same three parties abstained from running listeforbund in five of the constituencies. Apparently, they made their decisions on the basis of careful calculations. Simulations of 1985 vote distributions indicate that no additional seats would have been obtained by applying listeforbund in these constituencies. The Conservative party was involved in two alliances, in Østfold and in Telemark. This result clearly supports our main hypothesis. All alliances established included only close neighbors in the party system (see figures 1 and 2 and tables 1 and 2). However, in a system including seven parties, plus several miniparties, neighbors are numerous and one may wonder why other parties did not seize the opportunity to form alliances.

The problems involved in the application of listeforbund can best be illustrated by considering the two extreme parties, Socialist Left and Progress. Since they were both below the threshold of representation in a number of

TABLE 3. Application and Impact of *Listeforbund*

Province	Listeforbund	Seats Won	Taken from[a]
Østfold	Con+Cen	1	Labor
Akershus	ChrP+Cen+LPP	1	Con
Oslo	ChrP+Cen+LPP	1	Labor
Hedmark	None	—	—
Oppland	ChrP+Cen	Unchanged	—
Buskerud	ChrP+Cen	1	Con
Vestfold	ChrP+Cen	1	Con
Telemark	Con+LPP	Unchanged	—
	ChrP+Cen	1	Labor
Aust-Agder	ChrP+Cen	Unchanged	—
Vest-Agder	ChrP+Cen+LPP	Unchanged	—
Rogaland	None	—	—
Hordaland	ChrP+Cen+LPP	Unchanged	—
Sogn og Fjordane	None	—	—
Møre og Romsdal	None	—	—
Sør-Trøndelag	ChrP+LPP	1	Labor
Nord-Trøndelag	ChrP+LPP	1	Labor
Nordland	None	—	—
Troms	ChrP+Cen	1	Labor
Finnmark	ChrP+Cen+LPP	Unchanged	—

Source: Norwegian Election Study of 1985.

Note: Con = Conservative party; Cen = Center party; ChrP = Christian People's party; LPP = Liberal People's party.

constituencies, they would be in a position to capture many seats by combining their electoral support—provided they were competing in a policy-blind world. But since they were extreme antagonists along the left-right axis, an alliance between them would probably have caused most of their voters to defect from their respective parties. Actually, listeforbund between Socialist Left and Progress was never considered.

However, in both extreme parties, great interest was expressed in favor of listeforbund with their closest neighbors, Labor and the Conservatives, respectively. Again, possibilities of gaining seats could easily be demonstrated. When the listeforbund system was introduced, Labor intimated that it would respond by forming alliances with its leftist neighbor. But, on closer consideration, the threat was dropped. A similar relationship existed between the two parties of the right. However, list alliances between the two parties were never seriously considered. The interesting question of why the two wing parties were not included in list alliances will be discussed in the final section of the paper.

One might have expected that the three coalition parties would cooperate extensively at the election. The Conservative party was involved in listeforbund in only two constituencies, one of which being with a coalition partner. This may be a result of careful calculations by party strategists. They were, of course, aware that list alliances are most beneficial for the largest party.[9] A simulation of seat allocations in 1985 indicates that application of listeforbund between the three coalition parties and the tiny Liberal People's party in all constituencies would have resulted in net gains of five seats for the Conservatives. One of these seats would have come from the Socialist Left party and four from the Christian People's party and the Center party. Nonetheless, this difference would have given the coalition parties a total of 79 seats (out of 157) and a slight majority in the new Storting.[10] Attempts to create listeforbund between the three coalition parties in a few selected constituencies failed. It should be observed that in the summer of 1985, at the deadline for presenting the final electoral lists, opinion polls predicted a handsome bourgeois victory (Aardal and Valen 1989). Listeforbund between all coalition parties was hardly seen as necessary for maintaining the majority. Moreover, the idea was met with low enthusiasm in all camps.[11] In particular, the parties at the center were reluctant. As junior partners in the coalition, they wanted to strengthen their own position and preserve their identity by avoiding too close an affiliation with the largest party.

The Liberal party constitutes another puzzle. Despite its closeness to other parties at the center, the Liberals were not involved in a single alliance. This may have been a calculated decision. Being so much smaller than the Center party and the Christian People's party, the Liberals would have been in a disadvantaged position at the seat allocation.[12] Apparently, considerations of government alternatives were looming large in the relationships between this family of parties. While the Center party and the Christian People's party were involved in the coalition with the Conservatives, the Liberal party signaled support for a possible Labor government after the election. Consequently, the three parties entertained different goals regarding the distribution of seats in the new Storting. On the other hand, since the Labor party was, in principle, opposed to listeforbund, the Liberals were left more or less isolated, and at the election the party fell below the threshold of representation in all constituencies.

Although the listeforbund system was introduced as a reform that was to be universally applicable, only three parties at the center were sufficiently close, politically and ideologically, to take advantage of the system. Now the impact of the system may be briefly considered. As table 3 indicates, six of the alliances did not affect the distribution of seats—that is, the distribution would have been identical without listeforbund. But in nine cases, the alliances were successful. Labor lost six seats and the Conservatives three, but since the latter party won one seat due to its alliance with the Center party in the province of

TABLE 4.   Comparison of Actual Number with and without *Listeforbund* and the "Ideal" Seat Distribution, 1985

Party	Ideal # of Seats	Actual # with *Listeforbund*	Actual # without *Listeforbund*	Diff 1–2	Diff 1–3
Labor	64	71	77	+7	+13
Conservative	48	50	52	+2	+4
Christian People's	13	16	9	+3	–4
Center	10	12	11	+2	+1
Socialist Left	9	6	6	–3	–3
Progress	6	2	2	–4	–4
Liberal	5	0	0	–5	–5
Others	2	0	0	–2	–2

Source: Storting Elections 1985, vol. 1.

Østfold, the net gains for the parties at the center were eight seats. As in the 1930s, the main effect of the listeforbund was that the middle-sized parties obtained a number of extra seats at the expense of the larger parties.

Now we may go a step further and ask how the reform affected the proportionality of seat allocation. In answering this query, the actual number of seats will be compared with the ideal number, provided each vote counted equally. Table 4 indicates that when listeforbund is applied, the four largest parties—Labor, Conservative, Christians, and Center—are overrepresented by, jointly, fourteen seats. Socialist Left, Progress, Liberals, and other small parties are underrepresented, because they are below the threshold of representation in some or all constituencies. Since the latter parties have not applied the listeforbund—except for the tiny Liberal People's party—their underrepresentation would have been exactly the same, even without the reform. The reform did affect seat allocation among the larger parties, however. The listeforbund system reduced overrepresentation for the Labor party from thirteen to seven seats, and for the Conservatives from four to two seats. On the other hand, without listeforbund, the Christian People's party would have been underrepresented by four seats, and the Center party would have ended up with only one seat too many.

The Storting election of 1985 created an impasse between the two blocs in Norwegian politics. The bourgeois coalition parties lost their majority and obtained jointly 78 out of 157 seats. Labor and the Socialist Left obtained 77 seats, and the right-wing Progress party, with its two seats, arrived in a pivotal position. Parliamentary instability resulted. The four bourgeois parties were unable to form a majority coalition including the Progress party, because of big policy differences between this party and the other three. In particular, the distance was sizable between Progress and the two parties at the center (see tables 1 and 2). The coalition government remained in office after the election, but now as a minority cabinet. In April 1986, the Progress party joined the socialists in defeating the coalition. Labor took over as a minority government (Valen 1990). One may wonder whether this situation would have been avoided if the listeforbund had not been introduced. Due to the reform, Labor lost six seats, which would have given a comfortable socialist majority. However, if bourgeois parties had applied joint lists instead of listeforbund, some of the six seats would have been lost for Labor anyhow.

Voter Attitudes toward Listeforbund

Now we turn to the level of the electorate. The respondents were asked: "How do you regard the system of listeforbund: are you for or against retaining the system at future elections?" As indicated in table 5, less than one-third of the respondents wanted to maintain the system, and even fewer wanted to get rid of it, while the rest expressed no opinion.

Interestingly enough, opinion is almost identical in constituencies with and without listeforbund. However, respondents who have voted for some party involved in a listeforbund in their respective constituencies tend to take a more positive view than other voters on the reform. The proportion indicating no opinion is largest among respondents with low education, low political interest, and no membership in political parties. However, ignoring respondents with no opinion, there are practically no variations in attitudes for and against the reform in relation to the respective background variables.

A different pattern is observed when voter attitudes are considered in relation to electoral behavior. As indicated in table 6, opposition to the reform is strongest in the Labor, Socialist Left, and the Liberal parties. Attitudes are most positive in the Christian People's and the Center parties, while voters of the Conservative and Progress parties tend to indicate a midway position. The patterns observed are consistent with the position taken by the respective

TABLE 5. Maintenance of *Listeforbund* System

Position	Total Sample	Residence of Constituencies without *Listeforbund*	Residence of Constituencies with *Listeforbund*	Voted for Parties in *Listeforbund*
For	30%	30%	30%	52%
Both - and	14	11	15	16
Against	27	27	27	11
Don't know	29	32	28	21
Total	100	100	100	100
N	2,163	563	1,600	266

Source: Norwegian Election Study of 1985.

TABLE 6. Attitudes toward *Listeborbund* and Party

	Socialist Left	Labor	Liberal	Christian People's	Center	Liberal People's	Conservative	Progress
For	24%	19%	31%	52%	48%	—	41%	30%
Both - and	17	10	12	17	19	—	16	17
Against	37	43	41	8	12	—	15	20
Don't know	22	28	16	23	21	—	28	33
Total	100	100	100	100	100		100	100
N	106	704	68	180	129	8[a]	560	66

Source: Norwegian Election Study of 1985.

[a]Too few cases for computation of percentages.

parties when the reform was debated in the Storting. This consistency suggests that the political parties have been effective in communicating their position to their respective followers.

The reform of 1985, which was introduced about half a year before the election, triggered an intensive debate, both about ethical aspects of alternative voting, and about the political convenience of establishing listeforbund in given constituencies. The reform was indeed brought to the attention of the electorate. The listeforbund system implied a change in the structural framework within which an election is conducted. If listeforbund was not applied, the individual voter would be faced with a set of straight partisan lists—as before. If, on the other hand, a listeforbund appeared in a given constituency, the voter was invited to a conditional choice: a vote for one party in the alliance might be transferred to some other party. One crucial question, therefore, is whether the voter was aware of this specific choice. How did voter information affect attitudes towards the reform? And how did it affect electoral choice?

Voter Knowledge about Listeforbund

In the voter survey, the respondents were asked: "Do you know whether any so-called listeforbund between several parties was established at the election this year in [name of province]? If 'yes,' Which parties participated in the listeforbund in this constituency?" The result has been presented in table 7.

Table 7 confirms the well-known finding that voters, in general, are poorly informed about politics. Less than half of the respondents were able to answer correctly about the reform. As expected, voters who were directly affected by the reform were best informed. Thus, knowledge increased significantly with the occurrence of listeforbund in the province of residence. Best informed were voters who indicated that they had voted for some party directly involved in a listeforbund in their constituency: three out of four recognized the alliance, and only six percent responded incorrectly.

TABLE 7. Voter Knowledge of *Listeforbund*

Knowledge	Total Sample	Provinces without *Listeforbund*	Provinces with *Listeforbund*	Voted for Party in *Listeforbund*
Correct response	46%	35%	50%	72%
Incorrect response	10	16	8	6
Don't know	44	49	42	22
Total	100	100	100	100
N	2,180	564	1,616	266

Source: Norwegian Election Study of 1985.

TABLE 8. Knowledge of *Listeforbund* and Background in the System

Knowledge	Primary/Lower Sec. School	Education Part of Gymnas I	Gymnas completed II	Univ.	Political Interest Low	High	Party Membership No	Yes
Correct response	36%	45%	46%	61%	36%	60%	42%	63%
Incorrect response	9	11	12	11	10	11	11	10
Don't know	55	44	42	28	54	29	47	27
Total	100	100	100	100	100	100	100	100
N	622	674	482	356	1,301	862	1,835	328

Source: Norwegian Election Study of 1985.

Three more independent variables have been introduced in the analysis: whether the respondents belong to the active elite of the electorate, measured by questions about dues-paying party membership and level of interest in politics,[13] and education. The results are presented in table 8.

Consistent with findings from several other studies (Rokkan and Campbell 1960; Martinussen 1973), table 8 indicates a strong increase of political information with increasing education. The proportion of correct responses nearly doubles as we move from those with only obligatory education to university level. A similar gap is evident between respondents indicating low and high interest in politics and between ordinary voters and dues-paying party members. The data suggest that information about the reform was much higher among political and social elites than in the rest of the electorate.

Obviously, some of the variables applied in tables 7 and 8 are strongly interrelated, such as education and political interest, and party membership and political interest. In order to assess their joint impact upon voter knowledge, an additive index has been created combining party membership, education, political interest, and occurrence of listeforbund.[14] The result has been presented in figure 3.

As the curve indicates, extent of information increases with increasing number of resources, ranging from 26 percent correct responses among persons with low resources to 77 percent for those who score high on all indicators. Thus the degree of information about the listeforbund is highest among voters who come into most direct contact with the reform through their location in the political system. Having said this, it is nevertheless remarkable that

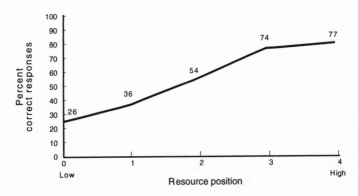

Fig. 3. Knowledge about listeforbund and number of resource positions. The curve indicates proportion of correct responses.

TABLE 9. Attitudes toward *Listeforbund* and Voting: By Knowledge of *Listeforbund* in Own Constituency

	Correct Answer on *Listeforbund*			Incorrect Answer or Don't Know		
	Socialist	Center	Right	Socialist	Center	Right
For	20%	64%	50%	19%	30%	32%
Both - and	12	18	17	10	19	15
Against	55	8	17	32	12	15
No opinion	13	10	16	39	39	38
Total	100	100	100	100	100	100
N	358	192	241	452	125	342

Source: Norwegian Election Study of 1985.

Note: Socialist comprises Labor party and Socialist Left; Center comprises Christian People's party, Center party, and Liberal party; Right comprises Conservative party and Progress party.

almost one out of four in the top group did not know that a listeforbund had been applied in their own constituency.

Now, let us return to the question of attitudes towards the reform. Table 6 indicates great party differences in support of the listeforbund system. To what extent are attitudes conditioned by knowledge of the reform? This query is considered in table 9. Reasonably enough, respondents who are well informed are most inclined to state a definite opinion, and the pattern of party variations is most marked in this group. Nonetheless, the same *pattern* is also evident among respondents who are poorly informed. The data suggest that the position taken by the parties centrally is communicated to the rank and file, more or less regardless of the information level of the voters.

Listeforbund and Electoral Behavior

Voters living in constituencies in which listeforbund does exist may be faced with a problem, provided their party is involved in the alliance, and provided they know of the listeforbund. This being the case, the question is how voters feel about other parties included in the alliance. If they like the partners, they are most likely to vote for their own party and accept the consequences of the listeforbund. If, on the other hand, they dislike some party in the listeforbund, they may express their feelings in their electoral choice. Norwegian voters in 1985 had three options for expressing their protest: (1) they might reserve themselves against the listeforbund (they could indicate on the list that they voted only for a party and not for the listeforbund, which meant that their vote would not be transferred to some other party); (2) they might vote for another party; and (3) they might abstain from voting. Since our respondents were not asked whether they had indicated reservations, the first option cannot be examined.[15] This is most unfortunate, since a surprisingly high number actually did opt for this solution. Nearly ten thousand voters indicated reservations–3.2 percent of those voting for parties involved in listeforbund in constituencies concerned (*Stortingsvalget 1985,* 1:78).[16] Our analysis has to be restricted to reported partisan choice. It is very difficult to identify voters who have abstained from voting due to the listeforbund. Moreover, the number of potential abstainers is so low that analysis is prohibited. Consequently, change in partisan choice is the only protest we are able to explore.

After electoral behavior had been ascertained, respondents living in constituencies in which listeforbund had been applied were asked: "Would you have voted differently if there had been no listeforbund?" Only eighteen persons responded in the affirmative—only about one percent of respondents in the provinces concerned. The figure is, of course, too low for a meaningful analysis. However, as margins are small in the final allocation of seats (see *Stortingsvalget 1985,* vol. 1), we cannot exclude the possibility that even small divergences among voters may have political consequences. A closer look at the eighteen respondents discloses that half of them would have voted either Labor or Conservative if no listeforbund had existed. Although this distribution most likely is due to sampling error, it is tempting to consider the possibility that some voters tended to vote for one of the large parties, instead of wasting their vote on some minor party that might be below the threshold of representation. Assuming that this explanation is correct, one should expect that parties at the center have gained additional votes as a result of their participation in listeforbund. In order to test this hypothesis, the proportion of votes obtained in 1981 and in 1985 is compared for each of the parties concerned. For this purpose, the constituencies have been combined into two groups, according to whether the respective parties were involved in listeforbund in 1985. The result is, however, that electoral changes from 1981 to 1985 are almost identical in the two types of constituencies. Thus, the analysis suggests that the reform did not at all affect party preferences of the electorate.

In a preceding section, it was hypothesized that if their party enters into an alliance with some party they dislike, voters are likely to shift party. Our data on electoral behavior do not provide a sufficient test of this hypothesis. An attempt has been made to apply attitudinal data as a substitute. Instead of classifying voters according to dislike of other parties, second party preference has been applied (see table 2). We are particularly interested in voters whose parties did actually apply listeforbund—that is, the Christian People's party, the Center party, and the Conservative party. Since second choice indicates a short distance between the parties concerned, we expect that voters of the three parties are more favorably disposed towards the reform if they rank one of the other listeforbund parties as their second preference than if they find their second choice outside this family of parties. The data presented in table 10 do, indeed, support this hypothesis. In order to obtain sufficiently large groups, the

TABLE 10.   Attitudes toward *Listeforbund* by Party and Second Choice: Percentage in favor of the reform

Second preference	Voting			
	Socialist	Christian and Center parties	Conservatives	Progress Party
Socialist	20%	31%	33%	—a
Christian and Center parties	25	60	44	—
Conservatives	13	52	—	—
Progress party	—	—	39	—

Source: Norwegian Election Study of 1985.

parties of the center, as well as socialist parties, have been combined. It is not surprising that support for listeforbund is highest in the Christian and Center parties (see table 9), but within these parties, variations are great. Respondents who rank another party of the center or the Conservatives as their second choice are far more inclined than those preferring some socialist party in the second place to support the reform. Within the Conservative camp, the picture is complementary: Support for listeforbund is highest among those who favor the parties at the center. On the other hand, socialist voters tend to reject the reform, regardless of their second party preference. The responses reported in table 10 confirm the inclination of the electorate to take up a position consistent with that of their respective parties: The main message is that listeforbund is supported by those who are able to apply it profitably.

Concluding Remarks

The purpose of electoral alliances is to improve the representation of participating parties. But although access to forming alliances is universal in character, only a few parties are able to take advantage of the system. The main concern of this chapter has been to study the impact of such alliances on parties and voters. Operating within a rational choice framework, two hypotheses have been proposed: First, consistent with coalition theory, only parties which are similar regarding policies and ideology are able to form list alliances. Second, consistent with spatial theory, voters disliking some party in the alliance are inclined to defect from their preferred party.

The introduction of a system of list alliances (listeforbund) in Norway in 1985 made it possible to study reactions of leaders, as well as of voters. The findings from this case study support our main expectations concerning the behavior of parties:

1. The reform was applied almost exclusively by three parties at the political center (i.e., close neighbors in the party spectrum);

2. Due to the listeforbund, two of the parties, the Center and the Christian People's parties, greatly increased their representation at the expense of the two large parties, Labor and the Conservatives;

3. Other neighboring parties (e.g., Conservative/Progress and Labor/Socialist Left) were unable to form alliances. Several small parties were too different to take advantage of the listeforbund system, and consequently, their representation was not at all affected by the reform.

Interesting regularities were also observed on the electoral level:

4. Attitudes towards the reform reflected a pattern of party differences that closely corresponded to the position taken by various parties on the national level. The consistency was evident even among voters who were uninformed about list alliances in their respective constituencies.

5. On the average, voter knowledge about the reform was not very high. However, great variations were evident, in the sense that knowledge increased sharply with background in the system and with the degree to which the individual voter was affected by the reform.

6. Data on electoral behavior were inconclusive concerning the hypothesis that voters might defect from their preferred party due to participation in list alliances, but by applying attitudinal data in conjunction with ranking of other parties (second choice), the hypothesis could be tested indirectly. The analysis indicated that, within given parties, voter attitudes towards the listeforbund system were conditioned by feelings towards other parties. The tendency was most striking in parties at the center that did apply the reform. Favorable attitudes occurred far more frequently among voters ranking some other party applying listeforbund as their second choice than among those who preferred anti-listeforbund parties. By reversing the wording of the hypothesis, we may state that voters favorably disposed towards other parties in the alliance are most inclined to accept the listeforbund and, consequently, also their own party. On the other hand, it may be subsumed that voters disliking other parties in the alliance are inclined to reject the listeforbund system.

The main conclusion for voters, as well as for parties, is that the listeforbund system is supported by those who are able to apply it profitably. In this sense, reactions are indeed rational on both levels. There are, however, some interesting deviations from this picture. Let us first consider the level of parties. We should have expected a more extensive use of list alliances between the three coalition parties. Not only did they share government responsibility at the time of the election, they also committed themselves to continue the coalition if they obtained sufficient support from the electorate. Why, then, did these parties not pursue a similar cooperative strategy regarding list alliances? Another interesting deviation concerns the relationship between the two big parties, Labor and the Conservatives, and their neighboring wing parties, the Socialist Left and the Progress party, respectively. One should have expected that both pairs of parties would apply listeforbund, considering their location along the left-right axis (see figs. 1 and 2) and the fact that, in both cases, the possibilities of capturing additional seats were evident. Why were the wing parties never included in any list alliance? The answer may be found in cost/benefit calculations made by the individual party. Let us return to concepts introduced in the first part of this paper to illuminate this point. What motivates parties when they choose their strategy? Let us first consider the relationship between the three coalition parties. If the parties were purely office-seekers, they would most likely have taken full advantage of the listeforbund system. As demonstrated above, the three parties would jointly have obtained a slight majority in the new Storting by extensive use of list alliances. In the early summer of 1985, however, when election lists had to be finalized, opinion polls predicted a solid victory for the coalition parties. Thus, the parties may have felt that they did not actually need the extra seats they might have obtained by including the Conservatives in the list alliances.

On the other hand, polls are not elections. Political parties, being well aware of this, might have wanted to secure their majority by maximizing their share of the seats. Thus, their decisions seem somewhat inconsistent with rational behavior. However, as observed above, parties have more complex motivations than just office seeking. In terms of policies, some differences have traditionally been evident between the Conservatives, on the one hand, and the two parties at the center, on the other (see figs. 1 and 2 and tables 1 and 2). By calculating on the basis of the preceding election, the parties at the center had undoubtedly discovered that listeforbund, when applied to several parties of varying strength, is most beneficial for the largest party. In fact, our simulation of the 1985 election, assuming listeforbund between the three coalition parties throughout the country, indicates that the Conservatives would have obtained five additional seats, while the Christian People's party would have lost one seat and the Center party three. By allowing the Conservatives more seats, the parties at the center would have weakened their own bargaining position in subsequent policy negotiations within the coalition. Thus, what seems to have been rational for the coalition, as such, was not necessarily a rational choice for the individual party. Apparently, the two parties at the center, which were most similar, calculated that by maximizing their number of seats, they would be in a position to contain the strength of their more conservative senior partner.

Somewhat different motives seem to apply for the two dominant parties, Labor and the Conservatives, in relation to their respective wing parties. Their avoidance of alliances may partly have been due to policy considerations. Policy differences between Labor and the Socialist Left could not easily be bridged, and in particular the anti-NATO foreign policy of the Socialist Left would have become a liability for the pro-NATO Labor party. A similar relationship existed between the two parties of the right. By forming list alliances with the Progress party, the Conservatives would have had to share responsibility for the populist ideas of the other party. In addition, it should be recalled that the Progress party was very unpopular with the parties at the center (see table 2). Listeforbund between the two parties of the right might have been perceived as a menace by the two traditional coalition partners of the Conservatives. Yet, despite some visible policy differences, it should be noted that in several policy areas, the voting record in parliament is consistent between the two dominant parties and their respective wing parties, particularly regarding issues related to the left-right axis. Thus, policy considerations can hardly have been an exclusive motivation for avoiding list alliances.

Panebianco (1988) offers an interesting theory that might apply to the situation described. Contrary to other coalition theories, Panebianco suggests that coalitions will be formed between parties that are *opponents,* in some respects (ideologically distant), rather than by *competitors* (ideologically similar). Panebianco's main argument is that competition may imply a threat to a party's identity. In order to preserve its identity, a party will be inclined to avoid alliances with ideologically similar parties. Consequently, party leaders tend to take an even more aggressive and hostile position towards competitors than towards their official opposition (Panebianco 1988, 217). The almost traditional hostility between competing socialist parties is a classical example of the situation described. In parliament, they may pursue more or less similar policies, but since they share the electoral hunting ground, they have a strong need for defending their identity and uniqueness in relation to potential voters. Thus, entering into electoral alliances with close competitors might be hazardous. Electoral studies in Norway have demonstrated that the Labor party, as well as the Conservatives, are consistently challenged by their respective wing parties. A number of voters move back and forth between Labor and Socialist Left and between the Conservatives and the Progress party (Aardal and Valen 1989, 161–64). The parties at the center, on the other hand, are close neighbors along the left-right axis (see figs. 1 and 2), but they both have a rather stable and distinct following. The Christian People's party draws most of its strength from members of the lay religious and temperance movements, while the

Center party obtains most of its support from the farm population (Aardal and Valen 1989).

The important theoretical point resulting from this discussion is easily recognized: Coalition building involves both cooperation and competition. This is a result of the dynamic interactions between parties and voters, or what has been called mass-elite linkages (Putnam 1976, 133; Miller 1988; Tsebelis 1990). Tsebelis uses the term *nested games* to characterize this situation. His underlying assumption is that political leaders participate in games in two arenas, the parliamentary and the electoral, which are different and yet connected. The dynamics between the two levels is reflected in the coexistence of different strategies pursued by the parties involved. The individual party may pursue two alternative strategies: it may cooperate with its partner or defect from him. Cooperation means promoting the interests of the coalition, while defection means promoting partisan interests.

As to the electoral level, the lack of reactions in terms of protest voting against the reform was observed with surprise. The explanation may possibly be that our measuring instruments were not fully adequate. Unfortunately, one important type of protest was not observed in the study: reservations against the listeforbund by people voting for parties applying it. It should be noted, however, that in order to react rationally, the voters needed to be informed about the reform. Thus, the result may partly be an effect of low voter information. On the other hand, it has been demonstrated that voters tended to share the position taken by their respective parties toward the listeforbund reform. The lack of protest voting may simply mean that voters, by and large, were conforming with leadership opinion.

The choice of strategy is a matter of elite decision, but sentiments in the electorate cannot be neglected, since the electoral arena is characterized by competition among parties, and the strength of a given party depends upon its support at the polls. The purpose of list alliances is to maximize the number of seats, rather than the number of votes. Basically, party strategists must be concerned with possible effects of list alliances upon the allocation of seats. At the same time, the application of such alliances might conceivably affect the distribution of votes. An alliance might have a mobilizing effect upon the electorate by creating enthusiasm within a given family of parties. On the other hand, the alliance might create frustrations among voters and thus reduce electoral support for the parties concerned. In order to prevent defections, political leaders who have decided to enter into a list alliance are likely to inform potential supporters about their strategy and explain it to them.

Our analysis suggests that elite strategies have effectively penetrated the electorate, despite a modest level of voter information. Since the proposal to reintroduce the listeforbund system reappeared on the agenda only a few months before the election, the consistency in attitudes between parties and voters implies that parties possess great ability to communicate policy positions to their supporters. The fact that voters were willing to go along with their respective parties suggests responsiveness on the voter level to elite strategies. This analysis illuminates the importance of mass-elite linkages in the study of political processes. In his scholarly works, Warren Miller has made a great contribution to elucidating these problems.[17]

Students of elections (Rokkan 1968; Grofman and Lijphart 1986; Taagepera and Shugart 1989) have called for more research on institutional change of electoral systems. The analysis on the preceding pages demonstrates that the introduction of the listeforbund system did have a considerable impact upon the allocation of seats at the Storting election of 1985. This election resulted in an impasse in Norwegian politics, with increasing parliamentary instability. It is debatable to what extent this was a result of the listeforbund, since other forms of electoral cooperation were also available for parties concerned. In any event, the reform triggered a process of reconsideration of the electoral system. By a new reform of 1988, a system with eight nationwide supplementary seats was introduced, in order to improve proportionality among parties. At the same time, the listeforbund was prohibited for the future by a constitutional amendment.

NOTES

This chapter is a modified version of a chapter on "Listeforbund" which appeared in B. Aardal and H. Valen 1989. I am grateful to the following colleagues who have read the manuscript and made valuable suggestions: Donald R. Matthews, Bernt Aardal, Hanne Marthe Narud, Warren Miller, Roy Pierce, M. Kent Jennings, Ola Listhaug, Steven Rosenstone, Walter Stone, and Erik Wickstrøm. But the author assumes full responsibility for the contents.

1. Observe, however, that several majority election systems only permit a restricted number of parties to run candidates at reelections (e.g., the two parties that obtained the highest number of votes at the first election). Under such conditions, the system is less conducive to forming electoral alliances (Nohlen 1978).

2. This idea was discussed at length by the commission which prepared the reform introducing proportional representation in Norway. See *Valgordningskommisjonen av 1917* 1919, 18. The demand for equity was also the main argument in the Storting debates when listeforbund was introduced in Norway in 1930 and in 1985. See *Stortingsforhandlingene* 1930 and 1985, respectively.

3. Parties of the left argued particularly strongly against the idea of forcing voters into an alternative choice of parties (*Valgordningskommisjonen av 1917* 1919). See also Kristvik and Rokkan 1964.

4. According to the d'Hondt formula, the votes of a given party are divided successively by 1, 2, 3, 4, etc., after each seat obtained. The Sainte Laguë method prescribes division by odd numbers—1, 3, 5, 7, etc. The d'Hondt method tends to

overrepresent large parties in the event of great variation in size of the competing parties. The pure Laguë method, on the other hand, overrepresents small parties. The modified Laguë method that is applied in the Scandinavian countries prescribes that the total vote for all parties is first divided by 1.4. The vote is then divided successively by 3, 5, 7, etc., for each seat obtained.

5. Electoral law in Norway does not require a specific number of votes for obtaining representation in the constituencies, but a threshold is implied in the representation formula. In order to obtain representation, a party needs a sizable proportion of the votes, but this proportion varies from one constituency to another, depending upon the number of competing lists, the number of seats, and the size of the electorate.

Party fragmentation occurred in 1972–73 after the very divisive debate on Norway's entry into the European Community. Thus, the old Liberal party (the Left) was split into two miniparties, the Liberals and the Liberal People's party; a new Progress party emerged on the right wing of the system, and a tiny Marxist-Leninist party (AKP) appeared on the left wing.

6. This constellation dates back to 1963, when a bourgeois coalition government was established for the first time. The bourgeois coalitions of the 1960s consisted of the Conservatives, the Agrarians, the Christian People's party, and the Liberals. The latter party broke out of the alliance after the split in 1972.

7. The three scales presented above are not available for the leadership level. However, other measures suggest that political leaders tend to perceive the political space in about the same way as the voters do. Thus, a local study in 1957 of voters and leaders indicates that, in attitudes on political issues, party differences are very similar for the two levels (Valen and Katz 1964, 258–64). H. Rommetvedt (1991) has studied voting patterns of different parties in Storting committees for the postwar period. By applying extent of similarity of voting as a measure of closeness between parties pairwise, he has demonstrated that party distances on the parliamentary level correspond nicely to our three measures of voter perceptions.

8. Leaders of the coalition parties in 1985 confirm that the question of listeforbund was discussed at national, as well as at province, level, but they are not willing to give detailed information about proceedings and political considerations involved. The author is entirely responsible for the subsequent analysis of the parties' behavior with regard to list alliances.

9. Consistently with the rules, joint seats won by a list alliance should be distributed among the participating parties according to the modified Laguë formula, which tends to overrepresent the largest party in cases where the number of votes differs greatly.

10. The result would have been exactly the same if the Liberal People's party had been excluded from the alliance.

11. According to information from leading people in the three parties concerned.

12. A simulation has been conducted on the basis of the vote distribution in 1985, assuming list alliances between the four parties at the center throughout the country. The Liberals, as well as the Liberal People's party, would have remained unrepresented. The Center party would have gained three more seats, one from the Conservatives and two from Labor. Jointly, the three coalition parties would have gained eighty seats, and majority in the new Storting.

13. Questions: "Are you at present a dues-paying member of some political party?" Sixteen percent of the respondents indicated membership. "Would you say that you in general are very interested in politics, fairly interested, only slightly interested, or not interested at all?" Those answering either very interested or fairly interested have been classified here as having a "high" degree of interest, while respondents in the other categories are classified as "low."

14. Each of the four indicators has been classified into two categories, low and high, following the patterns in tables 7 and 8. For education, a distinction has been made between university level and lower level.

15. At the time when the questionnaire was worked out, the number of reservations was expected to be minuscule. This expectation was based upon experiences from 1930–45, when less than 0.01 percent of the electorate reserved themselves against the listeforbund (according to electoral statistics). However, during this period, rules for reservation were different, in the sense that every vote cast for some party in listeforbund would automatically be transferred to allied parties, disregarding possible reservations.

16. Reported reservations did not at all affect allocation of seats, according to electoral statistics for 1985.

17. In addition to his book on mass-elite linkages in presidential politics (1988), his works on political leadership and political representation are highly relevant.

REFERENCES

Aardal, B., and H. Valen. 1989. *Velgere, Partier, og Politisk Avstand* (Voters, parties, and political distances). Oslo: Central Bureau of Statistics.

Andeweg, R. B. 1989. "Institutional Conservatism in the Netherlands: Proposals for and Resistance to Change." *West European Politics* 12 (1): 42–60.

Austen-Smith, D., and J. Banks. 1988. "Elections, Coalitions, and Legislative Outcomes." *American Political Science Review* 82:405–22.

Axelrod, R. 1970. *Conflict of Interest.* Chicago: Markham.

Converse, P. E., and H. Valen. 1971. "Dimensions of Cleavage and Perceived Party Distances in Norwegian Voting." *Scandinavian Political Studies* 6:105–52.

de Swaan, A. 1973. *Coalition Theories and Cabinet Formation.* Amsterdam: Elsevier.

Dodd, L. C., W. H. Flanigan, and E. Vogelman. 1987. "Representation in Parliamentary Regimes 1900–1976." Paper presented at the Midwest Political Science Convention, Chicago.

Downs, A. 1957. *An Economic Theory of Democracy.* New York: Harper and Brothers.

Duverger, M. 1954. *Political Parties.* Translated by Barbara and Robert North. London: Methuen. Originally published as *Les Parties politiques* (Paris: Colin, 1981).

Gamson, W. 1961. "A Theory of Coalition Formation." *American Sociological Review* 26:373–82.

Grofman, B., and A. Lijphart, eds. 1986. *Electoral Laws and Their Political Consequences.* New York: Agathon Press.

Kristvik, B., and S. Rokkan. 1964. *Valgordningen.* Bergen: Chr. Michelsen Institute, Bergen. Mimeo.

Laver, M. 1989. "Party Competition and Party System Change: The Interaction of Electoral Bargaining and Party Competition." *Journal of Theoretical Politics* 1:301–25.

Laver, M., and N. Schofield. 1990. *Multiparty Government: The Politics of Coalitions in Europe.* Oxford: Oxford University Press.

Leiserson, M. 1966. "Coalitions in Politics." Ph.D. diss., Yale University.

Lijphart, A. 1984. *Democracies.* New Haven, Conn.: Yale University Press.

Macdonald, S. E., O. Listhaug, and G. Rabinowitz. 1991. "Issues and Party Support in Multiparty Systems." *American Political Science Review* 85 (4): 1107–31.

Martinussen, W. 1973. *Fjerndemokratiet.* Oslo: Gyldendal. Translated by Martinussen, under the title *Distant Democracy* (London: Wiley, 1977).

Miller, W. E. 1988. *Without Consent: Mass Elite Linkages in Presidential Politics.* Lexington: University Press of Kentucky.

Nohlen, D. 1978. *Wahlsystem der Welt.* Munich: Piper.

Panebianco, A. 1988. *Political Parties: Organization & Power.* Cambridge: Cambridge University Press.

Pierce, R. 1956. "The French Election of 1956." *The Journal of Politics* 19:391–422.

Pridham, G., ed. 1986. *Coalitional Behaviour in Theory and Practice.* Cambridge: Cambridge University Press.

Putnam, R. 1976. *The Comparative Study of Political Elites.* Englewood Cliffs, N.J.: Prentice-Hall.

Riker, W. 1962. *The Theory of Political Coalitions.* New Haven, Conn.: Yale University Press.

Rokkan, S. 1968. "Elections: Electoral Systems." In *International Encyclopedia of the Social Sciences,* ed. David L. Sills. New York: Collier-Macmillan-Crowell.

Rokkan, S., and A. Campbell. 1960. "Citizen Participation in Political Life: Norway and the United States of America." *International Social Science Journal* 12 (1): 69–99.

Rommetvedt, H. 1991. *Partiavstand og partikoalisjon* (Party distances and party coalitions). Ph.D. diss., University of Bergen.

Sjöblom, G. 1968. *Party Strategies in a Multi Party System.* Lund: Studentlitteratur.

Stortingsforhandlingene. 1930. (The official report of Storting proceedings.) Oslo: Storting.

Stortingsforhandlingene. 1985. (The official report of Storting proceedings.) Oslo: Storting.

Stortingsvalget 1985 (Storting elections of 1985). 1985. Vol. 1. Oslo: Central Bureau of Statistics.

Strøm, K. 1990a. "A Behavioral Theory of Competitive Political Parties." *American Journal of Political Science* 34 (2): 565–98.

———. 1990b. *Minority Government and Majority Rule.* Cambridge: Cambridge University Press.

Taagepera, R., and M. S. Shugart. 1989. *Seats and Votes.* New Haven and London: Yale University Press.

Tsebelis, G. 1990. *Nested Games: Rational Choice in Comparative Politics.* Berkeley and Los Angeles: University of California Press.

Valen, H. 1981. *Valg og politikk* (Elections and politics). Oslo: NKS-forlaget.

————. 1990. "Coalitions and Political Distances." In *People and Their Polities,* ed. R. Sänkiaho et al. Helsinki: Finnish Political Science Association.

————. 1991. "Equity of Representation: Territorial versus Partisan Distortion." Paper presented at a symposium on electoral reform, arranged by the Tokai University, Copenhagen, March 27–28.

Valen, H., and D. Katz. 1964. *Political Parties in Norway.* Oslo: Universitetsforlaget.

Valen, H., and S. Rokkan. 1974. "Conflict Structure and Mass Politics in a European Periphery: Norway." In *Electoral Behavior,* ed. R. Rose. New York: Free Press.

Valgordningskommisjonen av 1917 (Electoral Commission of 1917). 1919. Report 1. Published as appendix to *Ot. prop.* nr. 37 (Oslo: Stortinget, 1920).

von Beyme, K. 1985. *Political Parties in Western Democracies.* Aldershot: Gower.

Williams, P. M. 1964. *Crisis and Compromise: Politics in the Fourth Republic.* London: Longmans.

Contributors

David W. Brady is Bowen H. and Janice Arthur McCoy Professor of Ethics, Political Science, Business and the Changing Environment at Stanford University.

Richard A. Brody is professor of political science at Stanford University.

Ivor Crewe is Professor of Government at the University of Essex.

Leon D. Epstein is Hilldale Professor Emeritus of Political Science at the University of Wisconsin, Madison.

Heinz Eulau is William Bennett Munro Professor of Political Science, Emeritus, at Stanford University.

Valerie D. Heitshusen is a research fellow in the governmental studies program at The Brookings Institution and assistant professor of political science at the University of Missouri.

M. Kent Jennings is professor of political science and research scientist at the Center for Political Studies, University of Michigan, and professor of political science at the University of California, Santa Barbara.

Sören Holmberg is professor in political science/election research and director of the Swedish Election Studies Program in the Department of Political Science at Göteborg University.

Max Kaase is research professor for the Comparative Study of Democratic Regimes, Research Area III on Social Change, Institutions and Mediating Processes at the Social Science Research Center, Berlin.

Anthony King is professor of government at the University of Essex.

Hans-Dieter Klingemann is professor of political science, Freie Universität Berlin; Director, Research Unit "Institutions and Social Change," Wissenschaftszentrum Berlin für Sozialforschung.

Thomas E. Mann is director of the governmental studies program and W. Averell Harriman Senior Fellow in American Governance at The Brookings Institution.

J. Merrill Shanks is professor of political science and director of the Computer-assisted Survey Methods Program at the University of California, Berkeley.

John Sprague is professor and chair of the Department of Political Science at Washington University in St. Louis.

Jacques Thomassen is professor of politics, Department of Public Policy and Public Administration at the University of Twente, The Netherlands.

Henry Valen is a professor at the Institute for Social Research in Oslo.

Raymond Wolfinger is professor of political science at the University of California, Berkeley.

Index

Aardel, B., 293, 295, 315, 316
Abelson, Robert P., 37n
Abramowitz, Alan I., 282
Abramson, Paul R., 67n, 111, 159
Absentee ballots, 86n
Achen, Christopher H., 244, 255
Age-related factors. *See also* Generational factors: in East German elections, 133–34; in party identification, 110–13
Aggregation of data, 18, 25–26, 33, 58–59, 65n, 208, 210, 215–19, 230; identification problem in, 227–29, 231; for modeling social context of voting behavior, 220–27; in voter perception of parties, 260n
Aldrich, John, 6, 83–84, 85n
Alford, John, 160
Alliance 90, 128, 129, 131, 140, 147
American Commonwealth, The, 62n, 93
American Political Science Association, 251, 267
American Voter, The, 4, 19, 36n, 41, 58, 59, 62–63n; explanatory variables in, 27, 28, 29
Andeweg, R. B., 290
Arterton, F. Christopher, 276
Asher, Herbert, 36n
Associated Press, 85n
Austen-Smith, D., 292
Australia, 186, 203
Austria, 127

Baer, Denise L., 282
Bain, Richard C., 274
Banks, J., 292

Barker, Lucius, 274, 276
Barnes, Samuel, 118n, 243, 245, 255
Bartels, Larry M., 37n
Barton, A., 114
Bauer, Petra, 152
Baum, Lawrence, 12, 157
Bean, Clive, 186, 187, 202, 203
Beck, Paul Allen, 7, 12, 157
Benson, Lee, 49
Berelson, Bernard, 39, 43, 62n, 123, 211
Berns, Walter, 62n
BFD. *See* Union of Free Democrats (Germany)
Bibby, John F., 283
Birch, A. H., 238, 240, 241, 251
Blackhurst, James, 278
Blalock, Hubert M., 68n
Block recursive model, 30–31
Bluck, Carlton, 133
Boll, Bernhard, 127, 129
Bositis, David, 277, 282
Boudon, Raymond, 213, 218
Bowler, Shaun, 76, 77
Brady, David, 160
Brody, Richard A., 37n, 94, 157
Brown, Barbara Leavitt, 282
Bruce, John M., 278, 282
Bryan, William Jennings, 266
Bryce, James, 39, 62n, 272
Buchanan, William, 10, 239
Budge, Ian, 94, 124
Burke, Edmund, 238–43, 250, 260n
Bush, George, 17, 63n, 65n, 164, 185, 283
Butler, David, 182, 183, 187